THE E.U. STRUCTURAL FUNDS

ANDREW EVANS

OXFORD
UNIVERSITY PRESS

OXFORD
UNIVERSITY PRESS
Great Clarendon Street, Oxford OX2 6DP

Oxford University Press is a department of the University of Oxford.
It furthers the University's objective of excellence in research, scholarship,
and education by publishing worldwide in

Oxford New York
Athens Auckland Bangkok Bogotá Buenos Aires Calcutta
Cape Town Chennai Dar es Salaam Delhi Florence Hong Kong Istanbul
Karachi Kuala Lumpur Madrid Melbourne Mexico City Mumbai
Nairobi Paris São Paulo Singapore Taipei Tokyo Toronto Warsaw
with associated companies in Berlin Ibadan

Published in the United States
by Oxford University Press Inc., New York

First published 1999

British Library Cataloguing in Publication Data
Data available

Library of Congress Cataloging in Publication Data
Evans, Andrew, Ph.D.
The EU structural funds / Andrew Evans.
p. cm.
Includes bibliographical references (p.) and index.
1. Economic development projects—Law and legislation—European
Union countries. 2. Regional planning—Law and legislation—
European Union countries. 3. Economic assistance, Domestic—Law
and legislation—European Union countries. 4. Structural adjustment
(Economic policy)—European Union countries. I. Title
KJE6436.E93 1999 338.94—dc21 99–23249

ISBN 0–19–826828–9

1 3 5 7 9 10 8 6 4 2

Typeset in Times
by Hope Services (Abingdon) Ltd.
Printed in Great Britain
on acid-free paper by
Biddles Ltd.,
Guildford & King's Lynn

Preface

This book examines the law concerning the Structural Funds and other financial instruments of the European Union. In doing so, it deals with issues of major social importance involving the use of substantial financial resources. The nature of the context in which the issues arise and of the procedures whereby they are tackled in Union practice means that reliance on traditional legal sources may be inadequate for effective analysis. In this sense, judgments of the European Courts, on which most analysis of Union law focuses, constitute little more than tips of icebergs. The materials examined in the course of the research for this book include Union legislation, soft law, judgments of the European Courts, official publications of the Union and Member States, as well as legal and social scientific literature.

The issues raised are topical because of the challenges to Union practice entailed by the introduction of a single currency, the 'Euro', and the planned future accession of several countries of Central and Eastern Europe to the Union.

The book is written for students and teachers of advanced courses in European Law, European Politics, and related areas. It should also be of interest to lawyers, in the public and private sectors, who require an introduction to sources of Union finance for their employers or clients. These sources are substantial. Over the period 1993 to 1999 a total of Euro 176 billion is to be made available from the Structural Funds alone.

Financial support for the research on which the book is based has been provided by the Tercentenary Fund of the Bank of Sweden and the European University Institute.

AE

Marian Glas,
November 1998

Contents

Part One: Structural Funds

Part Two: Other Financial Instruments

Part Three: Procedures

Tables

Treaties

ECSC Treaty

Convention on the Transitional Provisions

EC Treaty

General Agreement on Tariffs and Trade

Union Legislation and Administrative Decisions

Regulations

Directives

Decisions

ECSC Decisions

Recommendations

Opinions

National Legislation

Italy

EFTA Standing Committee Decisions

Judgments of the European Courts

Court of Justice

Court of First Instance

Judgment of the EFTA Court

Judgments of National Courts

Italy

Abbreviations

AJDA	Actualité Juridique, Droit Administratif
Bull EC	Bulletin of the European Communities
BYIL	British Yearbook of International Law
CAP	Common Agricultural Policy
CCT	Common Customs Tariff
CDE	Cahiers de Droit Européen
CES	Comité Economique et Social
CFI	Court of First Instance
CFP	Common Fisheries Policy
CMLR	Common Market Law Reports
CMLRev	Common Market Law Review
Cmnd	Command Papers (British Government Publication)
COA	Court of Auditors
COM	Communication from the European Commission
COR	Committee of the Regions
CSF	Community Support Frameworks
Débs PE	Débats du Parlement Européen
DG	Directorate-General (of the Commission)
EAGGF	European Agricultural Guidance and Guarantee Fund
ECJ	European Court of Justice
ECLR	European Competition Law Review
ECR	European Court Reports
ECSC	European Coal and Steel Community
ECU	European Currency Unit
EFTA	European Free Trade Association
EIB	European Investment Bank
EIF	European Investment Fund
EJIL	European Journal of International Law
ELR	European Law Review
EMS	European Monetary System
EMU	Economic and Monetary Union
EP Debs	European Parliament Debates
EP Doc	European Parliament Working Document
ERDF	European Regional Development Fund
ESC	Economic and Social Committee
ESF	European Social Fund
ETF	European Technology Facility
EUA	European Unit of Account
EuR	Europa Recht

Euratom	European Atomic Energy Community
Eurostat	Statistical Office of the European Communities
FIFG	Financial Instrument for Fisheries Guidance
GATT	General Agreement on Tariffs and Trade
HL	House of Lords
ICLQ	International and Comparative Law Quarterly
IDP	Integrated Development Programme
IMP	Integrated Mediterranean Programme
JCMS	Journal of Common Market Studies
JO	Journal Officiel des Communautés Européennes
JOCECA	Journal Officiel de la Communauté Européenne du Charbon et de l'Acier
JRC	Joint Research Centre
LIEI	Legal Issues of European Integration
MEPs	Members of the European Parliament
MGP	Multiannual Guidance Programme
MLR	Modern Law Review
OECD	Organization for Economic Co-operation and Development
OCT	Overseas Countries and Territories
OJ	Official Journal of the European Communities
Pedip	European Programme for the Development of Portuguese Industry
PHARE	Poland and Hungary: Assistance for Economic Restructuring
R & D	Research and Development
RDE	Rivista di Diritto Europeo
Rec	Recueil de la Cour de Justice des Communautés Européennes
RFSP	Revue Française de Science Politique
RGDIP	Revue Générale de Droit International Public
RMC	Revue du Marché Commun
RMUE	Revue du Marché Unique Européen
RTDD	Research and Technological Development, including Demonstration
RTDE	Revue Trimestrielle de Droit Européen
SEA	Single European Act
SEC	Internal Document from the Secretariat-General of the European Commission
SEDOC	Système Européen de Diffusion des Offres et des Demandes d'Emploi Enregistrés en Compensation Internationale
SG	Secretariat-General of the European Commission
SMEs	Small and medium-sized enterprises
SPD	Single Programming Document
TEN	Trans-European Network
TEU	Treaty on European Union

UA	Unit of Account
YBEL	Yearbook of European Law
ZaöRV	Zeitschrift für ausländisches öffentliches Recht und Völkerrecht

1

Introduction

This book concerns the Structural Funds and other financial instruments of the European Union (that is, the 'Union funds'[1]). Each fund has its own characteristics, which will be systematically examined in the book. What all the funds have in common, however, is that they provide financial assistance designed to support the attainment of objectives favoured by the Union. The provision of such assistance is said, in fact, to seek modification of the existing economic structure, in order to direct market forces towards an improved configuration.[2] In other words, promotion of what the EC Treaty calls 'economic and social cohesion'[3] is sought. According to Article 159 of the Treaty, the Union funds are all to support achievement of such cohesion.

Cohesion is not defined in the Treaty. However, Article 158 of the Treaty makes it clear that cohesion requires, 'in particular', the reduction of disparities between the levels of development of the various Union regions and the backwardness of the least favoured regions or islands, including rural areas. The implication is that pursuit of cohesion and, therefore, the operations of the Union funds are bound up with the concept of equality.[4] However, perceptions of the requirements of cohesion and equality may evolve and may vary as between Union institutions and Member States. In other words, the meaning of the relevant provisions may not only vary in time. Their meaning may also vary depending on the institutional context of their operation.

Ultimately, the variations may be attributable to differences in legal interpretations of social demands. However, the law may possess an internal capacity to reconcile the differences and to obscure underlying problems in the legal system. The significance or even the existence of such problems may remain obscured, unless regard is paid to the social context of the law.

As the Commission report, *Agenda 2000*,[5] recognizes, the social demands

[1] This expression is used throughout the book to denote the Structural Funds and other financial instruments generally.

[2] cf P Bianchi, 'La Réorientation des politiques structurelles de la CEE' (1991) RMC 599–603, 599.

[3] Art 159 EC.

[4] The equality principle is described as an essential legal criterion applicable to the grant of Union assistance. See R Priebe, 'Le Droit communautaire des structures agricoles' (1988) CDE 3–38, 31. See, more particularly, Joined Cases T–551/93 & 231–234/94 *Industrias Pesqueras Campos SA* [1996] ECR II–247, II–293 and II–307; and Case C–132/95 *Bent Jensen v Landbrugsministeriet—EF-Direktoratet* [19 May 1998]. Cf, regarding equality and time limits, Case T–81/97 *Regione Toscana v EC Commission* [16 July 1998].

[5] Bull EC, Supp 5/97, 21.

on both the Structural Funds and the other financial instruments are now rendered particularly pressing by moves towards admission of Central and East European countries to the Union. According to the Commission, the need is implied for major reforms to Union legislation governing their operations, particularly with a view to securing more efficient use of Union assistance.[6]

1.1 STRUCTURAL FUNDS

The Structural Funds currently comprise: the European Regional Development Fund (ERDF), the Guidance Section of the European Agricultural Guidance and Guarantee Fund (EAGGF), and the European Social Fund (ESF).[7] These Funds are examined in Part One of the book.

In particular, Chapter 2 examines the European Regional Development Fund. According to Regulation 2081/93,[8] this Fund is responsible for 'Objective 1' and 'Objective 2' of the Structural Funds, and is also involved in 'Objective 5b' operations.[9] Objective 1 is 'promoting the development and structural adjustment of regions whose development is lagging behind'. Objective 2 is 'converting the regions, frontier regions, and parts of regions seriously affected by industrial decline'. Redefinition is now proposed by the Commission, so that Objective 2 will be 'supporting the economic and social conversion of areas facing structural difficulties'.[10]

Objective 5b is 'promoting rural development by facilitating the development and structural adjustment of rural areas'.[11] In addition, the Fund contributes to 'Objective 6' operations.[12] Objective 6 is to 'promote the development and structural adjustment of regions with an extremely low population density'.[13]

It is proposed that these two Objectives will be brought within the scope of Objective 2 or Objective 1, respectively. A reduction in the number of Objectives is entailed. This reduction is designed to increase the concentration

[6] Explanatory memorandum to the Proposal of 19 Mar 1998 for a regulation laying down provisions on the Structural Funds, COM(97)131, 9.

[7] Art 2(1) of Reg 2081/93 (OJ 1993 L193/5) amending Reg 2052/88 on the tasks of the Structural Funds and their effectiveness and on the co-ordination of their activities between themselves and with the operations of the EIB and the other existing financial instruments.

[8] ibid.

[9] ibid, Art 3(1).

[10] Proposal of 19 Mar 1998 (OJ 1998 C176/1) for a regulation laying down provisions on the Structural Funds, Art 1.

[11] Art 1 of Reg 2081/93 (OJ 1993 L193/5).

[12] Objective 1 rules apply to areas covered by Objective 6. See Art 4 of Prot 6 to the Accession Agreement with Austria, Finland, and Sweden, as amended by Dec 95/1 (OJ 1995 L1/1) adjusting the instruments concerning the accession of new Member States to the EU. The Structural Funds, the FIFG, and the EIB 'shall each contribute in any appropriate fashion' to achievement of Objective 6 (ibid, Art 1).

[13] ibid.

of Union assistance and to simplify the operations of the Structural Funds.[14] In other words, greater efficiency is sought.[15]

Chapter 3 turns to the Guidance Section of the European Agricultural Guidance and Guarantee Fund. It is primarily responsible for 'Objective 5a'. Objective 5a is 'promoting rural development by speeding up the adjustment of agricultural structures in the framework of the reform of the common agricultural policy'. The Guidance Section is also involved in activity relating to Objective 1 and Objective 5b.[16]

It is now proposed that assistance from the Guidance Section will be limited to pursuit of Objective 1 and to regions covered by this Objective.[17] Objective 5a will be abolished, though assistance to the structural adjustment of agriculture will be provided by the Guarantee Section of the Fund.[18]

Finally, Chapter 4 examines the European Social Fund. Its primary responsibility is for 'Objective 3' and 'Objective 4', though it is also to provide support for Objectives 1, 2, and 5b.[19] Objective 3 concerns 'combating long-term unemployment and facilitating the integration into working life of young people and of persons exposed to exclusion from the labour market'. Objective 4 concerns 'facilitating the adaptation of workers of either sex to industrial changes and to changes in production systems'.[20]

It is now proposed that these two Objectives will be merged, to form a new Objective 3. This will be 'supporting the adaptation and modernization of policies and systems of education, training, and employment'.[21] The European Social Fund will contribute to all three new Objectives.[22]

Total Structural Fund spending over the period from 1994 to 1999 is to be almost Euro 170 billion. This sum represents around one-third of the Union Budget and around 0.4 per cent of Union gross domestic product. For 2000 to 2006, spending of up to Euro 218.4 billion is proposed.[23]

1.2 OTHER FINANCIAL INSTRUMENTS

The 'other financial instruments' of the Union are the subject of Part Two of the book. Union legislation[24] expressly treats as instruments of this kind:

[14] Proposal of 19 Mar 1998 (OJ 1998 C176/1) for a regulation laying down provisions on the Structural Funds, 4th recital in the preamble.

[15] *Agenda 2000*, Bull EC, Supp 5/97, 22.

[16] Art 2(1) of Reg 2081/93 (OJ 1993 L193/5).

[17] Proposal of 19 Mar 1998 (OJ 1998 C176/1) for a regulation laying down provisions on the Structural Funds, Art 2(2).

[18] *Agenda 2000*, Bull EC, Supp 5/97, 33.

[19] Art 3(2) of Reg 2081/93 (OJ 1993 L193/5).

[20] ibid, Art 1.

[21] Proposal of 19 Mar 1998 (OJ 1998 C176/1) for a regulation laying down provisions on the Structural Funds, Art 1.

[22] ibid, Art 2(2).

[23] ibid, Art 7(1).

[24] Art 3(1) of Reg 2082/93 (OJ 1993 L193/20) amending Reg 4253/88 laying down provisions for implementing Reg 2052/88 as regards co-ordination of the activities of the different Structural

European Coal and Steel Community (ECSC) assistance in the form of readaptation aid, loans, interest subsidies, and guarantees; European Investment Bank (EIB) loans and guarantees;[25] New Community Instrument (NCI) loans and guarantees; Euratom loans and guarantees; the Cohesion Fund; and Budgetary resources (particularly 'other actions for structural purposes').[26] The Budgetary resources treated as financial instruments include those associated with: measures accompanying reform of the common agricultural policy; Framework Programmes for research and technological development; trans-European networks; and Phare.[27]

In addition, there are the Financial Instrument for Fisheries Guidance (FIFG),[28] the Financial Instrument for the Environment (LIFE),[29] and the EFTA Financial Mechanism.[30] These seem classifiable as 'other financial instruments', since they are concerned with the structural development of the Union. Various other Budgetary resources, though not expressly so classified by the legislation, also seem classifiable as such instruments, since they too are concerned with the structural development of the Union. For example, the resources allocated to the Leonardo programme for vocational training[31] may be so classified.[32] Instruments of this kind may be contrasted with the Guarantee Section of the European Agricultural Guidance and Guarantee

Funds between themselves and with the operations of the EIB and the other existing financial instruments. Cf the Proposal of 19 Mar 1998 (OJ 1998 C176/1) for a regulation laying down provisions on the Structural Funds, Art 2(5) and (6).

[25] According to Art 2(6) (ibid), the EIB shall contribute to achieving the three new objectives.

[26] Ch B2–2 of the 1997 Budget (OJ 1997 L44/3) was headed 'Other Structural Operations' and included Pedip, IMPs, and the Community programme in the coal and steel sector.

[27] 3rd recital in the preamble to Reg 2082/93 (OJ 1993 L193/20). Phare may concern cross-border activities between regions of the Union and regions of Central and Eastern European countries. See, eg, Notice laying down guidelines for operational programmes in the framework of a Community initiative concerning border development, cross-border cooperation, and selected energy networks (OJ 1994 C180/60), para 19. See, generally, Reg 622/98 (OJ 1998 L85/1) on assistance to the applicant states in the framework of the pre-accession strategy, in particular on the establishment of Accession Partnerships; and Regional cooperation in Europe, COM(97)659. See also the Proposal of 19 Mar 1998 (OJ 1998 C176/1) for a regulation laying down provisions on the Structural Funds, 35th recital in the preamble.

[28] Reg 2080/93 (OJ 1993 L193/1) laying down provisions for implementing Reg 2052/88 as regards the FIFG. The FIFG is included in ch B2–1, headed 'Structural Funds', of the 1998 Budget (OJ 1998 L44/3), though inclusion within this heading is inconsistent with existing legislative terminology. It is now proposed, however, that the FIFG should be formally classified as a Structural Fund. See the Proposal of 19 Mar 1998 (OJ 1998 C176/1) for a regulation laying down provisions on the Structural Funds, Art 2(1). It will contribute to Objective 1 (ibid, Art 2(2)).

[29] Reg 1973/92 (OJ 1992 L206/1) establishing a financial instrument for the environment, as amended by Reg 1404/96 (OJ 1996 L181/1).

[30] Art 116 EEA.

[31] Item B3–1021 of the Budget for 1998 (OJ 1998 L44/3); and Dec 94/819 (OJ 1994 L340/8) establishing an action programme for the implementation of an EC vocational training policy.

[32] See, eg, the Ninth annual report of the Structural Funds 1997, COM(1998)562, 133.

Fund,[33] which is primarily responsible for price support in agricultural markets,[34] and with the administrative expenditure of the Union institutions.[35]

The instruments may be sectoral or 'horizontal'. Sectoral instruments are examined in Chapter 5. They are concerned with particular industrial sectors and include, for example, ECSC assistance and the Financial Instrument for Fisheries Guidance. Horizontal instruments are examined in Chapter 6. They may seek to assist the attainment of horizontal policies of the Union, that is, policies defined other than by reference to region or industrial sector. They include, for example, the Financial Instrument for the Environment and the Framework Programmes for research and technological development. Horizontal instruments may, as in the case of the operations of the European Investment Bank, have even more general objectives. This Bank is to contribute 'to the balanced and steady development of the common market'[36] and to economic and social cohesion.[37]

1.3 COMPLEMENTARITY AND ADDITIONALITY

The operations of the Union funds may be subjected by the terms of Union legislation to the principles of 'complementarity' and 'additionality'. According to the former principle, the provision of Union assistance presupposes complementary national assistance.[38] This principle is considered necessary to avoid 'fiscal illusion' and to ensure that spending reflects needs within Member States.[39]

According to the additionality principle, Union assistance should not lead Member States to reduce their own cohesion efforts, but should be additional to these efforts.[40] Hence, such assistance may not be used simply to replace

[33] Subsect B1 of the Budget for 1998 (OJ 1998 L44/3).

[34] It is now envisaged that it will contribute to the achievement of Objective 2. See the Proposal of 19 Mar 1998 (OJ 1998 C176/1) for a regulation laying down provisions on the Structural Funds, Art 2(3).

[35] Part A of the Budget for 1998 (OJ 1998 L44/3). Cf the distinction between 'an operating budget' and 'a financial policy instrument' in Opinion 1/94 *Competence of the Community to Conclude International Agreements concerning Services and Protection of Intellectual Property* [1994] ECR I–5267, I–5395.

[36] Art 130 EEC and Art 267 EC.

[37] Para 13 of the Protocol on Economic and Social Cohesion.

[38] Art 4(1) of Reg 2081/93 (OJ 1993/5). It is now proposed that 'Community action shall complement or contribute to comparable national operations'. See Art 8(1) of the Proposal of 19 Mar 1998 (OJ 1998 C176/1) for a regulation laying down provisions on the Structural Funds.

[39] D Costello, 'The Redistributive Effects of Interregional Transfers: A Comparison of the European Community and Germany' in *The Economics of Community Public Finance* (1993) 5 *European Economy* (EC Commission, Brussels, 1993) 269–294.

[40] 15th recital in the preamble to Reg 724/75 (OJ 1975 L73/1) establishing an ERDF. See also JA Winter, 'The ERDF and the Principle of Additionality' in *In Orde, Liber Amicorum Pieter Verloren van Themaat* (Kluwer, Deventer, 1982) 365–380.

public (or comparable) expenditure for structural purposes[41] undertaken by the Member State concerned in the whole of the territory eligible for assistance.[42] In principle, this means that in any given period for which Union assistance is 'programmed', the Member State is required at least to maintain its expenditure at the level of the previous programming period.[43] However, this requirement may be relaxed. According to Regulation 4253/88,[44] in the application of the requirement, account was to be taken of 'macroeconomic circumstances'. This relaxation was broadened by Regulation 2082/93.[45] According to this legislation, account is also to be taken of 'specific economic circumstances'. These comprise privatization, an unusual level of public structural expenditure in the previous programming period, and business cycles in the national economy.

It is now proposed that the Commission and the Member State will determine the level of expenditure to be maintained. As a general rule, this level will have to be at least equal to the level in the previous programming period.[46] For Objective 1 relevant expenditure will be public structural expenditure. For Objectives 2 and 3 it will be expenditure on active labour-market policies.[47]

These principles imply for the Union institutions what the European Commission describes as 'leverage'.[48] It derives from the tendency of national governments and financial institutions to favour interventions of a kind which qualify for Union assistance, because the burden and risk of financing the interventions will not fall exclusively on their own resources. As a result, national policies may be significantly affected by the availability of Union assistance. For example, the conditions which the Union attaches to the grant of assistance from the European Regional Development Fund are said to have a significant influence on the shape of the regional policies of the Member States, though the influence would be even greater if the additional-

[41] 'Le spese pubbliche o assimilabili a finalità strutturale'. Note that the English version of this provision does not make sense.

[42] Art 9(1) of Reg 2082/93 (OJ 1993 L193/20). According to Art 10(1) of the Proposal of 19 Mar 1998 (OJ 1998 C176/1) for a regulation laying down provisions on the Structural Funds, in order to achieve a genuine economic impact, the appropriations of the Funds may not replace public or other equivalent structural expenditure.

[43] Art 9(2) of Reg 2082/93 (OJ 1993 L193/20). See also New regional programmes 1997–9 under Objective 2, COM(97)524, 12.

[44] Laying down provisions for implementing Reg 2052/88 as regards co-ordination of the activities of the different Structural Funds between themselves and with the operations of the EIB and the other existing financial instruments (OJ 1988 L374/1), Art 9.

[45] Amending Reg 4253/88 (OJ 1993 L193/20), Art 9(2).

[46] Art 10(2) of the Proposal of 19 Mar 1998 (OJ 1998 C176/1) for a regulation laying down provisions on the Structural Funds.

[47] Explanatory memorandum to the Proposal of 19 Mar 1998 for a regulation laying down provisions on the Structural Funds, COM(98)131, 25.

[48] First cohesion report, COM(96)542, 114.

ity principle were fully implemented.[49] In other words, harmonization of national policies or even of the conduct of undertakings which benefit from Union assistance may take place.[50] Indeed, the Commission describes the regional policies of Member States as 'the Union's primary instruments for achieving cohesion'.[51] A less sanguine view is that the operations of the Union funds may have the effect of 'crowding out . . . plausible, alternative social policy solutions to the Union's regional problem'.[52]

1.4 OPERATIONAL FRAMEWORK

The limitations of language,[53] social demands, and their status as elements in the framework established by the Treaties[54] imply that the meaning of provisions governing the Union funds may not necessarily depend simply on their terms.[55] Their meaning may also depend on conclusions which the Union institutions draw from this framework. In other words, the operations of Union funds may be affected by 'fundamental' principles of the Treaties.[56]

The multiplicity of objectives embodied in the Treaties and the consequent necessity of evaluation entail that, in referring to the framework established by the Treaties, the Union institutions may enjoy wide discretion.[57] The discretion entailed may be so broad that, for example, the Commission may picture the requirements of the law differently from the Council of the Union.[58]

[49] Committee on Regional Policy and Regional Planning of the European Parliament, Report on the tenth annual report on the activities of the ERDF, EP Doc A2–76/86, 6.

[50] The Commission implicitly admits that, by providing finance, it influences the investment decisions of undertakings. See Commission Reply by Mr Millan to WQ 251/91 (OJ 1991 C227/15) by Mrs Cristiana Muacandini.

[51] First cohesion report, COM(96)542, 6.

[52] JJ Anderson, 'Structural Funds and the Social Dimension of EU Policy: Springboard or Stumbling Block?' in S Leibfried and P Pierson (eds), *European Social Policy* (Brookings Institution, Washington, 1995) 123–158, 124.

[53] It may be asserted that 'the tasks performed by rules are tasks for which the primary tool is the specific linguistic formulation of a rule' (F Schauer, 'Formalism' (1988) 97 Yale LJ 509–548, 510). However, it may also be admitted that 'legal terms possess a core of settled meaning and a penumbra of debatable meaning' (ibid 514) and that the choice of meaning may be determined by 'external factors' (ibid 516).

[54] cf Opinion 1/91 *Draft Agreement with the EFTA Countries relating to the Creation of the EEA* [1991] ECR I–6079, I–6103.

[55] A-G Roemer in Joined Cases 10 & 18/68 *Società 'Eridania' Zuccherifici Nazionali v EC Commission* [1969] ECR 459, 496.

[56] See, eg, regarding ECSC assistance, Case 8/57 *Groupement des Hauts Fourneaux et Aciéries Belges v ECSC High Authority* [1957–8] ECR 245, 253; and Case 13/57 *Wirtschaftsvereinigung Eisen- und Stahlindustrie, Gußstahlwerk Carl Bönnhoff, Gußstahlwerk Wilten, Ruhrstahl, and Eisenwerk Annahütte Alfred Zeller* [1957–8] ECR 265, 278.

[57] A-G Roemer in Joined Cases 63–69/72 *Wilhelm Wehrhahn Hansamühle v EC Council* [1973] ECR 1229, 1261.

[58] cf, in connection with Art 33(1) EC, AG Cosmas in Case C–122/94 *EC Commission v EU Council: aid to wine producers* [1996] ECR I–881, I–907.

In so far as such differences occur, the highly selective nature of the law's 'internal models of social reality'[59] may be demonstrated.[60]

Even so, in referring to the framework provided by the Treaties, the Union institutions may seek to use their discretion to achieve a consistency in decision making which would otherwise be precluded by the numerous variables involved in the application of individual Union law provisions. However, propelled as it is by social demands, the framework is evolutionary rather than static. It is for this reason that changes in the operations of the Union funds may reflect changes to the Union itself.[61]

For the purposes of the book, evolution of the operational framework for the Union funds is seen as being associated with establishment of the common market, development of the common market, and the search for cohesion. In the case of ECSC assistance, the relevant market is that for coal and steel. In the agricultural sector establishment and development of the common market has been subsumed by, or perhaps transformed into, establishment and development of common organizations of the agricultural markets.

In part, the evolution may reflect the 'internal logic' of the integration sought by the Treaties and acts of the Union institutions. In part, it may reflect the outcomes of intergovernmentalism, that is, bargaining between Member States. Such bargaining takes place mainly[62] during the drafting and amendment of the Treaties. Since the bargaining is 'framed' by the Treaties or their drafts, it may also be presented in integration terms. However, such presentation may obscure problems, which may materially affect the pursuit of cohesion, in the real relationship between these two evolutionary processes.

The problems revolve around the possibility that regulation of the use of Union assistance by the Union institutions may not be the sole function of the relevant Treaty provisions. These provisions may also have the function of giving effect to the outcomes of bargaining between Member States. In their latter function their meaning and the kind of equality sought may differ from those favoured by Union institutions.

[59] G Teubner, 'Autopoiesis in Law and Society: A Rejoinder to Blankenburg' (1984) 18 *Law and Society Review* 291–301.

[60] cf, regarding 'policy choices', Joined Cases T–480 & 483/93 *Antillean Rice Mills NV v EU Council and EC Commission* [1995] ECR II–2305, II–2340–2.

[61] P Cheshire, R Camagni, J-P de Gaudemaar, and JR Cuadrado Roura, '1957 to 1992: Moving Toward a Europe of Regions and Regional Policy' in L Rodwin and H Sazanami (eds), *Industrial Change and Regional Economic Transformation: The Experience of Western Europe* (Harper Collins Academic, London, 1991) 268–300, 268.

[62] cf, regarding the opportunities for Member States to 'participate in Commission decisions', the *Twenty-Fourth Report on Competition Policy* (EC Commission, Brussels, 1995) 78.

1.5 ESTABLISHMENT OF THE COMMON MARKET

Establishment of the common market sought the elimination of barriers to economic activity between Member States. Under the ECSC Treaty this process was to be limited to the coal and steel industries. It was to be accompanied by the provision of ECSC assistance to these industries.

Under the EEC Treaty barriers to economic activity generally were to be eliminated between Member States. According to this Treaty, the process was to be accompanied by the provision of assistance to farmers from what came to be called the Guidance Section of the European Agricultural Guidance and Guarantee Fund. Express provision was also made for assistance to workers from the European Social Fund and for assistance to undertakings from the European Investment Bank. No specific reference was made to a European Regional Development Fund. However, an early proposal for the creation of such a fund was submitted by the Commission to the Council under Article 235 of the EEC Treaty.[63] According to this provision, the Council, acting unanimously, might adopt acts which were necessary in the operation of the common market for the attainment of Treaty objectives and could not be based on any other Treaty provision.

1.5.1 ECSC Assistance

ECSC assistance was seen as having the limited functions of correcting 'market failure'[64] and enabling coal and steel undertakings to adjust to establishment of the common market in coal and steel.[65] For example, assistance under Articles 25 to 27 of the Convention on Transitional Provisions, adopted with the ECSC Treaty, was permissible for the restructuring of coal companies. The assistance had to be designed to enable the companies 'to meet competition on the common market'.[66]

Hence, the legality of assistance depended primarily on its impact on competition.[67] Implied constraints on the provision of assistance might be reinforced by concern to limit distortions of competition associated with the raising of sums to finance the assistance.[68]

[63] Now Art 308 EC.

[64] ie the failure of the market to ensure efficient allocation of resources. See R Quadri, R Monaco, and A Trabucchi, *Trattato istitutivo della Comunità europea del carbone e dell'acciaio: Commentario* (Giuffré, Milan, 1970) ii. 708.

[65] Case 9/55 *Société des Charbonnages de Beeringen v ECSC High Authority* [1954–56] ECR 311, 328.

[66] AG Lagrange in Case 8/55 *Fédération Charbonnière de Belgique v ECSC High Authority* [1954–56] ECR 245, 282.

[67] Case 12/57 *Syndicat de la Sidérurgie du Centre-Midi v ECSC High Authority* [1957–58] ECR 375, 386, 388.

[68] See the argument of the German Government, referring to Art 3(d) ECSC, in *Procedure for the Amendment of the Treaty pursuant to Art 95(3) and (4) ECSC* [1960] ECR 39, 45.

1.5.2 Proposed ERDF

The preamble to the EEC Treaty referred to reducing the differences existing between the various regions and the backwardness of the less favoured regions.[69] The apparent concern was with regional difficulties rather than regional development.[70] Thus the Treaty did not expressly require the adoption of a regional policy. Rather, the Treaty authors apparently regarded the establishment of the common market as in itself generally favourable to regional development.[71]

However, Member States tended to adopt divergent approaches to their regional problems. The very divergence of these approaches might be damaging to the undistorted competition sought through establishment of the common market.[72] The response of the Commission was to propose the creation of a European Regional Development Fund in 1969.[73] According to the Commission, such a Fund was needed to assist the reduction of regional disparities in a manner consistent with establishment of the common market. Specifically, by co-ordinating national action[74] the operations of the Fund could protect Member States from feeling compelled to bid against each other for mobile investment through the grant of state aid.[75] In other words, the thrust of the Commission proposal was to secure greater consistency between the regional development efforts of Member States and the requirements of establishing the common market. However, this early proposal was not accepted by the Council.

1.5.3 EAGGF, Guidance Section

The Guidance Section of the European Agricultural Guidance and Guarantee Fund was created explicitly as an integral element in the establishment of the common agricultural policy. As was judicially recognized, at their initiation the common organizations of agricultural markets might not completely measure up to the objectives of this policy, as listed in Article 39

[69] 5th recital in the preamble to the EEC Treaty.

[70] F Massart-Pierard, 'La Dialectique européanisation–régionalisation' in *L'Europe et ses régions* (Faculté de Droit de Liège, The Hague, 1975) 289–310, 294.

[71] PSRF Mathijsen, 'The Role of Regional Policy in the European Economic Integration Process' in S Bates, W Finnie, JA Usher, and H Wildberg (eds), *In Memoriam JDB Mitchell* (Sweet and Maxwell, London, 1983) 171–183. See also Anderson, n 52 above, 135.

[72] Proposal of 17 Oct 1969 (JO 1969 C152/6) on the organization of Community means of action in the regional policy field.

[73] ibid.

[74] cf European Parliament Resolution of 11 May 1967 (JO 1967 2059) inviting the Council to take the initiatives necessary to ensure a better balance in the economic development of the various regions of the Community.

[75] Commissioner Thompson (EP Debs No 158, 41, 13 Feb 1973).

of the EEC Treaty. Rather, they might contain gaps capable of endangering market stability in a part of the Community.[76]

Accordingly, this Section of the Fund was during the transitional period for establishment of the common market[77] to support action undertaken according to Community rules for attaining the objectives set out in Article 39 of the Treaty, including structural changes necessitated by the establishment of the common market.[78] In practice, its work during the transitional period was to be limited to coping with such changes.[79]

1.5.4 ESF

The European Social Fund originally had the function of facilitating establishment of the common market. According to Article 123 of the EEC Treaty, the Fund was to act 'to improve employment opportunities for workers in the common market'. By providing assistance to migration it would contribute to realizing the potential of the common market to reduce unemployment in the less developed regions and to improve the welfare of individual workers and the general economy. In other words, it would counter distortions of competition associated with the 'imperfect mobility of labour as a factor of production'.[80]

1.5.5 EIB

The European Investment Bank apparently owed its creation to a concern that undertakings should not be denied opportunities to participate in the common market by their lack of access to investment capital.[81] Hence, Article 130(b) of the EEC Treaty gave the Bank the task of financially supporting 'projects for modernizing or converting undertakings or for developing fresh activities called for by the progressive establishment of the common market'. Such support was expected to be consistent with the free competition sought through establishment of the common market, because the Bank only provided finance through interest-bearing loans.[82]

[76] Case 153/73 *Holtz and Willemsen GmbH v EC Council and EC Commission* [1974] ECR 675, 695.

[77] Art 8 EEC provided for a transitional period of twelve years.

[78] Art 3(1)(d) of Reg 25/62 (JO 1962 991) on the financing of the CAP.

[79] AG Capotorti in Joined Cases 117/76 & 16/77 *Albert Ruckdeschel & Co and Hansa-Lagerhaus Stroh & Co v Hauptzollamt Hamburg-St Annen* [1977] ECR 1753, 1783.

[80] See, regarding this 'market imperfection', 'State Aid Control in the Context of Other Community Policies' (1994) 4 *European Economy*, Supp A, 4.

[81] M Keating, 'Europeanism and Regionalism' in B Jones and M Keating (eds), *The European Union and the Regions* (Clarendon Press, Oxford, 1995) 1–22, 17.

[82] DA Pinder, 'Small Firms, Regional Development, and the European Investment Bank' (1986) 24 JCMS 171–186, 172.

1.5.6 Equality

Practice in the provision of assistance reflected approaches to equality embodied in the Treaties. For example, limitations to the functions of ECSC assistance might be found to be demanded by Article 4(b) of the ECSC Treaty. It prohibited measures or practices, including those of the ECSC institutions, which discriminated between producers, between purchasers, or between consumers in the coal and steel sectors.[83] The implication drawn from the terms of this provision was that ECSC assistance was not arbitrarily to discriminate regarding 'conditions of competition'.[84]

The proposal for creation of a European Regional Development Fund was based on comparable thinking. According to this thinking, in so far as increased regional equality was desirable, it was essentially dependent on the liberalization sought through establishment of the common market. To promote such liberalization, uncoordinated interventions by individual Member States were to be curbed. In essence, liberal equality, that is, equality which results from the limitation of public intervention in the market,[85] was favoured.

Equality issues were addressed more directly in connection with the Guidance Section of the European Agricultural Guidance and Guarantee Fund. Where two different products were equally suitable for a particular purpose whilst one was intrinsically more costly than the other, the Guidance Section could not be used artificially to equalize the costs. Such use of the Fund would, it was thought, have conflicted with the objective of improving agricultural productivity in Article 39(1)(a) of the EEC Treaty and with the prohibition of discrimination between consumers or producers in Article 40(3) of the Treaty.[86]

The question whether discrimination was entailed by assistance from the Communities was thus approached by assessing the impact of the assistance on competition.[87] This impact was assessed by reference to the compatibility of the assistance with the terms of individual Treaty provisions.

[83] cf, regarding Art 4(c) ECSC, Quadri, Monaco, and Trabucchi, n 64 above, i. 103.

[84] Case 13/57 *Wirtschaftsvereinigung Eisen- und Stahlindustrie, Gußstahlwerk Carl Bönnhoff, Gußstahlwerk Wilten, Ruhrstahl, and Eisenwerk Annahütte Alfred Zeller v ECSC High Authority* [1957–58] ECR 265, 301, 311 (AG Lagrange).

[85] Community assistance was treated as of public-law character. See Joined Cases 4–13/59 *Mannesmann AG v ECSC High Authority* [1960] ECR 113, 131; and Case 18/60 *Louis Worms v ECSC High Authority* [1962] ECR 195, 204.

[86] A-G Capotorti in Joined Cases 117/76 & 16/77 *Albert Ruckdeschel & Co and Hansa-Lagerhaus Ströh & Co v Hauptzollamt Hamburg-St Annen* [1977] ECR 1753, 1783.

[87] Case 15/57 *Cie des Hauts Fourneaux de Chasse v ECSC High Authority* [1957–58] ECR 211, 228.

1.5.7 Intergovernmentalism

Practice implied that assistance from the Communities would essentially support individual actions by Member States,[88] which considered themselves to be in a better position than the Commission to identify, evaluate, and act on claims for assistance.[89] It also implied that the assistance would not take on broader functions which might have been regarded by Member States as encroaching on their powers.[90] In other words, the assistance was to promote the 'interests of the common market' without jeopardizing the 'fundamental economic interests' of Member States.[91]

Such treatment of Community assistance may have reflected the outcomes of intergovernmental bargaining between Member States. For example, in such bargaining creation of the European Social Fund might be presented as being necessary to 'compensate' Italy for the social costs likely to result from the exposure of undertakings in the Mezzogiorno to competition from more industrialized parts of the Community.[92] Such compensation might be used by Member States to implement national policies which, in reality, had little to do with establishment of the common market.[93] Implicit problems in the use of the assistance for such purposes might be obscured by the assumption that the legality of assistance was determinable by reference to the compatibility of the assistance with the terms of particular provisions governing its use.[94] Through limiting consideration of the social impact of the assistance, this assumption obviated the need to examine the significance of the variations in the meaning attributed to these provisions by the Community institutions and Member States, respectively.

1.6 DEVELOPMENT OF THE COMMON MARKET

Progress in the elimination of barriers to economic activity between Member States exposed problems which, it was felt, could not be addressed simply through the application of provisions prohibiting such barriers. This feeling was reinforced by realization that establishment of the common market did

[88] Bianchi, n 2 above, 600. See, more particularly, regarding the ERDF, Cheshire, Camagni, de Gaudemaar, and Cuadrado Roura, n 61 above, 283.

[89] Anderson, n 52 above, 135.

[90] See the argument of the German Government in *Procedure for the Amendment of the Treaty pursuant to Art 95(3) and (4) ECSC* [1960] ECR 39, 44.

[91] A-G Lagrange in Joined Cases 2 & 3/60 *Niederrheinische Bergwerks-Aktiegesellschaft and Unternehmensverband des Aachener Steinkolenbergbaues v ECSC High Authority* [1961] ECR 133, 153.

[92] Cheshire, Camagni, de Gaudemaar, and Cuadrado Roura, n 61 above, 279.

[93] Anderson, n 52 above, 134.

[94] Case 12/57 *Syndicat de la Sidérurgie du Centre-Midi v High Authority* [1957–58] ECR 375, 386–388.

not in itself offer a solution to economic problems faced by Member States. In particular, it did not offer a solution to problems arising from changes in international economic conditions, such as the 1973–4 'oil shock' and its aftermath.[95] Hence, Community efforts to fashion economic policies were associated with development of the common market.[96] A more policy-oriented role for Community assistance was implied.[97]

1.6.1 ERDF

The European Regional Development Fund was established by Regulation 724/75.[98] This measure was adopted under Article 235 of the EEC Treaty.

The rationale for creation of the Fund, as expressed by the Commission, had evolved. According to the Commission, it was an illusion to hope for the convergence of Member States' economies as long as regional problems continued to weigh so heavily on certain economies. Hence, the development of Community regional policy was considered to be one of the conditions of continuing economic integration.[99] In practice, however, the operations of the Fund might owe less to regional policy considerations than to the requirements of other, more articulated Community policies.

Competition policy

According to Article 92(1) of the EEC Treaty,[100] save as otherwise provided in this Treaty, any aid granted by a Member State or through state resources in any form whatsoever which distorted or threatened to distort competition by favouring certain undertakings or the production of certain goods should, in so far as it affected trade between Member States, be incompatible with the common market.[101] However, the principles of complementarity and additionality meant that assistance from the Fund might not simply encourage what might be characterized, from the perspective of Article 92(1), as financial interventions distorting competition. The same principles meant that, in granting assistance, the Fund might also increase the scale or scope of the kind of interventions with which this provision was concerned. For example,

[95] *Eleventh EC General Report* (EC Commission, Brussels, 1978), 137–138. Cf the explanatory memorandum to the proposal for a regulation amending Reg 724/75, COM(81)589.

[96] According to Art 2 EEC, Community objectives were to be achieved not only through establishment of the common market but also through the approximation of national economic policies.

[97] cf the arguments concerning the 'programming' of Community legislative activity by policy in Case 13/83 *European Parliament v EC Council: transport policy* [1985] ECR 1513.

[98] Establishing an ERDF (OJ 1975 L73/1). See, generally, L van Depoele, 'Het Europees Fonds voor Regionale Ontwikkeling' (1975) *SEW* 387–394.

[99] *Community Regional Policy—New Guidelines*, Bull EC, Supp 2/77, 6.

[100] Now Art 87(1) EC.

[101] cf, regarding Art 81 EC and the allocation of Union assistance, T–369/94 & 85/95 *DIR International Film Srl v EC Commission* [19 Feb 1998].

Fund assistance might lead Member States to provide complementary aid in regions where Directorate General IV, the Commission Directorate General responsible for competition policy, considered that aid was prohibited by Article 92(1).[102]

Resolution of such contradictions in Community practice might be seen as dependent on adaptation of Fund operations to competition policy requirements. Certainly, it was noted that in the application of Article 92 the Commission co-ordinated regional aid granted by Member States. Such co-ordination was selective, in that account was taken of the differing intensity of the problems facing different regions.[103] The Community would have been inconsistent, it was argued, if the same selectivity was not shown in the operations of the Fund.[104]

This argument might lead to claims that the Community itself was bound by Article 92, when it granted 'pecuniary advantages' to individual undertakings.[105] Certainly, Article 19(1) of Regulation 1787/84[106] seemed consistent with Commission objections under Article 92 of the Treaty to state aid which merely kept inefficient undertakings in operation.[107] It required that investment projects in industry or the craft or service sector which might be assisted by the Fund were to relate to economically sound activities intended to help create or maintain permanent jobs. Moreover, this Regulation did 'not prejudice the application of Articles 92 to 94 of the EEC Treaty, particularly as regards establishing and modifying the areas aided by national regional aid schemes'.[108]

In practice, the result might be a preference for assisting infrastructure and training, because such assistance was regarded as less likely to distort competition than other kinds of assistance.[109] However, such assistance might not necessarily have been the most appropriate for regional development purposes.[110]

[102] A Evans, *EC Law of State Aid* (Oxford Series in EC Law; Clarendon Press, Oxford, 1997) 201–205. The problem continues. See eg COA annual report for 1996 (OJ 1997 C348/1), para 6.66.

[103] First Resolution of 20 Oct 1971 (JO 1971 C111/1) of the representatives of the governments of the Member States, meeting within the Council, on general systems of regional aid, Annex, para 7.

[104] ESC Opinion of 29 Apr 1982 (OJ 1982 C178/38) on the proposal for a regulation amending Reg 724/75, para 8.4.

[105] A-G Verloren van Themaat in Joined Cases 213–215/81 *Norddeutsches Vieh- und Fleischkontor Herbert Will, Trawako, Transit-Warenhandels-Kontor GmbH & Co, and Gedelfi Grosseinkauf GmbH & Co v Bundesanstalt für Landwirtschaftliche Marktordnung* [1982] ECR 3583, 3617.

[106] On the ERDF (OJ 1984 L169/1).

[107] Evans, n 102 above.

[108] OJ 1984 L169/1, Art 44. See also Commission Reply by Mr Sutherland to WQ 2058/86 (OJ 1987 C157/29) by Mr Rheinhold Bocklet. Cf, now, Art 7(1) Reg 2081/93 (OJ 1993 L193/1); and Art 11 of the Proposal of 19 Mar 1998 (OJ 1998 C176/1) for a regulation laying down provisions on the Structural Funds.

[109] Evans, n 102 above.

[110] A Cutler, C Haslam, J Williams, and K Williams, *1992—the Struggle for Europe* (Berg, New York, 1989) 79.

Sectoral policies

The *Guidelines for Community Regional Policy* envisaged 'regional impact assessment.'[111] In all the major policy fields the Commission would take account of the regional effects which its proposals might have, especially as regards employment. Where necessary, it would propose appropriate additional measures to permit the achievement of the policy aims concerned and the correction of any unfavourable effects on the regions. In particular, assistance from the Fund would be used to facilitate application of the relevant policy or to correct any effects likely to jeopardize the 'proper functioning of the Community'.[112] Equally, Recommendation 79/535[113] stated that the regional aspects of sectoral policies had to be taken into account in regional development programmes, which were to be drawn up by Member States and on which the grant of assistance from the Fund was to be planned.[114]

In practice, attention focused on policies for 'crisis' sectors. Thus research was undertaken into the regional impact of Community policies for textiles, steel, and shipbuilding.[115] It was observed, for example, that the problems of the shipbuilding industry were particularly serious because of the current high levels of unemployment and because the shipyards were generally to be found at coastal locations where there were few alternative job opportunities.[116] Accordingly, a special assessment was made of the regions likely to be most severely affected by the restructuring of this industry.[117]

Regulation 214/79,[118] which amended Regulation 724/75,[119] reflected such practice. It enabled the Fund to intervene where the Communities had become responsible as a result of a decision in one of their areas of competence, such as external relations, agricultural policy, or industrial policy, which had regional consequences.[120] Accordingly, the Commission began to perform analyses designed to make it possible to determine which regions would be affected by such policies and to propose intervention by the Fund.[121]

111 Bull EC, Supp 2/77, 9.

112 ibid, 12.

113 On the regional development programmes (OJ 1979 L143/9), para 4.

114 See, regarding such programmes, sect 7.4.1 below.

115 *EC Eleventh General Report* (EC Commission, Brussels, 1978) 140.

116 *Seventh Report on Competition Policy* (EC Commission, Brussels, 1978) 140. Cf the Council Resolution of 19 Sept 1978 (OJ 1978 C229/1) on the reorganization of the shipbuilding industry, paras 1 and 4.2.

117 *EC Thirteenth General Report* (EC Commission, Brussels, 1980) 127.

118 Amending Reg 724/75 (OJ 1979 L35/1), Art 2.

119 OJ 1975 L73/1.

120 Proposals of 15 Oct 1979 for regulations instituting specific Community regional development projects under Art 13 of the ERDF Regulation, COM(79)540, 2.

121 Report of the Committee on Regional Policy and Regional Planning on action taken on the European Parliament's resolutions in the field of regional policy since 1979, EP Doc A 2–65/86, 11.

A consequence was that the Fund might be employed more to tackle regional problems associated with implementation of sectoral policies[122] than to promote regional development.[123]

1.6.2 EAGGF, Guidance Section

In the agricultural sector the idea developed that the Guidance Section of the European Agricultural Guidance and Guarantee Fund acted 'in the higher interest of the proper functioning of . . . market organizations'.[124] According to this idea, assistance from the Guidance Section was to relate to 'the structural modifications required' for the proper functioning of these organizations.[125] The emphasis was on implementation of the common agricultural policy.

1.6.3 Equality

The equality concept retained importance for the operations of the funds. In the case of the Guidance Section of the European Agricultural Guidance and Guarantee Fund, the prohibition of discrimination in Article 40(3) of the EEC Treaty still had to be respected.[126] However, perceptions of the requirements of this provision had evolved. In *Holtz*,[127] for example, special Community assistance had been provided to Italian millers, but not to millers in other Member States. According to the Court of Justice, such assistance might lawfully distinguish[128] by reference to regional or other conditions of production or consumption. The distinctions had to be based on objective criteria, which ensured a proportionate distribution of advantages and disadvantages for those concerned without differentiating between the territory of Member States.[129] In other words, assistance which affected farmers

[122] Report of the Committee on Regional Policy, Regional Planning, and Transport on the guidelines for Community regional policy, EP Doc 307/77, 43.

[123] European Parliament Resolution of 18 Nov 1988 (OJ 1988 C326/289) on Community regional policy and the role of the regions, para 5. See also the ESC Opinion of 29 Jan 1986 (OJ 1986 C75/12) on national regional development aid, para 5.4.2; and the ESC Opinion of 29 Sept 1977 (OJ 1977 C292/5) on the guidelines for a Community regional policy, para 2.10.

[124] Case 97/76 *Merkur Aussenhandel GmbH & Co KG v EC Commission* [1977] ECR 1063, 1078.

[125] Art 2(2)(c) of Reg 25/62 (JO 1962 991) on the financing of the CAP.

[126] Case 192/83 *Greece v EC Commission: production aid for tomatoes and peaches* [1985] ECR 2791, 2811–2812. The granting of assistance which had ceased to be necessary also constituted an infringement of this provision. See Case 2/77 *Hoffmann's Starkfabriken v Hauptzollamt Bielefeld* [1977] ECR 1375, 1394.

[127] Case 153/73 *Holtz and Willemsen GmbH v EC Council and EC Commission* [1974] ECR 675.

[128] In the English version of the judgment 'be distinguished' is an inadequate translation of the German 'unterschiedlich ausgestaltet werden'.

[129] ibid, 695. See also A-G Capotorti in Joined Cases 117/76 & 16/77 *Albert Ruckdeschel & Co and Hansa-Lagerhaus Ströh & Co v Hauptzollamt Hamburg-St Annen* [1977] ECR 1753, 1780.

differently according to regional conditions was permitted, if it was 'determined on the basis of objective rules, formulated to meet the needs of the general common organization of the market, for all the products concerned'.[130]

In effect, the question of whether assistance was discriminatory increasingly came to depend[131] on the requirements of the relevant policies being developed by the Communities.[132] According to this emphasis on the development of policies, assistance now had to be provided in such a way as to confer uniform benefits on all persons who met the conditions contained in legislation implementing the policies.[133]

Pursuit of pluralist equality, according to which differential treatment might be justified 'on the basis of the requirements of the structural policy',[134] was entailed. For example, large undertakings might be found to be in a position by their own means to overcome the difficulties of adaptation with which they were confronted by development of the common agricultural policy. Hence, such undertakings might be denied assistance. On the other hand, assistance to a small undertaking might be justified. It might be justified, because the 'structural alterations which [would] be necessary during the next few years [might] . . . condemn it to death in the absence of external aid'.[135]

It was still felt that geography did not in itself constitute 'a prohibited kind of discrimination'. Rather, it was 'the consequence—that was not contrary to the rules of the Treaty—of a more advantageous location for certain undertakings'. However, it might be discriminatory for the provision of Community assistance to disregard geographical disadvantages and thereby effectively reinforce such disadvantages.[136]

Therefore, market conceptions of equality still implied constraints on the grant of assistance. However, assistance might be justified by virtue of the policy orientation of these conceptions.

[130] Case 179/84 *Piercarlo Bozzetti v Invernizzi SpA and Ministero del Tesoro* [1985] ECR 2301, 2323. See also Case 244/83 *Meggle Milchindustrie GmbH & Co KG v EC Council* [1986] ECR 1101, 1116. Cf, regarding Art 4(b) ECSC and state aid, Case C–99/92 *Terni SpA and Italsider SpA v Cassa Conguaglio per il Settore Elettrico* [1994] ECR I–541, I–558–559.

[131] As did the acceptability of state aid. See Case C–86/89 *Italy v EC Commission: aid for the use of wine musts* [1990] ECR I–3891, I–3908–3910.

[132] A-G Mischo in Case 15/85 *Consorzio Cooperative d'Abruzzo v EC Commission* [1987] ECR 1005, 1030. Cf, now, Joined Cases C–38 & 151/90 *R v Thomas Edward Lomas* [1992] ECR I–1781, I–1814.

[133] cf Case 265/78 *H Ferwerda BV v Produktschap voor Vee en Vlees* [1980] ECR 617, 628. Cf, in connection with Art 7 EEC and the Guidance Section of the EAGGF, the argument of the Commission in Case 152/79 *Kevin Lee v Minister for Agriculture* [1980] ECR 1495, 1504.

[134] A-G Roemer in Joined Cases 10 & 18/68 *Società 'Eridania' Zuccherifici Nazionali v EC Commission* [1969] ECR 459, 501.

[135] ibid.

[136] Joined Cases 63–69/72 *Wilhelm Wehrhahn Hansamühle v EC Council* [1973] ECR 1229, 1250. Note that the English translation ('prohibitive discrimination') of the original German ('*unerlaubte Diskriminierung*') is misleading.

1.6.4 Intergovernmentalism

The funds might be presented as compensating Member States, according to the outcomes of intergovernmental bargaining, for the social costs associated with their acceptance of Community policies. For example, the creation of the European Regional Development Fund might be presented as compensating the United Kingdom for the costs of implementing a common agricultural policy ill-adapted to the structure of its agricultural industry.[137] Its creation might also be presented as compensating Italy for the costs of implementing a policy ill-adapted to the composition of its agricultural production.[138] In reality, however, the funds might assist Member States in facilitating the economic restructuring which was in any case demanded by international economic conditions. Their use might have less to do with development of the common market than with assisting Member States.

The implicit conflict between interpretation of the relevant provisions according to the outcomes of such bargaining and the interpretation of the same provisions adopted by Union institutions tended to be obscured by policy orientation. On the one hand, Commission competition policy might be seen not only as making assistance to regional development more effective but also as ensuring that the assistance was not diverted from less favoured regions contrary to the outcomes of intergovernmental bargaining. On the other hand, the influence of sectoral policies pursued by the Union institutions meant that the assistance might be consistent with 'fair return' bargains reached by Member States in sectoral contexts.

1.7 COHESION

The concept of cohesion was formally introduced into the EEC Treaty by the Single European Act.[139] Its introduction reflected doubts over whether existing arrangements for Community assistance would be adequate to counteract the regional effects of completion of the internal market,[140] which the

[137] cf Reg 1888/84 (OJ 1984 L177/1) introducing special measures of Community interest in the field of employment; Reg 1889/84 (OJ 1984 L177/4) introducing special measures of Community interest relating to transport infrastructure; and Reg 1890/84 (OJ 1984 L177/7) introducing special measures of Community interest relating to energy strategy. All three measures involved the grant of Community assistance to the UK, though the last two also benefited Germany.

[138] C André, J-F Drevet, and E Landaburu, 'Regional Consequences of the Internal Market' (1989) *Contemporary European Affairs* 205–214; and Cheshire, Camagni, de Gaudemaar, and Cuadrado Roura, n 61 above, 279.

[139] OJ 1987 L169/1.

[140] The 'internal market' is defined in Art 14(2) EC.

Commission admitted were likely to be 'uneven'.[141] In particular, it was feared that increased competition would tend to favour the more developed, central regions of the Community at the expense of less developed, peripheral regions.[142] This tendency might, it was also feared, be reinforced by the deregulation of transport.[143]

Accordingly, seemingly important amendments to the EEC Treaty were introduced by the Single European Act.[144] Thus Article 130a of the Treaty now provided that to promote its overall harmonious development, the Community was to develop and pursue its actions leading to the strengthening of its economic and social cohesion. In particular, the operations of the funds were to aim at reducing disparities between[145] the various regions and the backwardness of the least favoured regions.[146] It was thus underlined that Union assistance was not to be limited to establishment and development of the common market. Rather, it was to meet cohesion requirements.

In fact, this provision meant that cohesion became an 'implicit objective' of the Treaty[147] rather than merely a consequence of policies pursued under the Treaty. It thereby created the need to transform the organization of Community assistance.[148]

The Treaty on European Union went further. Article 2 of this Treaty[149] expressly established that the strengthening of cohesion as well as the common market were both means of achieving the economic and social progress sought by the Union.[150] The same Treaty also amended the EC Treaty, so as to establish the promotion of cohesion as part of the 'task' of the European Community[151] and the strengthening of cohesion as one of its 'activities'.[152] Further amendments to the EC Treaty confirmed the fundamental character of cohesion, in the sense that cohesion requirements had to be respected in

[141] Completing the internal market, COM(85)310, 8. See, generally, I Begg, 'The Regional Dimension of the "1992" Proposals' (1989) *Regional Studies* 368–376.

[142] G Tichy, 'Theoretical and Empirical Considerations on the Dimension of an Optimum Integration Area in Europe' (1992) *Aussenwirtschaft* 107–137.

[143] Cheshire, Camagni, de Gaudemaar, and Cuadrado Roura, n 61 above, 287.

[144] OJ 1987 L169/1.

[145] The TEU later inserted 'levels of development of'.

[146] The TEU later added 'including rural areas', and the Amsterdam Treaty (OJ 1997 C340/1) inserted 'or islands'.

[147] cf, regarding the concept of 'solidarity', the argument of the Commission in Joined Cases T–551/93 & 231–234/94 *Industrias Pesqueras Campos SA v EC Commission* [1996] ECR II–247, II–313.

[148] C Mestre and Y Petit, 'La Cohesion économique et sociale après le Traité sur l'Union européenne' (1995) RTDE 207–243.

[149] Moreover, according to the 7th recital in the preamble to the TEU, the Member States are determined to promote economic and social progress for their peoples within the context of the accomplishment of the internal market and of reinforced cohesion and environmental protection.

[150] However, even if policy objectives are reconciled in accordance with this provision, conflicts between these means may remain. Cf, regarding 'conflict of method', T Frazer, 'The New Structural Funds, State Aids, and Interventions on the Single Market' (1995) ELR 3–19, 10.

[151] Art 2 EC.

[152] Art 3(j) EC (now Art 3(k) EC).

action under this Treaty generally.[153] Hence, cohesion is said to have been 'constitutionalized.'[154]

However, the practical significance of these legal developments for the operations of the Union funds is uncertain. In part, this uncertainty may reflect lack of definition of the 'social meaning' of cohesion. In part, it may reflect problems in the relationship between particular provisions on cohesion and the more general framework of the Treaties.

1.7.1 Definition of Cohesion

The meaning of cohesion may vary, depending whether political, social, or economic perspectives on its definition are favoured. Economic perspectives, however, seem generally to have been dominant in Union practice.

Political perspectives

From a political perspective, cohesion may be connected with the idea of solidarity.[155] It may be regarded as designed to demonstrate the value of Union membership to weaker regions.[156] In particular, it may be regarded as referring to the level of regional disparities which is found politically acceptable. Accordingly, the Economic and Social Committee considers that its meaning may vary historically and may become increasingly demanding, as economic union and political union are achieved.[157]

Social perspectives

From a social perspective, cohesion may be seen as seeking the convergence of basic incomes and equality of access to employment. It may even be seen as concerning 'the quality of life'[158] or, according to the Commission, 'the quality of European citizenship'.[159]

Economic perspectives

From an economic perspective, cohesion may be regarded as designed to allow all regions to compete in the internal market and in the monetary

[153] Art 130b EC (now Art 159 EC).

[154] A Valle Galvez, 'La cohesion economica y social como objetivo de la Union europea: analisis e perspectivas' (1994) *Revista de Instituciones Europeas* 341–378, 352. Cf, regarding the constitutionalization of 'social rights', E Szyszczak, 'Future Directions in European Union Social Policy Law' (1995) ILJ 19–32, 31.

[155] Dooge Report (interim report by the *ad hoc* Committee on Institutional Affairs), Bull EC 11–1984, 3.51.

[156] Keating, n 81 above, 18.

[157] Opinion of 27 Feb 1992 (OJ 1992 C98/50) on economic and social cohesion, para 12.1.1.

[158] J Scott, *Development Dilemmas in European Community Law* (Open University Press, Buckingham, 1995).

[159] First cohesion report, COM(96)542, 13–14. See also the European Parliament Resolution of 18 June 1998 (OJ 1998 C210/189) on *Agenda 2000: economic and social cohesion*, preamble, recital D.

union[160] by endowing them with the requisite infrastructure and skills. In other words, it may be regarded as designed to ensure a fairer spread of the benefits of economic integration.[161] To these ends, the Commission considers that redistributive action, involving the transfer of resources to less favoured regions, is required.[162]

Attempts may be made in Union practice to present such action as being reconcilable with the requirements of the competitiveness sought through the common market. It may be said, for example, that competitive Union industry can contribute to cohesion and that cohesion can provide industry with the benefits of a wider commercial and geographical base.[163] Again, assistance to research and technological development, including assistance to promote the full use of the capabilities of less favoured regions, is regarded as equivalent to encouraging European industry to become more competitive.[164]

A formal basis for such reconciliation is apparently provided by the EC Treaty. According to Article 159 of the Treaty,[165] the formulation and implementation of Union policies, presumably including competition policy, shall take into account cohesion objectives and contribute to their achievement,[166] as shall Union actions and the implementation of the internal market.

However, the potential for conflict is implicitly admitted in the Treaty. Article 157(3) provides that action to promote the competitiveness of European industry 'shall not provide a basis for the introduction by the Community of any measure which could lead to a distortion of competition'.

Conflict between cohesion and other Union concerns may be most acute in moves towards economic and monetary union.[167] In particular, the convergence criteria,[168] to be met by Member States adopting the single currency (the 'Euro'), require public expenditure to be limited. On the other hand, the principles of complementarity and additionality mean that Union assistance

[160] J de Ruyt, *L'Acte unique européen* (University of Brussels, 1987) 195.

[161] HW Armstrong, 'The Role and Evolution of European Community Regional Policy' in Jones and Keating, n 81 above, 23–53, 23.

[162] The EIB, the other financial instruments, and strengthening economic and social cohesion, COM(88)244, 3.

[163] Dec 96/413 (OJ 1996 L167/55) on the implementation of a Community programme to strengthen the competitiveness of European industry, para 9.

[164] *Evaluation of the Effects of the EC Framework Programme for Research and Technological Development on Economic and Social Cohesion in the Community* (EC Commission, Brussels, 1991) 13.

[165] Prior to the Amsterdam Treaty, it was Art 130b EC.

[166] cf Art 6 EC, which requires that environmental protection requirements must be integrated into the definition and implementation of other Union policies. In contrast, Art 178 EC merely requires that the Union 'shall take account' of development co-operation objectives in the policies it implements that are likely to affect developing countries.

[167] See the link made with cohesion in Dec 90/141 (OJ 1990 L78/23) on the attainment of progressive convergence of economic policies and convergence during stage one of EMU, 1st recital in the preamble.

[168] Art 121(1) EC and the Protocol on the convergence criteria.

encourages such expenditure. The relationship between the cohesion sought by Union assistance and convergence is only partly reconciled by the Cohesion Fund.[169] This Fund seeks to assist certain Member States with a programme for meeting the convergence criteria to tackle their cohesion problems. The legislation governing this Fund abandons the additionality principle, though it maintains the complementarity principle.[170]

The Commission considers that more radical efforts at reconciliation are required. According to the Commission, overall reductions in public expenditure necessary to meet the convergence criteria should be accompanied by a restructuring of expenditure, to improve the competitiveness of the weaker regions. Through Union assistance to improve their competitiveness, it is claimed, 'nominal convergence' (that is, compliance with the convergence criteria) and 'real convergence' (that is, cohesion) can be rendered mutually compatible objectives.[171]

Such claims exemplify the heavy demands implied for Union law by the evolution of the role expected of the Union funds. This evolution means that the operations of the funds are no longer governed by the terms of provisions concerning the establishment of the common market or by the requirements of Union policies. Rather, their operations are supposed to be determined by reference to the contribution which each fund may make to cohesion. As a result, the law needs, in regulating these operations, to absorb the various conceptions of cohesion and economic reasoning as to the most effective means of achieving it. This need is evident not only in Commission reports on the work of the funds. It is also evident in the criticisms of such work regularly made by the European Parliament, the Economic and Social Committee, and the Court of Auditors, as well as by national bodies, such as the House of Lords Select Committee on the European Communities.[172]

At the same time, the law may have need of information about the impact of the operations of the Union funds on cohesion.[173] Established Union procedures may not necessarily be adapted to provide the necessary information. In other words, the 'environmental exchange mechanisms'[174] of Union law may be ill adapted to realization of cohesion requirements. For example, according to the Court of Justice, it depends on the circumstances whether it is 'opportune' for the Commission to consult the competitors of those

[169] Reg 1164/94 (OJ 1994 L130/1) establishing a Cohesion Fund.

[170] ibid, 19th recital in the preamble and Art 7.

[171] Fifth periodic report on the social and economic situation and development of the regions of the Community, COM(94)322, 14.

[172] References to the criticisms will be made, as appropriate, in the following chapters.

[173] An analogy might be drawn with the effect given to the express requirement in Art 187 EC that association with the OCT be implemented on the basis of the principles set out in this Treaty and of the experience acquired in Joined Cases T–480 & 483/93 *Antillean Rice Mills NV v EC Council and EC Commission* [1995] ECR II–2305, II–2340–1.

[174] cf Teubner, n 59 above.

benefiting from Union assistance before granting it.[175] However, consultation of competitors and others may be a necessary precondition for appreciation of the likely impact of such assistance. Lack of such consultation contributes to the 'information deficit which imbues this area of policymaking'.[176]

1.7.2 Co-ordination

The demands made on Union law may be exaggerated when efforts are made to co-ordinate the operations of the Union funds. According to the legislation, the funds may be applied independently. They may also contribute, each according to the specific rules governing its operations, to any measure supported by one or more of the Structural Funds.[177]

It is a well-established view of the Union institutions that the impact of the Union funds may depend on such co-ordination.[178] According to the *Report and Proposals on Ways of Increasing the Effectiveness of the Community's Structural Funds*,[179] a problem was seldom exclusively agricultural, social, or regional. Hence, while due allowance should be made for the specific features of each Structural Fund, every opportunity should be taken to achieve synergy between these Funds and with the other financial instruments. Consistency in their operations should be strengthened, and incoherence and duplication, which could lead to the waste of resources, should be eliminated.

Thus, for example, Article 1 of Regulation 1787/84[180] envisaged co-ordination of Community policies, in so far as they affected regional development, taking account of the aims of each of those policies. Such co-ordination was also to take account of their regional impact.[181]

Article 130d of the EEC Treaty, as amended by the Single European Act,[182] itself required co-ordination of the work of the Structural Funds and other financial instruments. Regulation 2052/88[183] sought to meet this requirement. According to the preamble to this Regulation, the action taken through the Structural Funds, the European Investment Bank, and the other existing

[175] Joined Cases 10 & 18/68 *Società 'Eridania' Zuccherifici Nazionali v EC Commission* [1969] ECR 459, 501.

[176] Scott, n 158 above, 37.

[177] Art 2(3) of Reg 2081/93 (OJ 1993 L193/5).

[178] See eg the proposal of 3 June 1977 (OJ 1977 C161/17) for a regulation establishing an interest rebate scheme within the ERDF.

[179] COM(83)501, 19.

[180] OJ 1984 L169/1.

[181] Regional policy was said to have 'particularly high priority among Community policies, since it [could] serve to promote and safeguard effective integration of the Community'. See the ESC Opinion of 29 Sept 1977 (OJ 1977 C292/5) on the guidelines for Community regional policy, para 1.2.

[182] OJ 1987 L169/1.

[183] On the tasks of the Structural Funds and their effectiveness and on the co-ordination of their activities between themselves and with the operations of the EIB and the other existing financial instruments (OJ 1988 L185/9).

financial instruments formed part of a series of measures aimed at strengthening cohesion.[184] Article 161 of the EC Treaty now goes further and states that Union legislation may provide for the 'grouping' of the Structural Funds.[185]

In practice, however, 'dysfonctionnements' in co-ordination apparently remain.[186] For example, cases have been discovered of the European Regional Development Fund assisting projects creating the kind of environmental damage which assistance from the Financial Instrument for the Environment is designed to remove.[187]

1.7.3 'Integration'

Cohesion may require more than simply that Union funds do not work against each other. The operations of one fund may have to be modified to support the operations of others.[188] For example, according to the European Parliament, cohesion cannot be achieved by the European Regional Development Fund alone. Cohesion objectives must be considered integral to all Union policies and be taken into account in definition of their objectives.[189]

Formal legal support for such arguments may be found in the EC Treaty. In particular, Article 15 of this Treaty requires the Commission, in drawing up proposals for measures needed for completion of the internal market under Article 14, to take into account the extent of the effort that certain economies showing differences in development have to sustain.[190] The implications of this provision are clarified in Article 159 of the same Treaty,[191] the importance of which is stressed by the European Parliament.[192]

[184] ibid, 9th recital in the preamble.

[185] Radical action may be implied by such grouping. See the Report of the Committee on Regional Policy, Regional Planning, and Relations with Regional and Local Authorities on the annual report on the implementation of the reform of the Structural Funds in 1990, EP Doc A3–252/92, 26.

[186] C Pourre, 'Le Cumul d'aides' (1993) AJDA 444–450.

[187] See eg COA special report 3/92 (OJ 1992 C245/1) concerning the environment. See also J Scott, *EC Environmental Law* (Longman, London, 1998).

[188] cf, regarding policy consistency, the Proposal of 19 Mar 1998 (OJ 1998 C176/1) for a regulation laying down provisions on the Structural Funds, Art 2(5).

[189] Resolution of 18 Nov 1988 (OJ 1988 C326/289) on Community regional policy and the role of the regions, para 13.

[190] See, regarding the need 'on occasion' for cohesion requirements to be given priority over competition policy requirements, the Report of the Committee on Economic and Monetary Affairs and Industrial Policy on the twentieth report on competition policy, EP Doc A3–0338/91, 11–12.

[191] sect 1.7.1 above.

[192] Resolution of 24 June 1993 (OJ 1993 C194/221) on economic and social cohesion, recital G in the preamble; and Resolution of 22 Jan 1993 (OJ 1993 C42/232) on economic and social cohesion in the context of completion of the single market and EMU, para 6.

Obstacles to securing the 'integration' envisaged are apparent in both the 'institutional law' and the 'economic law' of the Union.[193] For example, as regards the former 'branch' of Union law, the 'vertical structure' of Commission Directorates General[194] may limit the possibility of policies evolved in one Directorate penetrating the thinking of others. Rather, the Commission has been said to be divided into 'watertight compartments which do not communicate with each other'.[195] This obstacle to effective pursuit of cohesion may not be overcome simply by changes in provisions on cohesion.[196] Rather, structured, systematic reform of Commission organization may be necessary.[197]

Obstacles in economic law are illustrated by *Wuidart*.[198] Here it was argued that Community legislation imposing an additional levy on milk production was contrary to Article 40(3) of the EEC Treaty. The legislation was allegedly contrary to this provision, because it took no account of structural and physical disparities between the different agricultural regions, as required by Article 39(2)(a) of the same Treaty. According to the latter provision, in working out the common agricultural policy, the Community was to take account of the particular nature of agricultural activity, which resulted from the social structure of agriculture and from structural and natural disparities between the various agricultural regions. However, the Court of Justice found the legislation compatible with the Treaty, because it allowed the Member States, in implementing the levy system, to take account of such disparities. In other words, Union sectoral policy should allow for account to be taken of regional disparities, but need not follow regional policy.[199]

True, certain regions were recognized as less favoured for the purposes of other Community legislation.[200] However, this recognition did not imply that such regions had to be treated differently from other regions for the purposes

[193] See, regarding these two 'branches' of the law, sect 1.8.2 below.

[194] See, regarding DGs, A Evans, *A Textbook on EU Law* (Hart Publishing, Oxford, 1998) sect 2.2.3.

[195] The future of rural society, House of Lords Select Committee on the European Communities, HL(1989–90)80–I, 33. See, more recently, COA annual report for 1996 (OJ 1997 C348/1), para 10.10.

[196] cf, regarding problems of 'departmental specialization' generally, JJ Hesse and LJ Sharpe, 'Local Government in International Perspective: Some Comparative Perspectives' in JJ Hesse (ed), *Local Government and Urban Affairs in International Perspective* (Nomos, Baden-Baden, 1991) 603–620.

[197] cf Fifth environmental action programme: integration of Community policies, House of Lords Select Committee on the European Communities, HL(1992–3)27, 7–8.

[198] Joined Cases C–267–285/88 *Gustave Wuidart v Laiterie Coopérative Eupenoise* [1990] ECR I–435.

[199] Indeed, sectoral policy rules may be regarded as *lex specialis*. Cf Dec 94/285 (OJ 1994 L122/30) relating to a procedure in application of Art 53(2) Euratom.

[200] Dir 75/268 (OJ 1975 L128/1) on mountain and hill farming, and farming in less favoured areas.

of the levy legislation. The need for such differentiation was not implied, because the two pieces of legislation had different purposes.[201]

Similarly, a measure adopted within the framework of a common organization of an agricultural market may affect a small holding more adversely than large holdings. However, the measure does not necessarily entail unlawful discrimination. It does not do so, if it is based on objective rules which are formulated to meet the needs of the common organization.[202] Unless thinking of this kind is revised, effective pursuit of cohesion may be jeopardized.

Such legal obstacles to pursuit of cohesion may be reinforced by the economic context. For example, it is said that use of Union assistance to raise standards regarding environmental protection and research and development cannot be regionally differentiated. The use of such assistance can merely be followed by actions to assist weaker regions to reach Union standards.[203] More fundamentally, there may be conflict between efficiency concerns in relation to global competition and equity concerns in relation to regional development. Thus policies to improve the international competitiveness of Union firms may be seen as counteracting efforts to secure cohesion and vice versa.[204]

1.7.4 Equality

The problems of securing cohesion may be expressed as those of establishing a 'positive' Union regional policy.[205] In other words, they are problems of interventionist equality, involving 'positive' or 'affirmative' action to reduce disparities and to create 'new economic states of affairs'.[206] Such equality is not simply a constraint on assistance. Rather, it is supposed to be the guiding principle for the grant of assistance.

Equality of this kind may not be attainable simply through budgetary transfers. Such transfers may be spent on imported goods rather than on investment. Hence, their lasting effects on productive capacity in beneficiary regions may be minimal.[207] Therefore, it is argued that greater equalization between levels of development and employment in the various regions should be sought. Such equalization should be sought through 'lending impetus to the most backward areas' potential for internally generated development'.[208]

201 [1990] ECR I–435, I–488.

202 Case T–119/95 *Alfred Hauer v EU Council and EC Commission* [14 July 1998].

203 R Hall and D van der Wee, 'Community Regional Policies for the 1990s' (1992) *Regional Studies* 399–404.

204 RJ Langhammer, *EC Integration Widening Towards Eastern Europe* (Working Paper No 524; University of Kiel, 1992) 12.

205 Keating, n 81 above, 17–18.

206 cf J Habermas, *Legitimation Crisis* (Polity Press, Cambridge, 1988) 53.

207 Hall and van der Wee, n 203 above.

208 Social dimension of the internal market, SEC(88)1148, 18. See also Committee for the Study of Economic and Monetary Union, *Economic and Monetary Union in the European Community* (EC Commission, Luxembourg, 1989) 22–23.

It may be objected that efforts at equalization conflict with exploitation of comparative advantages[209] and will lead to lower productivity.[210] However, dynamic conceptions suggest that distributional reforms and economic growth may mutually support each other by circular causation.[211]

The underlying issues may be touched upon, though not easily resolved, in judicial proceedings. For example, in *Debauve*[212] Belgian legislation prohibiting the transmission of advertisements by cable television was at issue. It was argued that the prohibition discriminated against broadcasting stations in other Member States, since their geographical situation allowed them to broadcast their signals only within their natural reception zone. The Court of Justice ruled that although differences attributable to natural phenomena did not constitute discrimination prohibited by the Treaty, the Union institutions might intervene to compensate for such differences.[213] Thus the Court implicitly acknowledged that Union pursuit of interventionist equality might be legitimate. Indeed, the Court has gone on to rule that the Union institutions have broad discretion in choosing measures appropriate to pursuit of such equality.[214] However, the Court has not found cause to address the fundamental problem, asserted in the literature, that the very inequality which cohesion opposes is inherent in the operation of the common market.[215]

1.7.5 Intergovernmentalism

The EEC Treaty amendments introduced by the Single European Act[216] owed much to bargaining between Member States. In particular, demands by the less developed Member States for compensation for the social costs likely to result from completion of the internal market were reflected in these amendments.[217]

Again, the amendments introduced by the Treaty on European Union and, more particularly, the creation of the Cohesion Fund[218] reflected demands from the less developed Member States for assistance in coping with the disciplines to be associated with establishment of monetary union and introduction of a single currency. Thus demands for assistance with pursuit of national policies continued to be presented by less developed Member States in integration terms. In reality, interventionist equality was treated as

[209] ie 'natural' advantages, which enable some actors to compete more successfully than others.

[210] V Curzon Price, *1992: Europe's Last Chance? From Common Market to Single Market* (Institute of Economic Affairs, London, 1988) 27–28.

[211] G Myrdal, *Economic Theory and Under-Developed Regions* (Duckworth, London, 1957) 120–121.

[212] Case 52/79 *Procureur du Roi v Marc JVC Debauve* [1980] ECR 833.

[213] ibid, 858.

[214] Case T–113/96 *Edouard Dubois et Fils v EU Council and EC Commission* [29 Jan 1998].

[215] Valle Galvez, n 154 above, 341–342.

[216] OJ 1987 L169/1.

[217] Bianchi, n 2 above, 600.

[218] Reg 1164/94 (OJ 1994 L130/1).

amounting to intergovernmental equality, which would promote the capacity of such Member States to intervene in their economies.

In accordance with such treatment, the introduction of Treaty provisions on cohesion may be seen as giving legal legitimacy to financial transfers between Member States. However, Member States may have limited interest in giving content to cohesion requirements, because interference with their pursuit of national policies may be entailed.

1.8 DECISION-MAKING PROCEDURES

Given the variety of definitions of cohesion and the complications in the relationship of cohesion with various Union policies and with differing conceptions of equality, the decision making involved in the pursuit of cohesion may be said to be of the 'multicriteria' kind.[219] Traditional approaches to designing appropriate procedures for such decision making are said to swing between two extremes. Either the decision maker should be given complete freedom, or restrictive assumptions should be introduced which allow decisions to be taken using the classical, single-criterion approach.[220] Such approaches may be unable to take account of the complexities involved, of which policy conflicts are particular manifestations rather than the essence. These complexities mean that the content of a policy cannot be separated from the decision-making procedures.[221]

The inference may often be drawn that only 'political' processes can give content to cohesion and to the action necessary to promote it.[222] However, the possibility may not be excluded of cohesion contributing to these processes as an 'interpretative principle' in Union law.[223] This possibility is considered in Part Three of the book, which concerns decision-making procedures related to the operations of the Union funds.

1.8.1 'Organic' Union Decision Making

'Organic' Union decision making is examined in Chapter 7. Such decision making originates in the practice of the Union institutions, which may be affected by their participation in various committees, and results in acts of these institutions. These acts may take the form of legislation, 'soft law', budgetary provision, contracts, individual administrative decisions, and judgments of the European Courts.

219 M Paruccini, *Decision Support Systems for Environmental Management* (EC Commission, Brussels, 1992).

220 J Spronk (ed), *Multiple Criteria Decision Methods and Applications* (Springer, Berlin, 1985).

221 Paruccini, n 219, 27.

222 Valle Galvez, n 154 above, 361.

223 ibid, 376.

1.8.2 Equality

The demands of institutional equality, that is, equality of participation in Union decision making, and pursuit of the evolving kinds of equality sought through the Union funds may not be separable.[224] It is true that, formally, the EC Treaty seeks to separate 'institutional law' procedures from the 'substantive economic law'. Thus Part Five of the Treaty[225] is headed 'Institutions of the Community' and lays down rules governing the composition, organization, and functions of the Union institutions. Part Three of the Treaty[226] is, in turn, headed 'Community Policies' and includes rules relating to the 'four freedoms',[227] competition policy, cohesion, and so on. If, however, this separation is not questioned in examination of the operations of the Union funds, critical problems in the law governing the Union funds, such as problems of the alleged 'constitutionalization' of cohesion, may be obscured.[228]

1.8.3 Intergovernmental Decision Making

Chapter 8 examines the contribution of intergovernmental decision making to the operations of the Union funds.[229] Amendments to the Treaties and Protocols and even Declarations attached thereto, as well as Accession Acts and Protocols and Declarations thereto, are examples of the outcomes of such decision making.[230]

Interactions may occur between such decision making and organic decision making.[231] The interactions may affect, and be affected by, the evolution of the 'economic law' governing the operations of the Union funds and, in particular, differing conceptions of cohesion as between Union institutions and individual Member States. The Union institutions, or at least the Commission, the European Parliament, and the Economic and Social Committee, may associate cohesion with interventionist equality entailing positive action to secure greater equality between regions. The Member States may see cohe-

[224] cf, regarding the 'feedback effects' of operations of the Union funds on decision making, Anderson, n 52 above, 128.

[225] Arts 189–280 EC.

[226] Arts 23–181 EC.

[227] ie, the free movement of goods, persons, services, and capital.

[228] cf DJ Gerber, 'The Transformation of European Community Competition Law' (1994) 35 Harvard International Law Journal 97–147, 98.

[229] See, generally, A Moravcsik, 'Negotiating the Single European Act' (1991) *International Organization* 19–56, 26.

[230] cf Gerber, n 228 above, 99, who distinguishes between 'those components of the system that operate as part of the process of establishing and applying generally applicable norms (here, the juridical components) and those that are the result of the political mediation of the interests of states and Community institutions'.

[231] cf the distinction between integration that takes place at the 'national' level and that which takes place at the 'supranational' level in EB Haas, *The Uniting of Europe* (Stanford University Press, Stanford, Calif, 1958).

sion as equalizing their capacity, despite differing financial positions, to adopt interventionist policies. However, the implementation of these policies may not necessarily be consistent with what the Union institutions consider as favouring regional equality.[232]

Therefore, fundamental issues about the relationship between Union law and the common market, the relationship between law and policy, and the relationship between economic law and institutional law may arise in analysis of practice concerning the Union funds. The issues raised are examined in greater detail in the following Chapters. Conclusions about these issues are drawn in Chapter Nine. Suggestions are also made as to the kind of reforms in Union law which may be appropriate to address problems in existing practice. At the same time, the fundamental legal obstacles to such reforms are considered.

[232] See eg regarding the operations of the Union funds and pursuit of low-wage growth strategies, Anderson, n 52 above, 152.

Part One
Structural Funds

2

European Regional Development Fund

2.1 INTRODUCTION

The European Regional Development Fund was the last of the three Structural Funds to be established, and only acquired an express legal basis in the Treaties as a result of the Single European Act.[1] However, in terms of the amount of resources used,[2] it has now become the most important of these three Funds.

2.2 ESTABLISHMENT OF THE COMMON MARKET

According to Article 2 of the EEC Treaty, a harmonious development of economic activities, a continuous and balanced expansion, an increase in stability, an accelerated raising of the standard of living, and closer relations between Member States were to be promoted. This provision could be read together with the fifth recital in the preamble to the Treaty. According to this recital, the Member States were anxious to strengthen the unity of their economies. They were also anxious to ensure their harmonious development by reducing the differences existing between the various regions and the backwardness of the less favoured regions.[3] Therefore, the Treaty expressed a commitment to balanced development of the Community as a whole, but also emphasized the need to develop 'backward' regions.

No specific role was envisaged for Community assistance in achievement of such development. This was partly because equity in the distribution of benefits from integration was expected to result from a 'package agreement'[4] embodied in the Treaty. This package entailed assistance for farmers from the European Agricultural Guidance and Guarantee Fund,[5] for workers from

[1] OJ 1987 L169/1.

[2] See the conclusions of the European Council meeting in Dec 1992 (Bull EC 12–1992, I.55).

[3] According to H Smit and P Herzog, *The Law of the European Economic Community: A Commentary on the EEC Treaty* (Matthew Bender, New York, 1990) i. 37, Art 2 EEC and the preamble required that economic 'growth . . . occur in an orderly fashion and . . . lead neither to overdevelopment of already developed regions nor to greater poverty in the areas already suffering from underdevelopment, but instead . . . equalize development throughout the Community'.

[4] L Tsoukalis, *The New European Economy: The Politics and Economics of Integration* (Oxford University Press, 1991) 234–235.

[5] See, regarding the EAGGF, sect 3.2 below.

the European Social Fund,[6] and for undertakings from the European Investment Bank.[7] Any problems of adjustment to establishment of the common market were to be tackled through such assistance.[8] Basically, however, it was anticipated that growth associated with establishment of the common market would resolve regional problems.

In reality, the establishment of the common market deprived Member States of protectionist instruments, such as tariffs and quotas. These instruments had been used to further national growth and, in so far as protected industries were regionally concentrated, regional growth. If they could no longer be used, it might be feared that the 'deglomeration effect of national agglomeration' would be weakened and that 'inter-European agglomeration' would be reinforced.[9] Such fears may explain why Member States increasingly resorted to state aid and sought to outbid one another with escalating offers to attract mobile investment.[10] This was a race that the poorer, worse-equipped, peripheral regions were bound to lose. The Commission drew the conclusion that the provision of Community assistance to such regions was necessary, if overall economic growth was not to be endangered.[11] Community assistance specifically for regional development thus came to be seen as necessary to correct distortions of competition arising from differences in national aid policies.[12]

2.2.1 Objectives of Assistance

Article 1(1) of the 1969 Commission proposal for organization of Community means of action in the regional development field[13] envisaged that Member States would draw up regional development plans. These plans were to take account of the implications of the common market, and their implementation was to be assisted by the Community. Thus the objective of such assistance was to ensure that regional development measures taken by Member States were organized consistently with the requirements of establishing of the common market.[14]

[6] See, regarding the ESF, sect 4.2 below.

[7] See, regarding the EIB, sect 6.2 below.

[8] cf *Memorandum on Regional Policy in the Community*, Bull EC, Supp 12/69, 15.

[9] H Giersch, 'Economic Union Between Nations and the Location of Industries' (1949–50) 16 *Review of Economic Studies* 87–97.

[10] J Jordan, 'The Compatibility of Regional Aid Systems with the Common Market' (1976) ELR 236–42.

[11] *Memorandum on Regional Policy in the Community*, Bull EC, Supp 12/69, 34.

[12] cf D Bureau and P Champsaur, 'Fiscal Federalism and European Economic Unification' (1992) 82 *American Economic Review* 88–108.

[13] Of 17 Oct 1969 (JO 1969 C152/6).

[14] ibid, 6th recital in the preamble.

2.2.2 Eligibility for Assistance

According to the European Parliament in 1960, Community assistance should concentrate on regions of a frontier or peripheral character.[15] However, broader conceptions of regional problems were not precluded, and in 1964 three reports were drawn up favouring action to enable all regions to contribute efficiently to establishment of the common market.[16] The thinking which underlay these reports seems to have been influential. For example, in 1966 the European Parliament maintained that certain regions should have priority for assistance. The regions concerned were: peripheral regions, 'regions in difficulty', regions near to frontiers between Member States, and regions situated on the eastern borders of Germany and Italy. Nevertheless, the Parliament insisted that assistance should concern all the regions of the Community.[17]

According to the Commission proposal itself, the need for assistance was urgent in the case of four kinds of regions. They were: regions which were undeveloped, above all because of the predominance of agriculture; regions in decline, because of the evolution of the predominant economic activities; regions suffering from structural unemployment; and border regions, where co-operation between Member States was particularly necessary.[18] Extension of assistance to other regions was implicitly left open as a future possibility.

2.2.3 Scope of Assistance

Community assistance was to concern: the co-ordination of national measures, particularly for frontier regions; infrastructure; agricultural restructuring; industrial policy and the need to avoid uneconomic activity; and vocational training and guidance.[19]

2.2.4 Forms of Assistance

Community assistance was to be limited to interest rebates and guarantees on loans from the European Investment Bank.[20]

However, the 1969 proposal was not adopted by the Council. Apparently, the latter was content to leave regional problems to individual Member States.

[15] Resolution of 17 May 1960 (JO 1960 827) on conjunctural, regional, and structural aspects of the long-term economic policy of the Community.

[16] *Rapports de groupes d'experts sur la politique régionale dans la CEE* (EEC Commission, Brussels, 1964).

[17] Resolution of 27 June 1966 (JO 1966 2427) on regional policy in the EEC.

[18] Art 1(1) of the proposal of 17 Oct 1969 (JO 1969 C152/6).

[19] ibid, Art 5.

[20] ibid, Arts 6 and 7.

2.3 DEVELOPMENT OF THE COMMON MARKET

Regional problems became more pressing as efforts were made to develop the common market. Indeed, the Commission maintained in the *EC Sixth General Report*[21] that Community assistance should be the vehicle for an overall economic policy aiming to guide the development of economic structures. Emphasis was placed on promoting the best use by regions of their own resources. Realization of all growth opportunities within the Community might thus be facilitated, and the stability and competitiveness of the Community might be ensured.[22]

2.3.1 Objectives of Assistance

According to the *Report on the Regional Problems in the Enlarged Community* ('the Thomson Report'), the objective of Community assistance should be to give areas suffering from regional imbalances the means to correct them and to enable them to put themselves on a footing of more equal competitiveness. It would then be possible for the various factors of production in the Community to be more fully utilized. In particular, it would be possible for the idle human resources and underused social capital and infrastructure to be more fully employed.[23]

Failure to achieve this objective would, it was argued, be undesirable for the Community as a whole. For example, according to the European Parliament, uncontrolled congestion and migration were more costly than measures to encourage the balanced development of the regions.[24] To entrepreneurs, expansion in an already crowded region might appear attractive, given the availability there of a network of suppliers and access to a mass market. However, such expansion could lead to the very congestion which the Parliament considered undesirable.[25]

The undesirable consequences were recognized as likely to go beyond the integration process in a purely economic sense. For example, the then President of the Commission told the European Parliament in May 1968 that an effective regional policy had become a *sine qua non* of integration in a broader sense. In his view, this policy should be in the Community 'as the heart is in the human body'.[26] According to the Thomson Report, no Community could maintain itself or have a meaning for the peoples which

[21] EC Commission, Brussels (1973) 115–116.

[22] cf, later, the Report of the Committee on Regional Policy and Regional Planning on the revision of the present regulation governing the ERDF, EP Doc A2–115/87, 10.

[23] Bull EC, Supp 8/73, 8.

[24] Resolution of 21 Apr 1977 (OJ 1977 C118/51) on aspects of the Community's regional policy to be developed in the future, part (a).

[25] ibid.

[26] PE Débs Nos 103, 126, 15 May 1968.

belonged to it, so long as some had very different standards of living and had cause to doubt the common will of all to help each Member State to improve the conditions of its people. Therefore, unless the Community's economic resources were moved where human resources were, thus sustaining living local communities, there was bound to be disenchantment over the idea of European unity.[27]

Such thinking was only partly reflected in Regulation 724/75,[28] which created the European Regional Development Fund. Article 1 of this Regulation provided that the Fund was intended to correct the principal regional imbalances within the Community resulting in particular from agricultural preponderance, industrial change, and structural underemployment. Article 6(1) added that the imbalances to be corrected were those likely to prejudice the attainment of economic and monetary union.

This reference to economic and monetary union reflected the conception of the Fund adopted by some at least of the Member States. They conceived of the Fund as a means of 'compensating' weaker Member States for the costs of their participation in such a union.[29]

However, from the 'regional policy' perspective of the Commission, the formulation of Fund objectives might be found too narrow. Certainly, a broader approach was favoured in Commission guidelines of 1977. According to these guidelines, the Fund should not only seek to reduce existing regional problems, which appeared both in the traditionally less developed regions and in regions undergoing industrial or agricultural reconversion. The Fund should also seek to prevent new regional imbalances arising from structural changes in the world economy or from policy measures adopted by the Community.[30]

These guidelines reflected a feeling that the economic and social context within which the Fund operated had changed fundamentally since its conception. The economic crisis had not only aggravated existing regional inequalities. It had also created additional problems of adaptation and development, which contained the seeds of new regional imbalances. Therefore, according to the Commission, the Fund had to be reviewed, and its objectives redefined.[31]

The Economic and Social Committee agreed. According to this Committee, the Fund could not be expected to eliminate regional imbalances completely. Even so, efforts should be made to reduce the imbalances to such an extent that they were on a par with those in the Member States which had

[27] *Report on the Regional Problems in the Enlarged Community*, Bull EC, Supp 8/73, 7.

[28] Establishing an ERDF (OJ 1975 L73/1). See, generally, L van Depoele, 'Het Europees Fonds voor Regionale Ontwikkeling' (1975) *SEW* 387–394.

[29] sect 8.2 below.

[30] *Community Regional Policy—New Guidelines*, Bull EC, Supp 2/77, 7.

[31] *Eleventh EC General Report* (EC Commission, Brussels, 1978) 137–138. Cf, later, the explanatory memorandum to the proposal for a regulation amending Reg 724/75, COM(81)589.

the highest degree of economic integration. To this end, there should be a comprehensive system of analysis and policy formulation. The system should not merely consider how regional disparities had developed. It should also investigate the interdependence between relatively rich and relatively poor regions. In particular, an assessment should be made of the extent to which transfers of resources from one region to another could contribute to balanced growth without endangering the situation in those regions from which transfers were effected. On the one hand, there were economic limits to such transfers. On the other hand, if poor regions remained underdeveloped, new problems might be created or existing ones exacerbated in richer regions.[32] At the same time, compensation for specific locational disadvantages had, as far as possible, to be neutral in its effect on competition.[33]

However, the existing formulation of the objectives of the Fund was essentially retained in Regulation 214/79,[34] Article 6 of Regulation 724/75[35] being only slightly modified. In its modified version it provided that the regional imbalances to be corrected were those which might prejudice the proper functioning of the common market and the convergence of the Member States' economies, with a view, in particular, to the attainment of economic and monetary union.

This provision was inadequate to meet the demands of the Economic and Social Committee. According to the Committee,[36] the purpose of the Fund was to ensure that the development of the common market and the progressive deepening of economic integration, leading eventually to economic and monetary union, did not work in such a manner that the prosperous regions of the Community enjoyed higher levels of employment and increasing prosperity, while the less advanced, peripheral regions suffered rising unemployment, emigration, and falling incomes. If the divergent pattern of economic development was not halted and reversed, certain disadvantaged regions would be effectively excluded from the gains of economic integration. Those Member States in which such regions were located might be compelled to renounce or resist the disciplines necessary for the creation of economic and monetary union. Indeed, the continued existence of the common market might be threatened.[37]

However, in Regulation 1787/84,[38] which replaced the earlier legislation on

[32] Opinion of 29 Sept 1977 (OJ 1977 C292/5) on the guidelines for Community regional policy, para 2.4.

[33] ibid, para 2.2.

[34] Amending Reg 724/75 (OJ 1979 L35/1).

[35] OJ 1975 L73/1.

[36] Opinion of 29 Apr 1981 (OJ 1981 C185/20) on the revision of the ERDF Regulation, paras 1.1–2.

[37] See, similarly, *Report of the Study Group on the Role of Public Finance in European Integration* (EC Commission, Brussels, 1977) i. 60.

[38] On the ERDF (OJ 1984 L169/1). See, generally, B De Witte, 'The Reform of the European Regional Development Fund' (1986) 25 CMLRev 419–440; J Elizade, 'La reforma del FEDER: Principios de una autentica politica regional comunitaria' (1985) *Revista de Instituciones*

the Fund, the implication was not drawn that any radical reformulation of the objectives of the Fund was needed. Article 3 of this Regulation defined the objective of the Fund as being to contribute to the correction of the principal regional imbalances within the Community. In pursuit of this objective, the Fund was to participate in the development and structural adjustment of regions whose development was lagging behind, and in the conversion of declining industrial regions.[39]

2.3.2 Eligibility for Assistance

The *Report on the Regional Problems in the Enlarged Community*[40] distinguished between 'agricultural problem areas' and 'areas suffering from industrial change'.[41]

'Agricultural problem areas' were defined in the Report as those which had a greater share of the workforce in agriculture than the Community average and a relatively low per capita income. They tended to be situated on the periphery of the Community, and over recent years they had experienced a sharp decline in the proportion of employment devoted to agriculture. They usually suffered from severe structural underemployment and often from high long-term unemployment.[42]

'Areas suffering from industrial change' were defined in the Report as those with at least 20 per cent of employment in declining industries, such as coal and textiles, persistently high unemployment (over 3.5 per cent or more than 20 per cent above the national average), or annual emigration exceeding 1 per cent over a long period. Such regions were usually those where there had been a high dependence for employment on ageing industries. Their problems of economic transformation were often underlined by a constantly slow rate of growth and by high levels of unemployment stretching over many years.[43] Such problems tended to be greater where integration led to inter-industry specialization (associated with exploitation of comparative advantage)[44] rather than intra-industry specialization.[45]

Such thinking as to definition of regions eligible for assistance was reflected in the 1973 proposal for creation of the European Regional Development Fund.[46] Article 3(1) of this proposal envisaged that the Council, on the basis of a Commission proposal, would adopt a list of regions eligible for Fund

Europeas 93–107. See also J Curral, 'Le Fonds européen de développement régional des origines jusqu'à l'acte unique européen' (1988) CDE 39–102.

39 Art 18(2) of Reg 1787/84 (OJ 1984 L169/1) followed Art 6 of Reg 214/79 (OJ 1979 L35/1).

40 Bull EC, Supp 8/73. 41 ibid 9. 42 ibid. 43 ibid.

44 A Sapir, *Regional Integration in Europe* (EC Commission Economic Papers, No 94; Brussels, 1992).

45 L Lundberg, 'Economic Integration, Inter- and Intra-Industry Trade: The Case of Sweden and the EC' (1992) *Scandinavian Journal of Economics* 393–408.

46 Proposal of 31 July 1973 (OJ 1973 C86/7) for a regulation establishing a Regional Development Fund.

assistance. According to Article 3(2), these regions would be chosen from those which benefited from a national system of regional aids and where the per capita gross domestic product was below the Community average. They were to include those with regional imbalances resulting from the preponderance of agriculture, industrial change, or structural unemployment. Account would be taken of: heavy dependence on agricultural employment; heavy dependence on employment in declining industrial activities; and persistently high unemployment[47] or net emigration.

These criteria were elaborated in a further proposal, drawn up to implement Article 3. According to this proposal, regions with a preponderance of agriculture were those with a percentage of the working population engaged in agriculture above the Community average[48] and a percentage engaged in industry lower than the Community average. Regions undergoing industrial change included: those with at least 20 per cent of the working population employed in the coal or textiles industry; those where unemployment had averaged at least 2 per cent over several years; and those where there had been net emigration over a long period. In the case of the last two categories of such regions, the number of persons employed in the coal or textiles industry had to have been at least 5,000. Regions with structural underemployment were those where unemployment was at least 20 per cent above the national average, representing at least 3.5 per cent of the working population, and where there had been net outward migration at an average annual rate of at least 1 per cent of the population over a long period. In addition, a region would qualify for assistance where its per capita gross domestic product was less than 50 per cent of the Community average.[49]

These proposals were criticized for failing adequately to require concentration of assistance on the most needy regions. The net result could even be to increase rather than decrease regional disparities, because Member States in the greatest economic difficulties had the fewest resources for carrying out the necessary restructuring.[50] Thus the European Parliament favoured a more systematic classification of all regions according to the relative seriousness of the imbalances found in relation to the Community average.[51]

[47] High unemployment and low per capita GDP tended to be closely linked. See the Second periodic report on the social and economic situation and development of the regions of the Community, COM(84)40, 2.4–4.

[48] Areas within ineligible regions would qualify where more than 11.3% were engaged in agriculture.

[49] Proposal of 11 Oct 1973 (OJ 1973 C106/26) for a regulation on the list of regions and areas referred to in the regulation establishing an ERDF; Bull EC 10–1973, 1303.

[50] Report of the Committee on Economic and Monetary Affairs on the fourth report on competition policy, EP Doc 164/75, 24.

[51] Resolution of 13 Dec 1973 (OJ 1974 C2/49) on the proposals for a regulation on the list of priority agricultural regions and areas referred to in the regulation on finance from the Guidance Section of the EAGGF for projects falling within development programmes in priority agricultural regions; and a regulation on the list of regions and areas referred to in the Regulation

Such criticism had no apparent impact on the terms of Regulation 724/75.[52] According to Article 3 of the Regulation, to be assisted by the Fund, regions simply had to be amongst those established by Member States in applying their own systems of regional aid.

The Commission itself subsequently sought more precise definition of eligible regions. It proposed the following indicators for assessment of the relative intensity of regional imbalances: the trend of unemployment rates during the preceding five years; the proportion of the active population occupied in agriculture; the proportion of the active population occupied in declining industrial sectors; the migration balance during the preceding five years; and the development and level of gross domestic product.[53] However, the Council did not favour the use of these indicators, and so they were not included in Regulation 214/79.[54]

Instead, Article 3 of Regulation 214/79[55] merely introduced provision for the Fund to grant certain assistance to regions other than those covered by national regional aid systems, if the Member State had granted aid or did so at the same time. The former regions were to be selected by the Council[56] in legislation adopting specific Community regional development measures.[57]

Similarly, Regulation 1787/84[58] provided that the only regions which could benefit from assistance to projects[59] or national programmes of Community interest[60] were those established by Member States in applying their systems of regional aid. Community programmes could cover other regions, where such coverage was appropriate for the solution of problems forming the subject of Community action, where the Member State concerned gave its consent, and where that Member State had also granted aid or did so at the same time.[61]

In other words, the legislation continued to rely essentially on national designations for determining eligibility. Particularly controversial was the continued failure of the legislation to address questions of the possible significance of peripherality and sectoral factors.

Peripherality

No specific reference to peripherality was made in the legislation. However, according to the *Second Periodic Report on the Situation and Socio-economic*

establishing an ERDF, para 7. See also the Resolution of 13 Mar 1974 (OJ 1974 C40/26) on Community regional policy, para 4.

52 OJ 1975 L73/1.

53 Art 2(2)(b) of the proposal of 3 June 1977 (OJ 1977 C161/11) for a regulation amending Reg 724/75.

54 OJ 1979 L35/1.

55 ibid.

56 ibid, Art 12(3)(b). The selection process was criticized in the European Parliament Resolution of 10 June 1983 (OJ 1983 C184/163) on the proposed regulations on a second series of specific Community regional development measures, paras 9 and 11.

57 sect 2.3.5 below.

58 OJ 1984 L169/1.

59 ibid, Art 17(3).

60 ibid, Art 11(3).

61 ibid, Art 9(3).

Development of the Regions of the Community, regions on the periphery of the Community tended to have a higher share of agricultural employment and a lower share of employment in manufacturing or service industries than the Community average. Moreover, in such regions agriculture was characterized by weak farm structures and low performance, while industrial activity tended to be of low productivity and concentrated in 'traditional' sectors.[62] The coincidence between peripherality and regions with these characteristics led to the conclusion that peripherality was a structural factor affecting development.[63]

True, certain disadvantages might arise from congestion in more central regions.[64] Nevertheless, distance from the main centres of economic activity was viewed as a considerable disadvantage for balanced development in peripheral regions and as a source of significant handicaps. Such handicaps included lack of access: to markets, suppliers, highly qualified manpower, and capital markets; to national and international networks; and to cost savings from increasing economies of scale.[65]

Certainly, a broad negative relationship was identified in many Member States between firm or plant size and regional peripherality. Moreover, firms in peripheral regions tended to be more dependent on local markets and intra-regional trade than those in central regions. The exceptions often concerned firms controlled from outside the region. Their production, however, was geared towards exports and often involved the application of labour-saving technologies. Their production also involved few significant intra-regional linkages or economies of scale.[66]

More particularly, the problems of border regions might be exacerbated by development of the common market, and the need for assistance there rendered more pressing.[67] Although most of these regions were situated in a central position in Europe, they were said to occupy a peripheral position with regard to their own country's economy.[68]

True, it was argued that there was no clear correlation between the development of a region and its spatial position. Research into economic growth

[62] COM(84)40, 4.4.3.

[63] First periodic report on the situation and socio-economic development of the regions of the Community, COM(80)816, 5.

[64] cf, regarding the need for 'decongestion' arrangements, the *Report on the Regional Problems in the Enlarged Community* (Bull EC, Supp 8/73, 8).

[65] Second periodic report on the social and economic situation and development of the regions of the Community, COM(84)40, 138.

[66] First periodic report on the situation and socio-economic development of the regions of the Community, COM(80)816, 58.

[67] See, regarding the problems of 'bottlenecks arising from delayed integration and from measures adopted on either side of the frontier', the 7th recital in the preamble to Rec 81/879 (OJ 1981 L321/27) on transfrontier co-ordination for regional development.

[68] European Parliament Resolution of 18 Nov 1976 (OJ 1976 C293/37) on the Community's regional policy as regards the regions at the Community's internal frontiers, para 5.

in Denmark, Germany, Norway, and Sweden between 1960 and 1970 revealed only a few sectors where geographical accessibility had a significant impact on regional growth. Rather, the main determinants of differences in regional growth appeared to be economies of scale, localization and urbanization diseconomies, and the national impact on regional growth.[69] Observed relationships with distance did not reflect current transportation or communication costs but rather the influence of the past on the contemporary spatial pattern of production and trade. However, the relevance for the Community as a whole of the data on which these views were based is questionable, because the data were taken from countries which were developed to a level above the average in the Community. Moreover, these countries contained few regions that could be classified as peripheral other than in a strictly geographical sense.

In short, therefore, the failure of the legislation squarely to address peripherality questions in determining regional eligibility for assistance was problematic.

Sectoral factors

No specific reference to sectoral factors was made in Regulation 724/75.[70] However, the 1977 Commission guidelines for regional policy emphasized the problems of regions requiring assistance to develop their agriculture or adapt their industries.[71]

Regulation 214/79[72] went some way towards more formal recognition of such factors. Article 13(1) provided 'in exceptional cases' for specific Community regional development measures intended to meet the structural consequences of particularly serious sectoral occurrences in certain regions. The aim of such measures would be to replace jobs lost and to create the necessary infrastructure for this purpose.[73]

The inference may be drawn that, in some cases at least, regional problems were regarded simply as consequences of sectoral dynamics. However, it was also admitted that the industrial mix of production, which varied widely from one region to another, only partly explained productivity gaps. The transformation of sectoral problems into regional problems depended on the general economic and social structure of the region and its flexibility of reaction.[74]

[69] K Peschel, 'Spatial Effects of the Completion of the European Single Market' (1990) *Built Environment Quarterly* 11–29.

[70] OJ 1975 L73/1.

[71] *Community Regional Policy—New Guidelines*, Bull EC, Supp 2/77, 12.

[72] OJ 1979 L35/1.

[73] See also the Report of the Committee on Regional Policy and Regional Planning on the contribution of the ERDF to the creation of jobs in the Community, EP Doc A2–120/86, 6.

[74] P Wäldchen, 'Industrial Change, New Technologies, and EC Regional Policy' in K Dyson (ed), *Local Authorities and New Technologies: The European Dimension* (Croom Helm, London, 1988) 49–58, 52.

The determining factor was overall economic development.[75] The leading sectors were created and developed in specific localities which provided for new technology and entrepreneurship not only in the physical sense but also through a stimulating natural, social, economic, and political environment. In other words, sectoral and regional changes were mutually interdependent.[76] However, the legislation failed to recognize the complexity of this relationship in its approach to determination of regional eligibility for assistance.

2.3.3 Allocation of Assistance

Assistance was to be allocated according to criteria laid down in Community legislation. However, application of these criteria was affected by national quotas and, later, 'ranges'.

Criteria

According to the 1973 proposal for the creation of a European Regional Development Fund,[77] assistance was to be allocated to regions[78] for projects[79] approved by the Commission with reference to the relative severity of the economic imbalance of the region.[80]

Such thinking was reflected in the preamble to Regulation 724/75.[81] According to the preamble, assistance was to be allocated on the basis of the relative severity of regional imbalances. Account was also to be taken of other factors affecting the importance of projects from the perspectives of the region concerned and the Community.[82]

According to the operative provisions of the legislation, assistance was to be allocated in the light of the relative severity of the economic imbalance in the region concerned and the direct and indirect effect of the project on employment.[83] Priority was to be given to projects in national priority areas,[84] taking account of the Community principles for the co-ordination of regional aid granted by Member States.[85] Special account was to be taken of the following: the consistency of the project with the regional development programmes to be drawn up by each Member State; the contribution of the project to the economic development of the region; the consistency of the pro-

[75] According to the Second periodic report on the situation and socio-economic development of the regions of the Community, COM(84)40, iv, this development should be the result of structural changes which were necessary if new production processes were to be adopted, and new sectors and new products developed.

[76] A Kuklinski, *Efficiency versus Equality: Old Dilemmas and New Approaches in Regional Policy* (European Policies Research Centre, Research Paper No 8; Glasgow, 1990), 2. Hence, regional disparities might be difficult to tackle solely by measures to change sectoral structures.

[77] OJ 1973 C86/7. [78] ibid, Art 3. [79] ibid, Arts 5 and 6.

[80] ibid, Art 13. [81] OJ 1975 L73/1.

[82] ibid, 10th recital in the preamble. [83] ibid, Art 5(1). [84] ibid, Art 3.

[85] First Resolution of 20 Oct 1971 of the Representatives of the Governments of the Member States, meeting within the Council, on general systems of regional aid (JO 1971 C111/1).

ject with the programmes or objectives of the Community; the situation of the economic sector concerned and the profitability of the project; whether the project fell within a frontier area of adjacent regions of separate Member States;[86] other contributions made by Community institutions or by the European Investment Bank, either to the same project or to other activities within the same region; and the effect of the project on the environment, particularly as regards living and working conditions.

Regulation 1787/84[87] added two new criteria for allocating assistance to projects. These additional criteria were: specific problems due to the island, landlocked, or peripheral character of the area in which the project was located; and the effects of the project on the region's natural resources.[88]

In allocating assistance to national programmes of Community interest under Regulation 1787/84, the Commission was to take account of similar criteria. It was also to take account of: the mobilization of the indigenous potential of the regions concerned; and the integrated use in appropriate cases of any other Community structural financial instruments.[89]

Quotas

Article 2(1) of Regulation 724/75[90] provided for assistance from the Fund to be allocated by national quotas. Concessions are said to have been made to the wish not to divide the Community into 'givers' and 'takers'. Hence, the quotas were calculated so that Member States with fewer regional difficulties would receive some—though limited—assistance from the Fund.[91] The implication drawn from the allocation of a quota to each Member State was that Community assistance should be used according to the regional policy pursued by the Member State concerned.

Certainly, by submitting a number of projects whose combined Fund-financing requirements approximated to the national quota, governments could effectively eliminate any scope for real Commission discretion. In 1980, for example, only 143 out of 3,252 applications for assistance were rejected by the Commission on 'substantive grounds', such as grounds related to sectoral or competition policy considerations.[92] Hence, the criteria for allocation of assistance laid down in the legislation might be only of formal significance.

The Commission had stressed the need for reform in the 1977 regional policy guidelines.[93] In the case of underdeveloped regions and declining regions,

[86] The Commission considered that frontier regions 'generally [felt] the effects of integration most acutely and so problems of development or conversion often [arose]'. See *Community Regional Policy—New Guidelines*, Bull EC, Supp 2/77, 12.

[87] OJ 1984 L169/1. [88] ibid, Art 21(1). [89] ibid, Art 11(2).

[90] OJ 1975 L73/1.

[91] Report of the Committee on Regional Policy and Transport on regional policy as regards the regions at the Community's internal frontiers (EP Doc 467/75), 13.

[92] *ERDF Sixth Annual Report* (EC Commission, Brussels, 1981) 21.

[93] *Community Regional Policy—New Guidelines*, Bull EC, Supp 2/77, 6.

remedial action should be taken by and through national governments. In the case of 'regional impact areas' and frontier areas, their situation inherently called for Community rather than national action. Fund resources should make separate provision for the first two categories on the one hand—complementing and not displacing national action—and for the second two categories on the other hand. Accordingly, the resources should be divided between a 'quota section', which would finance projects in the first two categories, and a 'non-quota section', which would be reserved for the second two categories.

Such thinking was reflected in Regulation 214/79.[94] Article 2(3) of this Regulation distinguished between 'quota measures' in support of regional policy measures taken by Member States (paragraph (a)) and 'non-quota measures' in the form of specific Community regional development measures (paragraph (b)). Allocation of assistance to the latter measures was not subject to the national quotas. However, according to Article 3, only 5 per cent[95] at most of Fund resources could be devoted to such measures.

Ranges

Increasing regional disparities as well as concern that the existing rules entailed a very limited power for the Commission to co-ordinate national regional policy measures[96] led the Commission to propose replacement of national quotas with regional quotas.[97] However, since this proposal was not acceptable to the Council, the Commission amended its proposal, so that Fund resources would be allocated according to ranges.[98]

Accordingly, Regulation 1787/84[99] provided for national quotas to be replaced by upper and lower limits for national allocations. For each Member State the lower limit constituted the minimum amount of Fund assistance it was guaranteed, if it submitted an adequate volume of applications for assistance which satisfied the conditions set out in the Regulation. The upper limits were calculated so that, except for Denmark, each Member State was theoretically able to obtain a larger share than under the quota system. Obviously, however, they could not all do so. In the case of that portion of the Fund resources falling between the lower and upper limits, allocations were to depend on the implementation of the priorities and criteria laid down

94 OJ 1979 L35/1.

95 The Commission had proposed in its preliminary draft budget for 1978 that 13% of ERDF finance should be available for 'non-quota measures'. The European Parliament objected that the figure adopted by the Council was too low and was not commensurate with the objectives of such measures. See the Resolution of 19 June 1981 (OJ 1981 C172/117) on the fifth annual report on the ERDF, para 9.

96 Report and proposals on ways of increasing the effectiveness of the Community's Structural Funds, COM(83)501, Annex, 8.

97 Proposal of 29 Oct 1981 (OJ 1981 C336/60) for a regulation amending Reg 724/75, Art 4(3).

98 Proposal of 18 Nov 1983 (OJ 1983 C360/1) for a regulation amending Reg 724/75, Art 4(3).

99 OJ 1984 L169/1.

in the Regulation.[100] In effect, it would be put up for competitive tender amongst Member States.

The Commission hoped that the increased competition for assistance would encourage Member States to submit a larger number of applications in order to improve their chances of obtaining the maximum possible allocation.[101] However, the total of the lower limits for each Member State, which had been 83.16 per cent of Fund resources in the amended Commission proposal,[102] amounted to 88.63 per cent in the Regulation itself. Only 11.37 per cent remained, therefore, to be allocated at the discretion of the Commission.[103]

2.3.4 Scope of Assistance

Assistance from the Fund might relate to productive investment, infrastructure investment, and 'endogenous development'.

Productive investment

Article 4(1)(a) of Regulation 724/75[104] envisaged Fund support for investments in industry, handicraft, or service activities which were economically sound and benefited from state regional aid. At least ten[105] new jobs had to be created or existing jobs maintained.[106] In the latter case the investments had to fall within the framework of a conversion or restructuring plan to ensure that the undertaking concerned became competitive. The only service activities which could be supported were those having a direct impact on the development of the region and the level of employment.

Such assistance was by no means unproblematic. Since the job-creating potential of investments was the main criterion for determination of their acceptability, applicants for assistance might tend to make exaggerated claims,[107] which might not be realized. Indeed, there were objections that

[100] ibid, Art 4(5).

[101] Eleventh report on the ERDF, COM(86)545.

[102] OJ 1983 C360/1.

[103] The Committee on Regional Policy and Regional Planning sought greater concentration through establishment of quotas for the weaker regions. See the Report on second-generation regional development programmes for 1981–85, EP Doc 2–63/85, 10.

[104] OJ 1975 L73/1.

[105] The Commission proposal (OJ 1973 C86/7) had required in Art 4(1) that investments had to exceed UA 50,000 and to involve the creation or maintenance of jobs (no figure was stipulated).

[106] This proviso was difficult for SMEs to meet (COA special report on job creation or maintenance in the granting of aid to regional investments (OJ 1982 C345/1), para 2.3), and the requirement was dropped in Reg 1787/84 (OJ 1984 L169/1). According to Art 17(1) (ibid), the investment had to cost more than ECU 50,000 and, according to Art 19(1) (ibid), be intended to help create or maintain jobs.

[107] COA special report on job creation or maintenance in the granting of aid to regional investments (OJ 1982 C345/1), para 3.5.4.

assistance was used to reduce the workforce[108] and, in particular, that the Fund might finance restructuring which led to redundancies but 'saved' the remaining jobs.[109]

In any case, job-creation forecasts were difficult to make because of cyclical factors and delays.[110] The Court of Auditors found in 1989 that in less than half (48 per cent) of the investments supported by the Fund were the forecasts fully achieved. Moreover, net jobs created by investments might differ considerably from the gross figure. In fact, the implementation of the investments, by reinforcing the competitiveness of companies in receipt of assistance, might result in job losses at other companies in the region concerned. Investments might still have indirect multiplier effects on regional employment, though lack of integration of projects into the regional economy might seriously limit such effects.[111]

In short, it proved difficult to ensure that Fund assistance to productive investments was optimal.[112] Indeed, by reducing the cost of capital for new investments, such assistance could artificially boost their capital intensity, thus substituting capital for labour.[113] This distortion of factor costs could lead to a misallocation of resources generating, for example, a capital-intensive pattern of development in regions with an abundance of labour.[114] Even when employment was increased in the unit of a company receiving assistance, the effect might be closure of a related unit or that an unassisted company elsewhere might be rendered uncompetitive.[115]

Infrastructure investment

The *Medium-Term Economic Policy Programme (1966–70)*[116] stressed problems of deficiencies in inter-regional infrastructures, especially in relation to transport. The Commission guidelines for regional policy of 1977[117] and

[108] Report of the Committee on Regional Policy and Regional Planning on the eleventh report on the ERDF, EP Doc 2–41/87, 7.

[109] Report of the Committee on Regional Policy and Regional Planning on the eighth and ninth annual reports on the ERDF, EP Doc A2–5/85, 15.

[110] There were also wide disparities in the costs of creating new jobs; eg one new job cost on average ECU 235,000 in Belgium and ECU 30,100 in Denmark (Report of the Committee on Regional Policy and Regional Planning on the efficiency of national regional policy instruments—conclusions regarding a new regional policy, EP Doc A2–66/86, 13–14).

[111] COA annual report for 1988 (OJ 1989 C312/1), paras 8.43–62.

[112] ESC Opinion of 29 Sept 1977 (OJ 1977 C292/5) on the guidelines for Community regional policy, para 4.6.

[113] COA special report on job creation or maintenance in the granting of aid to regional investments (OJ 1982 C345/1), para 4.1.

[114] RP Camagni, 'Development Scenarios and Policy Guidelines for the Lagging Regions in the 1990s' (1992) *Regional Studies* 361–374.

[115] Report of the Committee on Regional Policy and Regional Planning on the contribution of the ERDF to the creation of jobs in the Community, EP Doc A2–120/86, 11.

[116] JO 1967 1513, 1564.

[117] *Community Regional Policy—New Guidelines*, Bull EC, Supp 2/77, 12.

1981[118] maintained, more generally, that underdeveloped regions needed an economic and social infrastructure amenable to sustained growth. Low levels of infrastructure endowment were found in Ireland, Northern Ireland, and southern Italian and Greek regions.[119]

However, Article 4(1)(b) of Regulation 724/75[120] provided for the Fund to support only investments in infrastructures directly linked with the activities covered by Article 4(1)(a).[121] According to the former provision, as subsequently amended by Regulation 214/79,[122] no more than 70 per cent of Fund resources were to be available to infrastructure investments, unless the Council decided otherwise. In practice, this limit was never respected,[123] and it was formally relaxed in 1983.[124] Regulation 1787/84[125] itself merely provided that the Member States and the Commission were to endeavour to ensure that an appropriate proportion (if possible, 30 per cent) of Fund resources was available for investments in industry, crafts, and services.[126]

This emphasis on infrastructure investments was controversial.[127] On the one hand, it was argued by the Economic and Social Committee that infrastructural projects very often created the preconditions for industrial investment, particularly in weaker regions. By acting as a magnet for the attraction of further investments such projects also promoted the long-term development of such regions.[128] On the other hand, emphasis on infrastructure might lead to neglect of production weaknesses[129] and the particular needs of business at the local level.[130] Moreover, according to the European Parliament, industrial investments costing less than 10 million European units of account had created the largest number of jobs relative to the size of investments and

118 New regional policy guidelines and priorities, COM(81)152.

119 See eg Second periodic report on the social and economic situation and development of the regions of the Community, COM(84)40, 4.3.2.

120 OJ 1975 L73/1.

121 Art 4(2)(c) (ibid) imposed no similar restriction on infrastructure assistance in regions covered by Dir 75/268 (sect 3.3.4 below). Art 4(b) of the Commission proposal (OJ 1973 C86/7) had envisaged assistance for infrastructure required for the development of industrial or service activities.

122 OJ 1979 L35/1.

123 Between 1975 and 1984 assistance to industrial investment represented only 18% of total ERDF resources.

124 Dec 83/595 (OJ 1983 L340/24) enabling the ERDF to exceed the 70% limit for infrastructure investment projects for the period 1981–3.

125 OJ 1984 L169/1.

126 ibid, Art 35.

127 See, regarding doubts about the effectiveness of infrastructure expenditure in the promotion of regional development, AM Comfort, 'Alternatives to Infrastructure? Possible Ways Forward for the ERDF: A View from Luxembourg' (1988) *Regional Studies* 542–551. Cf the objection that ERDF financing of infrastructure work might amount to operating aid, in the COA annual report for 1986 (OJ 1987 C336/1), para 9.11.

128 Opinion of 22 Feb 1979 (OJ 1979 C133/27) on the ERDF third annual report, para 2.

129 R Hall and D van der Wee, 'Community Regional Policies for the 1990s' (1992) *Regional Studies* 399–404.

130 Second periodic report on the social and economic situation and development of the regions of the Community, COM(84)40, III.

the amount of the assistance from the Fund.[131] Hence, the Parliament recommended that assistance be directed to smaller industrial investments, which created more employment, rather than to infrastructure investments. In reality, there might be a 'chicken and egg' problem. Without adequate infrastructure there was little hope or purpose in investing in industry; without industry there was little use in providing supporting infrastructures.[132]

In practice, infrastructure projects might generate employment during their construction phase but little, if any—at least directly—after completion. Moreover, assistance to such projects might merely help to finance investments which would have been made anyway.[133] The Fund might thus make a contribution to general national budgets rather than stimulating additional regional development.[134]

These disadvantages of infrastructure assistance were exacerbated by the narrow view of infrastructure needs adopted in the legislation. In fact, the European Parliament had proposed that infrastructure investments 'in the broad sense, required for the development of a region within the framework of a regional development programme' should be covered.[135] Thus the Parliament, like the Economic and Social Committee,[136] considered that the Fund should go beyond assisting investments in physical infrastructure. According to the Parliament, infrastructure needs were more general and related, above all, to education and occupational training. The ability of firms to invest in the regions was considered to depend, first, on the availability of local people with the right skills or on the willingness of local people to acquire the right skills. Secondly, it was considered to depend on the availability of an efficient infrastructure.[137] In short, therefore, assistance should promote emergence of an industrial network sufficient to permit spontaneous development in the future.[138]

However, regional authorities, as a result of their weakness or their lack of resources, might not be able to use Fund assistance to carry through an adequate programme in respect of general infrastructures. The result would be the stabilization of industrial activity at a level falling a long way short of the

[131] Report of the Committee on Regional Policy and Regional Planning on the eighth annual report and the ninth annual report on the ERDF, EP Doc A2–5/85, 7.

[132] Report of the Committee on Regional Policy, Regional Planning, and Transport on the second annual report on the ERDF, EP Doc 452/77, 10.

[133] See, regarding the emphasis on road projects, the Report of the Committee on Regional Policy and Regional Planning on the tenth annual report on the ERDF, EP Doc A2–76/86, 6.

[134] Report of the Committee on Regional Policy and Regional Planning on the eighth annual report and the ninth annual report on the ERDF, EP Doc A2–5/85, 13.

[135] OJ 1973 C108/51 (amendment to Art 4(1)(b) of the Commission proposal).

[136] Opinion of 29 Apr 1982 (OJ 1982 C178/38) on the proposal for a regulation amending Reg 724/75, para 4.1.

[137] Report of the Committee on Regional Policy and Regional Planning on the eighth and ninth annual reports on the ERDF, EP Doc A2–5/85, 11. See, earlier, the European Parliament Resolution of 5 July 1973 (OJ 1973 C62/33) on Community regional policy, para 7.

[138] *La Politique industrielle de la Communauté* (EC Commission, Brussels, 1970) 270.

expectations initially raised by the setting-up of the industry concerned. This would be because the human resources necessary for the expansion or renewal of this industry would not be available on the spot.[139]

Particular problems could arise in the service sector linked to new communication and information technologies. Subscribers in the peripheral regions bore higher telephone, telex, and data communication costs for access to the rest of the Community because of distances and existing tariff structures and equipment.[140] Moreover, the growth of this sector generally favoured developed, urban regions and neglected less developed regions.[141] Unless corrective action was taken, infrastructure for the new technologies would tend to follow established patterns and concentrate in the most developed regions. Hence, it was argued that assistance should attach more emphasis to the promotion of such services.[142]

Article 4(4) of Regulation 214/79[143] went some way to meet such concerns, by extending the range of infrastructure investments that could be assisted by the Fund. Provided that the investment was justified by a regional development programme, support could be extended to an investment in any infrastructure contributing to the development of the region in which it was situated. This broadening of the definition of infrastructure investments eligible for assistance was, according to the preamble to the Regulation,[144] necessitated by the diversity of regional situations in the Community.

Similarly, Article 18(1) of Regulation 1787/84[145] provided that assistance could be granted to infrastructure projects which contributed to the development of the region. The Annex listed those categories of infrastructure which the Fund could not assist.

'Endogenous development'

The 'endogenous growth' approach to regional development seeks to develop the 'economic vocation' of each region.[146] This approach was felt to be necessitated by the perceived ineffectiveness of labour and capital subsidies[147] and

[139] Report of the Committee on Regional Policy and Transport on the proposals for a decision on the creation of a Committee for Regional Policy; a financial regulation relating to special provisions to be applied to the ERDF; and a regulation establishing the ERDF, EP Doc 178/73, 17.

[140] Second periodic report on the social and economic situation and development of the regions of the Community, COM(84)40, 4.6–2.

[141] ibid 3.5–16.

[142] ibid 7.3–4 and 7.3–8. See also the Report of the Committee on Regional Policy and Regional Planning on the efficiency of national regional policy instruments—conclusions regarding a new regional policy, EP Doc A2–66/86, 6.

[143] OJ 1979 L35/1.

[144] ibid, 11th recital in the preamble.

[145] OJ 1984 L169/1.

[146] Report of the Committee on Regional Policy and Transport on the proposals for a decision on the creation of a Committee for Regional Policy; a financial regulation relating to special provisions to be applied to the ERDF; and a regulation establishing the ERDF, EP Doc 178/73, 21.

[147] See eg A Whiting (ed), *The Economics of Industrial Subsidies* (HMSO, London, 1976).

increased exposure to international competition.[148] At the same time, with the prospect of higher unemployment levels in the years ahead and a decline in the number of jobs which could be transferred from the hitherto prosperous regions, the importance of encouraging indigenous enterprise through improvement of infrastructure in a broad sense became all the greater.[149]

According to this approach, a general reawakening in depth of the economic and social life of the less favoured regions should be sought. In other words, the conditions for the continuous recreation of a dynamic competitive advantage for such regions should be secured. To this end, it was felt that the basic preconditions for development (social overhead capital, human capital, and environmental capital), synergies among the different actors in each region, including external firms, and the establishment of external linkages at the inter-regional level had to be ensured.[150]

Hence, in its 1981 proposal concerning reform of the Fund the Commission favoured a broadening of the definition of infrastructure investment which could be supported. According to the Commission, the task was above all to use the local potential available, particularly by developing the latent capacities of undertakings. To this end, the Fund should provide information, research, and technical assistance.[151]

Articles 15 and 16 of Regulation 1787/84[152] duly provided for measures to exploit the potential for internally generated development of regions. In particular, Article 15(1) provided that, for the purposes of greater exploitation of such potential, the Fund might contribute to the financing of consistent sets of measures for existing undertakings, primarily small and medium-sized undertakings, in industry, craft industry, and tourism. Such assistance should seek to provide these undertakings with facilities enabling them to expand their activities and to obtain access to new technology. It should also seek to facilitate their access to the capital market. The originality of these measures was stressed by devoting to them a special chapter in the Regulation.

[148] The influence of external effects was advancing at the national level, but it was far more severe at the subnational regional level, especially after the elimination of national regulations that used to take a core set of social and constitutional conditions out of inter-regional competition. See W Streeck and PC Schmitter, 'From National Corporatism to Transnational Pluralism: Organised Interests in the Single European Market' (1991) *Politics and Society* 133–164. Moreover, 'institutional competition' might entail increased power for large corporations. See M Dunford and G Benko, 'Neo-Fordism or Post-Fordism? Some Conclusions' in G Benko and M Dunford (eds), *Industrial Change and Regional Development* (Belhaven Press, London, 1991) 286–305.

[149] ESC Opinion of 29 Apr 1982 (OJ 1982 C178/38) on the proposal for a regulation amending Reg 724/75, para 4.1.

[150] RP Camagni, 'Development Scenarios and Policy Guidelines for the Lagging Regions in the 1990s' (1992) *Regional Studies* 361–374. See also RP Camagni (ed), *Innovation Networks: Spatial Perspectives* (Belhaven Press, London, 1991).

[151] Explanatory memorandum to the proposal for a regulation amending Reg 724/75, COM(81)589, 4.

[152] OJ 1984 L169/1.

Such measures might still be regarded as too limited. According to the Committee on Regional Policy and Transport, individuals had to be prepared (through cultural and educational infrastructures) to take part in regional development. They also had to be trained (through vocational training infrastructures) for such participation.[153] In particularly depressed regions a policy of industrialization devoid of any attempt at improving attitudes or education could lead to the creation of an industrial strongpoint. Its creation could be at the expense of even greater depression in the region concerned. In such cases the region could become dependent on a single strongpoint. If the latter failed, the region would be left in an even more serious situation than before.[154]

Such thinking might imply the need for intervention going beyond the terms of the legislation governing the Fund. For example, Regulation 815/84[155] provided for 'exceptional Community financial support'[156] from the General Budget,[157] to assist Greece in the construction of vocational training centres. It also provided for assistance with the construction of centres for the rehabilitation of the mentally and physically ill and handicapped, with a view to helping them return to gainful employment.[158] This measure was a 'derogation from Fund rules'.[159]

2.3.5 Forms of Assistance

Assistance from the Fund might take the form of interest rebates on loans from the European Investment Bank[160] and the part-financing of projects. It might also take the form of national programmes of Community interest, specific Community regional development measures, Community programmes, and studies. Co-ordination of assistance from the European Regional Development Fund with operations of other Union funds might be sought

[153] Report on the proposals for a decision on the creation of a Committee for Regional Policy; a financial regulation for special provisions to be applied to the ERDF; and a regulation establishing a Regional Development Fund, EP Doc 178/73, 14.

[154] Report on the proposals for a regulation on the list of priority agricultural regions and areas referred to in the Regulation on finance from the Guidance Section of the EAGGF for projects falling within development programmes in priority agricultural regions; and a regulation on the list of regions and areas referred to in the Regulation establishing an ERDF, EP Doc 276/73, 19.

[155] On exceptional financial support in favour of Greece in the social field (OJ 1984 L88/1).

[156] ibid, Art 1.

[157] See eg Art 542 of the Budget for 1984 (OJ 1984 L12/1).

[158] See eg Dec 85/703 (OJ 1985 L30/31) on applications for assistance from the EC concerning exceptional financial support for Greece in the social field (1984).

[159] COA special report 5/90 (OJ 1990 C331/1) on the implementation of Reg 815/84, para 1.3.

[160] Art 4(2)(b) of Reg 724/75 (OJ 1975 L73/1). Cf, earlier, the proposal of 28 May 1971 (JO 1971 C90/23) concerning a European fund for interest rebates on regional development loans. Cf, later, the proposal of 3 June 1977 (OJ 1977 C161/17) for a regulation establishing an interest rebate scheme within the ERDF, which envisaged that the ERDF should be empowered to provide interest rebates on loans from the Community or from the EIB.

through Integrated Development Operations and Integrated Mediterranean Programmes.

Projects

The legislature sought gradually to subject project support to programming, which was supposed to increase Community influence over use of the assistance provided. According to the Commission, the financing of individual projects should be phased out in favour of a programme approach in which coherent groups of related projects would receive assistance over a period of years.[161]

In practice, support for individual projects remained the dominant form of assistance. Article 6 of Regulation 1787/84[162] provided that assistance for programme financing should 'as far as possible' be gradually increased to reach at least 20 per cent of total assistance within three years.[163] In the event, programmes received only 5.5 per cent of total Fund resources in 1985 and 7.7 per cent in 1986.

National programmes of Community interest

Regulation 1787/84[164] provided for the Fund to assist national programmes of Community interest. According to Article 10(1) of the Regulation, such a programme was to be defined at national level. It was to consist of a series of multiannual measures corresponding to national objectives and serving Community objectives and policies. In particular, it was to assist the convergence of Member States' economies through the reduction of regional disparities and thus to translate into operational commitments the indications contained in regional development programmes.[165]

According to the Commission, it was within the framework of national programmes of Community interest that the convergence of Community and national priorities and the organization of genuine joint action became possible.[166] On the other hand, the move from a project-based approach to a programme-based approach would, it was said, make it 'infinitely less easy to grasp the true nature of individual situations'.[167]

[161] New regional policy guidelines and priorities, COM(81)152; and the explanatory memorandum to the proposals for a regulation amending Reg 724/75, COM(83)649.

[162] OJ 1984 L169/1.

[163] The additional target of 40% after four years, contained in the proposal of 18 Nov 1983 (OJ 1983 C360/1), was not accepted by the Council.

[164] OJ 1984 L169/1.

[165] See sect 7.4.1 below, regarding such programmes.

[166] *ERDF Fourteenth Annual Report* (EC Commission, Brussels, 1990) 62.

[167] Report of the Committee on Regional Policy and Regional Development on the fifth annual report on the ERDF (EP Doc 1–181/81), 12.

Specific Community regional development measures

According to the Commission proposal for what became Regulation 214/79,[168] in view of the economic and social trends in the Community and particularly the economic crisis resulting from the increased cost of primary products, Fund assistance had to be diversified. The diversification should enable it to support not only regional policy measures taken by the Member States but also specific Community regional development measures in favour of regions experiencing problems of restructuring and of conversion.[169] The latter measures were to comprise, in particular: measures related to other Community policies or complementary thereto, intended to reinforce or to complement the convergent efforts of Community policies to correct structural imbalances in the regions, particularly in those covered by Directive 75/268;[170] measures made necessary by the regional consequences of other Community policies; measures to accelerate the creation of jobs in the Community's less developed regions or in conversion regions, particularly by facilitating the access of investors to the capital market and the location in the regions of investments originating outside them; development measures in frontier regions; and emergency measures to meet unforeseeable regional situations.[171]

Regulation 214/79[172] itself was more limited. Article 2(3)(b) provided for specific Community regional development measures to be adopted. According to Article 13(1), the measures should be linked with Community policies and with measures adopted by the Community, in order to take better account of their regional dimension or to reduce their regional consequences. In exceptional cases, they should be intended to meet the structural consequences of particularly serious occurrences in certain regions with a view to replacing jobs lost and creating the necessary infrastructures for this purpose.

Article 13(3) of the Regulation provided that the Council, acting unanimously, was to determine for each measure: the nature of the operations to which the Fund might contribute; the regions which the Fund might assist;[173] the national aid taken into consideration in granting Fund assistance; the contribution of the Fund; the categories of beneficiaries of Fund assistance; and the detailed rules for financing.

When adopting this Regulation, the Council declared its readiness to consider any request for assistance concerning frontier problems in the least

[168] Of 3 June 1977 (OJ 1977 C161/11) for a regulation amending Reg 724/75.

[169] ibid, 7th recital in the preamble. [170] sect 3.3.4 below.

[171] Art 13 of the proposal of 3 June 1977 (OJ 1977 C161/11).

[172] OJ 1979 L35/1.

[173] The Commission had proposed that the regions eligible should be decided by a qualified majority vote in the Council (Art 13 of the proposal of 3 June 1977 (OJ 1977 C161/11) for a regulation amending Reg 724/75).

favoured regions of the Community, submitted jointly by two or more Member States concerned.[174] Accordingly, Regulation 2619/80[175] provided for a measure to assist the border regions of Ireland and Northern Ireland.

Other measures concerned declining sectors and development of hydroelectric power and alternative energy sources in certain regions,[176] while Regulation 2615/80[177] sought to assist certain French and Italian regions in the context of Community enlargement, and Regulation 215/84[178] concerned Greek regions affected by enlargement. The emphasis was on assisting 'regions liable to be affected by the consequences of decisions and measures taken under other Community policies, especially outlying regions facing special problems to do with their remoteness'.[179] In other words, the measures were designed to assist regions where other Community policies caused or might cause major imbalances, so that the adverse regional consequences of these policies could be countered.[180]

In particular, Regulation 2616/80[181] concerned regions adversely affected by restructuring of the steel industry. According to Article 4, the Fund could assist programmes concerned with: improvement of run-down industrial areas; construction and modernization of housing to attract workers; establishment and development of consultancy firms; establishment and development of common services for a number of undertakings; promotion of innovation in industry and services; and better access for small and medium-sized enterprises to risk capital. Such programmes had to fall within a regional development programme[182] and be approved by the Commission.[183]

Regulation 2616/80[184] was amended by Regulation 216/84.[185] In particular, criteria were laid down to determine 'in principle' which regions would be eligible for assistance. The criteria were: number of jobs in the steel industry; dependence of employment 'in large measure' on the steel industry; major job

[174] Proposals of 15 Oct 1979 for Council regulations instituting specific Community regional development projects under Art 13 of the ERDF Regulation, COM(79)540, 3; and the Report of the Committee on Regional Policy and Regional Planning on the proposals for regulations instituting specific Community regional development projects, EP Doc 1–715/79, 16.

[175] Instituting a specific Community regional development measure contributing to the improvement of the economic and social situation of the border areas of Ireland and Northern Ireland (OJ 1980 L271/28).

[176] See sect 7.4.1 below.

[177] Instituting a specific Community regional development measure contributing to the development of certain French and Italian regions in the context of Community enlargement (OJ 1980 L271/1).

[178] Instituting a specific Community measure contributing to the development of certain regions of Greece in the context of Community enlargement (OJ 1984 L27/5).

[179] Ninth report on the ERDF, COM(84)522, 45.

[180] ESC Opinion of 13 Dec 1979 (OJ 1980 C83/4) on the proposal for regulations instituting specific Community regional development projects, para 3.1.

[181] Instituting a specific Community regional development measure contributing to overcoming constraints on the development of new economic activities in certain zones adversely affected by the restructuring of the steel industry (OJ 1980 L271/9).

[182] ibid, Art 3(3). [183] ibid, Art 3(6). [184] ibid. [185] OJ 1984 L27/9.

losses in the steel industry; eligibility under a regional aid scheme of the Member State concerned; the socio-economic situation assessed on the basis of per capita gross national product and structural unemployment; and an unexpected reduction in production capacity linked to implementation of restructuring programmes likely to worsen the regional employment situation.

A list was included of regions which were to be eligible from the start, if they conformed 'in principle' to these criteria. In addition, regions meeting 'in principle' the first three criteria would be eligible, when the Commission had adopted a position on the restructuring programmes for the steel industry under Decision 2320/81.[186]

Three additional forms of assistance were also provided for in Regulation 216/84.[187] They concerned: preparation of sectoral analyses for small and medium-sized enterprises; investment projects of such enterprises; and interest rebates on global loans in favour of small industrial projects, with the aim of encouraging the creation and development of such enterprises, the loans being granted under Article 56 of the ECSC Treaty.[188]

Regulation 2617/80[189] was limited to United Kingdom regions[190] adversely affected by the restructuring of the shipbuilding industry.[191] It was extended to similar German regions by Regulation 217/84.[192] Assistance from the Fund for development of new economic activities in such regions was envisaged. The same kind of measures could be assisted,[193] as under Regulation 2616/80. Provision for assistance to preparation of sectoral analyses and for assistance to small and medium-sized enterprises was added by Regulation 217/84.[194]

More generally, Regulation 219/84[195] concerned regions adversely affected by restructuring of the textile and clothing industry. The same kinds of assistance were envisaged as those for steel regions under Regulation 216/84,[196] though housing was not covered, and global loans under Article 56 of the ECSC Treaty were not available.[197] The regional eligibility criteria were also similar, though they were adapted to the textile industry.[198]

186 Establishing Community rules for aid to the steel industry (OJ 1981 L228/14).

187 OJ 1984 L27/9.

188 ibid, Art 4. See, regarding Art 56 ECSC, sect 5.3 below.

189 Instituting a specific Community regional development measure contributing to overcoming constraints on the development of new economic activities in certain zones adversely affected by restructuring of the shipbuilding industry (OJ 1980 L271/16).

190 ibid, Art 2.

191 The ERDF had already been involved in efforts to tackle the problems of shipbuilding regions. See *Community Regional Policy—New Guidelines*, Bull EC, Supp 7/77, 5.

192 OJ 1984 L27/15, Art 2.

193 ibid, Art 4.

194 ibid, Art 8.

195 Instituting a specific Community regional development measure contributing to overcoming constraints on the development of new economic activities in certain zones adversely affected by restructuring of the textile and clothing industry (OJ 1984 L27/22).

196 OJ 1984 L27/9.

197 ibid, Art 4.

198 ibid, Art 2(1).

Similarly, Regulation 3638/85[199] concerned regions adversely affected by the implementation of the common fisheries policy. The objectives of the measure were: the improvement of the physical environment; development of small and medium-sized enterprises and craft activities; and stimulation of economic activity in general and promotion of tourism.[200] The same kinds of assistance were envisaged as those for textiles regions.

Article 2(1) of the Regulation laid down the criteria for determining regions eligible for such assistance. They concerned: the number of jobs in the fisheries sector; the dependence for employment on this sector; job losses in this sector; the social and economic situation in the region in which the zone was situated, the situation being assessed on the basis of per capita gross domestic product and structural unemployment; and eligibility for a national regional aid scheme. The regions meeting these criteria were listed in Article 2(2) of the Regulation.

Regulation 2618/80[201] was somewhat different. It sought to assist reduction of dependence on imported petroleum and to promote regional development. The thinking was that Community energy policy sought to reduce petroleum imports, which would particularly affect regions with a substantial energy deficit and a heavy dependence on petroleum imports.[202] It applied to the Mezzogiorno, particularly its mountain areas. These areas required the installation of new activities with consequent increased electricity consumption. However, they suffered high power losses due to long-distance transmission of electricity produced in the North.[203] The aim was to help improve the development conditions of these areas by strengthening the security of their energy supplies. To this end, better use of hydroelectric resources would be sought through making possible, by improved techniques, the reutilization of abandoned or obsolete works and a better use of alternative energy sources. At the same time, an information campaign and feasibility studies would be supported, with a view to encouraging private users themselves to exploit hydroelectric and alternative energy sources. Finally, the assistance would seek to create jobs linked to the upkeep of these installations.[204]

Regulation 218/84[205] extended the measure to the Greek islands, except for Salamina, which was not covered by a national aid scheme.[206] The justification for the extension was that Greece also suffered from a substantial energy

[199] Instituting a specific Community regional development measure contributing to the development of new economic activities in certain zones affected by implementation of the common fisheries policy (OJ 1985 L350/17). According to Art 3(3) (ibid), there was to be close co-ordination with the EAGGF, 'other financial instruments of the fishing sector', the ESF, the EIB, and the NCI.

[200] More details of these objectives were given in Art 4 (ibid).

[201] Instituting a specific regional development measure contributing to improving security of energy supply in certain Community regions by way of improved use of new techniques for hydro-electric power and alternative energy sources (OJ 1980 L271/23).

[202] ibid, 10th and 11th recitals in the preamble.

[203] ibid, Art 2.

[204] ibid, Art 3(2).

[205] Amending Reg 2618/80 (OJ 1984 L27/15).

[206] ibid, Art 2.

shortfall and heavy dependence on oil imports. Moreover, the cost of energy was particularly high in the Greek islands. The development of those islands entailed increased energy consumption, which also stemmed from the operation of the water-supply systems serving agriculture, industry, and tourism. It was, therefore, necessary to encourage the installation there of a new generating capacity exploiting local alternative energy sources.[207]

Particular attention was paid to the need to encourage entrepreneurship in the framework of such measures.[208] For example, Article 3 of Regulation 3638/85[209] provided for the improvement of the physical environment, development of small and medium-sized enterprises and craft activities, stimulation of economic activity in general,[210] and promotion of tourism. The aim was to encourage new, employment-creating activities in fishing regions. It was not only the supply of skilled labour and capital but also the demand for them which had to be improved. Thus the entrepreneurial factor and capacity for adaptation had to be enhanced.[211]

However, the Economic and Social Committee considered such legislation too limited. In particular, the Committee sought reforms to enable the Community to intervene quickly and efficiently and to have the discretion to employ a wide range of measures where regions were faced with a sudden rundown of their basic industries. According to the Committee, this implied that part of the quota-free section should be set aside for such emergency action.[212]

Community programmes

Regulation 1787/84[213] provided that the Fund could assist Community programmes and that they should have priority in Fund operations.[214] Such a programme was defined as a series of consistent, multiannual measures directly serving Community objectives and the implementation of Community policies.[215] In contrast to the specific Community regional development

[207] ibid, Art 5. The relevant sources were also extended to include geothermal energy.

[208] European Parliament Resolution of 12 July 1985 (OJ 1985 C229/135) on proposals for specific Community regional development measures, para 21.

[209] OJ 1985 L350/17.

[210] The importance of 'aid for initiative' rather than 'capital aid' was stressed in the European Parliament Resolution of 11 Mar 1980 (OJ 1980 C85/24) on the proposals for regulations instituting specific Community regional development projects.

[211] R Camagni and R Cappellin, 'Policies for Full Employment and More Efficient Utilization of Resources and New Trends in European Regional Development' (1981) *Lo Spettatore Internazionale* 99–135, 119.

[212] Opinion of 23 Mar 1983 (OJ 1983 C124/2) on the second series of specific Community regional development measures, para 1.4. See also the Opinion of 29 Apr 1982 (OJ 1982 C178/38) on the proposal for a regulation amending Reg 724/75, para 5.1.

[213] OJ 1984 L169/1.

[214] ibid, Art 7(6). The Commission had originally proposed that 20% of ERDF resources should be devoted to them (proposal of 29 Oct 1981 (OJ 1981 C336/60) for a regulation amending Reg 724/75).

[215] Art 7(1) of Reg 1787/84 (OJ 1984 L169/1).

measures, these programmes were to be adopted by a qualified majority in the Council.[216] In practice, these programmes generally sought to counteract the regional impact of other Community policies. However, one programme—Star[217]—seems to have been designed, more positively, to assist regional participation in implementation of the relevant Community policy.

The Resider programme was established for steel regions by Regulation 328/88.[218] This programme sought to improve the infrastructure and the physical and social environment in the regions concerned. It also sought to promote the establishment of new activities, the growth of small and medium-sized enterprises, and innovation.[219]

Eligibility for assistance was to depend on the first five criteria established by Regulation 216/84,[220] with thresholds being applied to determine whether the criteria were met.[221] According to these thresholds, the minimum number of jobs in the steel industry had to have been 'of the order of 3500' on 1 January 1986; the rate of dependence on employment in the steel industry had to be 10 per cent or more; job losses 'in the order of 1500' had to have occurred as from 1 January 1986; and the socio-economic situation was to be assessed by a 'joint indicator' with a threshold of 120. Indicators reflecting an unfavourable employment situation (particularly, a high level of employment) were also to be applied.

In principle, eligibility would also be limited to regions covered by a regional aid scheme of the Member State concerned. Other regions would only be eligible if the Member State concerned was willing to provide aid and such aid was compatible with Article 92 of the EEC Treaty, governing state aid.

The Commission was to decide, on application by a Member State, those of its regions which were eligible for assistance.[222] By way of exception, the steel area of Luxembourg would be eligible, provided that it met the first three criteria.[223] The steel areas of Greece and Ireland would also be eligible, should the partial or total closure of steel works lead to major job losses.[224]

Assistance to such regions related to the kinds of actions covered by the specific Community regional development measures, except for actions relating to housing and global loans. In addition, infrastructure 'contributing to

[216] Art 7(4) of Reg 1787/84 (OJ 1984 L169/1).

[217] See sect 7.4.1 below.

[218] Instituting a Community programme to assist the conversion of steel areas (OJ 1988 L33/1).

[219] ibid, Art 2.

[220] ibid, Art 3(1).

[221] ibid, Art 4(1), though Art 3(3) (ibid) provided that certain regions of Spain were eligible without requiring a demonstration that they met the thresholds.

[222] ibid, Art 3(2). See eg Dec 89/317 (OJ 1989 L133/29) concerning the areas referred to in Art 3(2) of Reg 328/88.

[223] Dec 89/559 (OJ 1989 L305/30) concerning the steel area of Luxembourg referred to in Art 4(2) of Reg 328/88.

[224] Art 4(2) of Reg 328/88 (OJ 1988 L33/1).

the creation, development, and adaptation of job-creating productive activities' as well as tourist activities could now be assisted.[225]

Similarly, the Renaval programme was established by Regulation 2506/88.[226] Eligible regions were those which had experienced substantial job losses in shipbuilding in the past three years and not earlier than 1 January 1984[227] or were currently experiencing or threatened with such losses, whenever this sector determined their economic development, such losses resulting in a serious aggravation of unemployment in these regions. Other regions could also benefit, provided that they satisfied the sectoral criterion and the general criteria for qualification as an Objective 2 region,[228] as could adjoining regions.[229] In addition, the areas in Portugal and Spain in which major job losses in shipbuilding had occurred in the years preceding the above period were covered.[230] The areas concerned were Murcia in Spain and Setubal in Portugal.[231]

The programme was to contribute, in the regions concerned, to the removal of obstacles to the development of new, job-creating activities. To this end, the programme was to aim at improving the infrastructure and the physical and social environment in these regions. It was also to promote the establishment of new activities, the growth of small and medium-sized undertakings, and innovation. A better link was thereby sought between Community objectives for the conversion of regions and the objectives of Community policy on shipbuilding.[232]

The Star programme, established by Regulation 3300/86,[233] was different. According to Article 2 of the Regulation, the objectives of this programme were to contribute to strengthening the economic base in the regions concerned, to foster job creation, and to help raise technological standards in those regions. It was to seek these objectives through improving the supply of advanced telecommunications services and by integrating these regions into large telecommunications networks. The programme was thereby to provide

[225] ibid, Art 5.

[226] Instituting a Community programme to assist the conversion of shipbuilding areas (OJ 1988 L225/24).

[227] Failure to allow for losses of jobs that had occurred earlier meant that no account was taken of existing negative regional consequences and any existing need for regional restructuring which might result from such job losses (ESC Opinion of 19 Nov 1987 on shipbuilding—industrial, social and regional aspects, CES(87)1074, 9).

[228] sect 2.4.2 below.

[229] Areas eligible for assistance were determined by Commission decisions. See, eg, Dec 91/91 (OJ 1991 L50/24) on the areas referred to in Art 3(2) of Reg 2506/88.

[230] Art 3 of Reg 2506/88 (OJ 1988 L225/24).

[231] Dec 89/164 (OJ 1989 L61/56) and Dec 89/470 (OJ 1989 L233/29) concerning the areas referred to in Art 3(2) of Reg 2506/88.

[232] ibid, Art 2.

[233] Instituting a Community programme for the development of certain less favoured regions of the Community by improving access to advanced telecommunications services (OJ 1986 L305/1).

a better link between the Community's objectives for the structural development of regions and the objectives of Community telecommunications policy.

Eligible regions were those which satisfied four criteria simultaneously. The criteria were: a particularly difficult economic situation compared with the Community as a whole; peripheral or insular geographical location; inadequate supply of telecommunications services, notably advanced services for the productive sector; and, as a general rule, eligibility under a national regional aid scheme.[234] The regions meeting these criteria were in France, Greece, Ireland, Italy, Portugal, Spain, and the United Kingdom. They were listed in Article 3(2) of the Regulation.

According to Article 4 of the same Regulation, the Fund might assist establishment of the basic equipment needed for advanced telecommunications services. It might also promote the supply of, and the demand for, advanced telecommunications services.[235]

Finally, the Valoren programme was established by Regulation 3301/86.[236] This programme concerned regions facing serious energy problems affecting their socio-economic situation. The regions also had to be located in Member States which, because of their structural economic difficulties, found it difficult to meet the energy objectives laid down in the Council Resolution of 16 September 1986.[237] According to Article 2 of the Regulation, the programme sought to contribute to strengthening the economic base in the regions concerned. It sought to do so by: improving local energy-supply conditions on satisfactory economic terms, while respecting the objectives of the Community environmental policy; fostering job creation; and raising technological standards in those regions. The programme was thereby to provide a better link between the Community's objectives for the structural development of regions and its energy policy objectives.

Eligible regions had to have a particularly difficult economic situation compared with the Community as a whole. They also had to be located either in Member States that had considerable leeway to make up as regards attainment of the energy objectives set for the Community as a whole, or on island territory with high energy costs and heavily dependent on external energy supplies. As a general rule, they also had to be eligible under a regional aid scheme of the Member State concerned.[238] Article 3(2) of the Regulation

[234] Art 3(1) of Reg 3300/86 (OJ 1986 L305/1). The first programme to be approved was that for Greece. See Dec 88/55 (OJ 1988 L30/33) approving the intervention programme for Greece implementing the Star programme.

[235] The compatibility of such assistance with the concern of competition to end cross-subsidization of telephone calls has been doubted. See A Cutler, C Haslam, J Williams, and K Williams, *1992—the Struggle for Europe* (Berg, New York, 1989) 86.

[236] Instituting a Community programme for the development of certain less favoured regions of the Community by exploiting endogenous energy potential (OJ 1986 L305/6).

[237] Concerning new Community energy policy objectives for 1995 and convergence of the policies of the Member States (OJ 1986 C241/1).

[238] Art 3(1) of Reg 3301/86 (OJ 1986 L305/6).

listed the regions in France, Greece, Ireland, Italy, Portugal, Spain, and the United Kingdom which met these conditions.[239]

The European Parliament considered such action to be too limited. In particular, the Parliament called for a Community programme to improve the contribution of education and vocational training to regional development. It was suggested that the programme should: be co-ordinated with the projects assisted by the European Social Fund and the other financial instruments of the Community; aim to increase the number and the rate of growth of small and medium-sized enterprises; help to establish new centres specially equipped to deal with the problems of such enterprises, co-operatives, and craft businesses, particularly in regions without a tradition of small industries; promote an awareness within the educational system of the employment opportunities offered by the local economy; enlist the support of the above-mentioned centres in building up co-operation and exchanges of experience between schools, vocational training centres, universities, research centres, regional and local authorities, trade unions, and employers, with the aim of ensuring that the economic resources of the regions were used to best advantage; and take into account and be adapted to national variations in systems of education and vocational training, seeking to assist their development and modernization.[240] No such programme was adopted.

Studies

Article 1(1) of the 1973 proposal[241] envisaged that studies undertaken on the initiative of the Commission could be assisted. However, Article 10 of Regulation 724/75[242] stipulated that assisted studies had to be 'closely related to the operations of the Fund and undertaken at the request of a Member State'.[243] The requirement that they be requested by a Member State was removed by Regulation 1787/84.[244]

Integrated development operations

Integrated development operations[245] were first advocated by the Commission in 1978. They were designed to increase the impact of Community

[239] The first programme to be approved was that for Greece. See Dec 88/48 (OJ 1988 L30/25) approving the intervention programme for Greece implementing the Valoren programme.

[240] Resolution of 9 Mar 1987 (OJ 1987 C99/15) on regional development, education, and training, para 14.

[241] OJ 1973 C86/7.

[242] OJ 1975 L73/1.

[243] Art 14 of Reg 214/79 (OJ 1979 L35/1) removed the ceiling of 50% on Commission contributions to the financing of studies.

[244] Art 24 of Reg 1787/84 (OJ 1984 L169/1) provided that studies could be funded up to a maximum of 0.5% of the annual ERDF endowment.

[245] G Bernardini, 'Les Operations integrées de développement communautaire' (1982) RMC 265–271.

interventions, particularly in regions affected by serious problems.[246] At the same time, they might be seen as countering undesirable compartmentalization between assistance for infrastructure and assistance to productive activities.[247] To these ends, assistance from the Structural Funds and other Community financial instruments for structural purposes was to be combined.[248]

Such operations may be thought to have been essential for the effectiveness of the European Regional Development Fund, given the link between regional problems and problems with which the other funds were concerned. They might, however, be less attractive to at least some Member States, if arrangements for allocation of assistance established by legislation governing the individual funds were undermined. Such legislation, though ostensibly favourable to integrated operations, was careful to avoid prejudicing the 'individuality' of the various funds.

The operations could take the form of development programmes, assisted by the Guidance Section of the European Agricultural Guidance and Guarantee Fund under Article 6(1) of Regulation 729/70.[249] Indeed, Regulation 355/77[250] introduced priority for projects which fell within such programmes and formed part of an integrated approach.[251]

Moreover, in 1981 the Commission introduced priority treatment for operations jointly financed by two or more funds, in the Guidelines for the Management of the European Social Fund.[252]

More particularly, in the management of the European Regional Development Fund, investments and measures which were part of an integrated development approach, for example, in the form of integrated operations or programmes,[253] might, according to Article 34(1) of Regulation 1787/84,[254] have priority for assistance. Article 34(2) of the Regulation defined an integrated development operation as

[246] Procedures and content for the implementation of an integrated approach, COM(86)401. See also the Commission Reply by Mr Varfis to WQ 1877/87 (OJ 1989 C202/2) by Mr José Garcia Raya.

[247] ESC Opinion of 12 July 1989 (OJ 1989 C221/3) on the ERDF thirteenth annual report, para 3.5.

[248] *Fifth Annual Report on the ERDF* (EC Commission, Brussels, 1980), 27; *Eighth Annual Report on the ERDF* (EC Commission, Brussels, 1983), 79. Four preparatory studies were initiated in 1982 (ibid, 80).

[249] On the financing of the CAP (JO 1970 L94/13).

[250] On common measures to improve the conditions under which agricultural products were processed and marketed (OJ 1977 L51/1).

[251] Art 3(1)(f) (ibid) required information regarding the relationship of the programme to any other measures to encourage the harmonious development of the overall economy of the region in question.

[252] para 1.1.2 of the Guidelines for 1981–82 (OJ 1981 C110/2).

[253] The concept of 'integrated programmes' did not appear in the Commission proposal of 18 Nov 1983 (OJ 1983 C360/1) for a regulation amending Reg 724/75. In mentioning this concept, the Council may have been thinking of the IMPs, which were discussed at the time and were subsequently established.

[254] OJ 1984 L169/1.

a coherent set of public and private measures and investments which [had] the following characteristics: (a) they relate[d] to a limited geographical area affected by particularly serious problems involving, in particular, delayed development or industrial or urban decline and likely to affect the development of the region in question; (b) the Community, through the joint use of various structural financial instruments, and the national and local authorities in Member States contribute[d] in a closely co-ordinated manner to their implementation.

The Member State concerned was to ensure concerted use of Community and national financial resources and close co-ordination between the various public authorities involved in the execution of the operation.[255] The Commission was, likewise, to ensure concerted use of the Structural Funds and other financial instruments of the Community.[256]

Integrated Mediterranean Programmes

In the case of the Integrated Mediterranean Programmes, unified arrangements for the three Structural Funds were embodied in legislation. Such programmes were introduced by Regulation 2088/85.[257] This measure was enacted pursuant to three different EEC Treaty provisions: Article 235 (the original legal basis for the European Regional Development Fund), Article 43 (agricultural policy), and Article 127 (operations of the European Social Fund).[258]

According to Article 1 of the Regulation, the object of the programmes was to improve the socio-economic structures of the Mediterranean regions,[259] particularly those of Greece. The programmes were thereby to facilitate the adjustment of these regions to the new conditions created by Community enlargement in the best possible conditions. Article 2(1) required that the programmes were to be adopted by the Commission rather than the Council.[260] They should comprise multiannual operations which were consistent with one another and with Community policies. According to Article 2(2), the operations had to relate, in particular, to investments in the productive sector, the creation of infrastructures, and better use of human resources.

Finance for the programmes might be drawn from the European Regional Development Fund, the European Social Fund, the Guidance Section of the European Agricultural Guidance and Guarantee Fund, European Investment Bank loans, New Community Instrument loans, and from additional resources.[261] In particular, Article 551 of the General Budget[262] could be used to provide assistance above the thresholds laid down by the

[255] ibid, Art 34(3).
[256] ibid, Art 34(4).
[257] Concerning the IMPs (OJ 1985 L197/1).
[258] See eg Dec 86/477 (OJ 1986 L282/21) approving an IMP for Crete.
[259] The geographical scope of the IMPs was defined by Annex I to Reg 2088/85 (OJ 1985 L197/1).
[260] ibid, Art 7.
[261] ibid, Art 3.
[262] General Budget for 1985 (OJ 1985 L206/3).

provisions governing the Structural Funds. It could also be used for providing assistance outside the geographical scope of the Funds. However, the programmes were to be consistent with other Community policies. Thus agricultural operations carried out under such a programme were to remain in keeping with the general objectives of production management defined by the common agricultural policy.[263]

These arrangements were said to constitute a 'qualitative leap forward' from the integrated development operations. They established as a precondition for assistance a programme,[264] the purpose of which was to direct the bulk of available resources towards specific objectives in given regions.[265]

On the other hand, Article 12 of the Regulation provided that loans from the European Investment Bank should be granted according to the specific criteria and procedures applicable to such loans. This provision laid the foundations for a separation of the preparation and management of the programmes from the contribution provided by the Bank.[266] Thus financing by a combination of grants and loans was accepted as a general principle but not put into effect.[267] Even in the case of the former kind of assistance, co-ordination problems arose.[268] Assistance from the European Regional Development Fund and assistance under Article 551 of the General Budget were managed globally by annual instalments in respect of which advance payments were made. In contrast, assistance from the European Social Fund and assistance to the fisheries sector under Regulation 4028/86[269] were provided on the basis of specific projects.[270]

2.4 COHESION

The European Regional Development Fund is now treated as the principal instrument for achieving cohesion. Article 160 of the EC Treaty provides that the purpose of the Fund is to help to redress the main regional imbalances[271] in the Union. It is to do so through participation in the development and structural adjustment of regions whose development is lagging behind and in

263 OJ 1985 L197/1, Art 4.

264 ibid, Art 5.

265 Report of the Committee on Budgetary Affairs on the IMPs, EP Doc A3–0340/91, 7.

266 See, regarding a general lack of EIB interest in the programmes, the European Parliament Resolution of 17 Dec 1993 (OJ 1994 C20/515) on the Commission's fifth progress report on IMPs, para 11.

267 Report of the Committee on Budgetary Affairs on the IMPs, EP Doc A3–0340/91, 12.

268 COA special report 4/90 (OJ 1990 C298/1) on the IMPs. Cf COA special report 2/88 (OJ 1988 C188/1) on the integrated approach to Community financing of structural measures.

269 On Community measures to improve and adapt structures in the fisheries and aquaculture sector (OJ 1986 L376/7).

270 IMPs 1988 progress report, SEC(89)1665, 25.

271 Before amendment by the TEU, this provision referred to the 'principal' regional imbalances.

the conversion of declining industrial regions. Accordingly, the 'essential task' of the Fund is to support Objectives 1 and 2. It shall also participate in Objective 5b operations[272] and contribute to Objective 6 operations.[273]

To avoid previous administrative difficulties,[274] Article 14(3) of Regulation 2081/93[275] now provides that a region can be eligible under only one of these Objectives.[276] To promote full coherence between Objectives 2 and 5b, the Commission also considers that the lists of eligible regions should as far as possible be decided at the same time.[277]

2.4.1 Objective 1

Objective 1 is promoting the development and structural adjustment of regions whose development is lagging behind.[278] It is Objective 1 regions to which the bulk of Union assistance is directed.[279] For the four Member States eligible for assistance under the Cohesion Fund,[280] resources available under this Fund and Objective 1 were to be doubled in real terms between 1992 and 1999.[281]

Resources available for 2000 to 2006 are envisaged as being Euro 218.4 billion.[282] Around two-thirds of these resources are to be directed to Objective 1 regions.[283]

272 Art 3(1) of Reg 2081/93 (OJ 1993 L193/5) amending Reg 2052/88 on the tasks of the Structural Funds and their effectiveness and on the co-ordination of their activities between themselves and with the operations of the EIB and the other existing financial instruments.

273 Prot 6 to the Accession Agreement with Austria, Finland, and Sweden, as amended by Dec 95/1 (OJ 1995 L1/1) adjusting the instruments concerning the accession of new Member States to the EU, Art 1.

274 Community Structural Fund operations 1994–99, COM(93)67, 14.

275 Amending Reg 2052/88 on the tasks of the Structural Funds and their effectiveness and on the co-ordination of their activities between themselves and with the operations of the EIB and the other existing financial instruments (OJ 1993 L193/5).

276 No Objective 1, 2, or 5b regions were originally designated in the former GDR. Apparently the question was whether it should be classified under Objective 1 or 2. See EEC regional development policy, House of Lords Select Committee on the European Communities, HL(1991–92)20, Evidence, 6. It can be characterized in its entirety as an old industrial area, according to K Peschel, 'European Integration and Regional Development in Northern Europe' (1992) *Regional Studies* 387–397, 392. According to Art 2(5) of Reg 3575/90 (OJ 1990 L353/19) concerning the activities of the Structural Funds in the territory of the former GDR, by way of exception, given the absence of appropriate statistical information on the territory in question, Structural Fund measures would be implemented without previous classification of that territory in line with the regional and rural objectives. In practice, this meant that assistance was granted as in Objective 1 regions. Objective 1 status is now formally recognized. See sect 2.4.1 below.

277 Community Structural Fund operations 1994–99, COM(93)67, 14.

278 Art 1.1 of Reg 2081/93 (OJ 1993 L193/5). 279 ibid, Art 12(2).

280 See sect 6.5 below.

281 Art 12(4) of Reg 2081/93 (OJ 1993 L193/5). This provision accords with the conclusion of the European Council meeting in Dec 1992 (Bull EC 12–1992, I.55), that Objective 5a (see sect 3.4.1 below) commitments outside Objectives 1 and 5b regions were not to increase in real terms. See, regarding the problems involved, COA annual report 1995 (OJ 1996 C340/1), para 5.25.

282 Proposal of 19 Mar 1998 (OJ 1998 C176/1) for a regulation laying down provisions on the Structural Funds, Art 7(1).

283 ibid, Art 7(2).

Eligibility for assistance

The Commission originally envisaged that account would be taken of the situation of each Member State in determining whether any of its regions qualified for assistance under Objective 1. Hence, a Commission Statement was contained in Annex 2 to the March 1988 version of the proposal for what became Regulation 2052/88.[284] According to this statement, per capita gross domestic product of the Member State would be taken into account together with the per capita gross domestic product of the region in designating Objective 1 regions.[285]

Regulation 2052/88,[286] as adopted by the Council and subsequently amended by Regulation 2081/93,[287] makes no reference to the per capita gross domestic product of Member States. Article 8(1) provides that the regions concerned by Objective 1 shall be regions at NUTS[288] Level II. Their per capita gross domestic product in purchasing-power parities,[289] on the basis of the figures for the last three years,[290] must be less than 75 per cent of the Union average.[291] Northern Ireland, the five new German *Länder*, East Berlin,[292] the French overseas departments, the Azores, the Canary Islands, and Madeira shall be covered. Other regions whose per capita gross domestic product is close to that of the regions mentioned may be covered by Objective 1 for 'special reasons'. Moreover, in view of their unique adjacent position to Hainaut in Belgium and their regional gross domestic product, at NUTS III Level, the Council agreed that the *arrondissements* of Avesnes, Douai, and Valenciennes[293] should 'exceptionally' be covered. The Council also agreed that Argyll and Bute, Arran, the Cambrae, and western Moray should be covered.

284 COM(88)144.

285 It was also specified that Ireland would be included in those regions.

286 On the tasks of the Structural Funds and their effectiveness and on the co-ordination of their activities between themselves and with the operations of the EIB and the other existing financial instruments (OJ 1988 L185/9).

287 OJ 1993 L193/5.

288 Nomenclature of Territorial Units for Statistical Purposes. Cf the definition of 'region' in Art 1 of Dir 79/109 (OJ 1979 L29/20) amending Dec 64/432 as regards brucellosis.

289 21st recital in the preamble to Reg 2052/88 (OJ 1988 L185/9).

290 The European Parliament has complained about the lack of a transitional period for regions whose per capita GDP rises slightly above this figure. See the Resolution of 22 Jan 1993 (OJ 1993 C42/211) on Community structural policies: assessment and outlook ('mid-term review'), para 53. The Council decided in Art 8(1) of Reg 2081/93 (OJ 1993 L193/5) that Abruzzi, where the GDP figure had risen to 89%, would be eligible from 1 Jan 1994 to 31 Dec 1995.

291 The figures for the new *Länder* and Eastern Berlin are not included in the calculation of this average.

292 Its inclusion accords with the conclusions of the European Council in Dec 1992 (Bull EC 12–1992, I.55).

293 No GDP figures were available for these regions. See Commission Reply by Mr de Silguy to WQ E–4196/97 (OJ 1998 C323/17) by José García-Margallo y Marfil.

Article 8(2) of Regulation 2081/93[294] provides that the list of regions concerned by Objective 1 is given in Annex I.[295] This list includes regions which are neither specifically mentioned in Article 8(1) nor, in principle, meet the gross domestic product criterion laid down therein. In particular, it includes Hainaut in Belgium, with a per capita gross domestic product of 77 per cent. It also includes Merseyside and the Highlands and Islands of Scotland in the United Kingdom, both with a figure of 79 per cent.[296]

Inclusion of Flevoland in the Netherlands, which had a per capita gross domestic product of 62 per cent of the Union average, was not proposed by the Commission. According to the Commission, there were 'a lot of anomalies' in the position of this region.[297] Its low gross domestic product figure was largely a consequence of a disassociation between the place of work and the place of residence of the active population. Moreover, except for one city, this region was not eligible under the Dutch regional aid scheme.[298] Nevertheless, its inclusion in the list was agreed by the Council.[299] The impression given is that Council negotiations, which preceded enactment of the legislation, were affected by concern to maximize the number of Member States which could benefit under Objective 1.

Even so, eligible regions are those which are underdeveloped by reference to the average gross domestic product per capita for the Union as a whole. Use of this criterion is defended on the grounds that it reflects the economic performance of the regions. In contrast, an unemployment indicator can reflect only the manifest disequilibria on the labour market. Thus it cannot take into account underemployment.[300] Besides, differences between the social policies of governments lead to different definitions of unemployment. Differences in activity rates also affect the comparability of unemployment between different regions.

However, it is not universally accepted that gross domestic product figures alone are adequate to identify Union regions with the most serious problems. It may be objected, for example, that gross domestic product is only one of a number of relevant indicators, such as employment, emigration, and

[294] OJ 1993 L193/5.

[295] A new list may be established by the Council, on a Commission proposal and after consulting the European Parliament, from 2000 (ibid, Art 8(3)).

[296] COA annual report 1995 (OJ 1996 C340/1), table 5.3. The idea that Molise in Italy and the French island of Corsica, where the figure was also 79%, should be removed from the list (*European Report* 1831 (30 Jan 1993)) was not pursued. These regions were peripheral and rural and were originally included in the list because of specific reasons of a technical and political nature. See Structural Funds: amendment of Regs 2052/88 and 4253/88, SEC(93)651, 3.

[297] *European Report* 1831 (30 Jan 1993).

[298] Structural Funds: amendment of Regs 2052/88 and 4253/88, SEC(93)651, 3.

[299] The inclusion of Cantabria, where the per capita GDP was 73% of the Community average (COA annual report 1995 (OJ 1996 C340/1), table 5.3), was also agreed by the Council.

[300] Second periodic report on the social and economic situation and development of the regions of the Community, COM(84)40, ii.

poverty.[301] In itself it is also too restrictive to permit proper assessment of the level of development of the regions.[302] In particular, it may be objected that the principal indicators of regional problems are not the disparities in per capita gross domestic product but the disequilibria in the utilization of regional resources.[303]

The only response to such objections seems to have been flexible application of the 75 per cent threshold and acceptance of the eligibility of regions smaller than NUTS Level II.[304] This response did little to address the underlying methodological problems in determination of regional eligibility.

These problems are not addressed in the latest Commission proposals. According to these proposals, the 75 per cent criterion will be more strictly applied, so as to reduce the percentage of the Union population covered by Objective 1 from 25 per cent to 20 per cent.[305] Thus, in principle, the list of eligible regions is to be drawn up by the Commission (rather than the Council) strictly in accordance with this criterion. Even so, Objective 6 regions are to be brought within Objective 1,[306] by virtue of 'special arrangements'.[307] The most remote regions (the French overseas departments, the Canary Islands, and Madeira) will also be covered,[308] though only on 'an *ad hoc* basis'.[309] In addition, transitional assistance will be available in favour of regions previously covered by Objective 1 which are found no longer to be eligible.[310]

This proposal apparently takes no more account of the methodological problems involved than did earlier practice. Rather, it is designed to limit the coverage of Objective 1 to regions where state aid may be authorized under Article 87(3)(a) of the Treaty.[311]

[301] ESC Opinion of 25 May 1992 (OJ 1992 C106/20) on the annual report on the implementation of the reform of the Structural Funds, para 2.2.5.

[302] Opinion of the Committee on Economic and Monetary Affairs and Industrial Policy on the proposal for a regulation amending Reg 4254/88 (EP Doc A3–0191/93), 13.

[303] R Camagni and R Cappellin, 'Policies for Full Employment and More Efficient Utilization of Resources and New Trends in European Regional Development' (1981) *Lo Spettatore Internazionale* 99–135, 120.

[304] The Commission considered that the stronger concentration of Structural Fund operations on Objective 1 (around 70% of total allocations in 1997) should be accompanied by increased flexibility in terms of both the rate of assistance and the eligibility criteria. See Community finances between now and 1997, COM(92)2001, 24. According to Commissioner Millan, 'political considerations' should come into play in the application of the criterion (*Europe* 5927, 25 Feb 1993).

[305] Explanatory memorandum to the Proposal of 19 Mar 1998 for a regulation laying down provisions on the Structural Funds, COM(98)131, 18.

[306] Proposal of 19 Mar 1998 (OJ 1998 C176/1) for a regulation laying down provisions on the Structural Funds, para 12 of the preamble and Art 3(1). Cf the ambiguous approach envisaged in the explanatory memorandum to this Proposal, COM(98)131, 14.

[307] *Agenda 2000*, Bull EC, Supp 5/97, 22.

[308] This coverage reflects Art 299(2) EC (ibid, 22).

[309] ibid, 22.

[310] Proposal of 19 Mar 1998 (OJ 1998 C176/1) for a regulation laying down provisions on the Structural Funds, Art 3(2).

[311] *Agenda 2000*, Bull EC, Supp 5/97, 22. See, regarding this provision, A Evans, *EC Law of State Aid* (Clarendon Press, Oxford, 1997), ch 4.

Definition of regions

NUTS regions basically reflect national administrative classifications.[312] These classifications may mean that the size and structure of NUTS regions vary considerably between Member States. Such variations may affect the comparability of gross domestic product figures.[313] More particularly, parts of large, relatively stronger NUTS Level II regions may have serious problems but be 'lost' within such regions. Conversely, Flevoland gives the impression of being 'cut to measure' to meet eligibility conditions. Moreover, the Highlands and Islands include areas containing around one hundred thousand persons who were not within the original administrative region. Again, the treatment of Ireland as a single NUTS Level II region means that comparatively prosperous areas benefit from Objective 1 treatment.

Manipulation of the classifications continues. For example, Devon and Cornwall have previously been treated as a single NUTS Level II region. This treatment obscured the serious economic problems of Cornwall. However, the division of the two counties into two separate NUTS Level II regions has now apparently been accepted by the Commission. As a consequence, Cornwall, with a per capita gross domestic product of 69 per cent will, presumably, qualify for the first time for Objective 1 coverage.[314] Similarly, serious economic problems in parts of Wales may have been obscured. However, the creation of a new NUTS Level II region, to be known as 'West Wales and the Valleys', is now envisaged. This new region may also have a per capita gross national product less than 75 per cent of the Union average and thus qualify for the first time for such coverage.[315] Thus the uncritical Commission view that the 'NUTS system is generally stable over time, as changes only arise from the alteration of the administrative structure of a Member State'[316] seems questionable.

A more rational approach to definition of regions has been demanded,[317] to ensure a proper identification of the regions with the most serious problems from a Union perspective. Such a definition, it is argued, should be based on functional considerations.[318]

[312] eg *Länder* in Germany and standard regions in the UK are Level I regions; counties in the UK, regions in France and Italy, and provinces in Belgium and the Netherlands are Level II; and *nomoi* in Greece, *Kreise* in Germany, and *Maakunat* in Finland are Level III.

[313] Second periodic report on the social and economic situation and development of the regions of the Community, COM(84)40, 1.12.

[314] *European Report* 2329 (4 July 1998). [315] ibid.

[316] Commission Reply by Mrs Wulf-Mathies to WQ E–0840/98 (OJ 1998 C323/81) by José Barros Moura.

[317] cf the footnote to Regional and urban planning: Commission invitation to submit proposals (OJ 1991 C12/12), where regions were defined as 'geographical areas which represent[ed] coherent entities in economic, social, or energy terms, and not necessarily a particular administrative region'.

[318] Opinion of 30 June 1982 (OJ 1982 C252/20) on the regions of Europe—first periodic report on the social and economic situation of the regions of the Community, paras 2.3–4.

According to the Economic and Social Committee, 'labour market regions' may provide the clearest indication of regions with the most serious problems. They may do so in regions where there are relatively dense populations, where the pattern of travelling to work is identifiable, and where there exist metropolitan areas with an adequate, if not ideal, infrastructure. This definition of regions is considered particularly appropriate for the purposes of promoting endogenous development, which depends on the 'local industrial milieu'.[319]

Technically, a definition based on labour-market regions may also have the advantage that the data may be more accurate. For example, the data for gross domestic product will be more representative of the relative prosperity of a region, if the errors in attribution as between those who work and those who live in a particular region disappear. Such 'spillover' problems are particularly pronounced in regions such as Hamburg and Bremen. On the one hand, in such tightly drawn city regions official gross domestic product figures may overvalue the economic situation, because part of the production is contributed by commuters from adjoining regions. On the other hand, the gross domestic product per head of the regions from which people commute may be undervalued.

However, many Union regions, including agricultural, mountain, border, cross-border, and underdeveloped regions, are of a type where labour markets have little or no meaning. In such cases Level III—or even Level IV—regions should, it is argued, be aggregated into new regions requiring the same kind of development policies.[320]

Denominator problems

Fund assistance is supposed to raise regional incomes through improving the capacity of the regions to generate factor incomes and not by increasing transfer incomes. Moreover, effective integration into the Union economy of the weaker regions can only be achieved in the long run, if firms in these regions take as reference points levels and changes in international prices.[321] Such considerations favour the use of regional gross domestic product by reference to international exchange rates to determine regions eligible for assistance.

On the other hand, purchasing-power parities take into account the evolution of internal prices which may differ from those used in international markets. Hence, calculation of per capita gross domestic product in terms of such parities is expected to assist the building-up of a picture of the situation in the regions.[322] Therefore, this denominator is employed in the legislation.[323]

319 ibid, para 2.5.1.

320 ibid, para 2.6.1–2.

321 Report on the situation and socio-economic development of the regions of the Community, COM(80)816, 40.

322 ibid 42.

323 21st recital in the preamble to Reg 2052/88 (OJ 1988 L185/9). Introduction of the Euro may render use of this denomination increasingly problematic. See F Wishlade, 'Competition

Problems of averages

Use of the Union average may be too simplistic for the purposes of Fund operations. For example, the concept of the average may lead to false conclusions of increasing cohesion, although the conditions in the poorer regions may have become more serious in absolute terms.[324] The Economic and Social Committee, therefore, has argued that this average alone should not determine eligibility for assistance.[325]

Need for dynamic indicators

A dynamic approach to indicators may be considered desirable. If regional disparities reflect growth disparities, 'growth indicators', the relative regional growth of productivity and employment, are necessary to identify problem regions. Indicators should be recorded in graphical form for a period of five years at least. A projection of data for a further period of five years should also be attempted.[326]

Need for qualitative data

Figures for gross domestic product alone cannot describe the problems and opportunities of particular regions. In particular, such figures may not reveal the problems of traditional industrial areas which are in decline.[327] Thus data concerning, for example, infrastructure provision, educational opportunities, climate, fertility of soil, opportunities for tourist development, and socio-cultural attitudes to enterprise are needed.[328]

Demographic factors may also be important.[329] For example, population growth may mean that increased output is not fully reflected in per capita gross domestic product figures. Conversely, depopulation may mean that reduced output does not fully show up in the trend of such figures.[330]

Again, population density may be an important factor. The least densely populated regions tend also to have low incomes, high shares of agriculture

Policy or Cohesion Policy by the Back Door: The Commission Guidelines on National Regional Aid' (1998) ECLR 343–357, 348.

324 Opinion of 30 June 1982 (OJ 1982 C252/20) on the regions of Europe—first periodic report on the social and economic situation of the regions of the Community, para 9.5.

325 ibid, para 9.6.

326 ibid, para 6.3.

327 European Parliament Resolution of 15 Nov 1985 (OJ 1985 C345/406) on the proposal for a regulation amending Reg 1787/84, para 5.

328 ESC Opinion of 30 June 1982 (OJ 1982 C252/20) on the regions of Europe—first periodic report on the social and economic situation of the regions of the Community, para 7.2.

329 The First periodic report on the situation and socio-economic development of the regions of the Community, COM(80)816, 38, found that the regions with the highest demographic pressure included the Mezzogiorno, Ireland, and Northern Ireland. See, more recently, the Fifth periodic report on the situation and socio-economic development of the regions of the Community, COM(94)322, 29.

330 Second periodic report on the social and economic situation and development of the regions of the Community, COM(84)40, 3.2–1.

in output and employment, and poor infrastructure. In such regions a low population density in itself acts together with natural and man-made factors to handicap economic performance.

The significance to be attached to peripherality may remain more controversial. For example, Greek regions are said to be handicapped by an excessive centralization of population and economic activity in the main urban conglomerations of Athens and Thessaloniki. These handicaps are said to be exaggerated by: the distance of Greek regions from the main centres of Union economic activity; their lack of land frontiers with other Member States; a mountainous relief which renders internal communications difficult and impedes the development of a modern agriculture; a high level of indebtedness; and a low level of professional and vocational training and, consequently, an insufficiently qualified workforce.[331]

Transportation costs for such regions may in themselves have become less important because of technical improvements in transportation facilities, higher density of traffic infrastructure, and the diminishing importance of heavy goods. On the other hand, more general communication costs have increased importance, but only some elements of such costs depend on distance. Thus it may be argued that peripherality should be measured by reference to regional accessibility to economic activity in terms of distance costs of all kinds.[332] Such costs may result not only from poor transport infrastructure.[333] They may also result from lack of access to national and international information networks, including access to information emanating from the headquarters offices which cluster in the central regions.[334]

At the same time, the effect of completion of the internal market may be to further the concentration of economic activity in central regions,[335] where cost reductions and scale savings are used to the best advantage.[336] In other words, central location is likely to become of increasing importance, as the productive capacity of firms expands in line with economies of scale, and each firm becomes able to supply a larger market.[337] As a result, relative

[331] European Parliament Resolution of 22 Nov 1991 (OJ 1991 C326/262) on the Community's regional development activities to assist Greece, recital A in the preamble.

[332] D Keeble, J Offord, and S Walker, *Peripheral Regions in a Community of Twelve Member States* (EC Commission, Luxembourg, 1988).

[333] K Peschel, 'European Integration and Regional Development in Northern Europe' (1992) *Regional Studies* 387–397, 391–392.

[334] cf Case C–225/91 *Matra SA v EC Commission* [1993] ECR I–3203, I–3257.

[335] The effect will depend on: the degree of centrality in relation to the 'heart' of the Union; per capita GDP, as an indicator of past and existing prosperity; and unemployment rates, as an indicator of structural problems. See J Bachtler and K Clement, *Regional Peripherality in the Single European Market, with Particular Reference to Ireland and Scotland* (European Policies Research Centre, Research Paper No 10; Glasgow, 1990), 19.

[336] M Quévit, 'The Regional Impact of the Internal Market: A Comparative Analysis of Traditional Industrial Regions and Lagging Regions' (1992) *Regional Studies* 349–360, 350.

[337] N Vanhove and LH Klaassen, *Regional Policy: A European Approach* (Saxon House, London, 1980), 235.

centrality-peripherality at Union level may accelerate national centre-periphery influences.[338]

However, to equate regional problems with geographical peripherality may be an oversimplification.[339] For example, while Ireland is peripheral relative to central parts of the Union, in a global context it is part of a very prosperous trading area. Also its perceived peripherality is a reflection of its marginal position relative to the centres of economic and political decision making and to the internal flows of commerce and finance. This position results from relatively poor infrastructure in the form of transport connections with the rest of the Union.[340]

Moreover, certain factors are considered favourable to development in peripheral regions of the Union, such as those of Greece. In the case of Greece these factors include: a climate which serves to attract visitors and, potentially, new residents; an unrivalled archaeological and historical heritage; an environment which remains relatively unspoilt outside the main conurbations; a population with close links to the outside world through commercial and maritime activities on the one hand and through a tradition of emigration on the other; and a geographical position which, while distant from the existing centres of economic activity, may serve as a base for expanding Union links with the Balkans, the Middle East, and the Mediterranean countries, if political differences will allow.[341]

Problems of services

In areas where public services dominate, gross domestic product may generally be underestimated. In areas where there are mainly private services and manufacturing, gross domestic product is usually overestimated. Such overestimation is particularly likely in manufacturing sectors, such as oil refining[342] and tobacco, where taxes on consumption are significant. As a result, in the calculation of gross domestic product, accuracies of better than plus or minus 15 per cent are thought to be unlikely in any Member State.[343] If errors

[338] Second periodic report on the social and economic situation and development of the regions of the Community, COM(84)40, 4.4–1. Cf C Clark, F Wilson, and J Bradley, 'Industrial Location and Economic Potential in Western Europe' (1969) *Regional Studies* 197–212.

[339] eg the impact of the single market on transport costs, which are high for peripheral economies, and the significant Irish dependence on small firms, for which trade barriers were relatively high, suggest that Irish exporters may improve their competitive position relative to other Union competitors. See A Foley and B Griffith, 'Indigenous Manufacturing Enterprises in a Peripheral Economy and the Single Market: The Case of the Republic of Ireland' (1992) *Regional Studies* 375–386, 383.

[340] Bachtler and Clement, n 335 above, 53.

[341] European Parliament Resolution of 22 Nov 1991 (OJ 1991 C326/262) on the Community's regional development activities to assist Greece, recital B in the preamble.

[342] See, regarding Groningen, the First periodic report on the situation and socio-economic development of the regions of the Community, COM(80)816, 4.

[343] In some countries GDP due to services is not measured but simply attributed on a population basis. Errors also occur from the difficulty of estimating the GDP stemming from the black economy (ibid, 42–43).

between Member States are conservatively estimated to add a further plus or minus 5 per cent, possible errors could be at least 20 per cent.[344]

Problems of capital intensiveness

Activities leading to a relatively high gross domestic product per head tend to be capital intensive (except for service industries in metropolitan areas). Those leading to a relatively low gross domestic product tend to be labour-intensive. Although all industries must be, or become, more efficient to survive competition from outside the Union, the less developed regions require labour-intensive industries. If, instead, new technologies are introduced in such regions, they may well experience a rapid increase in gross domestic product. As a consequence, they may fail to qualify as Objective 1 regions, even though unemployment rates rise at the same time.[345]

Allocation of assistance

Article 12(6) of Regulation 2052/88[346] provided that to facilitate the planning of assistance in the regions concerned, the Commission should, for a period of five years and as a guide, establish allocations by Member State of 85 per cent of Fund resources. These allocations were to be based on the socio-economic criteria determining the eligibility of regions for Fund assistance under Objectives 1, 2, and 5b. The Commission was also to ensure that there was a substantial increase in assistance in Objective 1 regions, particularly the least prosperous ones.

The allocations were originally established by Decision 89/250.[347] They might not be entirely uncontroversial. For example, the Northern Ireland authorities were disappointed that their allocation did not reflect the doubling of the Structural Funds. They complained that Northern Ireland had been granted Objective 1 status for non-economic reasons but the Commission based the allocation largely on economic criteria. According to the Commission, the allocation could not be increased, because Northern Ireland was the most prosperous of the Objective 1 regions.[348]

Article 12(4) of Regulation 2081/93[349] now provides that the Commission shall, using transparent procedures, make indicative allocations by Member State for each of Objectives 1 to 4 and 5b of Structural Fund assistance. Full account, 'as previously', is to be taken of national prosperity; regional prosperity; population of the regions and the relative severity of structural prob-

[344] ESC Opinion of 30 June 1982 (OJ 1982 C252/20) on the regions of Europe—1st periodic report on the social and economic situation of the regions of the Community, para 3.4.

[345] ibid, para 3.7.

[346] OJ 1988 L185/9.

[347] Fixing an indicative allocation between Member States of 85% of the commitment appropriations of the ERDF under Objective 1 (OJ 1989 L101/41).

[348] EEC regional development policy, House of Lords Select Committee on the European Communities, HL(1991–92)20, 19.

[349] OJ 1993 L193/5.

lems, including the level of unemployment; and, as appropriate, the needs of rural development. These criteria are to be 'appropriately' weighted in the allocation of assistance.

In practice, the allocations, as established by Decision 93/589,[350] are apparently distorted by 'non-transparent factors'. For example, the allocations to Greece and Portugal are identical. However, there are considerable disparities between these two Member States, as regards population, gross domestic product, rate of unemployment, and rate of industrial activity.[351]

More fundamentally, Council definition of each Objective and, more particularly its determination of regions covered by Objective 1, may limit the scope of effective Commission discretion in application of the criteria for establishing the allocations. In fact, Member States apparently insist on firm guarantees regarding their allocations before adopting any Commission proposals in the Council.[352] To this extent, the real distinction between indicative allocations and the original quotas[353] should not, perhaps, be exaggerated.

It is now proposed that 'indicative breakdowns' by Member States should be made in respect of 90 per cent of the resources available to the Structural Funds.[354] The remaining 10 per cent is to be allocated at a mid-term review, on the basis of objective, simple, and transparent criteria. These criteria are to be basically the same as those applied under existing legislation.[355] They must be such as to reflect efficiency in the use of the assistance and the quality of management and financial execution.[356]

2.4.2 Objective 2

Objective 2 is converting the regions, frontier regions, or parts of regions (including employment areas and urban communities) seriously affected by industrial decline.[357] According to the preamble to the original version of Regulation 2052/88,[358] action in favour of Objective 2 regions could cover up to 15 per cent of the Community population living outside Objective 1 regions.[359] As amended by Regulation 2081/93,[360] the preamble now refers simply to 15 per cent of the Union population.[361]

350 Fixing an indicative allocation between Member States of the commitment appropriations of the Structural Funds and FIFG under Objective 1 (OJ 1993 L280/30).

351 COA annual report 1995 (OJ 1996 C340/1), table 5.3, n (e).

352 *European Report* 1872 (3 July 1993).

353 sect 2.3.3 above.

354 Proposal of 19 Mar 1998 (OJ 1998 C176/1) for a regulation laying down provisions on the Structural Funds, Art 7(3).

355 *Agenda 2000*, Bull EC, Supp 5/97, 22.

356 Proposal of 19 Mar 1998 (OJ 1998 C176/1) for a regulation laying down provisions on the Structural Funds, 52nd recital in the preamble.

357 Art 1.2 of Reg 2081/93 (OJ 1993 L193/5).

358 OJ 1988 L185/9.

359 ibid, 22nd recital in the preamble.

360 OJ 1993 L193/5.

361 ibid, 22nd recital in the preamble.

Redefinition is now proposed, so that Objective 2 will be supporting the economic and social conversion of areas facing structural difficulties.[362] The regions covered must not include more than 18 per cent of the total Union population.[363] The Commission also considers that the percentage of the Union population covered by Objectives 1 and 2 together should be reduced from 51 per cent to between 35 and 40 per cent.[364]

To ensure that the limit to population coverage for Objective 2 is respected, the Commission will draw up a population ceiling for each Member State. In drawing up the ceilings, the Commission will take account of three factors. These factors are: the total population in NUTS III regions of Member States which meet the eligibility criteria; the severity of structural problems at national level in each Member State as compared with the other Member States concerned; and the need to ensure that each Member State makes a fair contribution to achieving the concentration of resources required by the 18 per cent limit.[365]

Eligibility for assistance

The first paragraph of Article 9(2) of Regulation 2081/93[366] provides that regions may be found by the Commission to be eligible for assistance, if they represent or belong to a NUTS Level III region and satisfy three criteria. First, the average rate of unemployment recorded over the last three years must have been above the Union average. Secondly, the percentage share of industrial employment in total employment must have equalled or exceeded the Union average in any reference year from 1975 onwards. Thirdly, there must have been an observable fall in industrial employment compared with that reference year.

The second paragraph of Article 9(2) of Regulation 2052/88[367] originally provided that assistance might also be granted to:

- adjacent areas meeting the same criteria;
- urban communities with an unemployment rate at least 50 per cent above the Community average which had recorded a substantial fall in industrial employment; and

[362] Proposal of 19 Mar 1998 (OJ 1998 C176/1) for a regulation laying down provisions on the Structural Funds, Art 1.

[363] ibid, Art 4(2). In addition, 2% of the Union population which is eligible for Objective 1 transitional aid and meeting Objective 2 criteria will be covered. See the Explanatory memorandum to the Proposal of 19 Mar 1998 for a regulation laying down provisions on the Structural Funds, COM(98)131, 18.

[364] Communication on the links between regional and competition policy—reinforcing concentration and mutual consistency (OJ 1998 C90/3), para 3.2.

[365] Proposal of 19 Mar 1998 (OJ 1998 C176/1) for a regulation laying down provisions on the Structural Funds, Art 4(2).

[366] OJ 1993 L193/5.

[367] OJ 1988 L185/9.

- other areas which had recorded substantial job losses over the last three years or were experiencing or threatened with such losses in industrial sectors which were vital to their economic development, with a consequent serious worsening of unemployment in those areas.[368]

At the same time, Article 9(4) provided that assistance should be genuinely concentrated on the regions most seriously affected, at the most appropriate geographical level, taking into account the particular situation of the regions concerned.

More particularly, according to the March 1988 version of the Commission proposal for what became Regulation 2058/88,[369] the sectors affected by the second paragraph of Article 9(2) were to be coal, steel, textiles and clothing, and shipbuilding. Other sectors might be considered for assistance where the Commission so decided, having regard to the general developments in those sectors in the Community. The Council, however, was opposed to listing relevant sectors, and so this part of the proposal was not approved by the Council.

While the Council was apparently unwilling to limit Objective 2 to regions with problems in given sectors, it was willing in Article 9(2) to limit this Objective to regions having industrial problems of some kind. Consequently, regions where the percentage of employed persons working in industry[370] was below the Community average fell outside Objective 2, even if unemployment there was far above the Community average.[371] For example, depressed coastal resorts fell outside, because tourism was not considered industrial.[372] Moreover, certain urban zones fell outside, because their economic and social problems could not be attributed to industrial decline.

The original list of regions falling within Objective 2 was adopted by the Commission in Decision 89/288.[373] The draft list covered 25 per cent of the Community population and had to be revised, in line with the '15 per cent principle', and limited to the parts of regions considered to be most seriously

[368] These criteria are less 'objective' than those employed for determination of eligibility for state aid under Art 87(3)(c) EC. See A Evans, *EC Law of State Aid* (Clarendon Press, Oxford, 1997) ch 4.

[369] Art 9(3), 2nd para of the amended proposal of 23 Mar 1988 (OJ 1988 C151/4).

[370] Industry is taken to refer to mining and quarrying and utilities, manufacturing, and building and civil engineering. Service industries are not taken into account. See Commission Reply to WQ 2955/90 (OJ 1991 C195/21) by Lord Inglewood.

[371] Commission Reply by Mr Millan to WQ 1445/92 (OJ 1992 C345/19) by Mr Max Simeoni.

[372] EEC regional development policy, House of Lords Select Committee on the European Communities, HL(1991–92)20, 16.

[373] Establishing an initial list of declining industrial areas concerned by Objective 2 (OJ 1989 L112/19). The Commission decided to maintain this list unchanged up to the end of 1993. See Bull EC 4–1991, 1.2.78. See, thereafter, Dec 94/169 (OJ 1994 L81/1). This Decision was amended, in the case of Austria and Finland, by Dec 95/47 (OJ 1995 L51/17) and, in the case of Sweden, by Dec 95/189 (OJ 1995 L123/18).

affected by industrial decline.[374] As a result, of the 900 regions proposed by the Member States for treatment as Objective 2 regions, only sixty were selected.[375] In 1990 the average unemployment rate in the latter was 1.25 percentage points higher than the Community average (9.5 per cent against 8.3 per cent).[376]

For the future, the Commission envisaged that the list of eligible regions would continue to be compiled on the basis of unemployment and industrial employment statistics. However, it was not possible to identify, on the basis of Community statistics, all the regions currently affected by industrial decline.[377] Nor was it possible to allow for the anticipation of the consequences of new industrial change. The Commission sought, therefore, a measure of discretion, to be used in consultation with the Member States concerned, but with no easing of the geographical concentration. Otherwise, strict interpretation of the statistics would make it impossible to assist the regions most in need of help.[378]

Accordingly, the third indent of the second paragraph of Article 9(2) has been amended by Regulation 2081/93.[379] It now includes a reference to job losses caused by industrial changes and changes in production systems, with a consequent serious worsening of unemployment in the areas concerned.[380] The aim is to introduce greater flexibility, allowing to be submitted for consideration areas which a Member State considers to be vulnerable to industrial decline.[381]

Moreover, two new indents have been added to the second paragraph of Article 9(2). The first new indent refers to areas, especially urban areas,[382] with severe problems linked to the rehabilitation of large numbers of derelict

[374] Fourth periodic report on the social and economic situation and the development of the regions of the Community, COM(90)609, 56.

[375] Annual report on the implementation of the reform of the Structural Funds, COM(90)516, 31.

[376] Fourth periodic report on the social and economic situation and the development of the regions of the Community, COM(90)609, 54.

[377] See, regarding some parts of Western Germany, the European Parliament Resolution of 22 Jan 1993 (OJ 1993 C42/228) on the regional and social redevelopment plan and the CSF for the areas of Germany included in Objective 2, para 10.

[378] From the Single Act to Maastricht and beyond: the means to match our ambitions, COM(92)2000; and Community structural policies: assessment and outlook, COM(92)84, 38.

[379] OJ 1993 L193/5.

[380] In addition, Art 9(5) of Reg 2081/93 (OJ 1993 L193/5) provided that West Berlin should continue to be eligible for three years. This provision reflected the inclusion of the new *Länder* and East Berlin in Objective 1 and the concern of the Commission to secure coherence in the development efforts for Berlin and Brandenburg as a whole (Community Structural Fund operations 1994–99, COM(93)67, 13).

[381] ibid, 10. The Commission proposal that a reasoned request from the Member State concerned should be necessary (Proposal of 10 Mar 1993 (OJ 1993 C118/21)) was not accepted by the Council.

[382] eg an area of Madrid with a population of 5,000 persons is now covered by Objective 2. See Dec 96/472 (OJ 1996 L193/54) establishing the list of declining industrial areas covered by Objective 2 for the programming period 1997–9.

industrial sites. The second new indent refers to other industrial or urban areas where the socio-economic impact of restructuring of the fisheries sector, assessed on the basis of objective criteria, justifies assistance.

In applying this paragraph, the Commission is to take account of how the national situations with respect to unemployment, industrialization, and industrial decline compare with the Union average. This reference to the Union average was introduced at the request of Italy. The German argument that application of the criteria should depend on national averages[383] was not accepted by the Council.

These changes to eligibility criteria have been accompanied by procedural reforms. Originally, a list of eligible regions was to be established by the Commission after consulting an advisory committee of representatives of the Member States.[384] The procedure for determining regional eligibility is now laid down in Article 9(3) of Regulation 2081/93.[385] According to this provision, Member States, taking into account the concentration principle in Article 9(4),[386] propose to the Commission regions to be treated as covered by Objective 2. The Commission decides on the basis of their proposals. It does so after consulting an advisory committee composed of representatives of the Member States. It also takes account of national priorities and situations in close consultation with the Member State concerned. This procedure constitutes a compromise between the above two approaches favoured by Italy and Germany, respectively. As the Commission puts it, Objective 2 designations are based on 'Community socio-economic criteria and national criteria'.[387] However, the role of the Commission in drawing up the list of eligible regions for Objective 2 has been reduced by the new legislation. In practice, 'the Member States propose the regions and negotiate with the Commission'.[388] The outcome of the negotiations, which may be lengthy,[389] has been an increased geographical spread of regions found to be eligible.[390]

The negotiations are, presumably, complicated by the fact that many data relevant to the application of the second paragraph of Article 9(2) are not comparable at Union level. Hence, the data only enable comparisons to be made within each Member State. Therefore, it is not possible to say whether the principle in Article 9(4) is respected.[391]

It is now proposed that Objective 2 regions must face structural problems of socio-economic conversion and that their population or territory must be

[383] *Europe* 6006 (23 June 1993).

[384] Art 9(3) of Reg 2052/88 (OJ 1988 L185/9).

[385] OJ 1993 L193/5.

[386] This provision follows Article 9(4) of Reg 2052/88 (OJ 1988 L185/9).

[387] Communication on the links between regional and competition policy—reinforcing concentration and mutual consistency (OJ 1998 C90/3), para 2.1.

[388] ibid.

[389] New regional programmes 1997–99 under Objective 2, COM(97)524, 4.

[390] Commission Reply by Mrs Wulf-Matthies to WQ E-0303/97 (OJ 1997 C367/11) by Amedeo Amadeo. See also COA annual report 1995 (OJ 1996 C340/1), para 5.27.

[391] ibid, para 5.29.

sufficiently substantial. They shall include: areas undergoing socio-economic change in the industrial and service sectors; declining rural areas; urban areas in difficulty; and depressed areas dependent on fisheries.[392]

'Industrial areas' must represent or belong to a NUTS Level III region which satisfies three criteria. First, the average rate of unemployment recorded over the last three years must have been above the Union average. Secondly, the percentage share of industrial employment in total employment must have equalled or exceeded the Union average in any reference year from 1985 onwards. Thirdly, there must have been an observable fall in industrial employment compared with that reference year.[393]

Rural areas must also represent or belong to a NUTS Level III region which satisfies two criteria. First, they must have either a population density of less than 100 persons per square kilometre or a percentage share of agricultural employment in total employment which has been at least twice the Union average in any reference year from 1985. Secondly, they must have either an average unemployment rate over the last three years above the Union average or a decline in population since 1985.[394]

The population within areas qualifying as industrial or rural, according to these 'purely Community criteria', must, in principle, be at least half of the total population eligible for Objective 2 assistance in each Member State. However, this requirement only applies, 'where this is objectively possible'.[395]

Urban areas are densely populated areas which meet at least one of the following criteria: a long-term unemployment rate above the Union average; a high level of poverty, including precarious housing conditions; particular environmental damage; a high crime rate; or a low level of education among the population.[396]

Areas dependent on fisheries are those where two criteria are met. First, the number of jobs in fishing as a percentage of total employment must be significant. Secondly, there must be structural, socio-economic problems relating to restructuring of the fishing industry which result in a significant reduction in the number of jobs in that sector.[397]

Finally, areas whose population or area is significant and which fall within one of the following categories are eligible. The first category concerns areas meeting the criteria for industrial areas which are adjacent to a rural area. It also concerns areas which meet the criteria for industrial or rural areas which

[392] Proposal of 19 Mar 1998 (OJ 1998 C176/1) for a regulation laying down provisions on the Structural Funds, Art 6.

[393] ibid, Art 4(5).

[394] ibid, Art 4(6).

[395] ibid, Art 4(4). See also the Explanatory memorandum to the Proposal of 19 Mar 1998 for a regulation laying down provisions on the Structural Funds, COM(98)131, 15–16.

[396] Proposal of 19 Mar 1998 (OJ 1998 C176/1) for a regulation laying down provisions on the Structural Funds, Art 4(7).

[397] ibid, Art 4(8).

are adjacent to an Objective 1 region. The second category concerns areas with socio-economic problems arising from the ageing of the agricultural working population. The third category concerns areas facing or threatened by a high level of unemployment arising from an ongoing or planned restructuring of an activity of key importance for the agricultural, industrial, or service sector.[398]

It is envisaged that Member States will propose eligible regions to the Commission.[399] On the basis of the information provided, the Commission, in close consultation with the Member State concerned, will draw up a list of Objective 2 regions, with due regard to national priorities.[400]

The Commission will have to respect limits to the percentage of the Union population which can be included within each type of area. Thus industrial areas should cover no more than around 10 per cent of the Union population, rural areas 5 per cent, urban areas 2 per cent, and fisheries areas 1 per cent.[401]

As the Commission puts it, eligibility should in future be determined on the basis of 'Community agreed' criteria in partnership with the Member States, taking into account their regional priorities.[402] The Commission preference is to bring eligibility into line with rules regarding the permissible coverage of state aid. Thus, in principle, the Commission will not accept a region under Objective 2, unless it qualifies for regional aid granted by the Member state concerned under Article 87(3)(c) of the Treaty.[403] Exceptions may only be made where two conditions are met. First, no more than 2 per cent of the population not covered by Objective 1 may benefit. Secondly, there must be consistency with the general aim of concentration. In other words, the 35 to 40 per cent limit to the population coverage of Objectives 1 and 2 together must be respected.[404] However, the reduction of population coverage in each Member State should not exceed one-third of that previously covered by Objectives 2 and 5b.[405] Moreover, measures are also envisaged in favour of regions losing their Objective 2 status, but competition rules governing state aid must still be respected.[406]

[398] ibid, Art 4(9). [399] ibid, Art 4(3). [400] ibid, Art 4(4).

[401] ibid, 14th recital in the preamble.

[402] Communication on the links between regional and competition policy—reinforcing concentration and mutual consistency (OJ 1998 C90/3), para 3.2.

[403] 42.7% of the Union population are to be eligible for national aid under Art 87(3)(a) or (c) EC (ibid).

[404] ibid. See also the Proposal of 19 Mar 1998 (OJ 1998 C176/1) for a regulation laying down provisions on the Structural Funds, 15th recital in the preamble.

[405] ibid, 14th recital in the preamble. The aim is 'to ensure that each Member State contributes to the overall effort towards concentration' of resources. See the Explanatory memorandum to the Proposal of 19 Mar 1998 for a regulation laying down provisions on the Structural Funds, COM(98)131, 15.

[406] Communication on the links between regional and competition policy—reinforcing concentration and mutual consistency (OJ 1998 C90/3), para 3.3.

A region may be eligible under only one of Objectives 1 or 2.[407] The list of eligible regions is to be valid for seven years. However, it may be amended in 2000, if there is a serious crisis in a region.[408]

Allocation of assistance

According to Commission Decision 89/289,[409] most Objective 2 assistance was allocated to the United Kingdom, Spain, and France. However, all the more developed Member States received some assistance.

There was no direct proportionality between the allocations and the seriousness of unemployment in the regions concerned.[410] In the case of Luxembourg, the national unemployment rate had been around 1.6 per cent since 1983. However, the employment situation in the two cantons concerned by the Community Support Framework,[411] which could not be measured directly, was 'masked' by the national figure. In the period from 1986 to 1989 alone, over 2,700 jobs had been lost, and new reductions (of about 2,000 jobs) had been announced by the steel industry for 1990 to 1992. Moreover, the economic situation in the south of the country had implications for the industrial areas just across the border, especially in view of the close links with the Longwy area. On these grounds, the allocation of assistance was considered justified.[412]

The Commission based its current allocation of Objective 2 assistance[413] on the population in each Member State's eligible regions compared with the total Union population eligible for such assistance. It then combined these figures with the unemployment rate of each region as a proportion of the average unemployment rate across all the Objective 2 areas.[414]

2.4.3 Objective 5b

According to Article 1 of the original version of Regulation 2052/88,[415] Objective 5b was concerned with promoting rural development by facilitating the structural adjustment of rural areas. As amended by Regulation 2081/93,[416] this provision now states that Objective 5b is concerned with pro-

[407] Proposal of 19 Mar 1998 (OJ 1998 C176/1) for a regulation laying down provisions on the Structural Funds, Art 4(10).

[408] ibid, Art 4(11).

[409] Fixing an indicative allocation between Member States of 85% of the commitment operations of the ERDF under Objective 2 (OJ 1989 L113/29).

[410] COA annual report for 1991 (OJ 1992 C330/1), 122.

[411] See sect 7.4.4 below, regarding CSFs.

[412] *CSF 1989–91 for Converting the Regions Affected by Industrial Decline, Luxembourg* (EC Commission, Brussels, 1990) 11.

[413] Dec 94/176 (OJ 1994 L82/35) fixing an indicative allocation by Member State of Structural Fund commitment appropriations under Objective 2; and Dec 96/468 (OJ 1996 L192/29).

[414] *European Report* 1921 (29 Jan 1994).

[415] OJ 1988 L185/9.

[416] OJ 1993 L193/5.

moting rural development by facilitating the development and structural adjustment of rural areas.[417]

According to the economics literature, rural amenity may be regarded as a 'public good'. Hence, assistance to rural areas may be economically justified, if it corrects the failure of market forces adequately to recognize the social value of particular types of rural activity. In practice, however, it is also said that it may be difficult to measure their social value and that the imperative which leads to such assistance has generally been political in origin.[418]

It is now envisaged that assistance under this Objective will be replaced by assistance under the new Objective 2.[419] However, the European Parliament argues that rural areas should, along with fishing areas, be a 'sub-category' within the new Objective 2.[420]

Eligibility for assistance

Article 11(2) of Regulation 2052/88[421] provided that Objective 5b regions were to be selected by the Commission after consultation of a management committee.[422] The Commission was to take into account, in particular: the degree to which these regions were rural in character; the number of persons occupied in agriculture; their level of economic and agricultural development; their degree of peripherality; and their sensitivity to changes in the agricultural sector, especially in the context of reform of the common agricultural policy. They did not have to be NUTS Level III regions.

More details were provided in Regulation 4253/88.[423] According to Article 4(1), the regions that might receive assistance under Objective 5b had to satisfy each of three criteria. First, there had to be a high share of agricultural employment in total employment. Secondly, there had to be a low level of agricultural income, notably as expressed in terms of value added by agricultural work unit. Thirdly, there had to be a low level of socio-economic development assessed on the basis of gross domestic product per inhabitant. Moreover, account had to be taken of socio-economic parameters which

[417] Establishment of Objective 5ba, which would have been concerned with conservation of the environment and the continuation of farming in certain mountain and less favoured regions, was advocated by the European Parliament in its Resolution of 20 May 1988 (OJ 1988 C167/443) on the amended Commission proposal for what became Reg 2052/88.

[418] J Marsh, 'Agriculture and Structural Policy' in K Burger, M Groot, J Post, and V Zachariasse (eds), *Agricultural Economics and Policy: International Challenges for the Nineties* (Elsevier, Amsterdam, 1991) 95–118, 103.

[419] Proposal of 19 Mar 1998 (OJ 1998 C176/1) for a regulation laying down provisions on the Structural Funds, Art 1.

[420] Resolution of 18 June 1998 (OJ 1998 C210/189) on Agenda 2000: economic and social cohesion, para 7.

[421] OJ 1988 L185/9.

[422] See, regarding such committees, sect 7.7.2 below.

[423] Laying down provisions for implementing Reg 2052/88 as regards co-ordination of the activities of the different Structural Funds between themselves and with the operations of the EIB and the other existing financial instruments (OJ 1988 L374/1).

indicated the seriousness of the general situation in the regions concerned and how it was developing.

It was also provided in Article 4(2) of the same Regulation that, on receipt of a reasoned request from a Member State, assistance might be extended to other rural regions with a low level of socio-economic development on the basis of one or more of the following criteria:

- low population density and/or a significant depopulation trend;
- peripherality in relation to major centres of economic and commercial activity in the Community;
- sensitivity to developments in agriculture, especially in the context of reform of the common agricultural policy, assessed on the basis of the trend in agricultural incomes and the size of the agricultural labour force;
- pressures exerted on the environment and on the countryside; and
- status as mountain or less favoured regions classified pursuant to Directive 75/268.[424]

Member States were required, in respect of the regions which in their view should be eligible, to provide the Commission with such information as might help it to determine their eligibility. On the basis of that information and its overall assessment of the proposals submitted, the Commission was to determine the regions eligible.

In determining these regions, the Commission was required by Article 4(4) of the Regulation to ensure that assistance was effectively concentrated on regions suffering from the most serious problems of rural development.[425] Subject to this general requirement, it seems that rural problems other than that of the low per capita gross domestic product traditionally associated with the peripheral regions could be tackled.

Certainly, the Commission considered that per capita gross domestic product was 'neither a sufficient measure of the gravity of the situation of the regions concerned nor a suitable instrument for determining the allocation of assistance among the various regions'.[426] 'Very qualitative' assessments, which left the authorities broad discretion and favoured political compromises, might be preferred.[427]

In the event, the regions originally selected, and listed by the Commission in Decision 89/426,[428] were in Belgium, Denmark, France, Germany, Italy, Luxembourg, the Netherlands, Spain, and the United Kingdom.

[424] sect 3.3.4 below. The ESC favoured establishment of an ERDF programme for upland areas in its Opinion of 28 Apr 1988 (OJ 1988 C175/47) on a policy for upland areas, para 6.4.4.

[425] Concentration was to take place within the context of reform of the CAP, but this requirement has been removed in Art 11a(4) of Reg 2081/93 (OJ 1993 L193/5).

[426] COA annual report for 1991, OJ 1992 C330/1, para 7.18 (Commission reply).

[427] D Gadbin, 'Le Droit communautaire des structures agricoles: organisation ou dilution?' (1991) RMC 218–230, 224.

[428] Selecting rural areas eligible to receive Community assistance under Objective 5b (OJ 1989 L198/1).

These regions were smaller than those of the NUTS III Level. Moreover, the Commission sought to reduce overlaps between Objective 2 and Objective 5b regions, while limiting the coverage of Objective 2 regions to 15 per cent of the Community population. A result was fragmentation of the regions found to be eligible under Objective 5b.[429]

Intervention in such regions needed, according to the Commission, to be 'boosted'. While assistance should be directed towards all rural regions of the Community, it should be concentrated where the needs were greatest and the capacity to contribute at the national level was weakest.[430] To this end, the criteria for what constituted an eligible region should be applied more flexibly and the range of measures broadened.[431] Particular attention should be paid to problems of rural exodus.[432] Accordingly, studies were carried out regarding definition of Objective 5b regions.[433]

However, the problems raised might not be simply those of such definition. In particular, Highlands and Islands Enterprise, the body responsible for development of the Highlands and Islands, argued that this was a region of extreme peripherality and sparsity of population. Hence, Objective 5b, under which it was originally classified, did not suit its needs. Objective 1 status would be far more appropriate. This argument was supported by the British Government, which stressed that it was the most sparsely populated region of the Community by a factor of three.[434] It was also a very peripheral region, containing the land which was furthest north within the Community, and had very considerable problems of insularity, in that one-third of the population lived on islands. It thus had unique infrastructure requirements.[435] Such considerations now seem to be recognized by the Council, in that this region has been included within Objective 1.[436]

On the other hand, only limited changes to the definition of Objective 5b regions have been made by Regulation 2081/93.[437] The regions that may now receive assistance under Objective 5b are those which have a low level of socio-economic development assessed on the basis of gross domestic product per inhabitant and satisfy at least two of the following criteria:

[429] COA annual report for 1991 (OJ 1992 C330/1), para 5.2.1.

[430] Commission Reply by Mr MacSharry to WQ 2860/91 (OJ 1992 C168/24) by Mr John Cushnahan.

[431] Community finances between now and 1997, COM(92)2001, 24.

[432] *Europe* 5927 (25 Feb 1993).

[433] Commission Reply by Mr MacSharry to WQ 1039/91 (OJ 1991 C315/26) by Mr Verbeek. See also Community Structural Fund operations 1994–99, COM(93)67, 13.

[434] This argument was not fully supported by the figures given in the Fifth periodic report on the situation and socio-economic development of the regions of the Community, COM(94)322, Table A27.

[435] EEC regional development policy, House of Lords Select Committee on the European Communities, HL(1991–92)20, 17–18.

[436] See sect 2.4.1 above.

[437] OJ 1993 L193/5.

- high share of agricultural employment in total employment;
- low level of agricultural income, notably as expressed in terms of agricultural value added by agricultural work unit;
- low population density and/or a significant depopulation trend.[438]

Other regions with a low level of socio-economic development may receive Objective 5b assistance,[439] if they are affected by one or more of six listed criteria. These criteria are the same as those in Article 4(2) of Regulation 4253/88,[440] except that the depopulation criterion has now been moved to the first paragraph, and two new criteria are added. The new criteria are the structure of agricultural holdings and the age structure of the gainfully employed agricultural labour force; and the socio-economic impact on the region, as measured by objective criteria, of the restructuring of the fisheries sector.[441]

These changes to eligibility criteria have been accompanied by procedural reforms. According to Article 11a(3) of Regulation 2081/93,[442] Member States propose to the Commission the regions which, in their view, meet these criteria and provide the Commission with all useful information to this end. On the basis of this information and its overall assessment of the proposals submitted, the Commission establishes the list of eligible areas.[443] It must take into account national priorities and situations, act in close consultation with the Member State concerned, and consult a management committee.

Allocation of assistance

Most assistance under Objective 5b is allocated to France and Germany.[444] However, the allocations have been criticized on the ground that the amount of assistance provided is calculated on a per capita basis.[445] In fact, it is calculated by reference to the total population of each region covered, adjusted to take account of the impact of the reform of the common agricultural policy on employment in the respective agricultural sectors. Hence, the more underpopulated is the region, the smaller will be the amount of assistance allocated.[446]

[438] OJ 1993 L193/5 Art 11a(1).

[439] A reasoned request from a Member State is no longer required.

[440] OJ 1988 L374/1. [441] Art 11a(2) of Reg 2081/93 (OJ 1993 L193/5). [442] ibid.

[443] Dec 94/197 (OJ 1994 L96/1) establishing, for 1994–99, the list of rural areas under Objective 5b. See also Dec 95/37 (OJ 1995 L49/65) establishing, for 1995–99 in Austria and Finland, the list of rural areas under Objective 5b; and Dec 95/43 (OJ 1995 L92/29) establishing, for 1995–99 in Sweden, the list of rural areas under Objective 5b.

[444] Dec 89/379 (OJ 1989 L180/54) fixing an indicative allocation between Member States of 85% of the commitment appropriations of the ERDF under Objective 5b; and Dec 94/203 (OJ 1994 L97/43) establishing the indicative allocation by Member State of the commitment appropriations from the Structural Funds for Objective 5b for 1994–99.

[445] The future of rural society, House of Lords Select Committee on the European Communities, HL(1989–90)80–I, 33.

[446] This criterion meant that the Highlands and Islands was effectively penalized by its sparsity of population. See EEC regional development policy, House of Lords Select Committee on the European Communities, HL(1991–92)20, 17.

A more particular problem for rural regions in more developed Member States may result from Article 13 of Regulation 2081/93.[447] According to this provision, assistance is to be differentiated taking into account, *inter alia*, the financial capacity of the Member State concerned. Such capacity is to be assessed in the light of, in particular, the relative prosperity of that Member State.

2.4.4 Objective 6

The northern parts of Finland and Sweden comprise what the Commission describes as 'Arctic and sub-Arctic regions'.[448] They exhibit problems of low population density, unfavourable climate, and peripherality comparable with, though more severe than, those of the Highlands and Islands of Scotland. However, they may fail to qualify as Objective 1 or even Objective 5b regions by reference to per capita gross domestic product.[449] They may also benefit little from Objective 2 assistance, because there is limited industry to decline and unemployment problems may not be serious by Union standards.

To cater for these regional problems, Objective 6[450] has been created. This Objective covers regions of Finland[451] and Sweden[452] with a population density of no more than eight persons per square kilometre.[453] Objective 1 rules apply to regions covered by Objective 6.[454]

It is now envisaged that Objective 6 regions will be assisted under Objective 1.[455]

2.4.5 Scope of Assistance

The scope of the assistance which the European Regional Development Fund may provide is outlined in Article 1 of Regulation 2083/93.[456]

[447] OJ 1993 L193/5.

[448] *Opinion on Sweden's Application for Membership* Bull EC, Supp 5/92, 14; and *Opinion on Finland's Application for Membership*, Bull EC, Supp 6/92, 12.

[449] Note the GDP figures for Swedish regions published in *Norbotten inför EG-förhandlingen* (Lanstyrelsen Norbottens län, Luleå, 1992).

[450] *European Report* 1928 (23 Feb 1993).

[451] Dec 95/360 (OJ 1995 L208/13) on the approval of the SPD for Community structural assistance in the regions concerned by Objective 6 in Finland.

[452] Dec 96/116 (OJ 1996 L33/1) on the approval of the SPD for Community structural assistance in the regions concerned by Objective 6 in Sweden.

[453] Prot 6 to the Accession Agreement, as amended by Dec 95/1 (OJ 1995 L1/1) adjusting the instruments concerning the accession of new Member States to the EU.

[454] ibid, Art 4.

[455] Proposal of 19 Mar 1998 (OJ 1998 C176/1) for a regulation laying down provisions on the Structural Funds, Art 1.

[456] Amending Reg 4254/88 laying down provisions for implementing Reg 2052/88 as regards the ERDF (OJ 1993 L193/34).

Productive investment

The Fund may assist productive investment, to enable permanent jobs to be created or maintained.[457] However, the regional development impact of such investment may be limited, because the proportion of supplies bought within the assisted regions may not be significant. Hence, a substantial part of the income-multiplier effect of assistance to these regions may effectively benefit advanced regions.[458] Even where purchases within the former regions are reasonably important in quantitative terms, the products bought may be mainly raw materials or products which have only been slightly processed, with little exploitation of existing industrial capabilities being entailed. Therefore, the assistance may do little to secure the self-sustained growth of these regions.[459] The assistance may even adversely affect local labour markets, jeopardizing the small, local industrial activities already in existence.

Infrastructure investment

The Fund may assist the creation or modernization of infrastructure which contributes to the development or conversion of the regions concerned.[460] A broader range of investments may be supported in Objective 1 regions than in Objective 2 or 5b regions.

In Objective 1 regions, infrastructure investments contributing to increasing the economic potential, development, and structural adjustment of these regions may be supported. Where appropriate, investments contributing to the establishment and development of trans-European networks in the areas of transport,[461] telecommunications, and energy infrastructures may be included. Where the need is demonstrated, financing may also be provided for investments in education and health which contribute to structural adjustment.[462]

In Objective 2 regions the Fund may assist infrastructure investments relating to the regeneration of regions suffering from industrial decline, including inner cities. It may also assist infrastructure investments which provide the basis for the creation or development of economic activity in such regions. In Objective 5b regions the Fund may assist infrastructure investments directly linked to economic activity which creates jobs other than in agriculture,

[457] ERDF (OJ 1993 L193/34) Art 1(a).

[458] RP Camagni, 'Development Scenarios and Policy Guidelines for the Lagging Regions in the 1990s' (1992) *Regional Studies* 361–374.

[459] cf, regarding lack of lasting effects of Union assistance, COA special report 15/98 (OJ 1998 C347/1) on the assessment of Structural Fund intervention for the 1989–93 and 1994–99 periods, para 7.3.

[460] Art 1(b) of Reg 2083/93 (OJ 1993 L193/34).

[461] See also Trans-European networks 1997 annual report, COM(1998)391, 16.

[462] Art 1(d) of Reg 2083/93 (OJ 1993 L193/34). See also Art 3(1)(d) of Reg 2081/93 (OJ 1993 L193/5). Cf, earlier, the European Parliament Resolution of 9 Mar 1987 (OJ 1987 L99/15) on regional development, education, and training, para 14.

including communications infrastructure on which the development of such activity depends.

A more radical approach to infrastructure assistance has been advocated by the Economic and Social Committee. According to the Committee, the regions where the largest swathes of population are in greatest need also have the poorest social security cover and assistance. Such a situation might be perfectly logical in market-efficiency terms, but it may not be easily reconcilable with moves towards economic and political union. Hence, the Committee considers that infrastructure assistance should be more concerned with social welfare.[463]

However, it is open to question whether social policy and regional development can be so readily reconciled.[464] It is said, for example, that social policy measures will raise labour costs. According to such thinking, the less productive workers, who tend to be found in less developed regions, will be adversely affected by implementation of social policy.[465]

'Endogenous development'

The Fund may assist measures to exploit the potential for internally generated development of the regions concerned. Such measures are those which encourage and support local development initiatives and the activities of small and medium-sized enterprises. They may include: assistance towards services for firms, particularly in the fields of management, study and research of markets, and services common to several firms; financing the transfer of technology, particularly the collection and dissemination of information and the introduction of innovations in firms; improvement of access for firms to the capital market, particularly by the provision of guarantees and equity participation; direct assistance to investment; and the provision of small-scale infrastructure.[466]

More wide-ranging assistance to such development is advocated by the Economic and Social Committee. This Committee emphasizes the importance of 'human capital'. It is defined as the sum of knowledge about products, production technologies, innovation and research capacity, and marketing strategies, as well as social qualities deriving from general education, the ability to take independent decisions, flexibility, and interpersonal relations. According to the Committee, such capital is of crucial importance, if assistance from the Fund is to trigger self-sustaining growth. Societies which fully prepare their human capital for a high-efficiency, high-quality,

[463] ESC Opinion of 25 May 1992 (OJ 1992 C106/20) on the implementation of the reform of the Structural Funds, para 11.4.2.

[464] P Maillet and S Dormard, 'Social Europe and Economic Cohesion' in A Pijpers (ed), *The European Community at the Crossroads* (Nijhoff, Dordrecht, 1992) 71–90.

[465] JT Addison and WS Siebert, 'The Social Charter of the European Community: Evolution and Controversies' (1991) *Industrial and Labour Relations Review* 597–623.

[466] Art 3(1)(c) of Reg 2081/93 (OJ 1993 L193/5).

and high-innovation economy have an advantage over societies which leave human capital-formation largely to the limited resources which the individual is able and willing to mobilize to this end.[467] A 'modern social policy', particularly the social rights entailed, training[468] and social protection, labour-market organization, and industrial relations components, may thus be viewed not as a consequence of development, but as a precondition for it.[469]

An analogy may be drawn with development assistance to third countries. Experience has shown that such assistance should be directed towards giving a country the chance to make the most of its own capabilities, satisfy the basic needs of its population, increase its exports, and become a fair competitor in the world economy. According to this analogy, ensuring respect for social legislation and for workers' rights should be part of the thrust of cohesion efforts.[470]

Similarly, the European Parliament considers that the Fund should place greater emphasis on education and training, designed to mobilize the human resources of the regions concerned. The 'social economy', the co-operative movement, workers' access to the ownership of the means of production through association or self-management mechanisms, and the generation of self-employment among unemployed workers should also be promoted.[471]

At the same time, according to the Committee on Regional Policy and Regional Planning, Fund assistance should ensure that every Union citizen has access to a range of educational, cultural, postal, and commercial services. The availability of these services, whether public or otherwise, is regarded as an important factor in maintaining rural populations.[472] The living standards and living conditions of the inhabitants of the peripheral regions should, therefore, be brought into line with those of the inhabitants of the central regions of the Union.[473]

Current Union practice does little to ensure that Fund operations meet such demands. At least in the context of assistance to Objective 2 regions, the Fund has been criticized for paying insufficient attention to development of

[467] cf A Pfaller, 'The Issue' in A Pfaller, I Gough, and G Therborn, *Can the Welfare State Compete?* (Macmillan, London, 1991) 1–14, 10.

[468] The number of persons between the ages of 15 and 19 serving apprenticeships or undergoing training in the three least advanced Member States is only just over half the corresponding number for the three most advanced Member States. See From the Single Act to Maastricht and beyond: the means to match our ambitions, COM(92)2000.

[469] ESC Opinion of 27 Feb 1992 (OJ 1992 C98/50) on economic and social cohesion, para 4.5.2.

[470] ESC Opinion of 30 Apr 1992 (OJ 1992 C169/34) on the Commission document entitled 'From the Single Act to Maastricht and beyond: the means to match our ambitions', para 15.1.1.

[471] Resolution of 22 Nov 1991 (OJ 1991 C326/267) on the Perifra programme, para 10.

[472] Report on a concerted regional planning policy, EP Doc A3–245/90, 5.

[473] Report on a Community initiative to assist the most remote regions of the Community, EP Doc A 3–140/90, 7.

the endogenous potential of such regions.[474] According to this criticism, in periods of stagnation traditional infrastructure projects are unlikely to attract new industry to an assisted region and, in any case, other regions also have the necessary infrastructure.[475]

More particularly, in the case of Portugal, the European Parliament considers that Fund assistance should attach greater importance to the internal regional balance of this country. Such assistance should seek to counteract the continuing loss of population in the largely rural interior and the resulting increase of the population of the urban centres on the coast. Such demographic changes produce harmful social and economic consequences and, in particular, hamper the efficient use of all the resources of the country.[476] For example, the small, family farm is important to the economic and social structure of the Portuguese countryside and to the protection of the rural environment. Hence, the Union should seek solutions to the problems posed by low productivity that do not place this structure in jeopardy.[477] It is equally important, for social and environmental reasons, to assist the maintenance of small-scale fishing.[478]

Limited account of such criticism is taken in the latest Commission proposals. They envisage that more attention will be given to new forms of financial engineering and local services so as to provide instruments better adapted to innovation in the field of business investment and local development and employment initiatives.[479]

More fundamental criticism may be found in the literature. The literature admits the importance of internally generated development for mobilizing regional resources and creating a permanent, active network of small businesses, self-employment, and services. However, it may be argued that such development alone may not be sufficient to ensure the sort of intra-industry development that can make full use of the potential offered by the internal market. The build-up of a critical mass of new, small firms in regions without an entrepreneurial tradition is a very costly and time-consuming exercise, offering only limited short- to medium-term rewards. Such regions have suffered years of external control of their economies, and associated fragmentation and destruction of their industrial and entrepreneurial structures. As a result, they no longer possess the ability to recreate the regional institutions and traditions which have led to self-sustaining development in some new

[474] M Quévit, J Houard, S Bodson, and A Dangoisse, *Impact régional 1992: les régions de tradition industrielle* (De Boeck, Brussels, 1991) 338. Cf, regarding the concentration of ECSC assistance on restructuring, ibid 341, and regarding the concentration of EIB loans on physical infrastructure projects, ibid 344.

[475] In so far as such assistance goes to the productive sector, it relates to restructuring rather than conversion. See the COA annual report for 1986 (OJ 1987 C336/1), para 9.11.

[476] Resolution of 11 Oct 1991 (OJ 1991 C280/184) on the CSF for Portugal (1989–93), para 2.

[477] ibid, para 8.

[478] ibid, para 11.

[479] Explanatory memorandum to the Proposal of 19 Mar 1998 for a regulation laying down provisions on the Structural Funds, COM(98)131, 30.

industrial agglomerations. Extensive budgetary transfers and a growing public sector have, it is said, weakened the autonomy of such regions and quelled any inclination towards the development of new and efficient industrial enterprise. Therefore, an important role may remain for efforts to encourage major national and European companies to relocate—taking their capital assets, technology, and management capability with them. Such efforts may take the form of direct capital incentives and environmental improvements.

Other assistance

The Fund may assist the financing of two further kinds of investment. It may assist investment contributing to regional development in the field of research and technology.[480] It may also assist productive investment and investment in infrastructure aimed at environmental protection, according to the principles of sustainable development, where such investment is linked with regional development.[481]

2.4.6 Forms of Assistance

Assistance from the Fund is to be provided in a variety of forms, including non-repayable direct assistance, repayable assistance, interest-rate subsidies, guarantees, equity holdings, and venture-capital holdings,[482] that reflect the nature of the operations concerned.[483] By a qualified majority and on a proposal from the Commission, the Council may introduce other forms of assistance of the same type.[484]

Projects

The Fund may contribute to the financing of projects. The projects may concern productive investments, to enable permanent jobs to be created or maintained,[485] or investments in infrastructure.[486] Since the Commission exercises its monitoring and assessment rights at the level of programmes rather than projects, the latter are not themselves submitted to the Commission.[487]

It is now envisaged that the Fund may finance expenditure in respect of major projects. Such projects must meet two conditions. First, they must comprise an economically indivisible series of works fulfilling a precise tech-

[480] Art 1(e) of Reg 2083/93 (OJ 1993 L193/34). The original Commission proposal of 12 Mar 1993 (COM(93)67) had envisaged an express reference to the contribution of such measures to the implementation of the Framework Programmes for R & D.

[481] Art 1(f) of Reg 2083/93 (OJ 1993 L193/34).

[482] Art 27(3) of the Proposal of 19 Mar 1998 (OJ 1998 C176/1) for a regulation laying down provisions on the Structural Funds.

[483] Art 5(1) of Reg 2081/93 (OJ 1993 L193/5).

[484] ibid, Art 5(2). [485] ibid, Art 1(a). [486] ibid, Art 1(b).

[487] Commission Reply by Mr Steichen to WQ 3263/92 (OJ 1993 C185/38) by Jaak Vandemeulebroucke.

nical function and having clearly identifiable aims. Secondly, the total costs of the project must exceed Euro 50 million.[488]

Regional aid schemes

Fund assistance to regional aid schemes of Member States shall constitute one of the main forms of incentive to investment in firms.[489] To decide the financial participation of the Fund, the Commission shall examine, with the competent authorities designated by the Member State, the characteristics of the aid scheme concerned. Account is to be taken of: the relationship between the rate of aid and the socio-economic situation of the regions concerned and the consequent locational disadvantages for firms; the relationship between operating procedures and the types of assistance, including rates, and the needs to be met; the priority given to small and medium-sized enterprises and to the encouragement of services supplied to them, such as management advice and market surveys; the economic repercussions of the aid scheme; and the characteristics and impact of any other regional aid scheme in the same region.[490]

Regional operational programmes

The Fund may contribute to the financing of regional operational programmes.[491] Such a programme means the document approved by the Commission to implement a Community Support Framework. It must be composed of a consistent set of priorities and comprise multiannual measures. It may be implemented through recourse to one or more of the Structural Funds, one or more of the other financial instruments, and the European Investment Bank.[492]

Such a programme may be undertaken not only on the initiative of a Member State but also on the initiative of the Commission in agreement with the Member State concerned.[493] Where recourse is had to a Union fund additional to the European Regional Development Fund, an integrated approach may be employed.[494]

In Objective 1 regions programmes are usually to apply at NUTS Level II or in specific cases to one or more Level III regions or to several Level II regions.[495] In the case of Objective 2 regions, the programmes are usually to

[488] Art 24 of the Proposal of 19 Mar 1998 (OJ 1998 C176/1) for a regulation laying down provisions on the Structural Funds.

[489] Art 4(1) of Reg 2083/93 (OJ 1993 L193/34).

[490] ibid, Art 4(2).

[491] ibid, Art 3.

[492] Art 5(5) of Reg 2081/93 (OJ 1993 C193/5); and Art 9(1)(e) of the Proposal of 19 Mar 1998 (OJ 1998 C176/1) for a regulation laying down provisions on the Structural Funds.

[493] See pp 100—10 below, regarding programmes undertaken on the initiative of the Commission.

[494] Art 13(1) of Reg 2082/93 (OJ 1993 L193/20). Use of such an approach is to receive greater encouragement. See Explanatory memorandum to the Proposal of 19 Mar 1998 for a regulation laying down provisions on the Structural Funds, COM(98)131, 11–12.

[495] Art 3(1) of Reg 2083/93 (OJ 1993 L193/34).

apply at Level III.[496] Some decentralization of decision making, at least from the Commission to Member States, is implied.

Global grants

On the initiative of the Member State or the Commission in agreement with the Member State concerned,[497] the Fund may finance global grants.[498] Their management is entrusted to appropriate intermediaries,[499] including regional development bodies designated by the Member State in agreement with the Commission. These grants shall be used primarily to assist local development initiatives.[500] The intermediaries must be present or represented in the regions concerned, operate in the public interest, and associate adequately the socio-economic interests directly concerned by the implementation measures planned.[501]

The procedures for the use of global grants shall be the subject of an agreement, 'concluded in agreement with the Member State concerned', between the Commission and the intermediary concerned. These procedures shall detail, in particular: the types of measures to be carried out; the criteria for choosing beneficiaries; the conditions and rates of Fund assistance; and the arrangements for monitoring the use of the global grants.[502]

The importance of such grants in promoting endogenous development is often stressed.[503] They give public and private operators at the local level greater responsibility in the management of measures affecting the local economic base. In doing so, they assign to a decentralized body responsibilities that may previously have attached to the central authorities of Member States.[504]

Studies and pilot schemes

The Fund may, using up to 1 per cent of its annual budget, contribute to the financing of studies and pilot schemes.[505] According to Article 10(1)(a) of Regulation 2083/93,[506] such studies should be undertaken on the initiative of

[496] Art 3(1) of Reg 2083/93 (OJ 1993 L193/34) Art 9(2).

[497] See pp 100–10 below, regarding global grants introduced on the initiative of the Commission.

[498] Art 6(3) of Reg 2083/93 (OJ 1993 L193/34).

[499] In Ireland, eg, they are administered by Bord Fáilte Éireann and the Shannon Free Airport Development Company. See Commission Reply to WQ 2285/90 (OJ 1991 C161/9) by Mrs Jackson.

[500] See, regarding the role of such grants in supporting SMEs, Report on the ERDF 1991, COM(93)140, 2.

[501] Art 6(1) of Reg 2083/93 (OJ 1993 L193/34).

[502] ibid, Art 6(2).

[503] Though their use may not be without practical problems. See the COA annual report for 1994 (OJ 1995 C303/1), para 4.39–60.

[504] RP Camagni, 'Development Scenarios and Policy Guidelines for the Lagging Regions in the 1990s' (1992) *Regional Studies* 361–374.

[505] The regions concerned need not fall within the geographical scope of Objective 1, 2, or 5b. A list of studies and pilot projects financed under Art 10 of Reg 4254/88 (OJ 1988 L374/15) was provided in the Commission Reply to WQ 1866/90 (OJ 1991 C90/24) by Mr JG Urizza.

[506] OJ 1993 L193/34.

the Commission. They should aim to identify: the spatial consequences of measures planned by the national authorities, particularly major infrastructures, when their effects go beyond national boundaries; measures aiming to correct specific problems of the border regions within and outside the Union; and the elements necessary to establish a prospective outline of the utilization of Union territory.

Pilot schemes should, according to Article 10(1)(b) of the same Regulation, constitute incentives to the creation of infrastructure, investment in firms, and other specific measures having a marked Union interest,[507] particularly in border regions within and outside the Union. They should also encourage the pooling of experience, development co-operation between different Union regions[508] and innovative measures.[509]

For example, the Recite (Regions and cities of Europe) programme concerns co-operation networks for the realization of joint economic projects.[510] The selected projects are those designed to involve, as far as possible, networks representing partners from strong and weak regions.

Again, the Ecos-Ouverture (co-operation network with Central and Eastern European countries) programme[511] is designed to encourage regions, particularly the less developed regions of the Union, to establish links and to co-operate with counterparts in Eastern Europe. Under this programme the Fund, along with Phare,[512] has supported the establishment of various co-operation networks.[513]

Provision is now envisaged for innovative measures, studies, pilot projects, and exchanges of experience. They should contribute to the preparation of innovative methods and practices designed to improve the quality of assistance under Objectives 1, 2, and 3.[514] It is proposed that 0.7 per cent of Structural Fund resources may be allocated to innovative measures.[515] Consideration will be given to concentrating on significant projects and making implementation simpler and more transparent.[516] Moreover, 'a special

[507] See eg Call for proposals for pilot actions aiming at integrating the concept of the information society into regional development policies of less favoured regions (OJ 1996 C253/27).

[508] See eg Call for proposals from networks of regional and local authorities wishing to implement joint pilot inter-regional co-operation projects for economic development in the cultural field (OJ 1996 C253/26); and Networks of local regional authorities to carry out innovative and/or demonstrative pilot projects on spatial planning in specific areas (OJ 1996 C119/9).

[509] See eg Innovative measures: new sources of employment, particularly local employment initiatives—call for proposals (OJ 1996 C253/29).

[510] Call for network proposals from regional and local authorities wishing to carry out joint economic projects (OJ 1991 C198/8); and Recite II Call for proposals (OJ 1996 C326/9).

[511] *European Report* 1728 (11 Dec 1991); and Ecos-Ouverture 1997–9 (OJ 1997 C125/5). Cf the Med-Urbs programme (OJ 1993 C140/8), which supports co-operation between local authorities in the Union and those of Mediterranean non-Member States through networks.

[512] sect 6.6 below.

[513] See, now, Ecos-Ouverture 1998–2001 (OJ 1998 C183/26).

[514] Art 21(1) of the Proposal of 19 Mar 1998 (OJ 1998 C176/1) for a regulation laying down provisions on the Structural Funds.

[515] ibid, Arts 7(5) and 21.

[516] *Agenda 2000*, Bull EC, Supp 5/97, 24.

effort will be made to encourage financial engineering in the regions most deficient in that area'.[517]

Technical assistance

The Fund may finance, up to a limit of 0.5 per cent of its annual budget, preparatory, accompanying, and assessment measures necessary for implementation of Regulation 2083/93.[518] The measures may be carried out by the Commission or by outside experts.[519] They shall include studies, among them general studies concerning Union regional action, and technical assistance or information measures, including measures to provide information for local and regional development agents.[520] They may be embodied within sub-programmes of regional operational programmes or added to Community Support Frameworks.[521]

It is now envisaged that such assistance will be provided within programming[522] or on the initiative of the Commission.[523] Up to 0.3 per cent of Structural Fund resources may, it is envisaged, be allocated to technical assistance on the initiative of the Commission.[524]

Community initiatives

Community initiatives may be adopted by the Commission under Article 11(1) of Regulation 2082/93,[525] and Article 3(2) of Regulation 2083/93.[526] The former provision states that the Commission may, on its own initiative, propose to the Member States that they apply for assistance in respect of measures of significant interest to the Union which are not covered by regional development plans.[527] Up to 1.9 per cent of Structural Fund resources may be devoted to such initiatives.[528] It is now envisaged that the maximum will be raised to 5 per cent.[529]

For a limited part of the resources available, Community initiatives may apply to regions other than those eligible for assistance under Objectives 1, 2,

[517] Explanatory memorandum to the Proposal of 19 Mar 1998 for a regulation laying down provisions on the Structural Funds, COM(98)131, 17.

[518] OJ 1993 L193/34.

[519] ibid, Art 7(1).

[520] ibid.

[521] COA annual report for 1993 (OJ 1994 C327/1), para 7.68. See sect 7.4.4 below, regarding CSFs.

[522] ie 'the organizing, decision-making, and financing process carried out in a number of stages to implement on a multiannual basis the joint action of the Community and the Member States to attain the Objectives of the Structural Funds' (Art 9(1)(a) of the Proposal of 19 Mar 1998 (OJ 1998 C176/1) for a regulation laying down provisions on the Structural Funds).

[523] ibid, Art 2(4).

[524] ibid, Art 22.

[525] Amending Reg 4253/88 laying down provisions for implementing Reg 2052/88 as regards co-ordination of the activities of the different Structural Funds between themselves and with the operations of the EIB and the other existing financial instruments (OJ 1993 L193/20).

[526] OJ 1993 L193/34.

[527] See, regarding such plans, sect 7.4.1 below.

[528] Art 12(5) of Reg 2081/93 (OJ 1993 L193/5).

[529] Proposal of 19 Mar 1998 (OJ 1998 C176/1) for a regulation laying down provisions on the Structural Funds, Art 7(5).

and 5b.[530] In the view of the Commission, the flexibility entailed assists it in responding to new economic and social problems as they arise, including unforeseen industrial problems, which may not necessarily occur in eligible regions.[531] In other words, effective pursuit of cohesion may be found to demand exceptions from basic Union criteria for eligibility for assistance. However, this feature of Community initiatives, given the limited resources available for their implementation,[532] may be more an indication of, than a solution to, underlying problems in the legislation governing the operations of the Fund.

Such initiatives may even have relevance for third states. Certainly, co-ordination of such initiatives,[533] notably Interreg,[534] with Phare[535] activities is envisaged, particularly in the case of border regions affected by trade liberalization with Central and East European countries.[536]

The initiatives are designed: to help resolve problems common to certain categories of region; to help resolve serious problems directly associated with the implementation of other Union policies and affecting the socio-economic situation of one or more regions; or to promote the application of Union policies at regional level.[537] These three categories concern, respectively, regions with common problems, regions dependent on declining sectors, and regions which need assistance to implement Union policies.

It is now envisaged that they should concern three 'areas': cross-border, transnational, and inter-regional co-operation intended to encourage the harmonious and balanced development and spatial planning of the European territory; rural development; and transnational co-operation on new methods of combating all forms of discrimination and/or inequalities in access to the labour market.[538] Assistance concerning the first two areas may cover regions other than those covered by Objective 1 or 2.[539]

[530] Art 11(2) of Reg 2082/93 (OJ 1993 L193/20).

[531] Difficulties met in the implementation of the Interreg initiative (see pp 103–4 below), where cross-border co-operation between eligible and non-eligible areas was involved, may also be removed. See Community Structural Funds 1994–99, COM(93)67, 22.

[532] In practice, 'Member States' policies [remain] the Union's primary instruments for achieving cohesion'. See First cohesion report, COM(96)542, 6.

[533] 7th recital in the preamble to Reg 2082/93 (OJ 1993 L193/20) and the 3rd indent of Art 3(1) thereof.

[534] Future of Community initiatives under the Structural Funds, COM(93)282, 16.

[535] sect 6.6 below.

[536] The ESC considered that the Commission should put forward a separate proposal to provide additional assistance for Union regions bordering on the Czech Republic, Poland, and Slovakia. One of the primary purposes of this assistance should be to further the economic and political integration of eastern and south-eastern European countries into the Union. See the Opinion of 27 Nov 1991 (OJ 1992 C40/26) on the new *Länder*—CSF 1991–93, para 3.2.5.

[537] Art 3(2) of Reg 2083/93 (OJ 1993 L193/34).

[538] Art 19(1) of the Proposal of 19 Mar 1998 (OJ 1998 C176/1) for a regulation laying down provisions on the Structural Funds.

[539] ibid, Art 19(2).

Each such area is to be financed by a single Structural Fund. Thus the European Regional Development Fund is to be responsible for initiatives concerning cross-border, transnational, and inter-regional co-operation. The other two areas are to be the responsibility of the Guidance Section of the European Agricultural Guidance and Guarantee Fund and the European Social Fund, respectively.[540] In deciding the contribution of a Fund to an initiative, the Commission may 'amplify' the scope of the Fund as defined in the legislation specific to each Fund, but without broadening it, to include all measures required to implement the initiative concerned.[541] In other words, the scope of assistance of a single Fund may be extended to include that of the other Funds, where this is necessary for implementation of an initiative.[542]

Regions with common problems

The Regis initiative[543] concerns Guadeloupe, French Guyana, Martinique, Réunion, the Canary Islands, the Azores, and Madeira. These regions have been selected because of: their great distance from the rest of the Union; their economic dependence, in most cases, on tropical agriculture; and their proximity to third countries which are party to preferential trade agreements with the Union. The initiative is designed to speed up adaptation of the economies of the recipient regions, so that they may be better integrated into the internal market.

However, there are other Union regions, notably the Scottish islands and many of the Greek islands, which are also 'ultra-peripheral'. They experience many of the problems, such as isolation and underdevelopment, suffered by regions covered by this initiative. It has, therefore, been argued that they too should be covered by such an initiative.[544]

The Leader (Links between actions for the development of the rural economy) initiative[545] concerns rural regions more generally. It seeks to encourage integrated rural development at local level, through the allocation of global grants to local rural-development action groups. The grants are to be used to assist: the organization of rural development and the provision of information on all Union measures and finance likely to encourage rural

[540] Art 19(1) of the Proposal of 19 Mar 1998 (OJ 1998 C176/1) 35th recital in the preamble.

[541] ibid, Art 20(2).

[542] Explanatory memorandum to the Proposal of 19 Mar 1998 for a regulation laying down provisions on the Structural Funds, COM(98)131, 17. This part of the Proposal may be problematic. The Proposal is based on Art 130d EC, but the legislation concerning each Fund is based on other Treaty provisions (Art 130e EC).

[543] Notice laying down guidelines for operational programmes in the framework of a Community initiative concerning the most remote regions (OJ 1990 C196/15). See now Regis II, OJ 1994 C180/44.

[544] Committee on Regional Policy and Regional Planning, Report on a Community initiative to assist the most remote regions of the Community, EP Doc A 3–140/90, 12.

[545] Notice laying down guidelines for integrated global grants in the framework of a Community initiative for rural development (OJ 1991 C73/33).

development in the regions covered by the group; vocational training and employment measures; rural tourism; small firms, craft enterprises, and local services; and exploitation and marketing of local agricultural products.

The initiative covers all regions eligible under Objectives 1 and 5b. Decisions about the allocation of Union assistance are made in the light of the quality of the programmes presented by the groups and the proposals drawn up by the Member States, the extent of the rural parts of the region concerned, and the numbers of farmworkers and farms. Low population density and geographical features may also be taken into account.

The initiative recognizes that rural development calls for an approach firmly geared to local requirements and making use of available organizational capacity and expertise. Thus the action groups are to enjoy a substantial degree of flexibility in the management of the global grants.

However, the initiative may be perceived as an inadequate effort to deal with the consequences of reform of the common agricultural policy. According to the Economic and Social Committee, such reform will tend to reduce assistance to agriculture and will have serious implications for rural regions, particularly in terms of unemployment. At the same time, concentration of economic activity associated with completion of the internal market may result in increased transport costs and, consequently, will have a negative impact on such regions.[546]

In contrast, the Urban initiative[547] is mainly concerned with urban regions covered by Objective 1 or 2, though other urban regions may benefit.[548] In particular, it is directed towards regions that are densely populated, with a minimum size of population, a high level of unemployment, a decayed urban fabric, bad housing conditions, and a lack of social amenities.[549]

Finally, the Interreg initiative[550] concerns co-operation between regions. It aims: to assist both internal and external border regions of the Union in overcoming the special development problems arising from their relative isolation within national economies and within the Union as a whole, in the interests of the local population and in a manner compatible with the protection of the environment; to promote the creation and development of networks of co-operation across internal borders and, where relevant, the linking of these networks to wider Union networks, in the context of the completion of the internal market; to assist the adjustment of external border regions to their

[546] Opinion of 18 Oct 1990 on the Community initiative for rural development, CES(90)1223, 3.

[547] Notice laying down guidelines for operational programmes in the framework of a Community initiative concerning urban areas (OJ 1994 C180/6). The European Parliament had inserted Item B2–1405 in the Budget for 1994 (OJ 1994 L34/3), entitled 'urban policy', within the chapter on Community initiatives.

[548] para IV.18 of the Notice (OJ 1994 C180/6).

[549] ibid, para II.10.

[550] Notice laying down guidelines for operational programmes in the framework of a Community initiative concerning border areas (OJ 1990 C215/4).

new role as border regions of a single integrated market; and to respond to new opportunities for co-operation with third countries in external border regions of the Union.[551]

Three types of action are envisaged. They are: the joint planning and implementation of cross-border programmes; the introduction of measures to improve the flow of information across borders and amongst border regions and between public agencies, private organizations, and voluntary bodies; and the setting-up of shared institutional and administrative structures to sustain and promote co-operation.

Eligible regions include all Objective 1, 2, and 5b regions along the internal and external land borders of the Union. In exceptional cases Union assistance may also be given to networks which are established in the interests of the population of the border regions concerned, but concern other Objective 1, 2, or 5b regions.

The Interreg initiative has been extended by Interreg II,[552] which covers both cross-border co-operation and completion of energy networks.[553] All regions along the internal and external land borders of the Union are eligible, as are certain maritime regions.[554] However, Union assistance to cross-border co-operation in regions not covered by Objectives 1, 2, or 5b may only be a limited part of total Union assistance under this initiative.[555] A third 'strand'—transnational co-operation on spatial planning—has now been added to the initiative.[556]

Regions dependent on declining industries

Resider II[557] seeks to assist the conversion of steel regions. Eligible regions must be covered by Objective 1, 2, or 5b[558] and be steel production regions as defined under the ECSC Treaty. Moreover, at least 1,000 steel jobs must also have been lost since 1 January 1990; or the total number of steel jobs lost since then and future steel job losses publicly announced must be at least 1,000; or the total number of jobs lost since then and the number of jobs at risk must

[551] See, in connection with Andorra, the Commission Reply by Mrs Wulf-Matthies to WQ (OJ 1996 C280/65) by Joan Vallre.

[552] Notice laying down guidelines for operational programmes in the framework of a Community initiative concerning border development, cross-border co-operation, and selected energy co-operation (OJ 1994 C180/60).

[553] ibid, para I.3. It thus takes over from the Regen initiative (Notice laying down guidelines for operational programmes in the framework of a Community initiative concerning transmission and distribution networks for energy (OJ 1990 C326/7)).

[554] OJ 1994 C180/60, para II.8.

[555] ibid, para V.19.

[556] Communication laying down guidelines for operational programmes in the framework of a Community Interreg initiative concerning transnational co-operation on spatial planning (OJ 1996 C200/23).

[557] Notice laying down guidelines for operational programmes or global grants in the framework of a Community initiative concerning the economic conversion of steel areas (OJ 1994 C180/22).

[558] ibid, para II.5.

be at least 1,000. A limited number of other regions with a high dependence on the steel industry may, taking account of factors such as high unemployment, environmental degradation, isolation, or peripherality, also be eligible.[559]

Assistance may cover: environmental improvement; renovation and modernization of social and economic infrastructure; promotion of alternative economic activities; construction of new, advanced factory units and workshop premises; promotion of tourist activities, especially those based on industrial heritage; promotion of economic conversion bodies and regional development teams; and vocational training and employment measures.

Assistance may take the form of: interest rebates on ECSC loans for investments in small and medium-sized enterprises and for the reclamation of sites for industrial use; promotion of cross-border co-operation between former steel regions; and redeployment assistance under Article 56 of the ECSC Treaty.

Similarly, the Rechar II initiative[560] seeks to assist the conversion of coal-mining regions. It has been adopted because many such regions are amongst those which have been or are likely to be hardest hit by problems of industrial restructuring. They also have special difficulties in adjusting rapidly to changing economic circumstances.[561]

Eligible regions are those which satisfy one of three criteria. They must have lost at least 1,000 coal-mining jobs since 1 January 1990; the total of the jobs lost since that date and future coal-mining job losses publicly announced must be at least 1,000; or the total of jobs lost since the same date and the number of jobs at risk must be at least 1,000.[562] In addition, they must be included in a list of eligible regions drawn up by the Commission and, in principle, must fall within Objective 1, 2, or 5b.[563]

The adoption of this initiative has affected the operation of the Structural Funds even to the extent of requiring a redesignation of Objective 2 regions. This redesignation concerned certain parts of coal-mining regions in Germany, France, and the United Kingdom.[564] It highlights the possibility that in some cases at least, assistance from the European Regional Development Fund is employed to solve what are really sectoral problems. Such assistance is said to exacerbate regional inequality, since the poorest regions of the Union may have no eligible industries.[565]

559 ibid, para II.6.

560 Notice laying down guidelines for operational programmes in the framework of a Community initiative concerning the economic conversion of coal-mining areas (OJ 1994 C180/26). See, earlier, OJ 1990 C20/3.

561 OJ 1994 C180/26, para 3. 562 ibid, para II.6. 563 ibid, para II.5.

564 Dec 90/400 (OJ 1990 L206/26) amending Dec 89/288 establishing an initial list of declining industrial areas concerned by Objective 2.

565 *The Regional Impact of Community Policies* (Regional Policy and Transport Series No 17; European Parliament, Luxembourg, 1991) 11.

The Retex initiative[566] concerns regions heavily dependent on the textiles and clothing industries. However, unlike Resider II and Rechar II, it is not limited to assisting conversion. It may also assist modernization of the textile industry.[567]

Eligible regions must be covered by Objective 1, 2, or 5b, have at least 2,000 jobs in the textiles and clothing industries, and have a level of employment in these industries which is greater than 10 per cent of overall industrial employment.[568] It was envisaged that limited assistance might also be extended to regions not covered by Objective 1, 2, or 5b which were heavily dependent on the textile and clothing sector, if the necessary flexibility was introduced in the 1993 reform of the legislation governing the Structural Funds.[569] However, no such extension is envisaged in paragraph 2 of the current Commission Notice concerning this initiative.[570]

Assistance may be provided for: improving know-how; the formation of local associations and businesses and other co-operation schemes; the setting-up of a team to provide ideas and advice to sectors which comprise large numbers of small and medium-sized enterprises; temporary contributions towards paying engineers, technical staff, and managers recruited to help in implementing modernization plans; vocational training schemes; and the rehabilitation of industrial wasteland.[571]

There is doubt whether this initiative alone will be an adequate solution to the problems faced by the regions concerned.[572] In particular, both the Committee on Economic and Monetary Affairs and Industrial Policy of the European Parliament[573] and the Economic and Social Committee[574] advocate special co-ordination between the Retex initiative and other operations of the Union funds. Such co-ordination is considered necessary to allow better account to be taken of the time difference between the adjustments to be

[566] Notice laying down guidelines for operational programmes within the framework of a Community initiative for regions heavily dependent on the textiles and clothing sector (OJ 1992 C142/5).

[567] Improving the competitiveness of the Community's textile and clothing industry, COM(91)399.

[568] OJ 1992 C142/5, para 5.

[569] ibid, para 4. Such extension was supported by the European Parliament. See the Resolution of 10 Apr 1992 (OJ 1992 C125/276) on a Community initiative for regions heavily dependent on the textiles and clothing sector, para 16.

[570] Notice laying down guidelines for the Retex initiative (OJ 1994 C180/17).

[571] OJ 1992 C142/5, para 3.

[572] Applications for ERDF assistance in the textiles sector are assessed taking account of the code for state aid to this industry. See para 5(d) of the Annex to the Commission letter of 4 Feb 1977 (SEC(77)317).

[573] Report on restructuring the textile and clothing industry in the Community (EP Doc A3–0257/91), 19.

[574] Opinion of 29 Apr 1992 (OJ 1992 C169/25) on the draft guidelines for operational programmes within the framework of the Community initiative for regions heavily dependent on the textiles and clothing sector, para 2.1.2.

made by textile or clothing firms and the longer-term benefits of diversifying the economies of the regions concerned.

The Pesca initiative[575] concerns the restructuring of the fishing industry. It recognizes that changes in this sector are necessitated by a structural crisis of unprecedented seriousness.[576] It aims to enable these changes to be effected successfully, to help the sector to cope with the attendant social and economic consequences, and to contribute to the diversification of the regions concerned by developing job-creating activities.[577]

The initiative is designed principally for regions which are dependent on fisheries and are covered by Objective 1, 2, or 5b. However, in view of the specific problems and wide dispersion of fisheries activities, a maximum of 15 per cent of the appropriations allocated under Pesca in Objective 2 and 5b regions may be used outside these regions and Objective 1 regions.[578]

Finally, the Konver initiative[579] seeks to assist the diversification of economic activities in regions heavily dependent on the defence industry and to encourage the adjustment of commercially viable businesses in all industrial sectors. Eligible regions must meet one of the following criteria. They must have lost at least 1,000 jobs in defence activities since 1 January 1990; the total number of jobs lost in defence activities since that date and future job losses publicly announced in such activities must be at least 1,000; or the total number of jobs lost in defence activities since the same date and the number of such jobs at risk must be at least 1,000.[580] A maximum of 50 per cent of the total Union assistance under this initiative may be granted to regions not eligible under Objective 1, 2, or 5b.[581]

Regions needing assistance to implement Union policies

The Télématique initiative[582] concerned the accessibility of advanced telecommunications services. It was designed to promote the use of such services in Objective 1 regions, including improved access to advanced services located elsewhere in the Union. The emphasis was on services rather than on investments in infrastructure, which were considered only where they were

575 Notice laying down guidelines for global grants or integrated operational programmes within the framework of a Community initiative concerning the restructuring of the fisheries sector (OJ 1994 C180/1).

576 ibid, para I.4.

577 ibid, para I.6.

578 ibid, para III.7. See also the Call for proposals concerning transnational projects for co-operation and networking between areas dependent on fisheries (OJ 1998 C208/11).

579 Notice laying down guidelines for operational programmes or global grants in the framework of a Community initiative concerning defence conversion (OJ 1994 C180/18).

580 ibid, para III.5.1. See also the Notice laying down the list of new areas of France eligible pursuant to the Community initiative concerning the conversion of the defence industry (OJ 1997 C294/9), which was adopted pursuant to para III.7 of the Notice (OJ 1994 C180/18).

581 ibid, para III.8.

582 Notice laying down guidelines for operational programmes in the framework of a Community initiative for regional development concerning services and networks related to data communication (OJ 1991 C33/7).

directly linked to the promotion of the services targeted by this initiative. Three broad categories of measures were eligible for assistance. They were: development of the use by small and medium-sized enterprises of services linked to advanced telecommunications systems and of the supply of such services by enterprises of this kind; development of services in the public sector for data communication likely to contribute to regional development; and development of networks inside Objective 1 regions and between these regions and the rest of the Union.

Again, the Stride initiative[583] sought to strengthen the research, technological, and innovatory capacity of Objective 1 regions. The aim was to ensure that such regions were better placed to attract or retain technologically advanced activities in the productive sectors of the region and highly qualified personnel. Objective 2 regions could also be assisted through the stimulation of innovation in ways which encouraged diversification of the local economy.[584] This initiative was to be co-ordinated with other Union actions in favour of research and development,[585] especially those within the Community Support Frameworks,[586] the Framework Programme for research and development, and the Sprint programme.[587] According to the Commission, such co-ordination was a complicated process, requiring understanding and extensive communication between the relevant Commission services.[588]

The Prisma initiative[589] sought, in turn, to assist enterprises in Objective 1 regions to adapt to the completion of the internal market, so that they could benefit fully from the opportunities which arose. An essential feature was the promotion of a policy of quality assurance in the enterprises concerned. More specifically, efforts to develop certification and testing infrastructures received assistance. The aim was to enable businesses and laboratories to have access to or to possess facilities and services needed to show their clients that they were able to comply with technical quality standards. The aim was also to prepare small and medium-sized enterprises for the opening-up of

[583] Notice C(90)1562/2 (OJ 1990 C196/18) laying down guidelines for operational programmes in the framework of a Community initiative concerning regional capacities for research, technology, and innovation.

[584] The ESC recommended, *inter alia*, that, in drawing up the list of eligible Objective 2 regions, the Commission should recognize the importance of the impact of technological change for industrial sectors vulnerable to completion of the single internal market. See the Opinion of 28 Mar 1990 (OJ 1990 C124/22) on the declining industrial areas, para 2.5.

[585] para 3 of Notice C(90)1562/2 (OJ 1990 C196/18).

[586] sect 7.4.4 below.

[587] sect 6.3 below.

[588] *Evaluation of the Effects of the EC Framework Programme for Research and Technological Development on Economic and Social Cohesion in the Community* (EC Commission, Brussels, 1991) 27.

[589] Notice laying down guidelines for operational programmes in the framework of a Community initiative concerning the preparation of enterprises for the single market (OJ 1991 C33/9).

public procurement and for the suppression of measures under Article 134 of the Treaty.[590]

The SME initiative, for small and medium-sized enterprises, is designed to take over the tasks of Télématique, Stride, and Prisma. It aims to stimulate such enterprises, particularly in the less developed regions, to adapt to the single market and to ensure that they become internationally competitive.[591] The enterprises concerned are essentially those with fewer than 250 employees.[592] However, enterprises of between 250 and 500 employees, particularly in Objective 1 regions, may also be assisted.[593] Assistance is to be allocated to Objective 1, 2, or 5b regions, though small and medium-sized enterprises outside these regions may participate in networking activities linked with the initiative.[594] Basically, measures to improve the business know-how of small and medium-sized enterprises and to improve the business environment for such enterprises are to be supported.[595]

Finally, the Envireg initiative[596] acknowledged the link between regional development and the resolution of environmental problems. It aimed to help the least favoured regions to tackle their environmental problems and thereby put their economic and social development on a firmer footing. The specific objectives were: to reduce the pollution of coastal areas, particularly in the Mediterranean regions, whose economy depended significantly on tourism; to promote the planning of land use in coastal regions in such a way as to preserve natural beauty and protect and enhance biotopes in these regions; to contribute to the better control and management of toxic and hazardous industrial waste; to strengthen know-how relating to the design and management of facilities for reducing pollution; and, more generally, to improve the ways in which environmental problems were tackled.[597]

Eligible regions were, as regards the reduction of pollution and land-use planning and related know-how, coastal regions covered by Objective 1 and Mediterranean coastal regions covered by Objectives 2 and 5b. As regards toxic and hazardous waste and related know-how, eligible regions were all those covered by Objective 1.[598]

This initiative has not been continued.[599]

[590] According to this provision, in order to ensure that the execution of measures of commercial policy taken in accordance with the Treaty by a Member State was not obstructed by deflection of trade, or where differences between such measures led to economic difficulties in one or more of the Member States, the Commission might authorize Member States to take the necessary protective measures.

[591] Notice laying down guidelines for operational programmes or global grants in the framework of a Community initiative concerning the adaptation of SMEs to the single market (OJ 1994 C180/10).

[592] ibid, para III.6.1.

[593] ibid, para III.6.3.

[594] ibid, para IV.9.

[595] ibid, paras III.7 and 8.

[596] Notice laying down guidelines for operational programmes within the framework of a Community initiative concerning the environment (OJ 1990 C115/3).

[597] ibid, para 4.

[598] ibid, para 6.

[599] Though sustainable development measures may be assisted under the Communication

Integrated development operations

At the initiative of a Member State or of the Commission in agreement with the Member State concerned, assistance may be implemented as an integrated approach. Three conditions must be met for adoption of such an approach. First, financing by more than one Structural Fund or at least one Structural Fund and one financial instrument other than a loan instrument must be involved.[600] Secondly, the measures to be financed must be mutually reinforcing, and significant benefits must be likely to accrue from close co-ordination between all the parties involved. Thirdly, appropriate administrative structures must be provided at national, regional, and local level in the interests of integrated implementation of these measures.

The desirability of adopting an integrated approach should be considered when a Community Support Framework[601] is established or revised.[602] In the implementation of such an approach the Commission shall ensure that Union assistance is provided in the most effective manner, taking into account the special co-ordination effort required.[603] However, the Commission has been criticized for tending to rely more on 'multifund operational plans', made up of sub-programmes, each managed by one fund.[604]

It is now proposed that, as a general rule, assistance covered by a Community Support Framework shall be provided in the form of an integrated operational programme for each region.[605] Such a programme is defined as an operational programme financed by more than one Fund.[606]

2.4.7 Assistance Rates

The maximum rate of assistance from the European Regional Development Fund is 75 per cent of total project costs in Objective 1 regions. In regions benefiting from the Cohesion Fund the maximum rate may in exceptional cases be raised to 80 per cent and in the outermost regions and the outlying Greek regions to 85 per cent. Outside Objective 1 regions the maximum rate is 50 per cent.[607] In general, the Commission considers that the maximum

laying down guidelines for operational programmes in the framework of a Community Interreg initiative concerning transnational co-operation on spatial planning (OJ 1996 C200/23).

600 Art 13(1) of Reg 2082/93 (OJ 1993 L193/20). The IDO for Merseyside, eg, brought together the ERDF and the ESF to co-finance a programme for 1989–91. See the Commission Reply by Mr Millan to WQ 1776/91 (OJ 1992 C78/24) by Mr Kenneth Stewart.

601 sect 7.4.4 below.

602 Art 13(2) of Reg 2082/93 (OJ 1993 L193/20).

603 ibid, Art 13(3).

604 Report of the Committee on Budgetary Control on the management of the budget of the Structural Funds within the framework of the reform: assessment and outlook, EP Doc A–0191/92, 12.

605 Art 17(1) of the Proposal of 19 Mar 1998 (OJ 1998 C176/1) for a regulation laying down provisions on the Structural Funds.

606 ibid, Art 9(1)(e).

607 Art 13(3) of Reg 2081/93 (OJ 1993 L193/5).

should be 50 per cent of public expenditure in Objective 2 regions and 40 per cent in Objective 5b regions.[608] For investments in firms, up to 50 per cent of the total eligible costs may be covered in Objective 1 regions and up to 30 per cent of such costs in other regions.[609] In the case of preparatory studies and technical-assistance measures undertaken on the initiative of the Commission, 100 per cent of total costs may be covered.[610]

In all cases the actual rate of Union assistance is to be differentiated in the light of various factors. They are: the seriousness of the specific, notably regional or social, problems to be tackled; the financial capacity of the Member State concerned, taking into particular account the relative prosperity of that Member State; the special importance attaching to the operation concerned from a Union viewpoint and from a regional viewpoint; and the particular characteristics of that operation.[611]

The reduction of these rates is now proposed,[612] so as to bring them into line with the ceilings applicable to state aid.[613] More explicit attention should, it is also proposed, be paid to the need for the optimum utilization of financial resources.[614]

2.4.8 Assistance Periods

Eligibility for Objective 1[615] and 5b[616] assistance extends over a six-year period. In the case of Objective 2, however, assistance is planned and implemented on the basis of three-year periods.[617] A six-year programming period for Objective 2 operations has been advocated by the Commission.[618] The aim is to bring assistance periods into line with the financial perspectives agreed at the meeting of the European Council in Edinburgh in December 1992.[619] In practice, the Commission may seek to achieve this end through leaving largely unchanged its decisions on regions eligible for assistance under Objective 2.

608 Back-up policies: reform of the Structural Funds, COM(88)500, 31.
609 Art 17(3) of Reg 2082/93 (OJ 1993 L193/20).
610 Art 13(4) of Reg 2081/93 (OJ 1993 L193/5).
611 ibid, Art 13(1).
612 Art 28(4) and 37th recital in the preamble to the Proposal of 19 Mar 1998 (OJ 1998 C176/1) for a regulation laying down provisions on the Structural Funds.
613 ibid, Art 28(3).
614 ibid, Art 28(1)(f).
615 Art 8(3) of Reg 2081/93 (OJ 1993 L193/5).
616 Art 7 of Reg 2085/93 (OJ 1993 L193/44) amending Reg 4256/88 laying down provisions for implementing Reg 2052/88 as regards the EAGGF, Guidance Section.
617 Art 9(6) of Reg 2081/93 (OJ 1993 L193/5). Three years after entry into force of a list of eligible regions, the eligibility criteria laid down in Art 9(2) (ibid) may be amended by the Council (ibid, Art 9(7)).
618 Community Structural Funds 1994–99, COM(93)67, 8.
619 Bull EC 12–1992, I.51.

It is now proposed that the lists of regions eligible under Objective 1[620] or Objective 2[621] will be valid for seven years.

2.5 CONCLUSION

Practice regarding the European Regional Development Fund focuses more on questions of the distribution of assistance as between Member States than on ensuring that these resources are effectively used to promote cohesion. The basic criterion for eligibility for assistance from the Fund and, more particularly, for selection of Objective 1 regions, is per capita gross domestic product relative to the Union average. In principle, to qualify for Objective 1 assistance, regions must have a per capita gross domestic product which is less than 75 per cent of this average.

Application of this criterion has the advantage of apparent objectivity.[622] Certainly, in determining eligibility for assistance from the Fund, the Council and Commission have been concerned to use figures which are available throughout the Union on as nearly as possible a comparable basis. Figures are available, unreliable as they are admitted to be,[623] for gross domestic product.[624]

The criterion may also be claimed to secure the concentration necessary to ensure that limited resources are not so thinly spread as to lack real impact.[625] More particularly, it enables the assistance to be concentrated on regions in Member States which have sought 'side payments' for acceptance of the deepening of integration envisaged in the Single European Act[626] and the Treaty on European Union.[627] In this connection, it is notable that Ireland, Greece, Portugal, and Spain, as well as Italy, favour a strict application of the 75 per cent criterion for determining eligibility under Objective 1.[628]

The disadvantage of the criterion of per capita gross domestic product is that it does not enable account to be taken of the diverse and changing regional conditions within the Union. Community initiatives alone are unlikely to be sufficient to permit reconciliation of the need for concentration of funding emphasized by the above Member States with the need for flexibility to take account of such conditions.[629] From the start, therefore, the application of the criterion had to be relaxed in the case of Northern Ireland.

620 Art 3(2) of the Proposal of 19 Mar 1998 (OJ 1998 C176/1) for a regulation laying down provisions on the Structural Funds.

621 Proposal of 19 Mar 1998 (OJ 1998 C176/1) Art 4(11).

622 Note the objections of the French Government that Hainaut in Belgium was classified as an Objective 1 region, whereas neighbouring Hainaut-Cambresis in France, which was little better off, was to remain an Objective 2 region (*European Report* 1842 (10 Mar 1993)).

623 See also COA annual report 1995 (OJ 1996 C340/1), para 5.21.

624 EEC regional development policy, House of Lords Select Committee on the European Communities, HL(1991–92)20, Evidence, 7.

625 cf First cohesion report, COM(96)542, 117.

626 OJ 1987 L169/1.

627 ch 8 below.

628 *Europe* 6006 (23 June 1993).

629 cf Future of Community initiatives under the Structural Funds, COM(93)282.

Northern Ireland had a per capita gross domestic product of around 80 per cent of the Community average in 1986,[630] and the 'special reasons' for its original classification as an Objective 1 region essentially concerned its recent history of civil unrest.[631] The 1993 reforms entailed further relaxation in relation to Hainaut, Merseyside, and the Highlands and Islands of Scotland. These three regions 'are not areas of lagging development in the traditional sense but regions where the decline from relative prosperity based on industrial activity has been particularly acute. East Berlin and the new *Länder* . . . also represent a new type of problem—one of transition from a centrally planned to a market economy.'[632] Viewed against this background, introduction of Objective 6 seems to be more a recognition of a symptom of the underlying difficulties rather than a solution to these difficulties. The inference may be drawn that relaxation of criteria based on per capita gross domestic product may be necessary for the development of a Fund which genuinely addresses the diversity of cohesion problems within the Union.[633]

At the same time, adoption of more sophisticated criteria may be necessary, to curb the intergovernmental haggling over the designation of Objective 1 regions and over the eligibility criteria for Objectives 2 and 5b. Such haggling underscores how Union assistance can be abused by the Member States.[634] As the Commission admits, the distribution of such assistance reflects 'political compromises'.[635]

The Commission response to these problems is simply to call for a strict application of the criteria. However, this end is to be achieved essentially by limiting eligible regions to those where the Commission authorizes Member States to grant regional aid under Article 87(3) of the Treaty.[636] Thus eligibility is ultimately to be determined by reference to competition policy requirements[637] rather than by reference to cohesion requirements.[638] At the

[630] However, its unemployment rate was 1.7 times the Community average.

[631] EEC regional development policy, House of Lords Select Committee on the European Communities, HL(1991–92)20, 19.

[632] Fifth periodic report on the situation and socio-economic development of the regions of the Community, COM(94)322, 130.

[633] See eg Community Structural Fund operations, COM(93)67, 4.

[634] J Bachtler, 'Policy Agenda for the Decade' in S Hardy, M Hart, L Albrechts, and A Katos, *An Enlarged Europe* (Jessica Kingsley, London, 1995) 313–324, 317.

[635] First cohesion report, COM(96)542, 6.

[636] See, regarding current inconsistencies between regions covered by this provision and regions covered by Objectives 1, 2 and 5b, the Commission Reply by Mr Van Miert to WQ E–0473/98 (OJ 1998 C304/113) by Richard Howitt.

[637] cf the concern that there may be 'an excessive reduction in areas' covered by Objective 2 in the ESC Opinion of 27 May 1998 (OJ 1998 C235/38) on the new regional programmes 1997–99 under Objective 2, para 4.3.4. Cf, more generally, FG Wishlade, 'Competition Policy or Cohesion Policy by the Back Door: The Commission Guidelines on National Regional Aid' (1998) ECLR 343–357.

[638] cf the call for improved allocation of assistance, with particular attention being paid to the outermost regions, the ESC Opinion of 19 Mar 1997 (OJ 1997 C158/5) on the annual report of the Cohesion Fund 1995, para 4.1.

same time, 'political compromises' apparently remain influential, in that Objective 6 regions are to be treated as 'special cases'.[639]

Less attention is paid to ensuring that assistance, once it has been allocated to a Member State, is used effectively to promote cohesion. For example, much assistance concerns physical infrastructure,[640] even though such assistance may not be the most appropriate for regional development. Equally, assistance to productive investment may not necessarily be an effective means of reducing disparities between regions. Comparatively limited resources are devoted to 'endogenous growth' measures, which may be more successful in reducing such disparities.

[639] Communication on the links between regional and competition policy—reinforcing concentration and mutual consistency (OJ 1998 C90/3), para 3.2.

[640] In 1995 31.2% of assistance from the Structural Funds in Objective 1 regions went to infrastructure. See COA annual report for 1996 (OJ 1997 C348/1), para 6.6.

3

EAGGF, Guidance Section

3.1 INTRODUCTION

Article 33(1)(a) of the EC Treaty provides that the common agricultural policy shall seek to increase agricultural productivity. It shall seek to do so by promoting technical progress and by ensuring the rational development of agricultural production and the optimum utilization of factors of production, in particular labour.[1] At the same time, concern is expressed for social aspects of farming. According to Article 33(1)(b), the policy should seek to ensure a fair standard of living for the agricultural community, particularly by increasing the individual earnings of persons engaged in agriculture. Moreover, in the elaboration of this policy and the special methods for its application Article 33(2)(a) requires that account be taken of various factors. These include the particular nature of agricultural activity, which results from the social structure of agriculture and from structural and natural disparities between the various agricultural regions.

To these ends, common organizations of the markets for the various agricultural products may be established under Article 34(2).[2] Moreover, according to Article 34(4), one or more agricultural guidance and guarantee fund may be created. The rationale for providing for the creation of such funds is that a common organization may necessitate the grant of assistance to farmers. If the organization is really to be 'common' and there is to be 'equal burden sharing',[3] the grant of the assistance cannot be left to individual Member States.[4] Rather, the Union must play a central role in its grant. In particular, according to Article 36, the Council may authorize assistance:

(*a*) for the protection of enterprises handicapped by structural or natural conditions; and

(*b*) within the framework of economic development programmes.

Such assistance was sought primarily by Italy.[5] Special arrangements were also made for assistance to Luxembourg.[6]

[1] The agricultural and processed products concerned are defined in Annex II to the Treaty.

[2] Art 34(3) EC.

[3] See eg Case C–324/96 *Odette Nikon Petridi Anonymos Kapnemporiki v Athanasia Simou* [26 Mar 1998].

[4] R Quadri, R Monaco, and A Trabucchi (eds), *Trattato istitutivo della Comunità economica europea: Commentario* (Giuffré, Milan, 1965) i. 296.

[5] ibid.

[6] See the Protocol on Luxembourg, annexed to the EEC Treaty. This Protocol was invoked in the 8th recital in the preamble to Reg 541/70 (JO 1970 L68/3) on agriculture in Luxembourg, which provided for the grant of assistance by the Guidance Section to Luxembourg.

In addition, Article 35 envisages co-ordination of efforts in the spheres of vocational training, research, and dissemination of agricultural knowledge, to achieve the objectives of the common agricultural policy. Joint financing of projects or institutions may be entailed. This provision thus authorizes the provision of assistance to training[7] and research in the agricultural sector.[8]

All such assistance must be designed to secure 'permanent reconciliation' of the objectives of the common agricultural policy. However, contradictions between these objectives may arise, and in given cases one objective may have to be accorded the temporary priority demanded by economic circumstances.[9]

At the same time, there may be problems of reconciling assistance with competition policy. As the Commission recognizes, many factors affect the competitive position of farmers. The climate, soil types, rainfall, and proximity to population centres can be an advantage, or disadvantage, to particular farms or regions. Farmers may also be affected by the price of labour, land, or other inputs into the farming process, which may differ on a regional basis. According to the Commission, such differences cannot necessarily justify the provision of assistance.[10] Indeed, they may be perceived as fuelling the competitive process and as leading to the benefits that society gains from specialization and trade.[11]

3.2 ESTABLISHMENT OF THE COMMON ORGANIZATIONS

Regulation 25/62[12] created the European Agricultural Guidance and Guarantee Fund. It was designed to enable the common organizations of agricultural markets to attain their objectives.[13] Thus assistance was originally to be an 'accessory' to the establishment of the common organizations.[14]

[7] There were proposals of 3 Feb 1965 concerning Community grants towards the retraining of farmers wishing to change their occupation within agriculture; and concerning Community grants towards the training of advisers to provide information services for farmers and farmworkers wishing to change their occupation. Assistance from the General Budget (special ch on the CAP) was to be made available under Art 41 EEC (Bull EEC, Supp 3/65, 23 and 27).

[8] See eg Dec 73/127 (OJ 1973 L153/13) adopting a research programme for the EEC in the field of teledetection of earth resources, which was based on Arts 41 and 235 EEC. However, Dec 75/460 (OJ 1975 L199/37) adopting common research programmes and programmes for the co-ordination of research in the field of animal leucoses, livestock effluents, beef production, and plant protein protection referred only to Art 43 EEC. It was financed under ch 253 of Annex I to the General Budget (see for 1974, OJ 1974 L115/1).

[9] Case C–353/92 *Greece v EU Council: aid to cereal producers* [1994] ECR I–3411, I–3448–9.

[10] Distortions of competition in hothouse agriculture, COM(80)306, 32.

[11] State aids to agriculture, House of Lords Select Committee on the European Community, HL(1981–82)90, vi–vii.

[12] On the financing of the CAP (JO 1962 991).

[13] ibid, Art 1.

[14] D Gadbin, 'Le Droit communautaire des structures agricoles: Organisation ou dilution?' (1991) RMC 218–230, 218.

In March 1963 the Commission sought to go further and produced a proposal concerning a Fund for the Improvement of Agricultural Structures.[15] According to the explanatory memorandum to the proposal, establishment of the common organizations produced new problems.[16] It also rendered existing problems more difficult to tackle, because old solutions might be prohibited.[17] Hence, the proposed Fund was needed to stimulate and guide efforts to improve agricultural structures consistent with the requirements of this policy and thus to contribute to ensuring a balanced socio-economic situation.[18] To these ends, the Fund would be empowered to assist projects where the socio-economic situation, particularly in agriculture, suffered from backwardness threatening the implementation of the common agricultural policy. It would also be empowered to intervene, where the implementation of this policy led or would lead to a deterioration in the socio-economic situation.[19] Assisted projects had to be included in a regional development programme.[20] Assistance could take the form of interest rebates and loans,[21] though it was not to substitute aids normally granted by national authorities, or lead to their reduction.[22] However, the Commission had to abandon plans for the creation of this Fund in the face of Council objections.[23]

As a result, Regulation 17/64[24] simply divided the European Agricultural Guidance and Guarantee Fund into two Sections, the Guidance Section[25] and the Guarantee Section.[26] The Guarantee Section sought to affect market development in the short term through financing price-support, while the Guidance Section sought in the long term to affect structural conditions of production and marketing.[27] In other words, it was only the Guidance Section which was constituted as a Structural Fund.

3.2.1 Objectives of Assistance

The Guidance Section of the European Agricultural Guidance and Guarantee Fund was to finance common measures undertaken for attaining

15 Bull EEC, Supp 4/63.

16 cf Reg 742/67 (JO 1967 258/4) creating special sections I and II of the EAGGF concerning Community compensatory measures in favour of Germany, Italy, and Luxembourg and the grant of UA 4 million to Luxembourg, which provided three Member States with compensation to cover the losses of their cereal farmers following application of a common price in this sector. See also Dec 70/355 (JO 1970 L157/27) on the application by Germany of compensatory measures for cereal producers, which authorized complementary state aid under Art 93(2) EEC.

17 Bull EEC, Supp 4/63, paras 4–5.

18 ibid, Art 1(2).

19 ibid, Art 2.

20 ibid, Art 3(2)(a).

21 ibid, Art 5.

22 ibid, Art 6(b).

23 Quadri, Monaco, and Trabucchi, n 4 above, i. 297.

24 On the conditions for granting aid from the EAGGF (JO 1964 586).

25 See, generally, 'EAGGF: The European Community's Expenditure on the Common Agricultural Policy' (1986) 42 *Green Europe*.

26 Art 1 of Reg 17/64 (JO 1964 586).

27 R Priebe, 'Le Droit communautaire des structures agricoles' (1988) CDE 3–38.

the objectives set out in Article 39(1)(a) of the EEC Treaty,[28] including structural changes necessitated by the establishment of the common market.[29] Such measures were considered necessary because agricultural returns were often insufficient to finance the necessary changes.[30]

In a later Commission proposal for a regulation on the implementation of a Community programme for agricultural restructuring,[31] a rather more elaborate statement of the rationale for financing such measures was given. According to the preamble to this proposal, the rationale was that in much of the Community agriculture could not adapt to economic developments because of obstacles connected with land as a factor of production. Hence, it was thought that Community assistance for the rationalization of farms and labour-mobility was necessary to secure the restructuring which would lead to competitiveness. This proposal was not accepted by the Council, though it was revealing as to the considerations which underlay the provision of Community assistance to farming.

Similar considerations led to the common organization of the market in fishery products[32] being supplemented by structural assistance for the fishing industry.[33] The aim was to promote harmonious and balanced development of this industry within the general economy and to encourage rational use of the biological resources of the sea and inland waters.[34] Accordingly, assistance could be granted to promote the rational development of the fishing industry within the framework of economic growth and social progress. Assistance could also be granted to ensure an equitable standard of living for the population, which depended on fishing for its livelihood.[35] The Commission considered that such assistance should be directed towards alleviating the social costs of restructuring.[36]

3.2.2 Scope of Assistance

The Guidance Section was originally to receive one-third of the total resources made available to the European Agricultural Guidance and Guarantee Fund.[37] It was to assist adaptation and improvement of agricultural production. Similarly, it was to assist adaptation and improvement of

[28] Now Art 33(1)(a) EC. [29] Art 3(1)(d) of Reg 25/62 (JO 1962 991).

[30] 17th recital in the preamble to Reg 17/64 (JO 1964 586).

[31] Proposal of 19 June 1967 (JO 1967 254/20).

[32] Reg 2142/70 (JO 1970 L236/5) on the common organization of the market in fishery products. It was replaced by Reg 100/76 (OJ 1976 L20/1) and Reg 3796/81 (OJ 1981 L379/1).

[33] 5th recital in the preamble to Reg 2141/70 (JO 1970 L236/1) laying down a common structural policy for the fishing industry.

[34] ibid, Art 1. [35] ibid, Art 10(1). See, later, Art 9(1) of Reg 101/76 (OJ 1976 L20/19).

[36] Basic principles for a common policy in the fisheries sector 1966 (JO 1967 862), E.I.1; the proposal of 6 June 1968 (JO 1968 C91/1) for a regulation establishing a common structural policy for the fisheries sector; and the fishery management proposals of Sept 1976, COM(76)500, 18.

[37] Art 5(2) of Reg 25/62 (JO 1962 991).

the marketing of agricultural products. It was also to assist development of outlets for agricultural products.[38] Accordingly, assistance was granted: for Italian fruit and vegetable production;[39] for fruit production throughout the Community;[40] and for the 'integration of Luxembourg agriculture into the common market'.[41]

Moreover, assistance could be granted for projects for the adaptation or improvement of agriculture necessitated by the economic consequences of implementing the common agricultural policy. Assistance could also be granted for projects which sought to meet the requirements of that policy and to secure improvements in agricultural structures of lasting economic effect.[42] In addition, the Commission proposed that assistance should be granted to agricultural infrastructure,[43] but this proposal was not adopted by the Council.

Similarly, in the case of fishing, assistance related to sectoral development efforts,[44] though the assistance might not necessarily succeed in promoting such development. For example, assistance was granted for the construction and modernization of vessels for herring fishing. However, the Community sought to restrict herring fishing for conservation reasons.[45] As a result, many of the vessels in respect of which such assistance was granted had very limited use.[46]

3.2.3 Forms of Assistance

Assistance was to be granted to projects,[47] which were supposed to come within the framework of a Community programme.[48] The programmes were to be adopted by the Council,[49] taking into account the Council Decision of 4 December 1962 on the co-ordination of agricultural structures.[50] Each programme was to specify: the objective to be achieved and the nature of the

[38] Art 15(1) of Reg 17/64 (JO 1964 586). See, regarding the regional significance of such action, the *First EC General Report* (EC Commission, Brussels, 1968) 233.

[39] Reg 130/66 (JO 1966 2965) on the financing of the CAP, Arts 4 and 13.

[40] Reg 2517/69 (JO 1969 L318/15) laying down certain measures for reorganizing Community fruit production.

[41] Reg 541/70 (JO 1970 L68/3).

[42] Art 14(1) of Reg 17/64 (JO 1964 586).

[43] Proposal of 19 June 1967 (JO 1967 254/53) for a regulation on the implementation of a Community programme for the development of agricultural regions in difficulty or backward regions.

[44] cf Reg 2722/72 (JO 1972 L291/30) on the financing by the EAGGF, Guidance Section, of conversion projects in the salt cod-fishing industry.

[45] See eg Reg 2115/77 (OJ 1977 L247/2) prohibiting the direct fishing and landing of herring for industrial purposes other than human consumption.

[46] COA annual report for 1979 (OJ 1980 C342/1), para 5.17.

[47] See eg Grant of aid from the Guidance Section of the EAGGF for 1966 (JO 1967 181/9).

[48] Art 14(1)(a) of Reg 17/64 (JO 1964 586). See also the proposal of 19 June 1967 (JO 1967 254/18) for a regulation laying down general provisions concerning Community programmes for actions of the Guidance Section.

[49] Art 16(1) of Reg 17/64 (JO 1964 586).

[50] JO 1962 2892. See also Priebe, n 27 above, 5.

projects to be undertaken; the regions in which assistance should be concentrated; the percentages of assistance for each category of projects; and the total cost and estimated duration of the programme.[51] Projects would have priority for support, when they formed part of a comprehensive system of measures to encourage the harmonious development of the overall economy of the region concerned. They would have priority, because such projects had greater chances of effectiveness.[52] In practice, however, the tendency was for piecemeal financing of individual projects favoured by Member States.[53]

The European Parliament objected that such practice was inadequate for the development of agricultural regions in general and those which were depressed in particular. According to the Parliament, the Guidance Section should programme its operations to promote development of the latter regions, through concentrating its interventions and co-ordinating them with regional development programmes.[54] Continued failure so to programme the operations led to the Commission admission in the *Memorandum on the Reform of Agriculture in the European Economic Community*[55] that the social goals of the common agricultural policy were not being met. In particular, the holdings of the majority of farmers remained uneconomically small and inadequately equipped.[56] Therefore, an 'autonomous' Community structural policy was considered necessary.[57]

3.3 DEVELOPMENT OF THE COMMON ORGANIZATIONS

As the common organizations developed, interdependence between market policy and structural policy became increasingly apparent.[58] Thus Regulation 729/70[59] provided for assistance from the Guidance Section to facilitate the structural changes necessary for the proper working of the common market.[60] Such assistance was to take account of the Council Decision of 4 December 1962.[61] According to a Resolution of the Council and Representatives of the Governments of Member States of 21 March 1972,[62] it could be directed towards regional development.[63]

[51] Art 16(2) of Reg 17/64 (JO 1964 586).
[52] ibid, Art 15(1).
[53] cf Reg 2511/69 (JO 1969 L318/1) laying down special measures for improving the production and marketing of Community citrus fruits, which provided for Guidance Section assistance to be granted within the framework of plans drawn up by Member States and approved by the Commission (ibid, Art 2).
[54] Resolution of 27 June 1966 (JO 1966 2427) on regional policy in the EEC, para 12.
[55] Bull EC, Supp 1/69.
[56] ibid, 11.
[57] Priebe, n 27 above, 5.
[58] Gadbin, n 14 above, 219.
[59] On the financing of the CAP (JO 1970 L94/13).
[60] ibid, Art 6(1).
[61] JO 1962 2892. Art 6(3) of Reg 729/70 (JO 1970 L94/13) referred to this Decision.
[62] On the application of the Resolution of 22 Mar concerning the realization, in stages, of EMU (JO 1972 C38/3), para 2.
[63] Council Resolution of 25 May 1971 (JO 1971 C52/1) on new guidelines for the CAP, para VII. Assistance for cessation, modernization, training, and marketing improvements was envisaged (ibid, para II).

The importance of such assistance was stressed by the Commission in *Stock-taking of the Common Agricultural Policy*.[64] According to the Commission, price support through the Guarantee Section could not, on its own, solve the income and standard-of-living problems associated with agriculture. On the contrary, disparities in farm incomes might well be increased, if the support was not accompanied by a dynamic socio-structural policy and effective regional and social policies. Such policies should entail socially acceptable schemes for the gradual laying-off of workers and the establishment of a general economic infrastructure by means of a resolute regional development policy.[65]

3.3.1 Objectives of Assistance

According to Article 1(3) of Regulation 729/70,[66] the Guidance Section was to finance common measures adopted to achieve the objectives in Article 39(1)(a) of the EEC Treaty, including structural adaptation necessary for the proper working of the common market. The adaptation of agricultural structures sought through these measures was considered a 'basic factor' in the development of the common agricultural policy.[67] At the same time, the Commission considered that regional policy should 'underpin policy on agricultural structures in the less developed rural areas'.[68]

The objectives of such assistance were refined by Regulation 797/85.[69] This Regulation was concerned with reforming the common agricultural policy,[70] tackling problems of surplus production,[71] and taking account of the environment.[72] According to Article 1(1) of the Regulation, Community assistance was to encourage the continuous development of agriculture. In particular, the assistance was to help to improve the efficiency of holdings and

[64] Bull EC, Supp 2/75, 36.

[65] Moreover, according to the Commission, all assistance to the forestry sector should seek, *inter alia*, to reduce regional disparities. See para 6 in Annex I to the draft Council Resolution concerning objectives and lines of action for Community regional policy regarding forestry and forest-based industries, COM(83)222, 53–59.

[66] JO 1970 L94/13.

[67] Case 152/79 *Kevin Lee v Minister for Agriculture* [1980] ECR 1495, 1505. Thus eg the assistance could not apply to the provision of a water supply with a view to the construction of dwelling-houses (ibid, 1506).

[68] Report and proposals on ways of increasing the effectiveness of the Community's Structural Funds, COM(83)501, Annex, 3.

[69] On improving the efficiency of agricultural structures (OJ 1985 L93/1).

[70] Priebe, n 27 above, 4 and 6.

[71] Note, in particular, the restrictions on assistance to products in surplus (Arts 3(2), (3), (4) and (5) of Reg 797/85, OJ 1985 L93/1). This consideration was given increased emphasis in Reg 1760/87 (OJ 1987 L167/1) amending Regs 797/85, 270/79, 1360/78, and 355/77 as regards agricultural structures, the adjustment of agriculture to the new market situation, and the preservation of the countryside.

[72] Art 1 of Reg 797/85 (OJ 1985 L93/1). See also the 12th recital in the preamble to Reg 1760/87 (OJ 1987 L167/1); and P Godin, 'Environment and the CAP' (1987) 219 *Green Europe*.

to develop their structures, while at the same time ensuring the permanent conservation of the natural resources of agriculture.

According to the preamble to the Regulation, such assistance was to contribute to the overall economic and social development of each region concerned.[73] It was asserted that only through assistance to improve the efficiency of agricultural structures, especially in regions suffering very serious problems, could the objectives in Article 39(1)(a) and (b) of the EEC Treaty be met.[74] Accordingly, the results of such assistance were to be evaluated by reference to their effect on the structural changes necessitated by the common agricultural policy and on the harmonious development of Community regions.[75]

Thus the emphasis in the new legislation was on facilitating reform of the common agricultural policy. According to *Perspectives for the Common Agricultural Policy*,[76] price and market rules should regulate supply and demand more efficiently. If they were to do so, unacceptable social consequences for the agricultural population had to be avoided. Indeed, avoidance measures might be seen as a condition of the legality of agricultural reforms.[77] Accordingly, assistance would, as far as possible, be linked with social, regional, and environmental factors rather than with production.[78]

3.3.2 Eligibility for Assistance

Initially, assistance under Regulation 729/70[79] might be limited to farmers capable of reaching at the end of a development programme an income level comparable to that of average non-agricultural workers.[80] This limitation reflected concern that the modernization of holdings could be jeopardized if, on the basis of social or regional considerations, assistance was granted to farmers with few development possibilities. If they were assisted, those with better possibilities would not be given enough incentive to undertake structural improvements. Hence, assistance should be limited to farms from which 'the best results [were] to be expected from the point of view of structural policy'.[81] A consequence was that assistance tended to be more readily available

[73] OJ 1985 L93/1, 8th recital in the preamble.
[74] ibid, 5th recital in the preamble.
[75] ibid, Art 29.
[76] COM(85)333, 49. See also 'Un avenir pour l'agriculture européenne: Les Orientations de la Commission' (1985) 34 *Europe Verte* (*notes rapides*).
[77] Case C–353/92 *Greece v EU Council: aid to producers of cereals* [1994] ECR I–3411, I–3448.
[78] E Guth, 'European Agricultural Policy: Is There Really No Alternative?' (1985) *Intereconomics* 3–9, 7. However, some reforms, such as stabilizers, might penalize those who had failed to catch up in the past. See M Cuddy, 'Community Policy and the Periphery' (1984) 32 *Administration* 147–162, 157.
[79] JO 1970 L94/13.
[80] Art 4(2) of Dir 72/159 (JO 1972 L96/1) on the modernization of farms.
[81] A-G Reischl in Case 121/78 *Giuseppe Bardi v Azienda Agricola Paradiso* [1979] ECR 221, 243.

in developed regions than in regions where agricultural structures were backward and overall economic imbalance existed.[82]

Recognition of this problem led to removal of this limitation to eligibility in later measures, such as Directive 75/268.[83]

3.3.3 Allocation of Assistance

The Commission drew up a draft regulation listing agricultural regions having priority for assistance pursuant to Regulation 729/70.[84] However, the draft was not adopted by the Council. As a result, Community legislation failed to ensure that regions with underdeveloped agricultural structures received assistance in proportion to the gravity of their structural problems.[85]

The Commission did publish criteria for the selection of projects[86] for the improvement of processing and marketing to be supported under Regulation 355/77.[87] These criteria were designed to ensure a 'harmonious distribution' of assistance between Member States.[88] The Commission also adopted unpublished 'internal rules' governing rates of assistance.[89] However, even these arrangements failed to ensure that the development of the local processing industry in the less favoured regions was encouraged.[90]

Besides, the assistance granted by the Guidance Section was only a small proportion of total Fund spending. Price-support measures, financed by the Guarantee Section, used as their direct reference the quantity produced and thus tended to favour large, productive farms.[91] Moreover, in general, comparatively developed northern regions of the Community, because of the composition of their agricultural production (cereals, milk, and sugar), benefited from a higher level of support from the Guarantee Section than southern regions. In the latter regions production of fruit, vegetables, and wine was dominant.[92] In 1989, for example, assistance from the Guarantee Section was

[82] Report of the Committee on Regional Policy, Regional Planning, and Transport on aspects of the Community's regional policy to be developed in the future, EP Doc 35/77, 49.

[83] See sect 3.3.4 below.

[84] Proposal of 11 Oct 1973 (OJ 1973 C106/23) for a regulation on the list of priority agricultural regions and areas referred to in the regulation on finance from the Guidance Section of the EAGGF for projects falling within development programmes in priority agricultural regions.

[85] *Second Report on the ERDF* (EC Commission, Brussels, 1977) 46.

[86] OJ 1983 C152/2; OJ 1985 C78/7; OJ 1987 C79/3.

[87] On common measures to improve the conditions under which agricultural products were processed and marketed (OJ 1977 L51/1).

[88] Priebe, n 27 above, 24.

[89] Case 15/85 *Consorzio Cooperative d'Abruzzo v EC Commission* [1987] ECR 1005.

[90] Cuddy, n 78 above.

[91] ESC Opinion of 27 Nov 1991 (OJ 1992 C40/56) on the development and future of the CAP, para 2.7.2.

[92] First periodic report on the social and economic situation of the regions of the Community, COM(80)816, 73. See, regarding the failure of the Guarantee Section to promote regional equality, *The Regional Impact of Community Policies* (Regional Policy and Transport Series No 17; European Parliament, Luxembourg, 1991) 11. See, earlier, the *Study on the Regional Effects of the Common Agricultural Policy* (Regional Policy Series No 21; EC Commission, Brussels, 1981).

ECU 3,751 million for the Netherlands, where 4.7 per cent of the working population were engaged in agriculture. Only ECU 174 million was granted to Portugal, where 20.7 per cent of the population were so engaged.[93] Hence, the impact of the Guidance Section was outweighed by the general tendency of the common agricultural policy to perpetuate, if not exacerbate, regional inequality.[94] At the same time, additionality requirements[95] meant that assistance from this Section was, in practice, more accessible to Member States with strong economies and administrative organization.[96]

The Committee on Regional Policy and Regional Planning concluded that the Guidance Section needed to be radically strengthened. Only then could the structural changes which would make it possible to reorganize and modernize farms instead of abandoning them be effected.[97]

3.3.4 Scope of Assistance

Assistance was initially provided pursuant to 'horizontal' measures, which were designed to assist agricultural development throughout the Community. However, recognition of the inadequacy of these measures for structural purposes led to the gradual adoption of various measures designed to target assistance more effectively.

Modernization

Directive 72/159[98] provided for assistance to farmers whose incomes were below average non-agricultural earnings to modernize and so increase their income to at least a comparable level. The purpose of this Directive was to initiate reform of agricultural structures.[99] Thus, according to the fifth recital in the preamble, the assistance was to concern the formation and development of farms capable of adjusting to economic developments. Such farms were those: where the farmer had adequate occupational skill and competence; where profitability was verified by accounts; and where the adoption of rational methods of production would ensure a fair income and satisfactory working conditions.

Directive 73/440[100] allowed for regional differentiation of such assistance. It provided that a Member State might refrain from applying some or all of

[93] ESC Opinion of 25 May 1992 (OJ 1992 C106/20) on the annual report on the implementation of the reform of the Structural Funds.

[94] cf the ESC Opinion of 24 Oct 1979 (OJ 1980 C53/22) on the proposals on policy with regard to agricultural structures, para 1.3.

[95] sect 1.3 above.

[96] Priebe, n 27 above, 23 n 81.

[97] Report on the seventh annual report on the ERDF, EP Doc 1–768/83, 31.

[98] On the modernization of farms (JO 1972 L96/1).

[99] Case 107/80 *Giacomo Cattaneo Adorno v EC Commission* [1981] ECR 1469, 1486.

[100] On the general provisions for the regional differentiation of certain measures provided for in the Directives of 17 Apr 1972 on the reform of agriculture (OJ 1973 L356/85).

the measures envisaged in Directive 72/159.[101] However, it might do so only in those regions where a major part of the agricultural industry had already attained the objective of comparable income, or where land hitherto exploited for agricultural purposes was intended for other uses.[102]

Early retirement

Directive 72/160[103] sought to assist withdrawals from farming. It provided for the grant of an annuity or a lump sum to farmers aged between 55 and 65 years who took early retirement.[104] Special subsectoral schemes, such as assistance for cessation of milk production, might also be introduced.[105]

Vocational training

Directive 72/161[106] provided for the grant of assistance for: socio-economic guidance for the agricultural population;[107] acquisition of occupational skills by persons engaged in agriculture;[108] and, pending implementation of European Social Fund arrangements,[109] vocational retraining of persons engaged in agriculture who wished to take up an occupation outside agriculture.[110] This measure followed the Council Resolution of 25 May 1971[111] on new guidelines for the common agricultural policy. This Resolution called for the Member States and the Commission to assist the creation of new jobs in regions highly dependent on agricultural employment.[112]

However, without systematic efforts to promote the development of the region concerned, assistance under Directive 72/161 might have only a limited impact. Farmers could only move to jobs outside agriculture, if new jobs were created. In regions with a surplus of agricultural workers the most urgent need was for sectoral diversification. This need could not be satisfied adequately through a Directive adopted under the agricultural structural policy. At the same time, assistance under the Directive might run counter to efforts to maintain farming in difficult natural conditions.[113]

[101] JO 1972 L96/1.

[102] Similar requirements applied regarding regional differentiation of the application of Dirs 72/160 and 72/161 (see below).

[103] Concerning measures to encourage the cessation of farming and the reallocation of utilized agricultural areas for the purposes of structural improvement (JO 1972 L96/9).

[104] ibid, Art 2. Such assistance is now provided by the Guarantee Section of the EAGGF. See sect 5.6.2 below.

[105] Reg 1336/86 (OJ 1986 L119/21) fixing compensation for the definitive discontinuation of milk production.

[106] Concerning the provision of socio-economic guidance for persons engaged in agriculture and their acquisition of occupational skills (JO 1972 L96/15).

[107] ibid, Arts 1–4.

[108] ibid, Arts 5–6.

[109] Before new legislation came into force, the ESF could only assist vocational retraining of persons who were unemployed or whose companies were undergoing restructuring. See sect 4.3.2 below.

[110] Art 7 of Dir 72/161 (JO 1972 L96/15).

[111] JO 1971 C52/1.

[112] ibid, para VII.

[113] COA special report on the application of Dir 75/268 (OJ 1980 C358/1), para 3.1.1.

In recognition of the former problem the Commission proposed a specific allocation of assistance from the Fund over a five-year period to finance the creation of non-farming jobs in predominantly agricultural regions.[114] The aim was to support the creation of jobs outside agriculture which could be taken up by those who ceased agricultural work, and their descendants.[115] However, the proposal was not accepted by the Council.[116]

Preservation of farming under unfavourable natural conditions

Article 42(a) of the EEC Treaty[117] provided that the Council might authorize assistance for farmers handicapped by structural or natural conditions.[118] In accordance with this provision, Directive 75/268[119] was enacted. The objective of this Directive was to ensure the continuation of farming. A minimum population level or the conservation of the countryside in three categories of regions was thereby to be maintained.[120]

First, the Directive applied to mountain areas suffering from permanent natural handicaps. These were handicaps mainly associated with very difficult climatic conditions, the slope of the land, and a short growing season. They led to high production costs.[121] Secondly, less favoured areas in danger of depopulation were covered. These were areas where conservation of the countryside was necessary and which suffered from three disadvantages: infertility, a poor economic situation, and a low or declining population dependent on agriculture.[122] Finally, other areas affected by specific handicaps were covered. These included areas in which farming had to be continued: to ensure the conservation of the environment, to maintain the countryside, to preserve the tourist potential of the area, or to protect the coastline.[123]

According to the Economic and Social Committee, selection of the areas covered should be sufficiently flexible to take account of socio-economic and demographic changes. It should not, argued the Committee, be an immutable rule that 'less favoured areas' must suffer from both a low population density and unfavourable production conditions. Moreover, the criteria used should take account of the fact that poor land was taken out of farming more quickly in, for instance, more densely populated areas, although farming should con-

[114] Proposal of 28 May 1971 (JO 1971 C90/19) on the financing by the Guidance Section of the EAGGF of projects included within the framework of regional development operations in priority agricultural regions.

[115] ibid, Art 1.

[116] The Council was willing to do no more than adopt Reg 725/75 (OJ 1975 L73/8) on the transfer to the ERDF of UA 150 million out of the appropriations held in reserve by the Guidance Section of the EAGGF.

[117] Now Art 36(a) EC.

[118] See, more particularly, Reg 3606/86 (OJ 1986 L335/3) establishing a special emergency measure for the less favoured areas in Ireland; and Reg 1654/86 (OJ 1986 L145/13) introducing a common measure for replanting and converting olive groves damaged by frost in 1985 in certain regions of the Community, which was a common measure 'of an exceptional nature'.

[119] On mountain and hill farming and farming in less favoured areas (OJ 1975 L128/1).

[120] ibid, Art 1. [121] ibid, Art 3(3). [122] ibid, Art 3(4). [123] ibid, Art 3(5).

tinue there on environmental grounds.[124] However, the broadening of the availability of assistance sought by such arguments might encounter objections by reference to competition-policy requirements.[125]

Where assistance was available, it might take the form of a compensatory allowance.[126] It might also take the form of: development assistance,[127] including assistance for the development of a tourist or craft industry,[128] for which farmers would be ineligible under Directive 72/159;[129] assistance for joint investment schemes for fodder production and for improvement and equipment schemes for pasture and hill grazing land which was farmed jointly;[130] and investment assistance for farmers not capable of attaining the level of earned income required under Directive 72/159.[131]

Such assistance might be problematic. For example, the compensatory allowance might lead to the overstocking of mountain areas with sheep and, hence, to severe environmental damage.[132] At the same time, it did not necessarily preserve rural populations, since the recipient need not live on the farm.[133]

Moreover, in so far as such assistance simply reduced the costs of farmers, it might tend to reinforce distortions of competition associated with the common agricultural policy generally.[134] More particularly, assistance designed to compensate for permanent natural handicaps had itself to be permanent. It thus amounted to the kind of 'operating aid' to which the Commission in the application of competition policy was opposed.[135]

Improvement of processing and marketing

Regulation 355/77[136] provided for assistance to projects to improve the processing and marketing of agricultural products.[137] Projects had to contribute to improving the situation of the basic agricultural production sector in

[124] Opinion of 30 Jan 1975 (OJ 1975 C62/19) on the proposals for a directive completing the provisions under Title V of the Directive on mountain and hill farming and farming in certain less favoured areas; and for directives concerning the Community list of less favoured farming areas within the meaning of that Directive, para 6.

[125] J-V Schrader, 'EC Agricultural and Regional Policy: Consistent Interventions or Cumulative Inconsistencies' (1989) *Intereconomics* 167–173, 172.

[126] OJ 1975 L128/1, Arts 5–7.

[127] ibid, Arts 8–10.

[128] ibid, Art 10(2).

[129] JO 1972 L96/1.

[130] Art 11 of Dir 75/268 (OJ 1975 L128/1).

[131] ibid, Art 12.

[132] COA annual report for 1996 (OJ 1997 C348/1), para 8.46.

[133] Though Member States have discretion to impose a residence requirement on the recipient. See Joined Cases C–9 & 118/97 *Raija-Liisa Jokela and Laura Pitkäranta* [22 Oct 1998].

[134] COA annual report for 1996 (OJ 1997 C348/1), para 8.46.

[135] A Evans, *EC Law of State Aid* (Oxford EC Law Series; Clarendon Press, Oxford, 1997).

[136] OJ 1977 L51/1.

[137] See eg Reg 3974/86 (OJ 1986 L370/9) on the rationalization and improvement of health conditions in slaughterhouses in Belgium.

question[138] and to have a lasting beneficial effect on agriculture.[139] Moreover, they had to guarantee the producers of the basic agricultural product an adequate and lasting share of the resulting economic benefits.[140]

Priority was accorded to projects which would: guide production in a direction sought by the common agricultural policy or involve development of new outlets for agricultural production, particularly through the manufacturing of new products; lighten the burden on the intervention mechanisms of the common organization of the markets by meeting a need for structural improvement in the long term; assist regions experiencing particular difficulty in adjusting to the common agricultural policy, or benefit such regions;[141] shorten or improve the marketing channels for agricultural products or rationalize the method of processing such products; or contribute to improvement of the quality, presentation, and market preparation of products or the better use of by-products, in particular by the recycling of waste.[142]

Development of producer groups

Assistance for producer groups was introduced by Regulation 1360/78.[143] Such assistance was to remedy the structural deficiencies affecting the supply and marketing of agricultural products in certain regions of France, Belgium, and Italy. These deficiencies resulted from the absence of sufficient producer groups in the regions concerned. In these regions the market tended to be supplied by many holdings which were uneconomically small.[144]

Special arrangements for assistance of this kind were also made in certain sectors, such as hops,[145] fruit and vegetables,[146] cotton,[147] and fisheries.[148]

[138] ibid, Art 9(1). Agricultural structures might be indirectly altered. Cf AG Roemer in Joined Cases 10 & 18/68 *Società 'Eridania' Zuccherifici Nazionali v EC Commission* [1969] ECR 459, 495.

[139] 8th recital in the preamble to Reg 355/77 (OJ 1977 L51/1).

[140] They could be undertaken by the producers themselves. See Case 107/80 *Giacomo Cattaneo Adorno v EC Commission* [1981] ECR 1469, 1485.

[141] Art 17(2)(c) of Reg 355/77 (OJ 1977 L51/1) provided for a higher level of assistance to be granted in the case of such projects.

[142] ibid, Art 11(1).

[143] On producer groups and associations thereof (OJ 1978 L166/1).

[144] AG Jacobs in Case 77/88 *Stute Nahrungsmittelwerke GmbH & Co KG v Germany* [1989] ECR 1755, 1770. It was unclear whether non-producers were excluded from assistance. See ibid, regarding Art 3a of Reg 516/77 (OJ 1977 L73/1) on the common organization of the market in products processed from fruit and vegetables.

[145] Reg 1696/71 (JO 1971 L175/1) on the common organization of the market in hops.

[146] Reg 1035/72 (JO 1972 L118/1) on the common organization of the market in fruit and vegetables, Arts 14 and 36. See, now, Arts 14 and 15(6) of Reg 2200/96 (OJ 1996 L297/1) on the common organization of the market in fruit and vegetables; and Reg 411/97 (OJ 1997 L62/9) laying down detailed rules for the application of Reg 2200/96 as regards operational programmes, operational funds, and Community financial assistance.

[147] Reg 389/82 (OJ 1982 L51/1) on producer groups and associations thereof in the cotton sector. See also Greek requests in the cotton sector, COM(98)10.

[148] Reg 2142/70 (JO 1970 L236/5), Arts 6 and 22; Reg 100/76 (OJ 1976 L20/1), Arts 6 and 24; Reg 3796/81 (OJ 1981 L379/1), Arts 13 and 26; and Reg 3759/92 (OJ 1992 L388/1), Art 7b. The assistance is now provided by the FIFG. See sect 5.2 below.

Infrastructure improvement

Regulation 1760/78[149] provided for assistance to improve public amenities in rural areas of France and Italy. The areas had to suffer from infrastructural deficiencies. They also had to be covered by Directive 75/268[150] or be situated in the Mezzogiorno.

The assistance was extended to the West of Ireland by Article 4 of Regulation 1820/80,[151] to regions of Germany by Article 2 of Regulation 1938/81,[152] to Northern Ireland by Article 4 of Regulation 1942/81,[153] and to Greece by Article 4 of Regulation 1975/82.[154]

Regional development

Assistance might be granted for agricultural improvements in particular regions.[155] For example, assistance was granted for: the restructuring and conversion of vineyards in certain Mediterranean regions of France;[156] improving the rearing of beef cattle in certain less favoured areas of northern France;[157] a flood-protection programme in the Hérault Valley;[158] agricultural development in the French overseas departments;[159] irrigation in Corsica;[160] collective irrigation operations in the Mezzogiorno;[161] agricultural development in less favoured regions of northern Italy;[162] the development of agricultural advisory services in Italy;[163] the adaptation and modernization of the structure of production of beef and veal, sheepmeat,

[149] On a common measure to improve public amenities in certain rural areas (OJ 1978 L204/1).

[150] OJ 1975 L128/1.

[151] For the stimulation of agricultural development in the less favoured areas of the West of Ireland (OJ 1980 L180/1).

[152] On a common measure to improve public amenities in certain less favoured agricultural areas of Germany (OJ 1981 L197/1).

[153] For the stimulation of agricultural development in the less favoured areas of Northern Ireland (OJ 1981 L197/17).

[154] On the acceleration of agricultural development in certain regions of Greece (OJ 1982 L214/1).

[155] See, generally, Proposals on policy with regard to agricultural structures, COM(79)122.

[156] Dir 78/627 (OJ 1978 L206/1) on the programme to accelerate the restructuring and conversion of vineyards in certain Mediterranean regions in France.

[157] Reg 1400/86 (OJ 1986 L128/1) introducing a common measure for the encouragement of agriculture by improving the rearing of beef cattle in certain less favoured areas of France.

[158] Dir 79/174 (OJ 1979 L38/18) concerning the flood-protection programme in the Hérault Valley.

[159] Dir 81/527 (OJ 1981 L197/38) on the development of agriculture in the French overseas departments.

[160] Dir 79/173 (OJ 1979 L38/15) on the programme for the acceleration and guidance of collective irrigation works in Corsica.

[161] Reg 1362/78 (OJ 1978 L166/11) on the programme for the acceleration and guidance of collective irrigation works in the Mezzogiorno.

[162] Reg 1401/86 (OJ 1986 L128/5) introducing a common action for the encouragement of agriculture in certain less favoured areas of northern Italy.

[163] Reg 270/79 (OJ 1979 L38/6) on the development of agricultural advisory services in Italy.

and goatmeat in Italy;[164] a special emergency measure to assist stock farming in Italy;[165] agricultural development in certain Greek regions;[166] the seasonal transfer of sheep, goats, and cattle for grazing in Greece;[167] increasing the staff of the departments responsible for quality control of agricultural products in Greece;[168] improvement of the structures of the wine-making sector in Greece;[169] irrigation in Greece;[170] vine-growing in Portugal;[171] drainage operations in Ireland;[172] the development of sheep farming in Greenland;[173] agricultural development on Scottish islands;[174] agricultural development in the less favoured areas of Northern Ireland;[175] and improvement of the processing and marketing conditions in the cattlefeed sector in Northern Ireland.[176]

Sub-sectoral development

Assistance was granted for the development of various 'sub-sectors'. For example, assistance was granted for the restructuring of vineyards;[177] conversion from wine production to other activities;[178] abandonment of wine production;[179] early

[164] Reg 1944/81 (OJ 1981 L197/27) establishing a common measure for the adaptation and modernization of the structure of production of beef and veal, sheepmeat, and goatmeat in Italy.

[165] Reg 2969/83 (OJ 1983 L293/7) establishing a special emergency measure to assist stock farming in Italy.

[166] Reg 1975/82 (OJ 1982 L214/1) on the acceleration of agricultural development in certain regions of Greece.

[167] Reg 764/85 (OJ 1985 L86/4) introducing aid for the transhumance of sheep, goats, and cattle in Greece.

[168] Reg 765/85 (OJ 1985 L86/5) on increasing the staff of the departments responsible for quality control of agricultural products in Greece.

[169] Reg 895/85 (OJ 1985 L97/2) on a common measure to improve the structures of the wine-making sector in Greece.

[170] Reg 2968/83 (OJ 1983 L293/5) introducing a common measure for the acceleration of collective irrigation operations in Greece.

[171] Reg 2239/86 (OJ 1986 L196/1) on a specific common measure to improve vine-growing in Portugal.

[172] Dir 78/628 (OJ 1978 L206/5) on a programme to accelerate drainage operations in the less favoured areas of the West of Ireland.

[173] Reg 1821/80 (OJ 1980 L180/9) on the development of sheep farming in Greenland.

[174] Reg 1402/86 (OJ 1986 L128/9) introducing a common action for the encouragement of agriculture in the Scottish islands off the northern and western coasts with the exception of the Western Isles (Outer Hebrides).

[175] Reg 1942/81 (OJ 1981 L197/17) for the stimulation of agricultural development in the less favoured areas of Northern Ireland.

[176] Reg 1943/81 (OJ 1981 L197/23) on a common measure to improve the processing and marketing conditions in the cattlefeed sector in Northern Ireland.

[177] Reg 458/80 (OJ 1980 L57/27) on collective projects for the restructuring of vineyards.

[178] Reg 1163/76 (OJ 1976 L135/34) on the granting of a conversion premium in the wine sector.

[179] Reg 456/80 (OJ 1980 L57/16) on the granting of temporary and permanent abandonment premiums in respect of certain areas under vines and of premiums for the renunciation of replanting; Reg 777/85 (OJ 1985 L88/8) granting for the 1985/6 to 1989/90 wine years of permanent abandonment premiums in respect of certain areas under vines; and Reg 1442/88 (OJ 1988 L132/3) on the granting for the 1988/89 to 1995/96 wine years of permanent abandonment premiums in respect of wine-growing areas, which involved joint financing by both Sections of the EAGGF.

retirement from wine production;[180] and conversion from dairy to beef production.[181]

Measures were also adopted for the fishing industry. In particular, Regulation 1852/78[182] provided for assistance to the development of inshore fishing in regions where fishing potential made this possible. It also provided for assistance to the development of aquaculture in regions which were particularly suited to this activity.[183] Regulation 2908/83[184] went further. It introduced a common measure for restructuring, modernizing, and developing the fishing industry and for developing aquaculture. It was designed to meet the objectives set out in Article 39(1)(a) of the EEC Treaty. Accordingly, the Guidance Section was to finance projects within the framework of multiannual guidance programmes, designed to achieve a satisfactory balance between fishing capacity and fish stocks. In respect of aquaculture, it was to finance projects designed to achieve a substantial and economically profitable volume of production of fish, crustaceans, or molluscs.[185]

Further measures were adopted for forestry development.[186] For example, Regulation 269/79[187] provided for assistance to Mediterranean forestry. The assistance was to contribute to 'the conservation and improvement of the soil, the fauna, the flora, and the surface and groundwater balance'. It was also to contribute to 'the productivity of agricultural land by forming windbreaks and shelter belts and by affecting local water and weather conditions'.[188]

The linking of forestry development and regional development might, in the light of a Council Resolution of 1971,[189] be sought in measures relating to particular regions. For example, assistance to forestry development was provided for in Regulation 1820/80,[190] which was concerned with agricultural development in the less favoured areas of the West of Ireland.

[180] Reg 457/80 (OJ 1980 L57/23) establishing a system of premiums for the cessation of winegrowing in France and Italy.

[181] Reg 1353/73 (OJ 1973 L141/18) introducing a premium system for the conversion of dairy-cow herds to meat production and a development premium for the specialized raising of cattle for meat production. See also Reg 1078/77 (OJ 1977 L131/1) (OJ 1977 L313/1) introducing a system of premiums for the non-marketing of milk products and for the conversion of dairy herds.

[182] On an interim common measure for restructuring the inshore fishing industry (OJ 1978 L211/30).

[183] ibid, Art 1(1). Cf the proposal of 28 Nov 1975 (OJ 1976 C6/2) for a regulation on a programme for restructuring the non-industrial inshore fishing industry; and the amended proposal of 12 June 1978 (OJ 1978 C148/4) for a regulation on a common interim measure for restructuring the inshore fishing industry, Art 7(b).

[184] OJ 1983 L290/1.

[185] ibid, Art 3.

[186] *Forestry Policy in the EC*, Bull EC, Supp 3/79; and Community action programme regarding forestry and forest-based industries, COM(83)222, 48 and 51.

[187] Establishing a common measure for forestry in certain Mediterranean zones of the Community (OJ 1979 L38/1).

[188] ibid, 9th recital in the preamble.

[189] Resolution of 25 May 1971 (JO 1971 C52/1) on the new guidelines for the CAP, part III.

[190] For the stimulation of agricultural development in the less favoured areas of the West of Ireland (OJ 1980 L180/1), Arts 12 and 13.

However, assistance directed specifically towards forestry might entail a potential misuse of land, which might not benefit the overall efficiency of the industry. The assistance permitted marketing of timber below cost and in increased supply, thus reducing profitability and willingness to invest. Such willingness was in any case already affected by inadequate information in the market. Even if the assistance did promote efficiency, it would do little to sustain rural communities. Hence, it was argued that intervention in forestry should be primarily directed towards the protection of non-marketed benefits, such as environmental protection, the diversity of plant and animal species, and recreational services. However, in some cases, such as in the case of forest wetlands or where the introduction of fast-growing species was assisted, there might be a conflict between environmental protection and forestry development.[191]

Agricultural structures

Under Regulation 797/85[192] assistance might be granted to: investments in agricultural holdings;[193] the installation of young farmers;[194] other measures to assist agricultural holdings, such as the introduction of the keeping of accounts[195] and the establishment and operation of groups, services, and other facilities for the benefit of several undertakings;[196] specific measures to assist mountain and hill farming and farming in certain less favoured areas;[197] specific regional measures;[198] forestry measures on agricultural holdings;[199] adjustment of vocational training to the requirements of modern agriculture;[200] set-aside of arable land;[201] extensification;[202] conversion to production of non-surplus products;[203] and assistance to environmentally friendly farming in environmentally sensitive areas.[204]

191 S Wibe, 'Policy Failures in Managing Forests' in *Market and Government Failures in Environmental Management: Wetlands and Forests* (OECD, Paris, 1992) 45–82, 78.

192 OJ 1985 L93/1. Reg 870/85 (OJ 1985 L95/1) amending Reg 729/70 established the principle that there should be a five-year financial framework for the Guidance Section and allocated ECU 5,250 million for 1985–89.

193 Arts 2–6 and 8 of Reg 797/85 (OJ 1985 L93/1).

194 ibid, Art 7.

195 ibid, Art 9.

196 ibid, Arts 10–12.

197 ibid, Arts 13–17.

198 ibid, Art 18.

199 ibid, Art 20. See also Art 15(3) (ibid), in connection with continuation of compensatory allowances after afforestation in regions covered by Dir 75/268 (OJ 1975 L128/1).

200 Arts 21–22 of Reg 797/85 (OJ 1985 L93/1).

201 ibid, Art 1a, as introduced by Reg 1094/88 (OJ 1988 L106/28) amending Regs 797/85 and 1760/87 as regards the set-aside of arable land and the extensification and conversion of production.

202 Art 1b of Reg 797/85 (OJ 1985 L93/1), as introduced by Reg 1760/87 (OJ 1987 L167/1) and amended by Reg 1094/88 (OJ 1988 L106/28). Extensification consists in the reduction of the normal output of a holding. See Case C–255/95 *S Agri SNC and Agricola Veneta Sas v Regione Veneto* [1997] ECR I–25, I–53.

203 Art 1c of Reg 797/85 (OJ 1985 L93/1), as introduced by Reg 1094/88 (OJ 1988 L106/28).

204 Art 19 of Reg 797/85 (OJ 1985 L93/1), as amended by Reg 1760/87 (OJ 1987 L167/1).

3.3.5 Forms of Assistance

The forms of assistance evolved along with changes in the scope of assistance.

Common measures

According to Article 6(1) of Regulation 729/70,[205] assistance was to be provided in the form of 'common measures', adopted by the Council. When adopting such a measure, the Council was to determine: the objective to be attained and the nature of the projects to be assisted; the contribution of the Fund to the common measure; the estimated total cost of the common measure and the estimated time for its execution; the economic and financial conditions; and the necessary provisions concerning procedure.[206]

For example, Regulation 1820/80[207] introduced a common measure to stimulate the development of agriculture in the West of Ireland. According to the preamble to this Regulation, achievement of the objectives set out in Article 39(1)(a) and (b) of the EEC Treaty required the provision of assistance appropriate to the production conditions of less favoured areas.[208] The measure was to bring about a significant improvement in agricultural structures and in agricultural-production possibilities in the areas concerned.[209] To this end, assistance was to be provided for: the improvement of public amenities in rural areas; land improvement; the introduction of specific development action aimed at the orientation of farm production; the improvement of processing and marketing facilities; forestry development; and the provision of training facilities and specialized support services. All assistance granted was to fall within the framework of the regional development programme for Ireland.[210]

Specific programmes

Regulation 355/77[211] provided for common measures to take the form of 'specific programmes'. The programmes had to ensure a coherent improvement in the processing and marketing of agricultural products. They also had to contain a detailed analysis of the situation in the sector and of the improvements proposed.[212]

In particular, the programmes were to provide at least the following information: a definition of the geographical area and of the sector covered by the programme and the reasons for this definition; the initial situation and

205 JO 1970 L94/13.
206 ibid, Art 6(2).
207 For the stimulation of agricultural development in the less favoured areas of the West of Ireland (OJ 1980 L180/1).
208 ibid, 6th recital in the preamble.
209 ibid, Art 1(1).
210 Reg 1030/88 (OJ 1988 L102/1) amending Reg 1820/80 extended this measure to all the less favoured areas of Ireland for the purposes of Dir 75/268.
211 OJ 1977 L51/1.
212 ibid, 7th recital in the preamble.

the trends which might be inferred from it; the needs to be met by the programme; the economic importance of the programme for the products concerned and the implications of the programme for agricultural undertakings in the region concerned; the means proposed for achieving the objectives of the programme; the relationship of the programme to any other measures to encourage the harmonious development of the region in question; and the estimated time required for the execution of the programme, which in principle was not to be more than three to five years.[213]

Specific common measures

Article 18 of Regulation 797/85[214] provided for common measures to take the form of 'specific common measures'. Such measures might be adopted to help remove the structural or infrastructural handicaps suffered by agriculture in certain regions. They were to encourage agriculture in the regions concerned. At the same time, they were to 'harmonize' with any development schemes simultaneously undertaken in non-agricultural sectors and with the needs of the environment.[215] By doing so, they were expected to improve the efficiency of agricultural structures in the regions concerned.[216]

For example, Regulation 1118/88[217] introduced a specific common measure to encourage the development of agriculture in certain regions of Spain. It aimed to bring about a significant improvement in agricultural structures. It sought to do so through reducing production costs and maintaining agriculture in the regions concerned, which all faced major socio-structural handicaps, without favouring surplus production.[218] It was to cover the less favoured areas of Spain within the meaning of Directive 75/268.[219] Assistance concerned: the improvement of the agricultural infrastructure; irrigation works; the reparcelling of agricultural land; improvement of privately owned farmland as part of an overall scheme; forestry; and the improvement of farm housing.[220]

Integrated development programmes

Since agricultural development depended on the integration of farming into the economy as a whole,[221] such development could not be achieved through assistance to agriculture alone. The implication was that assistance from the Guidance Section had to be complemented by the operations of other

[213] OJ 1977 L51/1 Art 3(1).
[214] OJ 1985 L93/1.
[215] See also the explanatory memorandum to the proposals for regulations establishing a common measure for the acceleration of agricultural development in certain less favoured areas of France where beef cattle were reared; a common action for the promotion of agriculture in certain less favoured areas of northern Italy; and a common action for the promotion of agriculture in the Scottish islands off the northern and western coasts with the exception of the Western Isles, COM(85)759, 1–3.
[216] 23rd recital in the preamble to Reg 797/85 (OJ 1985 L93/1).
[217] OJ 1988 L107/3.
[218] ibid, Art 1(1).
[219] ibid, Art 1(2).
[220] ibid, Art 2.
[221] *Adjustment of the CAP*, Bull EC, Supp 4/83, 6.

Structural Funds. This implication was recognized by the adoption of integrated development programmes. Such programmes were seen by the European Parliament as a means of countering the tendency of expenditure by the Guarantee Section to favour the richer, more productive regions at the centre of the Community.[222] They were adopted for the Western Isles of Scotland,[223] Lozère,[224] and the less favoured regions of Belgium.[225]

For example, according to Article 2 of Regulation 1939/81,[226] the integrated development programme for the Western Isles was to cover not only measures to improve agriculture, including the afforestation of marginal land, operations to improve the marketing and processing of agricultural products, and measures to develop fisheries. It was also to cover measures relating to tourist amenities, crafts, industrial activities, and other complementary activities essential to the improvement of the general socio-economic situation of the Isles. Article 3(2) stipulated that all such measures had to fall within the framework of a regional development programme formulated according to Article 6 of Regulation 724/75,[227] as amended by Regulation 214/79.[228] The Guidance Section was to assist measures forming part of the programme and concerning: the improvement of the structure of agricultural production, excluding premiums granted on a unit-of-production basis; the planting of windbreaks for the protection of agriculture; operations for improving the marketing and processing of agricultural products; the improvement of the agricultural infrastructure; investments in landing-stages and other shore facilities for the inshore fisheries industry; and the development of aquaculture.[229] By assisting such measures the Guidance Section would supplement measures supported by the European Regional Development Fund and the European Social Fund.

Integrated development programmes might also involve assistance to forestry. For example, Regulation 1940/81[230] provided for assistance under the programme for Lozère for renovation of chestnut plantations intended for the production of sweet chestnuts.[231] Similarly, the fishing industry might benefit, as under the programme for the Western Isles of Scotland.[232]

These programmes aimed to ensure that agricultural structural measures and assistance from other Structural Funds were mutually supportive.[233]

222 Resolution of 17 Nov 1983 (OJ 1983 C342/88) on ways of increasing the effectiveness of the Community's structural funds, especially that of the EAGGF, Guidance Section, para 6.

223 Reg 1939/81 (OJ 1981 L197/6) establishing an IDP for the Western Isles of Scotland (Outer Hebrides).

224 Reg 1940/81 (OJ 1981 L197/9) on an IDP for the Department of Lozère.

225 Reg 1941/81 (OJ 1981 L197/13) on an IDP for the less favoured areas of Belgium.

226 OJ 1981 L197/6.

227 Establishing an ERDF (OJ 1975 L73/1).

228 OJ 1979 L35/1.

229 Art 5 of Reg 1939/81 (OJ 1981 L197/6).

230 OJ 1981 L197/1.

231 ibid, Art 5(1).

232 OJ 1981 L197/6.

233 See, regarding difficulties of co-ordination, the Report of the Committee on Agriculture on aspects of the Community's regional policy to be developed in the future, EP Doc 35/77, annex, 48–50.

However, achievement of this aim implied the need for redefinition of the tasks of the three Structural Funds. This need could not be met solely by adoption of an integrated programme.[234]

3.4 COHESION

The tasks of the Guidance Section are now, according to Article 3(3) of Regulation 2081/93:[235] strengthening and reorganizing agricultural and forestry structures, including those for the marketing and processing of agricultural and forestry products; helping to offset the effects of natural handicaps on agriculture; ensuring the conversion of agricultural production and fostering the development of supplementary activities for farmers; helping to ensure a fair standard of living for farmers; and helping to develop the social fabric of rural areas, to safeguard the environment, and to preserve the countryside by securing, *inter alia*, the conservation of natural agricultural resources.[236] These tasks are to be performed in pursuit of Objective 5a as well as Objectives 1 and 5b. Actions under Objective 5a and Objective 5b are intended to be complementary.[237]

It has been proposed by the Commission that assistance from the Guidance Section should in future be limited to pursuit of Objective 1 and to regions covered by this Objective.[238] The abolition of Objective 5a (as well as Objective 5b) is entailed. A greater contribution from agricultural spending to 'territorial development' and nature protection is sought through these proposed reforms.[239]

[234] COA special report 2/88 (OJ 1988 C188/1) on the integrated approach to Community financing of structural measures.

[235] Amending Reg 2052/88 on the tasks of the Structural Funds and their effectiveness and on the co-ordination of their activities between themselves and with the operations of the EIB and the other existing financial instruments (OJ 1993 L193/5).

[236] The European Parliament had proposed the creation of Objective 5c, which would have been concerned with conservation of the environment and continuation of farming in certain mountain and less favoured regions. See the Report of the Committee on Regional Policy and Regional Planning on the amended proposal for a regulation on the tasks of the structural funds and their effectiveness and on co-ordination of their activities between themselves and with the operations of the EIB and the other existing financial instruments, EP Doc A2–58/88, 6.

[237] Fourth periodic report on the social and economic situation and the development of the regions of the Community, COM(90)609, 55. See also Report on the EAGGF Guidance Section 1992, COM(94)261.

[238] Proposal of 19 Mar 1998 (OJ 1998 C176/1) for a regulation laying down provisions on the Structural Funds, Art 2(2).

[239] Explanatory memorandum to the Proposal of 19 Mar 1998 for a regulation laying down provisions on the Structural Funds, COM(98)131, 32.

3.4.1 Objective 5a

Objective 5a is promoting rural development by speeding up the adjustment of agricultural structures in the framework of the reform of the common agricultural policy. It is the responsibility of the Guidance Section of the Fund, though the Financial Instrument for Fisheries Guidance has now become responsible for fisheries.[240] In practice, this Objective is said to have been designed to compensate farmers for reduced price-support from the Guarantee Section.[241]

Eligibility for assistance

Where the Guidance Section provides assistance in pursuit of Objective 5a, eligibility depends on the functional requirements of the 'common measures' concerned.[242]

Allocation of assistance

Indicative allocations of assistance are made. They are based on the need for continuity[243] regarding the use of resources in the previous programming period and the specific structural needs of agriculture.[244]

Scope of assistance

In pursuit of Objective 5a, assistance may be provided for: market-policy accompanying measures contributing to re-establishing a balance between production and market capacity; measures to support farm incomes and to maintain viable agricultural communities in mountain, hill, or less favoured areas, such as compensation for natural handicaps; and measures to encourage the installation of young farmers. Provision for assistance to such measures implicitly confirms the rejection of the market mechanism as a resource-allocation device implicit in traditional arrangements for the grant of assistance by the Guidance Section. Other measures are aimed in part at assisting adjustment in a declining sector. They include equally traditional

[240] Art 2(1) of Reg 2080/93 (OJ 1993 L193/1) laying down provisions for implementing Reg 2052/88, as regards the FIFG.

[241] P Cheshire, R Camagni, J-P de Gaudemaar, and JR Cuadrado Roura, '1957 to 1992: Moving toward a Europe of Regions and Regional Policy' in L Rodwin and H Sazanami (eds), *Industrial Change and Regional Economic Transformation: The Experience of Western Europe* (Harper Collins Academic, London, 1991) 268–300, 292.

[242] Art 2 of Reg 2085/93 (OJ 1993 L193/44) amending Reg 4256/88 laying down provisions for implementing Reg 2052/88 as regards the EAGGF, Guidance Section.

[243] Dec 94/279 (OJ 1994 L120/50) establishing the indicative allocation by Member State of the commitment appropriations from the Structural Funds for the agricultural part of Objective 5a except for those fields covered by Objective 1 for 1994–99, as amended by Dec 98/524 (OJ 1998 L233/32); and Objective 5a: indicative breakdown by Member States of commitment appropriations from the Structural Funds, COM(94)268, 4.

[244] Art 12(4) of Reg 2081/93 (OJ 1993 L193/5).

measures to improve the efficiency of the structures of holdings; to improve the marketing and processing of agricultural products; and to encourage the establishment of producer groups.[245]

Accordingly, Regulation 950/97[246] provides for: assistance for investments in agricultural holdings;[247] setting-up assistance for young farmers;[248] assistance for the introduction of accounting practices;[249] setting-up assistance for farmers' groups;[250] setting-up assistance for farm relief services;[251] assistance for farm-management services;[252] assistance to farmers in less favoured agricultural areas;[253] and assistance for adjustment of vocational training to the requirements of modern agriculture.[254]

Moreover, Regulation 951/97[255] concerns the improvement and rationalization of the treatment, processing, and marketing of agricultural products. Assistance may be granted for: investments helping to guide production in keeping with foreseeable market trends or encouraging the development of new outlets for agricultural products; investments relieving the intervention mechanisms of the market organizations by furthering long-term structural improvement, where this is needed; investments in regions faced with special problems in adapting to the economic consequences of developments on the agricultural markets and investments of benefit to such regions; investments helping to improve or rationalize marketing channels or processing procedures for agricultural products; investments helping to improve the quality, presentation, and preparation of products or encouraging a better use of by-products, particularly by the recycling of waste; investments contributing to the adjustment of sectors facing new situations as a result of reform of the common agricultural policy; investments helping to facilitate the adoption of new technologies relating to environmental protection; and investments encouraging the improvement and monitoring of quality and of health conditions.[256] More detailed criteria for the grant of such assistance are provided by Decision 94/173.[257]

In the fisheries sector assistance to the formation and (for three years) the operation of producers' organizations may be provided under legislation on

[245] Art 2 of Reg 2085/93 (OJ 1993 L193/44); and Reg 952/97 (OJ 1997 L142/30) on producer groups and associations thereof. The latter measure applies to Austria, Belgium, Finland, parts of France, Greece, Ireland, Italy, Portugal, and Spain (ibid, Art 2).

[246] On improving the efficiency of agricultural structures (OJ 1997 L142/1).

[247] ibid, Arts 4–9.

[248] ibid, Arts 10–11.

[249] ibid, Art 13.

[250] ibid, Art 14.

[251] ibid, Art 15.

[252] ibid, Art 16.

[253] ibid, Arts 17–25. These provisions replace Dir 75/268 (OJ 1975 L128/1).

[254] OJ 1997 L142/1, Arts 26–28.

[255] On improving the processing and marketing conditions for agricultural products (OJ 1997 L142/22).

[256] ibid, Art 1(2).

[257] On the selection criteria to be adopted for investments for improving the processing and marketing conditions for agriculture and forestry products (OJ 1994 L79/29).

the common organization of the market in fishery products.[258] Moreover, under Regulation 4042/89[259] assistance could be granted for: improving the situation of the production sectors of fishery and aquaculture basic products; directing production and processing towards the objectives pursued by the common fisheries policy; improving the processing and marketing structures for fisheries and aquaculture products; improving the marketing and distribution networks for fisheries and aquaculture products; improving the hygiene, quality, preservation, or packaging of products or the use of by-products; promoting technical innovation; adapting processed products to consumer demand at reasonable prices; stabilizing the market for fishery and aquaculture products; and ensuring the regular and adequate supply of raw materials to the fishery and aquaculture-product processing sector. Assistance could also be granted to take account of the Community deficit in fishery products and the need for a balanced exploitation of the internal resources of the Community; cohesion requirements;[260] and the needs of Objective 1 regions.[261] Such assistance is now provided by the Financial Instrument for Fisheries Guidance under Regulation 3699/93.[262]

In the case of forestry, Regulation 867/90[263] provides that measures instituted by Regulation 866/90,[264] now substituted by Regulation 951/97,[265] may be applied to this sector. Assistance is to be directed preferably to small and medium-sized enterprises, where their restructuring and rationalization may contribute to the improvement and economic development of agriculture and rural areas.[266]

Forms of assistance

Under Regulation 950/97[267] the Guidance Section part-finances national aid schemes by reimbursing expenditure incurred by Member States.[268] Under Regulation 951/97[269] it provides assistance through operational programmes[270] and global grants.[271] It may also contribute to technical assistance and

[258] Arts 7 and 25 of Reg 3759/92 (OJ 1992 L388/1) on the common organization of the market in fishery and aquaculture products.

[259] On the improvement of the conditions under which fishery and aquaculture products were processed and marketed (OJ 1989 L388/1).

[260] ibid, Art 1(1)(a).

[261] ibid, Art 1(1)(b).

[262] Laying down the criteria and arrangements regarding Community structural assistance in the fisheries and aquaculture sector and the processing and marketing of its products (OJ 1993 L346/1). See sect 5.2.3 below.

[263] On improving the processing and marketing conditions for forestry products (OJ 1990 L91/7).

[264] On improving the processing and marketing conditions for agricultural products (OJ 1990 L91/1).

[265] OJ 1997 L142/22.

[266] Art 1(2) of Reg 867/90 (OJ 1990 L91/7).

[267] OJ 1997 L142/1.

[268] ibid, Art 2.

[269] OJ 1997 L142/22.

[270] Reg 860/94 (OJ 1994 L99/7) on plans and applications, in the form of operational programmes, for aid from the Guidance Section of the EAGGF for investments for improving the processing and marketing conditions for agricultural and forestry products.

[271] OJ 1997 L142/22, Art 9.

information operations, and support studies or pilot schemes concerning the adjustment of agricultural structures and the promotion of rural development at Union level.[272]

3.4.2 Objectives 1 and 5b

In pursuit of Objectives 1 and 5b, assistance may go beyond improving farm structures and the processing and marketing of agricultural products, as required under Objective 5a. Assistance under Objectives 1 and 5b may be provided to measures for the sustainable development of the rural environment. These measures may not only concern developing and strengthening agricultural and forestry structures. They may also concern maintaining, enhancing, and restoring the landscape.[273] In particular, assistance under Objective 1 should tackle the backwardness of agricultural structures.[274]

Eligibility for assistance

Where the Guidance Section provides assistance in pursuit of Objective 1 or 5b, regional criteria for eligibility are applicable.[275]

Allocation of assistance

Indicative allocations of assistance are made. They are based on the need for continuity regarding the use of resources in the previous programming period and the specific structural needs of agriculture. They may entail higher levels of assistance in Objective 1 regions than in Objective 5b regions.[276]

Scope of assistance

In pursuit of Objectives 1 and 5b, the Fund may support: the conversion, diversification, reorientation, and adjustment of production potential, including the production of non-food agricultural products; promotion of local agricultural and forestry products; development of rural infrastructures; encouragement of diversification; renovation and development of villages and the protection and conservation of the rural heritage, to the extent that financing is not provided by the European Regional Development Fund under Regulation 2083/93;[277] reparcelling and associated work; individual or

[272] Art 8 of Reg 2085/93 (OJ 1993 L193/44). See eg Call for proposals relating to the adjustment of agricultural structures and the promotion of rural development (OJ 1994 C303/17). Greater use of calls in relation to 'priority topics' is to be made. See the Commission Reply by Mr Fischler to WQ E–1791/96 (OJ 1996 C356/97) by Gerhard Botz.

[273] Art 3(1) of Reg 2085/93 (OJ 1993 L193/44).

[274] ibid, Art 3(2).

[275] sect 2.4 above.

[276] Reg 223/90 (OJ 1990 L22/62) fixing the rates of Community part-financing for the measures referred to in Regs 797/85, 1096/88, 1360/78, 389/82, and 1696/71.

[277] Amending Reg 4254/88 laying down provisions for implementing Reg 2052/88 as regards the ERDF (OJ 1993 L193/34).

collective land or pasture improvement; irrigation; encouragement for tourist and craft investments; restoration of agricultural and forestry production potential after natural disasters and the introduction of appropriate prevention measures in ultra-peripheral areas particularly at risk from such disasters;[278] development and exploitation of woodlands and protection of the environment; maintenance of the countryside and restoration of landscapes, to the extent that financing is not provided for under measures accompanying reform of the common agricultural policy;[279] development of agricultural and forestry advisory services and the improvement of facilities for agricultural and forestry vocational training; measures in the area of forestry technological research and development; and financial engineering measures for agricultural and agri-food businesses.[280]

Forms of assistance

Assistance pursuant to Objectives 1 and 5b is in the main to take the form of operational programmes, including those using integrated approaches, and global grants.[281] In addition, the Guidance Section can contribute up to 1 per cent of its resources to pilot projects concerning development of rural areas, including forestry development; technical assistance and preparatory studies; evaluation studies; demonstration projects for farmers; and measures necessary for diffusion of results of work and experience regarding improvement of agricultural structures.[282]

3.5 CONCLUSION

Union assistance to agriculture may have a *national* impact outweighing that of the European Regional Development Fund. For example, between 1973, when Ireland joined the Union, and 1991 the disparity of average income in Ireland relative to other Member States narrowed by three or four percentage points. This narrowing is regarded as more likely to have been the result of the common agricultural policy than of operations by the European Regional Development Fund.[283] Generally, however, comparatively developed northern regions of the Union have benefited from a higher level of support from

[278] cf, earlier, Reg 206/66 (JO 1966 3869) on the contribution of the EAGGF towards the repair of damage caused by catastrophic floods in certain regions of Italy during the autumn of 1966; and Reg 3222/88 (OJ 1988 L288/1) introducing a common measure for the re-establishment of olive groves damaged by frost in certain regions of Greece. The use of such assistance may be problematic. See eg the European Parliament Decision regarding the discharge to the Commission in respect of the implementation of the General Budget for 1994 (OJ 1996 L148/44), para 56.

[279] sect 5.6 below.

[280] Arts 5 and 6 of Reg 2085/93 (OJ 1993 L193/44).

[281] ibid, Arts 4 and 6.

[282] ibid, Art 8.

[283] EEC regional development policy, House of Lords Select Committee on the European Communities, HL(1991–92)20, 20.

the Guarantee Section of the European Agricultural Guidance and Guarantee Fund than southern regions.[284] In other words, this Section tends to work against the *regional* equality sought by cohesion. This tendency may be reinforced rather than countered by the operations of the Guidance Section of the same Fund. These operations give more emphasis to restructuring demanded by the common agricultural policy than to cohesion.

Some arrangements for assistance from the Guidance Section, notably those for assistance to farming under unfavourable natural conditions, do acknowledge that, in the case of some farmers, such restructuring may be impossible. At the same time, they implicitly recognize that agriculture and, more particularly, food production[285] are not the only output of rural resources.[286] Rather, 'public goods' may be involved.

The inference may be drawn that a balance should be sought between assisting agriculture and assisting alternative rural activities. On the one hand, rural development assistance must, it is said, be rooted in agricultural policy, since rural resources are irrevocably integrated with the dominant rural land use, agriculture.[287] On the other hand, assistance should be designed to reallocate some rural resources at the margin away from agricultural products.[288] However, such reallocation may be inhibited by price support from the Guarantee Section.[289] For this reason, the scope of the common agricultural policy is said to be operationally too limited, and its stated objectives are said to be too broad.[290] The Commission considers that the solution is to design assistance to: generate prospects for the future which will allow sufficient farmers to stay on the land; diversify employment in rural areas; contribute to better planning; favour local development; and protect the countryside.[291]

Accordingly, in the context of reforms to the common agricultural policy the social and regional role of assistance from the Guidance Section in facilitating adjustment by farmers is stressed.[292] In practice, however, the assistance is generally designed to restructure the agricultural sector in such a way that it becomes less dependent on price support.[293] Thus, for example, assis-

[284] This tendency has been reduced following the 1992 reforms of the CAP. See First cohesion report, COM(97)542, 8.

[285] Guidance Section assistance to Objective 2 regions has been criticized for its concentration on the food industry rather than on the restructuring of agricultural production and development of the rural infrastructure. See M Quévit, J Houard, S Bodson, and A Dangoisse, *Impact régional 1992: Les Régions de tradition industrielle* (De Boeck, Brussels, 1991) 350.

[286] J McInerney, 'Agricultural Policy at the Crossroads' (1986) *Countryside Planning Yearbook* 44–75, 51.

[287] ibid, 57. [288] ibid, 58. [289] ibid, 64. [290] ibid, 69.

[291] From the Single Act to Maastricht and beyond: the means to match our ambitions, COM(92)2000.

[292] cf the ESC Opinion of 23 Mar 1994 (OJ 1994 C148/12) on possible developments in the policy of arable land set-aside, para 8.3.

[293] J Rosenblatt, T Mayer, K Bartholdy, D Demekas, S Gupta, and L Lipschitz, *The Common Agricultural Policy of the European Community: Principles and Consequences* (IMF, Washington, D.C., 1988) 24.

tance is not to be granted where it may lead to an overall increase in production capacity in sectors where there are surpluses.[294]

As a result, criticism of the work of the Guidance Section continues. In particular, it is said that assistance from this Section may still favour sectors in a more advantageous structural, organizational, regional, and macroeconomic position. At the same time, 'the international context' demands the ever-increasing liberalization of markets and reductions in assistance. As a result, the weakest agricultural sectors may be permanently forced out of the market under the pressure of greater competition on the Union and international markets.[295]

The Economic and Social Committee infers that assistance from the Guidance Section should be graduated to reflect the special structural circumstances of different regions.[296] Accordingly, in the allocation of assistance differentiated parameters, which take account of factors that impede economic development and production in the less favoured and most outlying regions of the Union, should be used. Their use offers a way of reducing (if not eliminating) structural disparities and thus boosting cohesion.[297] More particularly, it has been argued that Objective 5a assistance should not always be denied in the case of a product in surplus. It should not be denied where the assistance is consistent with the objective of stimulating growth in the whole economy of the region, that is, not just agriculture, but also industry and commerce.[298]

Such arguments may have some judicial support. For example, in *Eridania*[299] the grant of assistance to Italian sugar refineries was challenged, because there was surplus production capacity in this sector. According to Advocate General Roemer, however, the principle of 'regional specialization', given the structural and climatic disadvantages of Italian refineries, justified the assistance. Even if the total capacity of the existing refineries was sufficient, their dimensions, their machinery, and their geographical dispersal might be such that they did not correspond to an adequate national structural

294 10th recital in the preamble to Reg 2843/94 (OJ 1994 L302/1) amending Regs 2328/91 and 866/90 with a view to expediting the adjustment of production, processing, and marketing structures within the framework of the reform of the CAP.

295 It has been urged that Union preference should be set at a level that will not increase the disadvantages faced by peripheral regions in competing with other areas of the Union. See the Report of the Committee on Agriculture, Fisheries, and Rural Development on the development and future of the CAP, EP Doc A3–0342/91/Part C, 31.

296 cf, regarding the need for 'regionalization' of assistance, the ESC Opinion of 10 Dec 1980 (OJ 1980 C353/8) on the ERDF, paras 11.2 and 13.1.

297 Opinion of 27 May 1992 (OJ 1992 C223/67) on the proposal for a regulation authorizing an enhanced aid system for the formation of producers' organizations in the French overseas departments, the Canary Islands, Madeira, and the Azores, para 2.

298 ESC Opinion of 21 Dec 1993 (OJ 1994 C52/26) on Objective 5a (1994–99), para 2.16.6.

299 Joined Cases 10 & 18/68 *Società 'Eridania' Zuccherifici Nazionali v EC Commission* [1969] ECR 459.

policy.[300] Thus the total capacity was not decisive. What was vital was the geographical dispersal of that capacity.[301]

The same kind of arguments also appear to have had some impact on the Commission. According to the latter, established hierarchies and innovations written into the EC Treaty, notably as regards the Objectives of the European Social Fund,[302] the role of rural development as a social phenomenon, and its part in the context of reform of the common agricultural policy, have to be reconsidered.[303] Indeed, in view of the special requirements of rural development, the Commission has advocated the creation of a specific instrument for such development. The new instrument 'in due course' would take over from the Guidance Section.[304]

Such thinking is only partly reflected in the latest legislative proposals, though they are apparently designed to direct assistance from both Sections of the Fund more towards disadvantaged regions. According to these proposals, Objective 5a (as well as Objective 5b) will be abolished, and assistance from the Guidance Section will be limited to pursuit of Objective 1.[305] At the same time, the Guarantee Section will contribute to achievement of Objective 2.[306]

[300] Joined Cases 10 & 18/68 *Società 'Eridania' Zuccherifici Nazionali v EC Commission* [1969] ECR 498.

[301] ibid, 503.

[302] sect 4.4.2 below.

[303] From the Single Act to Maastricht and beyond: the means to match our ambitions, COM(92)2000.

[304] Community structural policies: assessment and outlook, COM(92)84, 39.

[305] Proposal of 19 Mar 1998 (OJ 1998 C176/1) for a regulation laying down provisions on the Structural Funds, Art 2(2).

[306] ibid, Art 2(3). See also sect 5.6 below.

4

European Social Fund

4.1 INTRODUCTION

In Article 117 of the EEC Treaty, Member States agreed upon the need to promote improved working conditions and an improved standard of living for workers. They believed that such improvements would ensue not only from the functioning of the common market but also from the procedures provided for in the Treaty. Presumably, these procedures were to include the provision of assistance by the European Social Fund (ESF).

Articles 123 to 127 of the Treaty provided for the creation of this Fund. According to Article 123, the Fund was to improve employment opportunities for workers in the common market and to contribute thereby to raising the standard of living. To these ends, the Fund was to render the employment of workers easier and to increase their geographical and occupational mobility within the Community.[1]

More particularly, Article 49(3)(d) of the Treaty required the establishment of machinery to facilitate the achievement of a balance between supply and demand in the employment market. This was to be done in such a way as to avoid serious threats to the standard of living and level of employment in the various regions and industries. It led to the establishment of a system known as SEDOC,[2] which was designed to prevent new regional problems in countries of immigration.[3]

The apparent emphasis in these provisions was on increasing the mobility of workers rather than on assisting the economic development of regions of high unemployment. This emphasis may go some way towards explaining the need felt by Italy to secure the adoption of a Protocol to the Treaty. The

[1] Art 128 EEC also required the Council to 'lay down general principles for implementing a common vocational training policy capable of contributing to the harmonious development both of the national economies and the common market'. In Dec 63/266 (JO 1963 1338) determining general principles for the implementation of a common policy for vocational training, the 'fourth principle' emphasized the aim of promoting the geographical and professional mobility of workers. Note also the reference to Art 128 EEC in Art 1 of Reg 9/60 (JO 1960 1189) on the ESF.

[2] *Système européen de diffusion des offres et des demandes d'emploi enregistrés en compensation internationale.*

[3] Art 15(2) of Reg 1612/68 (JO 1968 L257/2) on freedom of movement for workers within the Community. This system has now been replaced. See Dec 93/569 (OJ 1993 L274/32) on the implementing of Reg 1612/68 as regards, in particular, a network entitled Eures (European Employment Services).

Protocol on Italy[4] envisaged use of the Fund and the European Investment Bank[5] to assist implementation of an Italian regional development programme.

4.2 ESTABLISHMENT OF THE COMMON MARKET

Article 125 of the EEC Treaty provided for the grant of assistance for training, resettlement, and conversion. This provision was narrower in scope than Article 123, and concerned only the 'immediate task' of the European Social Fund.[6] Such assistance was to be provided under Article 125 during the transitional period for establishment of the common market and could be abolished by the Council at the end of this period.[7] To implement this provision, the Council adopted Regulation 9/60.[8]

4.2.1 Objectives of Assistance

Apparently, the Fund was originally intended to alleviate the social costs of establishing the common market[9] and was thus viewed as essential for its establishment.[10] This view certainly seems to have been adopted in the Spaak Report, on the basis of which the EEC Treaty was negotiated. According to this Report, the Fund was to help workers adjust to the industrial restructuring which would be demanded by the establishment of the common market. Since the restructuring would lead to increased efficiency and thereby benefit the Community as a whole, it was considered justified for the social costs to be shared.[11] However, the impossibility of accurately determining when unemployment could be attributed to the establishment of the common market was acknowledged.[12]

[4] Protocols annexed to the Treaty by common accord of the Member States were an integral part of the Treaty. See Art 239 EEC.

[5] See sect 6.2 below.

[6] 6th recital in the preamble to Reg 9/60 (JO 1960 1189). The enactment of this Regulation did not prejudice other ESF tasks under the Treaty (ibid, 8th recital in the preamble).

[7] During the negotiation of the EEC Treaty there had been some support, particularly from France and Germany, for limiting ESF operations to this period. See S Neri and H Sperl, *Traité instituant la Communauté économique européenne* (Court of Justice of the European Communities, Luxembourg, 1960) 307.

[8] On the ESF (JO 1960 1189). It was 'technically' amended by Reg 47/63 (JO 1963 1605) and Reg 37/67 (JO 1967 526).

[9] D Collins, *The Operation of the European Social Fund* (Croom Helm, London, 1983); and P Hatt, 'Thirty Years of ESF Assistance', *Social Europe* 2/91, 78–91.

[10] R Quadri, R Monaco, and A Trabucchi (eds), *Trattato istitutivo della Comunità economica europea: Commentario* (Giuffré, Milan, 1965) ii. 961.

[11] Comité Intergouvernemental Crée par la Conference de Messine, *Rapport des Chefs de Délégation aux Ministres des Affaires Etrangères* (Secretariat of the Committee, Brussels, 1956) 83. At the Messina Conference it had been recognized that the establishment of a common market would require the creation of a 'readaptation fund'.

[12] Neri and Sperl, n 7 above, 308, 313.

At the same time, it was recognized that surplus labour exerted downward pressure on pay and working conditions. Establishment of the common market meant that this pressure would be exerted throughout the Community.[13] Hence, it would be of general benefit for the Fund to intervene where the retraining or re-employment of workers became necessary.[14]

In setting these limited objectives for the Fund, the Treaty authors may be said to have held an overly sanguine view of the self-regulating powers of the common market. In a context of overall economic growth, they reasoned, backward regions, assisted by decentralized, loosely co-ordinated measures that focused primarily on the labour market, would catch up with the more prosperous regions.[15]

4.2.2 Eligibility for Assistance

Assistance was available in respect of three categories of persons. They were: unemployed persons[16] receiving vocational training; unemployed persons changing their place of residence for employment purposes; and workers who required retraining because their company was undergoing conversion. In particular, assistance for vocational training was available in the case of workers who completed at least six months of productive employment in the occupation for which they had been retrained. Moreover, assistance for resettlement was available in the case of workers who completed at least six months of productive employment in their new place of residence. Finally, assistance for conversion was available in the case of workers who completed at least six months of full employment in the converted undertaking.[17]

4.2.3 Allocation of Assistance

The Protocol on Italy was referred to in the preamble to Regulation 9/60.[18] It was interpreted as meaning that the Fund should be used to assist the Italian Government in its efforts to reduce unemployment.[19] No reference to the particular needs of Italy was made in the operative provisions of the Regulation, though in practice many Italians benefited from Fund assistance during the first decade of its existence. In the period 1961 to 1972 the re-employment of

[13] J Tessier, 'Le Fonds social européen' (1960) RMC 325–337, 334.

[14] ibid, 325.

[15] JJ Anderson, 'Structural Funds and the Social Dimension of EU Policy: Springboard or Stumbling Block?' in S Leibfried and P Pierson (eds), *European Social Policy* (Brookings Institution, Washington, D.C., 1995) 123–158, 135.

[16] Persons clearly underemployed for a prolonged period were assimilated to the unemployed. See Art 2(3)(a) of Reg 9/60 (JO 1960 1189). See also Reg 12/64 (JO 1964 537) fixing the conditions of clear and prolonged underemployment within the meaning of Art 2(3)(a) of Reg 9/60.

[17] Art 125(2) EEC; and Arts 1 and 2 of Reg 9/60 (JO 1960 1189).

[18] ibid.

[19] ibid, 7th recital in the preamble.

more than 1.1 million jobless, including 850,000 Italians, and the resettlement of about 800,000 job applicants, half of whom were Italian, were assisted.[20]

4.2.4 Scope of Assistance

Article 125 of the EEC Treaty provided for the European Social Fund to assist two kinds of state measures. First, it was to meet 50 per cent of the cost of state measures to ensure productive re-employment of workers by means of vocational training[21] or resettlement allowances. Secondly, the Fund was to assist state measures in favour of workers whose employment was reduced or temporarily suspended, in whole or in part, as a result of the conversion of an undertaking to other production. Such measures, it was envisaged, would enable the workers to retain the same wage level pending their full re-employment. According to Regulation 9/60,[22] the conversion envisaged was that involving a change in the production programme of an enterprise. The change had to be designed to lead to the production of new goods differentiated from their predecessors by more than mere improvements or additions.[23] The first kind of measures were 'active' in character, and the second kind 'passive'.[24]

The Commission considered that the scope of assistance from the Fund should be wider. According to the Commission, the creation of a 'real' common market required that along with a customs union, an economic union be established. To this end, a social policy should be implemented,[25] so as to enable undertakings to adapt and to maintain a high level of employment. In particular, the actions of the Fund in favour of labour mobility should be intensified.[26] Hence, in 1965 the Commission proposed new legislation under Article 235[27] rather than Article 125 of the

[20] Hatt, n 9 above, 80. Though the proportion of Fund assistance received by Italy was lower than these figures might have led one to expect (Annex to the Commission Opinion of 10 June 1969 (JO 1969 C131/4) on reform of the ESF). See also A Gallizioli, *I Fondi strutturali delle Comunite europee* (CEDAM, Padua, 1992) 79.

[21] The ESC considered that the Fund should go beyond 'requalification' assistance and should support training generally. See the Opinion of 3 July 1963 (JO 1963 3039) concerning the Community action programme in the second stage, para 15.

[22] JO 1960 1189.

[23] ibid, Art 9. During the negotiation of the Treaty Germany had suggested that assistance should be conditional on its being shown that the conversion would promote establishment of the common market. See Neri and Sperl, n 7 above, 318.

[24] W Steinle, 'Labour Markets and Social Policies' in W Molle and R Cappellin (eds), *Regional Impact of Community Policies in Europe* (Avebury, Aldershot, 1988) 111–126, 115–116.

[25] The European Parliament also called for reform of the ESF, so that it could make a greater contribution to regional development. See the Resolution of 27 June 1966 (JO 1966 2427) on regional policy in the EEC, para 13.

[26] Preamble to the draft decision of 11 Nov 1964 (Bull EEC, Supp 1/65, 6) on certain aspects of social policy.

[27] According to this provision, if action by the Community proved necessary to attain, in the course of the operation of the common market, one of the objectives of the Community and the

Treaty.[28] According to the proposal, the Fund would have been able to provide assistance to: retrain persons in employment;[29] to maintain incomes of workers affected by conversion by way of the substitution of enterprises;[30] to construct, enlarge, and equip retraining centres;[31] and to construct housing.[32] This proposal was supported by the European Parliament[33] and the Economic and Social Committee,[34] but it was not adopted by the Council. Apparently, the Council considered that labour-market policy should be left essentially to individual Member States.

4.2.5 Forms of Assistance

Every year Member States were to present to the Commission estimates of their needs for Fund assistance for the following year.[35] These estimates were aggregated, and the contributions required of each Member State to finance the aggregate amount of estimated Fund expenditure[36] were calculated according to the scale laid down in Article 200(2) of the EEC Treaty.[37] The percentage contributions required of Italy and the Netherlands under this provision were lower than the percentage contributions which they were required to make to the General Budget under Article 200(1) of the Treaty. This disparity was justified by reference to the economic and social situation of the two countries at the time of adoption of the Treaty.[38] Each Member State was subsequently to claim from the Fund reimbursement of expenditure which it had actually incurred.

Therefore, the Fund did not take initiatives.[39] Rather, its assistance took the form of a 'clearing system'[40] or an intergovernmental compensation system for social risks entailed by the establishment of the common market.[41]

Treaty had not provided the necessary powers, the Council should, acting unanimously on a proposal from the Commission and after consulting the European Parliament, take the appropriate measures.

28 Draft supplementary regulation on the ESF of 27 Jan 1965 (Bull EEC, Supp 3/65, 13).

29 ibid, Arts 2–5.

30 ibid, Arts 6–13.

31 ibid, Arts 14–18.

32 ibid, Arts 19–20.

33 Resolution of 16 June 1965 (JO 1965 2006) on the Commission proposals for regulations to increase the effectiveness of ESF interventions. See also the Resolution of 1 Dec 1967 (JO 1967 307/24) on the evolution of the social situation in the Community in 1966, para 6(a).

34 Opinion of 26 May 1965 (JO 1965 2244) on the Commission proposals for regulations to increase the effectiveness of ESF interventions.

35 Art 16 of Reg 9/60 (JO 1960 1189).

36 More details of Art 125 EEC expenditure were provided in Arts 15–24 of the Financial Regulation of 31 Jan 1961 (JO 1961 509).

37 This expenditure was only included in the General Budget from 1971 (JO 1971 L62/1, Arts 451 and 452).

38 Annex to the Commission Opinion of 10 June 1969 (JO 1969 C131/4).

39 Quadri, Monaco, and Trabucchi, n 10 above, ii. 968.

40 See the German argument in Case 2/71 *Germany v EC Commission: ESF aid* [1971] ECR 669, 674. See, similarly, Quadri, Monaco, and Trabucchi, n 10 above, ii. 982.

41 Tessier, n 13 above, 325.

4.3 DEVELOPMENT OF THE COMMON MARKET

Despite the operations of the European Social Fund, structural unemployment persisted in certain regions and industrial sectors. Its persistence was considered attributable not simply to the relocation of job opportunities resulting from establishment of the common market, but also, more fundamentally, to the fact that much of the workforce lacked the qualifications and skills needed in an increasingly competitive world economy.[42] At the same time, migration for economic necessity came to be regarded as undesirable in terms of integration goals.[43] Greater emphasis, it was felt, should be placed on enabling workers to find employment in their own region.[44] In these circumstances, the targeting of assistance was considered necessary.

However, the Fund was empowered under Article 125 of the EEC Treaty only to assist state measures. The implication was that Member States could control the use of Fund assistance. As a result, such assistance tended to be used to tackle the most pressing, short-term problems of the Member States,[45] rather than being designed systematically to tackle what from the Community point of view were the long-term, structural problems. To overcome this tendency, the Commission sought transformation of the Fund into 'an instrument of economic policy'.[46] According to Commission plans, the Fund would be used to stimulate and guide national employment policies. In doing so, the work of the Fund would prevent Member States from protecting jobs through measures which would undermine the working of the common market.[47]

A legal basis for reform of the Fund was provided by Article 126 of the Treaty. According to this provision, after the end of the transitional period the Council, acting unanimously on a Commission opinion, could replace the original tasks of the Fund with new tasks within the framework of Article 123.[48] Following the call at The Hague Summit of December 1969 for reform

[42] Commission Opinion of 10 June 1969 (JO 1969 C131/4). See also A Gruber, 'Le Fonds social européen à la veille d'un bilan' (1982) RTDE 251–287, 255.

[43] The Communiqué issued by the Heads of State or Government on 20 Oct 1972 (Bull EC 10–1972, 14–23), para 3 stressed that economic expansion was not an end in itself but should result in an improvement of the quality of life as well as of the standard of living.

[44] Council Resolution of 21 Jan 1974 (OJ 1974 C13/1) concerning a social action programme aimed at achieving a policy of full and better employment in the Community as a whole and in the regions. See also the Resolution of 9 Feb 1976 (OJ 1976 C34/2) on an action programme for migrant workers and members of their families. Cf, earlier, the *Fifth EEC General Report* (EEC Commission, Brussels, 1962) 141.

[45] cf Dec 66/740 (JO 1966 4168) on the grant of a Community contribution to Italy to enable it to grant certain aids to sulphur miners affected by redundancy, and a certain number of scholarships to their children, which was adopted under Art 235 EEC.

[46] Opinion of 10 June 1969 (JO 1969 C131/4), preface.

[47] ibid, para 5.

[48] Thus the original tasks were 'provisional'. See Quadri, Monaco, and Trabucchi, n 10 above, ii. 977.

of the Fund within the framework of 'a closely concerted social policy',[49] this replacement was effected by Decision 71/66.[50]

4.3.1 Objectives of Assistance

Decision 71/66[51] stressed the interdependence of social and economic policies,[52] and aimed to assist restructuring associated with the development of the common market and Community policies.[53] According to the preamble to this Decision, account was to be taken of the demands of social progress in the face of technical development.[54] Hence, not only should efforts continue to remedy the structural unemployment and underemployment still existing in various Community regions.[55] Action should also be taken to prevent unemployment from arising in the first place.[56] At the same time, the Fund should seek more positively to secure for all workers employment that best corresponded to their abilities and to ensure continuity of employment and income for them.[57]

Decision 83/516[58] subsequently modified these objectives, with a view to making the Fund a more active instrument to promote employment policies.[59] Accordingly, the Fund was now to concentrate on assisting the implementation of policies designed to equip the workforce with the skills required for stable employment and to generate employment opportunities.[60] It was, in particular, to assist the socio-vocational insertion and integration of young people and disadvantaged workers, the adaptation of the workforce to labour-market developments and to technological change, and the reduction of regional imbalance in the labour market.[61]

4.3.2 Eligibility for Assistance

According to Regulation 2396/71,[62] five categories of persons were eligible for assistance. They were: the unemployed; those who would become unemployed after a specific period; those who were underemployed; those who had had to cease work in a self-employed capacity;[63] and those whose qualifications had to be adapted to permit them to pursue occupations requiring high

[49] Communiqué (Bull EC 1–1970, 11), para 12.
[50] On the reform of the ESF (JO 1971 L28/15).
[51] ibid.
[52] ibid, 3rd recital in the preamble.
[53] Gruber, n 42 above, 260.
[54] 2nd recital in the preamble to Dec 71/66 (JO 1971 L28/15).
[55] ibid, 4th recital.
[56] ibid, 6th recital.
[57] ibid, 17th recital.
[58] On the tasks of the ESF (OJ 1983 L289/38).
[59] ibid, 7th recital in the preamble.
[60] See also AG Da Cruz Vilaça in Case 84/85 *UK v EC Commission: assistance for part-time employment* [1987] ECR 3765, 3777.
[61] Art 1(1) of Dec 83/516 (OJ 1983 L289/38).
[62] Reg 2396/71 (JO 1971 249/54) implementing Dec 71/66.
[63] ibid, Art 1(2)(a).

qualifications.[64] Moreover, subject to the approval of the employment services of the Member State or Member States concerned, assistance could also be granted in respect of three further categories of persons. Thus it could be granted in respect of workers who were difficult to place in employment again on account of their age. It could also be granted in respect of women over 35 years who wished to pursue a professional or trade activity for the first time or whose qualifications were no longer in demand. Finally, it could be granted in respect of young people under 25 years who were unemployed through lack of qualifications or whose qualifications were no longer those in demand.[65] In addition, assistance might be granted generally for operations in favour of handicapped persons who might be able to pursue a professional or trade activity after medical rehabilitation, vocational training, or vocational retraining.[66]

The Fund might contribute to financing assistance to those within the above categories where they were to pursue activities as employed persons.[67] In special cases, to be determined by the Council, assistance could also be granted where they were to pursue activities as self-employed persons.[68] Since agriculture and textiles were treated as such cases by the Council, those who were to pursue self-employed activities in these sectors became eligible for assistance.[69] The distinction between persons who were to pursue employed activities and those who were to pursue self-employed activities was subsequently removed in 1977.[70]

Age acquired more central importance as a criterion of eligibility in Decision 83/516.[71] It was felt that to respond effectively to the requirements of the labour market, vocational guidance systems should be made more widely available to young people and job-seekers. As a precaution, they should also be available to those whose employment was threatened.[72] Accordingly, assistance could be granted generally in favour of persons under 25 years.[73] Those over 25 years were only eligible, if they were: unemployed or threatened with unemployment or underemployment; women wishing to return to work; handicapped persons capable of working in the open labour market; migrants; or employed persons, particularly those in small and

[64] Reg 2396/71 (JO 1971 249/54) implementing Dec 71/66 Art 1(2)(b).

[65] ibid, Art 1(2)(c).

[66] ibid, Art 1(3).

[67] Art 3(1) of Dec 71/66 (JO 1971 L28/15).

[68] ibid, Art 3(2).

[69] Art 1(2) of Dec 72/428 (JO 1972 L291/158) on assistance from the ESF for persons leaving agriculture to pursue non-agricultural activities; and Art 1(2) of Dec 72/429 (JO 1972 L291/160) on intervention by the ESF in favour of persons occupied in the textile industry.

[70] Art 1(2) Dir 77/801 (OJ 1977 L337/8) amending Dec 71/66. Assistance was made available to the self-employed by Reg 3824/85 (OJ 1985 L370/25) amending, with a view to its extension to cover self-employed persons, Reg 2950/83.

[71] OJ 1983 L289/38.

[72] Council Resolution of 27 June 1980 (OJ 1980 C168/1) on guidelines for a Community labour market policy, para II.2.

[73] OJ 1983 L289/38, Art 4(1).

medium-sized enterprises, who required retraining in new technology or improved management techniques.[74]

4.3.3 Allocation of Assistance

According to Regulation 2396/71,[75] in the allocation of assistance priority was to be given to eliminating long-term structural unemployment in regions which were either less developed or dependent on declining industries.[76] Hence, 60 per cent of the resources of the Fund not devoted to 'specific' operations[77] under Article 4 of Decision 71/66[78] were to be directed each year to operations in such regions.

Regulation 2893/77[79] reinforced the regional bias in allocations. The 60 per cent figure now became a minimum figure for the priority regions.[80] Moreover, Fund assistance was ordinarily limited to 50 per cent of eligible costs. However, regions might be designated as having especially serious and prolonged unemployment problems. Such designation was to be based, in particular, on the lower level of the economic and social development of such regions, their peripheral location in the Community, and their significance for their respective national economies.[81] In their case, the limit to Fund assistance was raised to 55 per cent.[82] They originally comprised: Greenland, the French overseas departments, Ireland, Northern Ireland, and the Mezzogiorno.[83]

Operations located in these regions were accorded 'first-level priority' by the 1977 Guidelines of the Commission for management of the Fund, which meant that assistance was 'virtually guaranteed'.[84] 'Second-level priority' was accorded to operations in other regions qualifying for assistance from the European Regional Development Fund.[85] These were operations which might not be carried out without assistance from the European Social Fund and were proposed for approval without delay.[86]

Decision 83/516[87] added an age-bias in the allocation of assistance. Operations for young people were to receive at least 75 per cent of the assistance from the Fund.[88] At least 40 per cent of the assistance for these operations was to be directed towards regions qualifying for the higher rate of

[74] ibid, Art 4(2). [75] JO 1971 L249/54. [76] ibid, Art 2.
[77] See sect 4.3.4 below, regarding such operations. [78] JO 1971 L28/15.
[79] Amending Reg 2396/71 (OJ 1977 L337/1). [80] ibid, Art 1.2.
[81] 5th and 6th recitals in the preamble to Reg 2895/77 (OJ 1977 L337/7) concerning operations qualifying for a higher rate of intervention by the ESF.
[82] Art 1.6 of Dec 77/801 (OJ 1977 L337/8).
[83] Reg 2895/77 (OJ 1977 L337/7). [84] OJ 1977 C141/2, para III.A.1.
[85] The Commission, however, considered that the distinction between these priority regions should be abolished (ibid, para B.2).
[86] ibid, para I.D.3. [87] OJ 1983 L289/38. [88] ibid, Art 7(1).

assistance,[89] which now included Greece.[90] The remainder was to support operations in respect of employment in other regions of high and long-term unemployment[91] and/or industrial restructuring.[92]

New Commission Guidelines[93] envisaged that Fund assistance would be concentrated on operations to further employment in regions qualifying for the higher rate of assistance and in two other categories of regions. The first category concerned regions of industrial and sectoral restructuring[94] assisted or proposed by the Commission to be assisted from the non-quota section of the European Regional Development Fund[95] or assisted under Article 56 of the ECSC Treaty.[96] The second category concerned regions of high and long-term unemployment. They were drawn up by reference to unemployment rates and per capita gross domestic product.[97]

However, there was a permanent disproportion between the applications for financing submitted and the resources available to the Fund. Consequently, allocations of assistance had to be reduced in line with priorities adopted in the legislation and the management guidelines.[98] Thus reductions applied to operations classified at the lowest level of priority for which appropriations were still available.[99] The reduction for each Member State might be weighted to take account of its unemployment rate and per capita gross domestic product.[100] However, for 1986 to 1988, where appropriations were insufficient to cover priority operations, a linear reduction was applied.

[89] OJ 1983 L289/38 Art 7(3).

[90] Reg 1989/81 (OJ 1981 L194/4) concerning operations qualifying for a higher rate of intervention by the ESF. Dec 85/568 (OJ 1985 L370/40) amending, on account of the accession of Spain and Portugal, Dec 83/516 added these two countries to the priority regions. It also raised the percentage of Fund resources reserved for such regions to 44.5%.

[91] In a Statement *ad* Art 6 of Dec 83/516 (OJ 1983 L289/38) the Council and Commission declared that special attention should be given to projects to promote employment in regions where the unemployment rate was exceptionally high compared with the national average.

[92] In a Statement *ad* Art 7 (ibid) the Council requested the Commission to prepare proposals regarding 'reliable statistical machinery, taking account, *inter alia*, of the criterion of GDP per capita'.

[93] Guidelines for the management of the ESF for 1984–86 (OJ 1984 C5/2), para I; and Dec 85/261 (OJ 1985 L133/26) on the Guidelines for the management of the ESF for 1986–88, para 1.1.

[94] Para 4.3 (ibid) introduced priority for operations outside the priority regions where the restructuring was of an exceptional scale and was located in an area of particularly high unemployment or where the public authorities had introduced exceptional measures to support vocational training and job creation.

[95] See sect 2.3.3 above.

[96] See sect 5.3 below.

[97] See, later, Dec 87/329 (OJ 1987 L167/56) on the Guidelines for the management of the ESF for 1988–90, para 1.1.

[98] AG Da Cruz Vilaça in Case 84/85 *UK v EC Commission: assistance for part-time employment* [1987] ECR 3765, 3779. See also the *Sixteenth Report on the ESF* (EC Commission, Brussels, 1989) 5.

[99] Guidelines for the management of the ESF for 1979–81 and transitional guidelines for 1978 (OJ 1978 C116/2), para D.1. See, earlier, para D.3 of the Guidelines for 1977 (OJ 1977 C141/2).

[100] Para I.D.2(c) of the Guidelines for the management of the ESF for 1980–82 (OJ 1979 C159/2); for 1981–83 (OJ 1980 C119/3), para 1.4; and for 1982–84 (OJ 1981 C110/3), para 1.3.

It was calculated in proportion to the financial volume of remaining applications by each Member State.[101]

In practice, the bulk of the assistance from the Fund went to regions with the highest unemployment and lowest per capita gross domestic product[102] within the Community and to restructuring regions eligible under the non-quota section of the European Regional Development Fund or the ECSC Treaty.[103] Hence, the geographical allocation of the assistance from the European Social Fund was largely determined by the requirements of regional policy pursued under the EEC Treaty and sectoral policies pursued under the ECSC Treaty.

In fact, the Community legislature had sought to develop the objectives of the Fund so as to make it a more active instrument to promote employment policies. However, increased unemployment produced patterns of assistance-allocation which suggested that the Fund still operated more as an equalization or compensatory mechanism.[104] In other words, there were contradictions between 'legislative dynamism' and practical constraints.[105]

4.3.4 Scope of Assistance

Decision 71/66[106] provided for the Fund to assist 'specific' and 'general' operations.[107] Specific operations were envisaged by the Commission in its Opinion,[108] on which the Decision was based. The provision for general operations was added by the Council.[109]

General operations were those which, according to Article 5(2) of the Decision, were to be undertaken pursuant to Regulation 2396/71.[110] Specific operations were those which, according to Article 4 of the Decision, required the enactment of specific Council measures authorizing them.

[101] Dec 85/261 (OJ 1985 L133/26) on the Guidelines for the management of the ESF for 1986–88, para 1.7. In the Guidelines for 1984–86 (OJ 1984 C5/2) a linear reduction method had already been applied in relation to assistance to the priority regions (para 6.3). See, generally, COA special report 1/88 (OJ 1988 C126/1) on national and Community systems and procedures relating to the management of the ESF.

[102] Thus eg because of its high per capita GNP Groningen was not a priority area for ESF assistance. See Commission Reply to WQ 1380/86 (OJ 1987 C82/25) by Mr Bran van der Lek.

[103] Commission Reply to WQ 2304/86 (OJ 1988 C140/2) by Mr Heinz Schreiber.

[104] Hatt, n 9 above, 90. Cf COA special report 1/88 (OJ 1988 C126/1) on national and Community systems and procedures relating to the management of the ESF, para 5.2.

[105] Gruber, n 42 above.

[106] JO 1971 L28/15.

[107] See also Notice concerning the presentation of requests for assistance from the ESF (JO 1972 C96/1); and Communication concerning the procedures laid down by the Member States for the submission of applications for assistance from the ESF and their transmission to the Commission (OJ 1982 C6/4).

[108] JO 1969 C131/4.

[109] J Mégret, JV Louis, D Vignes, M Waelbroeck, JL Dewost, P Brueckner, and A Sacchettini, *Le Droit de la Communauté économique européenne* (University of Brussels, 1973) vii. 57–58.

[110] JO 1971 249/54.

In the case of either kind of operation, the private sector[111] as well as the public sector could now receive assistance. Employment assistance to businesses, provided that there was no conflict with Community competition policy, could thus be provided.[112]

General operations

General operations were to be 'essentially of a remedial nature'.[113] According to Article 5 of Decision 71/66,[114] they concerned difficulties resulting indirectly from the working of the common market or impeding the harmonious development of the Community. In the case of such difficulties, assistance could be granted without the need for a specific Council decision. It could be granted: to eliminate long-term structural unemployment and underemployment; to train a labour force with the skills needed; and to assist the absorption and reabsorption into active employment of the disabled, older workers, women, and young workers.[115] Such operations were to receive not less than 50 per cent of total Fund resources. In the longer term, however, the greater part of the resources was to be reserved for specific operations.[116]

According to Article 1(1) of Regulation 2396/71,[117] the general operations were to:

(*a*) aim at solving the problems which arose in a region which, because it was less developed or there was a decline in the main activities, suffered a serious and prolonged imbalance in employment;

(*b*) aim at facilitating adaptation to the requirements of technical progress of those branches of economic activity in which such progress gave rise to substantial changes in manpower and professional knowledge or skill; or

(*c*) be undertaken because of substantial changes in conditions of production or disposal of products in groups of undertakings with similar or connected activities which were thus forced to cease, reduce, or transform their activities permanently.

In the context of these operations assistance could be provided for training programmes, resettlement expenses, tideover allowances, coun-

[111] Art 8(2) of Dec 71/66 (JO 1971 L28/15). See also the Communication concerning those public authorities which were empowered by Member States to provide financial assistance for operations by entities governed by private law, and which guaranteed the completion of such operations (OJ 1982 C6/2). The distribution as between public and private bodies between 1984 and 1988 was indicated in the Commission Reply by Mr Marin to WQ 676/88 (OJ 1989 C95/11) by Geoffrey Hoon.

[112] Commission Reply by Mr Richard to WQ 1304/82 (OJ 1982 C333/26) by Mrs Fuillet.

[113] 8th recital in the preamble to Dec 71/66 (JO 1971 L28/15). See also the Report of the Committee on Social Affairs and Employment on the proposal for a decision on assistance from the ESF to persons employed in the shipbuilding industry, EP Doc 86/74, 14.

[114] JO 1971 L28/15.

[115] ibid, Art 1(2) and (3).

[116] ibid, Art 9(2).

[117] JO 1971 249/54.

selling, removal of barriers to employment for disadvantaged (handicapped or elderly) groups of workers, and the improvement of working conditions in less developed regions.[118]

The scope of such assistance might be more closely defined in Commission guidelines. Thus 'adaptation operations'[119] under Article 1(1)(b) were accorded first-level priority in the guidelines where they: were carried out in sectors which manifested a reduction in the labour force, notably for reasons of technological changes in production; concerned small and medium-sized enterprises; or envisaged the introduction, in a given sector, of the first applications of a new technology.[120]

In the case of assistance to groups of undertakings facing changed conditions under Article 1(1)(c), first-level priority was accorded to operations which fell within sectors manifesting large-scale structural change of a long-term nature, particularly for reasons concerning product outlets, and were developed in line with guidelines for assistance to particular sectors. The same priority was accorded to operations carried out by groups of small and medium-sized enterprises, especially those which had a subcontracting or similar activity and were regarded as the most vulnerable.[121]

However, prospects of limited growth, demographic trends, and structural adjustment problems, particularly those resulting from the energy crisis, the introduction of new technologies, and changes in the international economy, implied the need for reform.[122] Without reform, the resources of the Fund would be too thinly spread, and its work rendered 'defensive' by economic conditions.

Accordingly, under Decision 83/516[123] general operations were to be carried out within the framework of the labour-market policies of the Member States.[124] Thus the 'Fund [was to] intervene in policy actions to promote employment adopted by the Member States'.[125] The operations were to include those intended to improve employment opportunities for young people, notably by means of vocational training measures after completion of full-time compulsory schooling.[126] Under Article 7(2) of the Decision at least 95 per cent of Fund resources were to be used for such operations.

The operations were now to concern: vocational training and guidance; recruitment and wage subsidies; resettlement and socio-vocational integration

118 ibid, Art 3(2).

119 Other Community policies, notably competition policy, meant that operations not opened up to the whole economic sector could not be assisted (para V.B of the 1977 Guidelines, OJ 1977 C141/2).

120 ibid, para V.B(a).

121 ibid, para V.B(b).

122 1st recital in the preamble to the Council Resolution of 27 June 1980 (OJ 1980 C168/1) on guidelines for a Community labour market policy.

123 OJ 1983 L289/38.

124 ibid, Art 3(1).

125 A-G Darmon in Case C–157/90 *Infortec Projectos & Consultadoria, Lda v EC Commission* [1992] ECR I–3525, I–3532.

126 Art 3(1) of Dec 83/516 (OJ 1983 L289/38).

in connection with geographical mobility; and services and technical advice concerned with job creation.[127]

Specific operations

Specific operations were to be concerned with improving the employment situation and preventing employment problems; adapting employment to structural developments in the industry concerned;[128] and adding to the effectiveness of Council decisions by alleviating social obstacles to their implementation.[129] According to Article 4 of Decision 71/66,[130] the Council could provide for the Fund to assist such operations. The Council could do so, when the employment situation was affected or in danger of being affected either by special measures adopted by the Council in the framework of Community policies or by 'jointly agreed operations' to further Community objectives. The Council could also provide for the Fund to assist such operations, when the employment situation called for 'specific joint action' to improve the balance between the supply of, and the demand for, manpower within the Community. The assistance was thus intended to meet situations arising from Community decisions or requiring action at Community level and to meet situations arising indirectly from the functioning of the common market or impeding the harmonious development of the Community.[131]

Accordingly, assistance was introduced to facilitate implementation of 'jointly agreed operations' for workers leaving the agricultural,[132] textile,[133] and clothing industries.[134] At the same time, assistance by way of 'specific joint actions' was made available in respect of the handicapped,[135] migrant workers,[136] young people,[137] and women.[138]

Article 4 of Decision 75/459[139] sought to give the former category of spe-

[127] Art 3(1) of Dec 83/516 (OJ 1983 L289/38), Art 1(2).

[128] See also the Report of the Committee on Social Affairs and Employment on the proposal for a decision on assistance from the ESF to persons employed in the shipbuilding industry, EP Doc 86/74, 14.

[129] See also Gruber, n 42 above, 262.

[130] JO 1971 L28/15.

[131] ibid, 11th recital in the preamble.

[132] Dec 72/428 (JO 1972 L291/158).

[133] Dec 72/429 (JO 1972 L291/160). For a critical analysis of such assistance, see MJ Macmillen and JS Chard, 'European Social Fund Aid to Textile Workers: The Early Experience' (1978) *European Economic Review* 269–290.

[134] Dec 76/206 (OJ 1976 L39/39) on intervention by the ESF in favour of persons occupied in the textile and clothing industries.

[135] Dec 74/328 (OJ 1974 L185/22) on action by the ESF for handicapped persons.

[136] Assistance towards courses of specialized teaching for children of migrant workers was provided for by Reg 1761/74 (OJ 1974 L185/1) amending Reg 2397/71. See, later, Dec 77/803 (OJ 1977 L337/12) on action by the ESF for migrant workers.

[137] Dec 75/459 (OJ 1975 L199/36) on action by the ESF for persons affected by employment difficulties. See, later, Reg 3039/78 (OJ 1978 L361/3) on the creation of two new types of aid for young people from the ESF.

[138] Dec 77/804 (OJ 1977 L337/14) on action by the ESF for women.

[139] On action by the ESF for persons affected by employment difficulties (OJ 1975 L199/36). The 1st recital in the preamble referred to para 26 of the Dec 1974 Summit Communiqué (Bull EC 12–1974, 1104).

cific operations a more systematic basis. It provided that by 30 November 1975 the Council would deliberate on a Commission proposal for persons who were or had been employed in sectors particularly affected by employment imbalances resulting from recession. Due regard was to be had to the regions most affected by employment difficulties.

The resulting proposal[140] envisaged assistance relating to sectors with an unemployment increase since the beginning of 1974 considerably above the Community average. Assistance was also envisaged in regions with an unemployment increase since the beginning of the same year considerably above the national average or in which unemployment in one of the above sectors affected a substantial part of the active population. Due account was to be taken of the absolute level of unemployment in the region concerned.[141]

More particularly, the Commission proposed that the Fund should assist persons affected by the restructuring of the shipbuilding industry.[142] Assistance was envisaged for operations designed to facilitate the employment and increase the geographical and occupational mobility of such persons,[143] where their jobs were, or risked being, directly affected by the restructuring of this industry.[144] Such assistance was to take the form of a specific programme designed to contribute towards the long-term improvement of the competitiveness of undertakings, so that they could compete on a worldwide basis.

The Committee on Social Affairs and Employment considered that the Fund should have a more positive role in promoting the development of Community shipyards through the training of workers. Rather than using the Fund to assist the mobility of the workers and their transfer to other industries and regions, the assistance should be used to provide vocational training for these workers and to qualify them for new types of work in modernized shipyards. Only by such means could the Fund achieve its basic objective. This was to provide better employment and better working and living conditions for the workers and not to subsidize their removal to other regions or cause them to be made redundant or prematurely retired.[145]

[140] Of 14 Oct 1975 (OJ 1975 C258/5) for a decision on intervention by the ESF in favour of vocational-training adjustment measures.

[141] ibid, Art 1.

[142] Proposal of 11 Jan 1974 (OJ 1974 C13/6) for a decision on assistance from the ESF to persons employed in the shipbuilding industry; and State of the shipbuilding industry in the Community (situation as at 1 Jan 1981), COM(81)432, 17.

[143] The European Parliament considered that the action envisaged should form part of a reorganization and investment policy co-ordinated at the Community level, due regard being given to regional policy. More particularly, workers in industries related to shipbuilding should be eligible for assistance. See the Resolution of 13 June 1974 (OJ 1974 C76/42) on the proposal for a decision on assistance from the ESF to persons employed in the shipbuilding industry, para 10.

[144] Art 1 of the 1974 proposal (OJ 1974 C13/6).

[145] Report on the proposal for a decision on assistance from the ESF to persons employed in the shipbuilding industry, EP Doc 86/74, 13. More recently, the Parliament sought unsuccessfully to amend the proposal for what became Dir 90/684 (OJ 1990 L380/27) on aid to shipbuilding, to

However, these proposals were not accepted by the Council. Consequently, the assistance to implementation of 'jointly agreed operations' remained limited to agriculture and textiles. These were sectors which had already been selected in Council enactments. Yet, the problems of other sectors and the need for Fund intervention therein might have been just as great.

Even in relation to agriculture and textiles, legislative arrangements for assistance from the Fund might be inadequate. Thus the Commission sought closer targeting of Fund assistance to agriculture than was required by the Council legislation through its guidelines for the management of the Fund. According to the Guidelines for 1977,[146] first-level priority was accorded to operations which: related to the consequences for agriculture of the implementation of the Directives of 17 April 1972;[147] included the same objectives; were carried out in Directive 75/268 regions[148] and concerned those leaving agriculture with a view to vocational retraining in the same regions; or were aimed at certain farm home-helps such as young persons, who had been unemployed or underemployed since leaving school, and wives of farmers seeking employment outside agriculture, even if their husbands remained in that sector.[149] Other operations in this sector might receive second-level priority.[150]

The Guidelines for 1978 to 1981[151] were more restrictive. Priority was accorded only to two kinds of operations. The first kind concerned operations on behalf of persons (farmers, hired agricultural workers, or family workers) who left farming—or had left more than two years previously—to take up employment in another sector. The second kind concerned operations on behalf of persons who wished to pursue an activity additional to farming, particularly tourism and craft activities. Both kinds of operations had to be carried out in Directive 75/268 regions or in regions with agricultural income below the Community average.[152] The Guidelines for 1982 to 1984 added priority for operations coming within the framework of specialized measures for the agricultural sector or for the rural environment.[153] Other operations were not accorded priority, which meant that they would be held over until the end of the year and their approval would be subject to finance being available.[154]

In the case of assistance to textiles and clothing, first-level priority was accorded by the 1977 Guidelines[155] to two categories of operations. First, it

provide for Community assistance to retraining. See the Resolution of 23 Nov 1990 (OJ 1990 C324/343).

146 OJ 1977 C141/2. 147 See sect 3.3.4 above. 148 ibid.

149 para III.A.1 of the Guidelines for the management of the ESF for 1977 (OJ 1977 C141/2).

150 ibid, para III.A.2.

151 Guidelines for the management of the ESF for 1979–81 and transitional guidelines for 1978 (OJ 1978 C116/2).

152 ibid, para II.A.

153 para 2.1.1.1 of the Guidelines for the management of the ESF for 1982–4 (OJ 1981 C110/2).

154 OJ 1977 C141/2, para I.D.3. 155 ibid.

was accorded to operations in favour of persons having to leave the textile and clothing sectors in order to pursue activities in another sector of economic activity. Such operations had to show clearly the scope of the employment problems to be resolved and the strategy to be implemented. Secondly, such priority was accorded to persons who, as a result of structural adjustment measures, left one job in this sector for another in a branch of the same sector showing prospects in due course of viability at Community level.[156]

The Guidelines for 1979 to 1981[157] added the requirement that the first category of operations was to be carried out in textile-producing regions with a particularly high rate of unemployment. They also introduced a proviso regarding operations of the second category. This proviso concerned training operations which led directly to employment in producing goods considered particularly sensitive because of a high-level of market penetration by cheap imports or because of a recognized crisis in the Community market. They could only be assisted, if the products involved were capable of reaching a satisfactory level of competitiveness, particularly in terms of average costs.[158] In other words, training was not to concern production which offered poor prospects of future employment.[159]

The Guidelines for 1982 to 1984[160] were more demanding and required that operations within the second category had to take place within the framework of a conversion or restructuring programme. Second-level priority was accorded to other operations, either for persons remaining in the sector or for those leaving it, when training corresponded to the requirements of jobs assured in advance by employers.[161] No priority was accorded to operations concerning products which were either in a critical situation with regard to intra-Community trade (synthetic fibres, tights and stockings, worsted yarn, and pullovers) or were identical to those supplied at low prices by certain 'third world' countries, when such operations were linked to increased productive capacity liable to create new employment problems.[162]

4.3.5 Forms of Assistance

Decision 71/66[163] envisaged that Member States would propose 'sets of specific measures' for assistance.[164] Accordingly, Regulation 2396/71[165] provided that, save in exceptional circumstances, Fund assistance had to contribute towards the implementation of a specific programme directed at remedying the causes of imbalance affecting employment. Such programmes were to be established for the region, sector, group of undertakings, or category of persons concerned. They were to indicate clearly the economic

[156] ibid, para III.B.1.
[157] OJ 1978 C116/2.
[158] ibid, para B.1.
[159] ibid, para 1.A(d).
[160] OJ 1981 C110/2.
[161] ibid, para 2.2.1.2.
[162] ibid, para 1.1.3.2.
[163] JO 1971 L28/15.
[164] ibid, Art 6.
[165] JO 1971 L245/54.

interrelationship of the operations being planned and were to state the objectives and methods for attaining them.[166]

Assistance could also take the form of preparatory studies and pilot schemes. These were to be designed to give guidance to the Council and Commission in the choice of interventions by the Fund. They were also to enable the Member States and those in charge of operations to choose the most effective assistance and to organize the implementation thereof to best effect.[167]

Decision 83/516[168] envisaged assistance from the Fund to operations,[169] including innovatory projects. Assistance to innovatory projects generally had to fall within a Council action programme. Studies and exchange of experience might also be assisted.[170]

4.4 COHESION

The search for cohesion has imposed new demands on the European Social Fund.[171] However, definition of these demands has not been without problems.

4.4.1 Original Objectives 3 and 4

The Single European Act[172] sought to develop the role of the Fund by making it an instrument of cohesion. A closer definition of Fund objectives was considered necessary. It was considered necessary to ensure that too few resources and too many priorities for assistance did not lead to use of the linear reduction method[173] in the allocation of assistance.

Objectives 3 and 4 were originally established for the Fund by Regulation 2052/88.[174] Objective 3 was 'combating long-term unemployment',[175] and Objective 4 was 'facilitating the occupational integration of young people'.[176] Both Objectives were to be pursued throughout the Community.

[166] JO 1971 L245/54 Art 1(4). [167] ibid, Art 7. [168] OJ 1983 L289/38.

[169] ibid, 1(2). See also Dec 88/319 (OJ 1988 L143/45) on the Guidelines for the management of the ESF for 1989–91, Annex, para 5.

[170] OJ 1983 L289/38, Art 3(2).

[171] Arts 130a and 130b EEC, as amended by the SEA (OJ 1987 L169/1). See, now, Arts 158 and 159 EC.

[172] OJ 1987 L169/1. [173] sect 4.3.3 above, regarding the linear reduction method.

[174] On the tasks of the Structural Funds and their effectiveness and on co-ordination of their activities between themselves and with the operations of the EIB and the other financial instruments (OJ 1988 L185/9).

[175] ibid, Art 1(3). [176] ibid, Art 1(4).

Eligibility for assistance

In principle, only assistance to persons unemployed for over twelve months could originally be supported under Objective 3, though this period could be reduced in specific cases to be decided upon by the Commission.[177] Assistance to persons under 25 years of age, however long or short the period during which they had been seeking employment, could be supported under Objective 4.[178]

Moreover, in Objective 1, 2, or 5b regions assistance could be granted in respect of four further categories of persons. They were: unemployed persons generally; persons threatened with unemployment; persons employed in small or medium-sized enterprises; and working persons involved in an operation which was essential to the achievement of the development and conversion objectives of an integrated programme.[179] In Objective 1 regions apprentices and vocational trainees at secondary school were also eligible.[180]

Allocation of assistance

Article 3(2) of Regulation 2052/88[181] provided that the Commission, when allocating assistance, should take into account 'the requirements of the labour market and the priorities laid down in employment policies within the Community'. In practice, most assistance was allocated to the United Kingdom, followed by Italy, Germany, and France.[182]

Scope of assistance

Regulation 4255/88[183] provided that the Fund could contribute to financing vocational training, recruitment into newly stable jobs, and the creation of self-employed activities.[184] Accordingly, throughout the Community the Fund could support training measures aimed at providing the skills necessary to carry out specific types of employment, except for apprenticeship schemes. Equally, it could support training with the relevant technology content required by technological change and developments in the labour market.[185]

In Objective 1, 2, or 5b regions any vocational training and further training required for the use of new production and/or management techniques in small and medium-sized enterprises could also be supported.[186] More particularly, in Objective 1 regions support could extend to the theoretical portion

[177] Art 2(a) of Reg 4255/88 (OJ 1988 L374/21) laying down provisions for implementing Reg 2052/88 as regards the ESF. The Commission responded positively to a request from the Member States for it to make use of this possibility. See Promoting economic recovery in Europe (the Edinburgh growth initiative), COM(93)164, 8–9.

[178] Art 2(a) of Reg 4255/88 (OJ 1988 L374/21).

[179] ibid, Art 2(b).

[180] ibid, Art 2(c).

[181] OJ 1988 L185/9.

[182] *Twenty-Third EC General Report* (EC Commission, Brussels, 1990) 191.

[183] Laying down provisions for implementing Reg 2052/88 as regards the ESF (OJ 1988 L374/21).

[184] ibid, Art 1(1).

[185] ibid, Art 1(3).

[186] ibid, Art 1(4).

of apprenticeship training given outside the firm. Again, in specific cases, to be defined according to the particular needs of the Member States and regions concerned, support could extend to that part of the national secondary (or corresponding) education system specifically devoted to vocational training following compulsory full-time schooling. It was stipulated that that part had to meet the challenges posed by economic and technological changes.[187] Finally, training under apprenticeship contracts and training under national secondary vocational education systems could be assisted.[188]

Moreover, in Objective 1, 2, or 5b regions assistance could be granted to measures to encourage job stability and to develop new employment possibilities for persons who were unemployed, threatened with unemployment, particularly within the context of restructuring requiring technological modernization or substantial changes in the production or management system, or employed in small and medium-sized enterprises. Assistance could also be granted to measures to facilitate vocational training for any working person involved in an operation essential to the achievement of the development and conversion objectives of an integrated programme.[189]

The scope of Fund assistance was thus to be somewhat broader in such regions than elsewhere in the Community. However, the horizontal nature of Objectives 3 and 4 was felt generally to preclude a priori the selection of measures to be financed on the basis of the regionalization of intervention.[190] Rather, the need to increase the impact of assistance implied rigorous selection, based essentially on qualitative factors, particularly the requirements and prospects of the labour market.[191]

Accordingly, Commission Guidelines[192] stated that assistance would be allocated preferentially to operations in Objective 1, 2, or 5b regions which were not directly linked to regional or rural development or industrial restructuring. The operations had to: demonstrate a special effort to take account of the needs and prospects of the labour market; be of transnational character; concern training in advanced technology; be of innovatory character; concern training and recruitment in the interests of modernization; concern improved and more efficient training structures; or concern operations for persons encountering special difficulties on the labour market.[193]

[187] Reg 4255/88 (OJ 1988 L374/21) Art 1(5). In the same regions, and for three years after the entry into force of the Regulation, recruitment assistance could, according to Art 1(6) (ibid), be extended to non-productive projects which fulfilled a public need involving the creation of additional jobs of at least six months' duration for the long-term unemployed aged over 25.

[188] ibid, Art 2(c). Persons employed within the framework of the operations referred to in Art 1(6) (ibid) might also be assisted.

[189] ibid, Art 2(b).

[190] Guidelines concerning ESF intervention in respect of action against long-term unemployment and occupational integration of young people (OJ 1989 C45/6), para III. 3.

[191] ibid. [192] ibid, para III. 4. [193] ibid, para V.

Forms of assistance

Operational programmes and global grants constituted the main forms of assistance.[194] The Fund could also participate, with up to 5 per cent of its resources, in financing: innovatory measures; transfer of knowledge between undertakings; guidance and advice for the reintegration of the long-term unemployed; and measures of preparation, accompaniment, and management necessary for implementation of Regulation 4255/88.[195] In addition, pilot projects might be assisted.[196]

More particularly, the Fund was involved in implementation of three Community initiatives.[197] The Euroform initiative was concerned with new skills and new employment opportunities created by the completion of the internal market and technological change.[198] The Now initiative was concerned with promoting equal opportunities for women in employment and vocational training.[199] The Horizon initiative was concerned with handicapped persons and certain other disadvantaged groups.[200] In addition, there was Youthstart, which concerned the labour-market integration of young people.[201]

4.4.2 New Objectives 3 and 4

Experience of pursuing the original Objectives 3 and 4 indicated a need for reform. According to the Commission, the legislation allowed for assistance applications to be presented with little justification other than that technically they met the eligibility criteria. In other words, the Fund passively assisted the financing of national policies.[202]

[194] Art 5 of Reg 2052/88 (OJ 1988 L185/9); and Art 6(1) of Reg 4255/88 (OJ 1988 L374/21).

[195] ibid, Art 1(2).

[196] See eg Call for proposals for the implementation of the 'Local Social Capital' pilot project—Art 6 of the ESF Regulation (OJ 1998 C228/15).

[197] cf Dec 90/267 (OJ 1990 L156/1) establishing an action programme for the development of continuing vocational training in the EC, which was designed to improve the quality and availability of continuous vocational training in the Community and, in particular, to improve the competitiveness of firms by improving the skills of their employees. It was adopted under Art 128 EEC and was financed under Items B3–1023 and B8–3123 of the General Budget for 1991 (OJ 1991 L30/3).

[198] Notice laying down guidelines for operational programmes/global grants in the framework of a Community initiative concerning new qualifications, new skills, and new employment opportunities (OJ 1990 C327/3).

[199] Notice laying down guidelines for operational programmes/global grants within the framework of a Community initiative to promote equal opportunities for women in the field of employment and vocational training (OJ 1990 C327/5).

[200] Notice laying down guidelines for operational programmes/global grants in the framework of a Community initiative concerning handicapped persons and certain other disadvantaged groups (OJ 1990 C327/9).

[201] Community initiative for the occupational integration of young people (Item B2–1423 of the Budget for 1998 (OJ 1998 L44/3)).

[202] Operation of the Community Structural Funds, COM(93)124, 11.

Arrangements of a 'more policy-driven' kind were favoured by the Commission.[203] Such arrangements would take into account economic developments, particularly the effects of further industrial changes on human resource needs.[204] At the same time, account had to be taken of the amendment to Article 123 of the EC Treaty,[205] introduced by the Treaty on European Union, and the Protocol on Economic and Social Cohesion. The Treaty amendment added 'adaptation [of workers] to industrial changes and to changes in production systems, in particular through vocational training and retraining' to the tasks of the Fund.[206] Moreover, the Protocol established the integration of persons excluded from the labour market as a 'Community policy'.[207] Accordingly, Regulation 2052/88[208] was amended by Regulation 2081/93,[209] and Regulation 4255/88[210] was amended by Regulation 2084/93.[211]

As a result of these amendments, Objective 3 now concerns combating long-term unemployment and facilitating integration into working life of young people and of persons exposed to exclusion from the labour market.[212] Objective 4, in turn, concerns facilitating the adaptation of workers of either sex to industrial changes and to changes in production systems.[213] According to the Commission, Objective 3 supports and strengthens policies which are already well established in Member States. In contrast, Objective 4 'represents a specific approach to the employment, training, and competitiveness problem'.[214]

Objective 4 seeks to forestall the effects of the relevant changes on unemployment.[215] Pursuant to this Objective, it is envisaged that the Fund will address the underlying causes of problems relating to industrial adaptation and not deal with short-term, market-related symptoms. At the same time, it should meet the general needs of workers resulting from changes in produc-

203 Operation of the Community Structural Funds, COM(93)124, 11.

204 Community Structural Fund operations 1994–99, COM(93)67, 4.

205 See, now, Art 146 EC.

206 From the Single Act to Maastricht and beyond: the means to match our ambitions, COM(92)2000.

207 Report of the Committee on Social Affairs, Employment, and the Working Environment on the European Parliament's approach to the revision of the ESF, EP Doc A3–57/93, 4.

208 OJ 1988 L185/9.

209 OJ 1993 L193/5.

210 OJ 1988 L374/21.

211 OJ 1993 L193/39.

212 See eg the Call for proposals for pilot actions aiming at integrating the concept of the information society into regional development policies of less favoured regions (OJ 1995 C253/27).

213 Art 1(3) and (4) of Reg 2081/93 (OJ 1993 L193/5). See eg the Call for proposals for pilot projects and demonstration projects concerning innovative schemes for women in agricultural and in rural areas (OJ 1996 C284/21).

214 ESF—the new Objective 4, COM(94)510, 3–4. See also, regarding 'incentive measures', Art 129 EC.

215 ESC Opinion of 30 Apr 1992 (CES(92)501) on the Commission document 'From the Single Act to Maastricht and beyond: the means to match our ambitions', 7. See, more particularly, the Council Resolution of 16 May 1994 (OJ 1994 C149/1) on the automobile industry, para I.9.

tion systems identified or predicted and not be designed to benefit a single firm or a particular industry.[216]

To avoid economically unsound, hidden subsidies to uncompetitive enterprises or sectors, which would in the long term be contrary to these Objectives, the assistance should, it is argued, primarily be 'people centred'. Where there is a need for enterprise or sector-specific assistance, it should chiefly benefit small and medium-sized enterprises and ancillary industries.[217] Unless it is so fashioned, Directorate General IV of the Commission may block proposed assistance, especially assistance to the training of persons threatened with unemployment in their company, on competition-policy grounds.[218]

It is now proposed that these two Objectives will be merged, to form a new Objective 3. It will be supporting the adaptation and modernization of policies and systems of education, training, and employment.[219]

Eligibility for assistance

Under the existing Objective 3 the following persons are eligible for assistance: unemployed persons exposed to long-term unemployment;[220] young people[221] in search of employment; persons exposed to exclusion from the labour market; and women not possessing vocational qualifications or returning to the labour market after a period of absence.[222]

Under Objective 4 persons of either sex needing to adapt to changed conditions are eligible. In particular, persons threatened with unemployment or faced with industrial changes and changes in production systems are eligible.[223]

It is now proposed that assistance under the new Objective 3 will only be available to persons outside regions covered by Objective 1 or 2.[224]

Allocation of assistance

At least 80 per cent of the total resources for the existing Objectives 3 and 4 must be allocated to Objective 3, 'in view of the seriousness of the unemployment problem'.[225] In other words, most of the resources of the Fund are to be

[216] Operation of the Community Structural Funds, COM(93)124, 15.

[217] Report of the Committee on Social Affairs, Employment, and the Working Environment on the European Parliament's approach to the revision of the ESF, EP Doc A3–0057/93, 9–10. Comparisons may thus be drawn with assistance provided under Art 56 ECSC (ibid 9–10). See sect 5.3 below, regarding such assistance.

[218] COA annual report for 1994 (OJ 1995 C303/1), para 5.32.

[219] Proposal of 19 Mar 1998 (OJ 1998 C176/1) for a regulation laying down provisions on the Structural Funds, Art 1.

[220] Rather than 'persons unemployed for more than 12 months'.

[221] There is no longer any express age limit.

[222] Art 1(1) of Reg 2084/93 (OJ 1993 L193/39).

[223] ibid, Art 1(2).

[224] Proposal of 19 Mar 1998 (OJ 1998 C176/1) for a regulation laying down provisions on the Structural Funds, Arts 1 and 5.

[225] Statement regarding Objective 3 in the Minutes of the meeting between the European Parliament, the Council, and the Commission of 12 July 1993 (OJ 1993 C255/17).

used to assist national employment policies. In practice, 35 per cent of spending under Objective 3 is targeted on promoting the occupational integration of young people.[226] Most assistance has been allocated to the United Kingdom and France.[227]

It is now proposed that the allocation should be based 'principally on the eligible population, the employment situation, and the severity of the problems, such as social exclusion, education and training levels, and participation of women in the labour market'.[228] Particular emphasis will be given to improving systems for anticipating and facilitating economic and social change as well as to improving the participation of women in the labour market. In practice, there will be an indicative allocation of 15 per cent of Fund resources for each of these two policy fields.[229]

Scope of assistance

In pursuit of Objective 3, the Fund is to assist: vocational training; temporary employment; and the development of appropriate training, employment, and support structures.[230] In pursuit of Objective 4, assistance is to cover: anticipation of labour-market trends and vocational qualification requirements; vocational training and retraining, guidance, and counselling; and the improvement and development of appropriate training systems.[231]

Further measures are envisaged in regions covered by Objectives 1, 2, or 5b. In these regions the Fund is to support employment growth and stability, particularly through continuing training and vocational guidance, and is to boost human potential in research, science, and technology.[232] More particularly, in Objective 1 regions it is also to strengthen and improve education and training systems and to contribute to development through the training of public officials.[233]

The Fund may grant assistance towards expenditure to cover the income and related costs as well as subsistence and travel costs of people participating in the above actions. It may also assist the preparation, management, and evaluation of operations in the Member States[234] and provide technical assistance.[235]

It is now proposed that the Fund will assist: developing active labour-market policies; promoting social inclusion and equal opportunities; developing education and training systems; improving systems to produce a

[226] Commission Reply by Mrs Cresson to WQ 0766/96 (OJ 1996 C297/25) by Thomas Megahy.

[227] *EU General Report 1994* (EC Commission, Brussels, 1995), 155.

[228] Art 7(3) of the Proposal of 19 Mar 1998 (OJ 1998 C176/1) for a regulation laying down provisions on the Structural Funds.

[229] Explanatory memorandum to the Proposal of 19 Mar 1998 for a regulation laying down provisions on the Structural Funds, COM(98)131, 31.

[230] Art 1(1) of Reg 2084/93 (OJ 1993 L193/39).

[231] ibid, Art 1(2).

[232] ibid, Art 1(3).

[233] ibid, Art 1(4).

[234] ibid, Art 2(1).

[235] ibid, Art 2(2).

skilled, trained, and adaptable workforce; and improving the participation of women in the labour market.[236] The Fund shall also contribute to promoting local development, including local employment initiatives and territorial employment pacts.[237] Account is to be taken of the social and labour-market dimensions of the information society.[238]

This broad definition of the scope of assistance is designed to facilitate effective dovetailing between the assistance provided and the national action-plans for employment. It is also designed to ensure that the assistance is appropriate to the national and regional priorities and policies of each Member State.[239]

Forms of assistance

The forms which assistance may take under the existing Objectives 3 and 4 are the same as in the case of the original Objectives.[240] However, two new initiatives—the Adapt initiative and the initiative on Employment and Development of Human Resources—have been adopted.

The Adapt initiative[241] is intended to serve as a catalyst for Union-wide innovation as well as for the organized transfer of expertise and the dissemination of good practice among Member States. It seeks: to accelerate the adaptation of the workforce to industrial change; to increase the competitiveness of industry, services, and commerce; to prevent unemployment by developing the workforce through improving the qualifications of workers and their 'internal and external flexibility' and ensuring greater occupational mobility; and to anticipate and accelerate the development of new jobs and new activities, particularly labour-intensive ones, including exploitation of the potential of small and medium-sized enterprises. Attention is to be given to actions aimed at promoting equal opportunities for women.[242] The initiative is applicable throughout the Union, but particular emphasis is to be placed on the needs of the 'less favoured regions'.[243]

A further 'priority' within this initiative—Adapt-bis—(building the information society) has been adopted.[244] It is to facilitate the transition to

[236] Art 2(1) of the Proposal of 19 Mar 1998 (OJ 1998 C176/39) on the ESF.

[237] ibid, Art 2(2).

[238] ibid, Art 2(3).

[239] Explanatory memorandum to the Proposal of 19 Mar 1998 for a regulation laying down provisions on the Structural Funds, COM(98)131, 17.

[240] See eg Call for proposals for innovatory measures under the ESF in the field of new job sources (OJ 1996 C323/13).

[241] Communication laying down guidelines for operational programmes or global grants within the framework of the Community initiative, Adaptation of the Workforce to Industrial Change, aimed at promoting employment and the adaptation of the workforce to industrial change (OJ 1994 C180/30).

[242] ibid, para 6.

[243] ibid, para 8.

[244] Communication laying down amended guidelines for the Adapt initiative (OJ 1996 C200/7).

the information society and minimize the social exclusion which can result from it.[245]

Eligible measures must have 'some specific features'. Thus they must encourage a more active and co-ordinated approach at local level. Such an approach is expected to secure a greater employment impact by involving in the planning, implementation, and evaluation of the measures all relevant actors designated by the Member State, including local and regional authorities, economic and social partners, and training bodies.[246]

The initiative on Employment and Development of Human Resources[247] aims, in turn, to contribute to the development of human resources and to improve the working of the labour market. It is thereby to enhance employment growth, to promote social solidarity in the Union, and to promote equal opportunities for women on the labour market.[248] It is applicable throughout the Union, but particular emphasis is to be given to the needs of less favoured regions. Hence, some measures are limited to Objective 1, 2, or 5b regions.[249] The allocation of assistance among Member States is based on the relative severity of structural problems, particularly unemployment levels, as well as on the quality of proposals submitted.[250]

This initiative has absorbed Now, Horizon, and Youthstart, and a further 'strand'—Integra—has been added. This strand is designed to promote measures to improve the access to the labour market and the employability of vulnerable groups who are excluded or risk being excluded from it.[251]

It is now proposed that the Fund will assist: operations of an innovatory nature and pilot projects; studies, technical assistance, and change of experience; technical assistance for the preparation, monitoring, evaluation, and control of Fund operations; operations regarding the transfer of special knowledge concerning areas of intervention by the Fund; and information activities.[252] In addition, the Fund is to be responsible for a Community initiative on new forms of combating all forms of discrimination and/or inequalities in access to the labour market.[253]

[245] (OJ 1996 C200/7) para 4. [246] ibid, para 7(d).

[247] Communication laying down guidelines for operational programmes or global grants within the framework of the Community initiative on Employment and the Development of Human Resources aimed at promoting employment growth mainly through the development of human resources (OJ 1994 C180/36).

[248] ibid, para I.3. [249] ibid, para III.7. [250] ibid, para VI.17.

[251] Communication laying down guidelines for operational programmes or global grants within the framework of the Community initiative on Employment and the Development of Human Resources aimed at promoting employment growth mainly through the development of human resources (OJ 1996 C200/13).

[252] Art 6(1) of the Proposal of 19 Mar 1998 (OJ 1998 C176/39) on the ESF.

[253] Art 19(1) of the Proposal of 19 Mar 1998 (OJ 1998 C176/1) for a regulation laying down provisions on the Structural Funds.

4.5 CONCLUSION

The European Social Fund is said to contribute to strengthening the human-resource base of the weaker regions, where the lack of a suitably trained workforce is a serious problem. By assisting with training the Fund, it is also said, helps such regions to develop their endogenous potential.[254] Substantial lasting effects on these regions are expected to result.[255]

In reality, such assistance may merely lead successful trainees to migrate to more prosperous regions where their acquired skills are in demand. As a result, national rather than regional development may be encouraged.

This problem has implicit recognition in a Treaty amendment. In particular, Article 3(i) of the EEC Treaty provided for the creation of a European Social Fund, to improve employment opportunities for workers and to contribute to the raising of their standard of living. As amended by the Treaty on European Union, it now provides for a policy in the social sphere comprising this Fund. The implication is that the role of the Fund is to be broadened.

In practice, however, the operations of the Fund may still have more to do with assisting labour-market interventions by Member States than with promoting the regional equality demanded by cohesion.[256] The continuing emphasis on assisting such interventions, particularly training,[257] means that 'those who regard the EC as a Community rather than as a market . . . must be rather disappointed'.[258]

[254] M Quévit, J Houard, S Bodson, and A Dangoisse, *Impact régional 1992: Les Régions de tradition industrielle* (De Boeck, Brussels, 1991) 347, 352.

[255] R Hall and D van der Wee, 'Community Regional Policies for the 1990s' (1992) *Regional Studies* 399–404.

[256] cf the contrast drawn between the operations of the Structural Funds and an 'entitlement based social policy' in Anderson, n 15 above, 149.

[257] A Cutler, C Haslam, J Williams, and K Williams, *1992—the Struggle for Europe* (Berg, New York, 1989), 81.

[258] J Harrop, *The Political Economy of Integration in the European Community* (Edward Elgar, Aldershot, 2nd edn, 1992) 167–168.

Part Two

Other Financial Instruments

5

Sectoral Instruments

5.1 INTRODUCTION

Sectoral instruments may be created as integral elements of common policies for which the EC or ECSC Treaty provides an express basis. They may also be created as responses in Union practice to the needs of 'growth' sectors[1] or the problems of declining sectors,[2] such as oil refining[3] or wool production.[4] Indeed, in October 1978 the Commission presented the Council with a proposal[5] to assist the restructuring of undertakings[6] in any sector where the Council considered assistance appropriate.[7] If the employment situation in the region of an undertaking being restructured was sufficiently serious and if jobs had not been found for the labour made redundant, assistance could also be granted for conversion to other sectors.[8] The assistance envisaged could take the form of investment grants or interest rebates on loans.[9] However, this proposal was not accepted by the Council.

Article 157(1) of the EC Treaty, as amended by the Treaty on European Union, now provides that the Union and Member States are to aim at speeding up the adjustment of industry to structural changes. The implication is that Union assistance may play a role in facilitating industrial restructuring generally.

The issues raised by such restructuring are, it is recognized, seldom exclusively sectoral or exclusively regional. Hence, 'synergy' between the operations of the Structural Funds and those of sectoral instruments is

1 See eg Dec 92/421 (OJ 1992 L231/26) on a Community action plan to assist tourism; and the proposal of 6 June 1996 (OJ 1996 C222/9) for a decision on a first multiannual programme to assist European tourism. Cf the Proposal of 28 May 1998 (OJ 1998 C211/18) for a decision establishing a single programming instrument for cultural co-operation.

2 See eg the European Parliament Resolution of 10 June 1983 (OJ 1983 C184/163) on a second series of specific Community regional development measures, para 16, regarding the need to assist sectors likely to be affected in the foreseeable future by drastic structural upheavals. See also the Resolution of 22 Apr 1982 (OJ 1982 C125/119) on the European Parliament's guidelines for the General Budget for 1983, para 20.

3 Budget for 1979 (OJ 1979 L23/3), Item 3751.

4 European Parliament Resolution of 19 Apr 1996 (OJ 1996 C141/250) on the need for support measures for producers and processors of European wool.

5 Proposal of 31 Oct 1978 (OJ 1978 C272/3) for a regulation on Community assistance for industrial restructuring and conversion. See also Item 3750 of the Budget for 1979 (OJ 1979 L23/3).

6 Art 1(1) of the proposal of 31 Oct 1978 (OJ 1978 C272/3).

7 ibid, Art 1(2).

8 ibid, Art 2(2).

9 ibid, Art 3.

sought.[10] Since sectoral adjustment is easier against a background of regional development and vice versa, there may be thought to be a natural compatibility of sectoral policy requirements and those of cohesion, which facilitates the search. In practice, however, achievement of compatibility may be problematic, because challenges to the legal and political entrenchment[11] of sectoral policies are implied[12] and basic conceptions of 'industrial policy' may be at stake.[13]

Such problems are discernible in the operations of the Financial Instrument for Fisheries Guidance, ECSC assistance, support for trans-European networks, Euratom loans and guarantees, measures accompanying reform of the common agricultural policy, and the use of 'other budgetary resources'.

5.2 FINANCIAL INSTRUMENT FOR FISHERIES GUIDANCE

Assistance to the fishing industry was originally provided by the Guidance Section of the European Agricultural Guidance and Guarantee Fund. However, specific features of this industry required increasing resort to 'other Budgetary resources' and, ultimately, led to the creation of the Financial Instrument for Fisheries Guidance.

5.2.1 Establishment of the Common Organization

It was recognized that structural adjustment of the fishing industry might be associated with establishment of the common organization for fisheries. However, it was apparently considered that the adjustment could satisfactorily be assisted by the Guidance Section of the European Agricultural Guidance and Guarantee Fund.[14]

[10] Ways of increasing the effectiveness of the Community's Structural Funds, COM(83)501, 19.

[11] eg according to the Report of the Committee on Agriculture on aspects of the Community's regional policy to be developed in the future, EP Doc 35/77, Annex, 4–5, the co-ordination of the Structural Funds must not be allowed to interfere with the specificity of agricultural structural policy.

[12] eg the Committee on Regional Policy and Regional Planning considers that the Commission should devise sectoral policies in such a way as to take account of their regional planning impact. See the Report on a concerted regional planning policy, EP Doc A3–245/90, 7. See also the European Parliament Resolution of 18 Nov 1988 (OJ 1988 C326/289) on Community regional policy and the role of the regions, paras 12–13.

[13] The DG for Industry maintains that the 'Commission does not pursue any policies which would a priori aim at benefiting any specific industrial sector in a particular region. Such a policy would conflict with the Community's approach to industrial policy intended to create a business environment in which industry increases its competitiveness and the economy in general can further flourish.' See the Commission Reply by Mr Bangemann to WQ E–3481/93 (OJ 1994 C268/42) by Sir James Scott-Hopkins.

[14] See sect 3.2 above.

5.2.2 Development of the Common Organization

As the common organization and structural policy for this sector developed, the inadequacy of the Guidance Section of the European Agricultural Guidance and Guarantee Fund for addressing the structural problems of the fishing industry became clear. For example, Directive 83/515[15] provided for assistance to facilitate adjustment of the production capacity of fishing fleets to reduced catch possibilities.[16] This measure was described as a 'measure of a specific character [which could] not therefore be treated as a common measure' of the kind supported by the Guidance Section.[17] Hence, specific provision for assistance from the General Budget was made.[18] At the same time, Regulation 2909/83[19] sought to encourage redeployment of capacity. It introduced assistance for exploratory fishing and co-operation through joint fishing ventures involving partners in a third country on the Mediterranean or West African coast. Again, specific provision for assistance from the General Budget was made.[20]

Regulation 4028/86[21] envisaged a more comprehensive approach to the restructuring of the fishing industry. Assistance granted pursuant to this measure was financed under chapter 47 of the General Budget for 1988,[22] which was entitled 'New Structural Measures for Fisheries and the Sea'.

Objectives of assistance

According to the preamble to Regulation 4028/86,[23] the objective of assistance was the balanced exploitation of internal resources in Community waters. Broad account was to be taken of the economic and social environment of the industry. More particularly, account was to be taken of the diversity and seriousness of structural problems at regional level.[24]

Eligibility for assistance

Eligibility for assistance depended on the functional requirements of operations to be financed under Regulation 4028/86.[25]

Allocation of assistance

The allocation of the assistance granted under Regulation 4028/86[26] was controversial. In particular, there were objections to the concentration of such

[15] Concerning certain measures to adjust capacity in the fisheries sector (OJ 1983 L290/15).
[16] ibid, Art 1(1).
[17] ibid, final recital in the preamble.
[18] Art 450 of the Budget for 1984 (OJ 1984 L12/5).
[19] On measures to encourage exploratory fishing and co-operation through joint ventures in the fishing sector (OJ 1983 L290/9).
[20] Art 451 of the Budget for 1984 (OJ 1984 L12/5).
[21] On Community measures to improve and adapt structures in the fisheries and aquaculture sector (OJ 1986 L376/7).
[22] OJ 1987 L226/3.
[23] OJ 1986 L376/7.
[24] ibid, 8th recital in the preamble.
[25] ibid.
[26] ibid.

assistance in regions where the problem of excess fishing capacity was most severe.[27] It was argued that regional and social considerations should have been given closer attention. According to this argument, regions most heavily dependent on fishing should have received more assistance.[28]

Scope of assistance

The Commission favoured assistance to: redeployment and reduction of capacity;[29] early retirement from the fishing industry generally;[30] the payment of unemployment benefits for fishermen made redundant as a result of restructuring sponsored by Community assistance;[31] vocational training;[32] and the maintenance or creation of jobs for fishermen in disadvantaged regions.[33]

Regulation 4028/86[34] turned out to be less socially oriented. It provided for assistance to: the restructuring and renewal of the fishing fleet through the purchase or construction of new ships;[35] the modernization of the fishing fleet;[36] the development of aquaculture and structural works in coastal waters;[37] exploratory fishing;[38] joint ventures;[39] adjustment of capacities;[40] provision of facilities at fishing ports;[41] and the search for new markets.[42] In addition, Article 28 of the Commission draft for this measure[43] envisaged a

[27] COA Special report 3/91 (OJ 1994 C2/1) concerning the implementation of the measures for the restructuring, modernization, and adaptation of the capacities of fishing fleets in the Community, para 3.36.

[28] European Parliament Resolution of 15 May 1992 (OJ 1992 C150/317) on the CFP and the adjustments to be made, para 28. See also the Resolution of 28 Oct 1992 (OJ 1992 C305/56) on the MGPs 1993–96, para 3.

[29] Proposal of 21 Oct 1977 (OJ 1977 C278/15) for a regulation on certain immediate measures to adjust capacity in the fisheries sector, Art 3.

[30] ibid, Art 18(1).

[31] ibid, Art 18(2).

[32] An appropriation for 'Actions leading towards the development of a Common Fisheries Training Policy' was included in the Budget for 1984 (OJ 1984 L27/5), Items 4300 and 4301. See also Commission Reply to WQ 1476/83 (OJ 1984 C109/10) by Ms Joyce Quin.

[33] See, generally, Social aspects in the Community sea fishing sector, COM(80)725.

[34] OJ 1986 L376/7.

[35] ibid, Arts 6–8. Having regard to the global overcapacity in the Community fishing fleet, the Commission decided not to grant assistance for the construction of fishing vessels. See Granting of Community assistance to the fisheries and aquaculture sector within the framework of Regulation 4028/86 (OJ 1992 L182/4).

[36] Arts 9–10 of Reg 4028/86 (OJ 1986 L376/7).

[37] ibid, Arts 11–12.

[38] ibid, Arts 13–17; and Reg 1871/87 (OJ 1987 L180/1) laying down detailed rules for implementing Reg 4028/86 as regards schemes to encourage exploratory fishing.

[39] Arts 18–21 of Reg 4028/86 (OJ 1986 L376/7); and Reg 1955/88 (OJ 1988 L171/1) laying down detailed rules for implementing Reg 4028/86 as regards joint ventures in the fisheries sector.

[40] Arts 22–26 of Reg 4028/86 (OJ 1986 L376/7).

[41] ibid, Arts 27–28; and Reg 3856/91 (OJ 1991 L362/61) laying down detailed rules for the application of Reg 4028/86 as regards measures for the provision of facilities at fishing ports.

[42] Arts 29–31 of Reg 4028/86 (OJ 1986 L376/7).

[43] Proposal of 18 Sept 1986 (OJ 1986 C279/3) for a regulation on Community measures to improve and adapt structures in the fisheries and aquaculture sectors.

retirement incentive scheme and a lay-off allowance for fishermen on vessels for which laying-up or final cessation premiums had been granted. However, no provision for such assistance was included in the Regulation.

In addition, assistance for improvement of the processing and marketing of fishery and aquaculture products was provided under Regulation 4042/89.[44]

Forms of assistance

Assistance was to be granted within the framework of multiannual guidance programmes,[45] which were to be adopted under Regulation 4028/86.[46] These programmes had to be designed, *inter alia*, to establish a viable fishing fleet in line with the economic and social needs of the regions concerned and the foreseeable catch-potential in the medium term. They also had to take account of the socio-economic consequences and the regional impact of sectoral developments.[47]

In addition, specific measures might be adopted, to deal with certain regional or sectoral situations.[48] Such measures might assist: the removal of structural handicaps which affected fishing activities in certain regions; the implementation of a structural project covering all the problems related to fishing activities in a particular region; or the implementation of concerted measures to alleviate difficulties affecting a specific aspect of fishing activities.[49] Assistance for research might also be provided in the form of Community programmes.[50]

5.2.3 Cohesion

Regulation 4028/86[51] was amended by Regulation 3944/90,[52] which stressed the importance for cohesion of assistance to small-scale fisheries. Such assistance, it was argued, helped to speed up development in the less favoured regions which were heavily dependent on fisheries.[53] Hence, assistance for restructuring and renewal of the fishing fleet, modernization of the fishing fleet,[54] and adjustment

[44] On the improvement of the conditions under which fishery and aquaculture products were processed and marketed (OJ 1989 L388/1).

[45] OJ 1986 L376/7, Art 1(2).

[46] ibid, Art 2(1).

[47] ibid, Art 2(2).

[48] ibid, 18th recital in the preamble.

[49] ibid, Art 32(1). See eg Dec 91/258 (OJ 1991 L126/17) on a specific measure to alleviate difficulties affecting whiting fishing in the North Sea.

[50] Reg 3252/87 (OJ 1987 L314/17) on the co-ordination and promotion of research in the fisheries sector; and Dec 87/534 (OJ 1987 L314/20) adopting Community research and co-ordination programmes in the fisheries sector for 1988–92. The assistance was to be provided under Art 440 of the Budget for 1988 (OJ 1988 L226/3).

[51] OJ 1986 L376/7.

[52] Amending Reg 4028/86 (OJ 1990 L380/1).

[53] ibid, 11th recital in the preamble.

[54] See eg Dec 92/30 (OJ 1992 L11/39) on the small-scale fisheries zonal plan (1991–92) submitted by Greece in accordance with Reg 4028/86.

of capacities[55] was limited by Article 1(4) of the new Regulation to small-scale fishing fleets.[56] At the same time, assistance was made available for the creation of joint enterprises[57] rather than joint ventures and for redeployment operations.[58]

The preamble to the new Regulation also stressed that no structural policy measures in the fisheries sector could be successful if, concomitantly, attention was not given to the socio-economic consequences of such measures, particularly as regards employment and the development of regions heavily dependent on fishing.[59] Indeed, the lack of social-support measures was said to have impeded implementation of the multiannual guidance programmes.[60] Therefore, it was considered necessary to identify those regions which were socially and economically dependent on fishing and related activities and which were likely to be the most seriously affected by the common fisheries policy. It was also considered necessary to define for those regions appropriate socio-economic flanking measures in order to improve cohesion. However, the operative part of the Regulation merely provided for assistance to small-scale pilot schemes to deal with representative cases of socio-economic problems of Community importance.[61]

The assistance actually granted was criticized for its failure[62] to reduce capacity[63] and for doing nothing to tackle the growing capability of the fleet

[55] See, for details of the assistance granted, the Commission Reply by Mrs Bonino to WQ E–0411/96 (OJ 1996 C280/25) by Raphael Chanterie. In practice, however, where such assistance was granted, 'the bulk of the capacity in question [was] effectively . . . relocated'. See COA special report 3/91 (OJ 1994 C2/1) concerning the implementation of the measures for the restructuring, modernization, and adaptation of the capacities of fishing fleets in the Community, paras 4.8 and 4.9.

[56] Such fleets were defined in Art 1(5) of Reg 3944/90 (OJ 1990 L380/1).

[57] ibid, Arts 21a–21d of Reg 3944/90 (OJ 1990 L380/1); and Reg 1956/91 (OJ 1991 L181/1) laying down detailed rules for implementing Reg 4028/86 as regards measures to encourage the creation of joint enterprises.

[58] Arts 17a–17d of Reg 3944/90 (OJ 1990 L380/1) and Reg 1859/91 (OJ 1991 L181/83) laying down detailed rules for implementing Reg 4028/86 as regards Community financial assistance for redeployment operations.

[59] 2nd recital in the preamble to Reg 3944/90 (OJ 1990 L380/1).

[60] ESC Opinion of 27 May 1992 (OJ 1992 C223/30) on the 1991 report on the CFP, para 2.6.3.

[61] 3rd indent of Art 32(1) of Reg 4028/86 (OJ 1986 L376/7), as amended. See eg Dec 91/566 (OJ 1991 L307/37) on a concerted measure for the implementation of a socio-economic pilot scheme in the fisheries and aquaculture sector in France; and Dec 92/50 (OJ 1992 L20/14) on a concerted measure for the implementation of a socio-economic pilot scheme in the fisheries and aquaculture sector in Denmark.

[62] eg, in the case of France, compare Dec 88/121 (OJ 1988 L62/21) on the MGP for the fishery fleet forwarded by France with Dec 90/229 (OJ 1990 L124/48) amending Dec 86/121 concerning the MGP for the fishing fleet (1987–91) forwarded by France.

[63] Report on the CFP, SEC(91)2288. Results remain mixed. See eg, Annual report on the results of the MGPs for the fishing fleets at the end of 1996, COM(97)352. But cf the view that aid to joint enterprises has been effective in reducing capacity in the COA annual report 1997 (OJ 1998 C349/1), 57 (Commission reply).

which resulted from technological advances.[64] Such criticism suggested that the main concern of assistance should be to encourage more effective efforts to reduce capacity. In connection with such efforts, Article 11 of Regulation 3760/92[65] required the Council to set the objectives and detailed rules for restructuring the sector. The Council was to do so with a view to achieving a sustainable balance between resources and their exploitation. Such restructuring was to take account on a case-by-case basis of possible economic and social consequences for fishing regions. However, in Decision 94/15[66] the Council simply set the same requirements as to reduction in fishing capacity for each Member State.[67]

At the same time, criticism was levelled against the failure of the legislation to ensure that adequate account was taken of regional and social considerations. According to the European Parliament, a more efficient social policy, particularly in the least favoured maritime regions, was needed to alleviate the impact of the restructuring of the Community fleet.[68]

Similar views were expressed by the Economic and Social Committee. According to this Committee, neglect of the social dimension impeded restructuring. Although a reduction of capacity was bound to affect employment, little effort was made to cushion the social effects through the grant of Community assistance.[69]

The impact of such criticism is uncertain. Assistance is now provided for in Regulation 3699/93[70] and is funded by the Financial Instrument for Guidance in the Fisheries Sector.[71] Such funding seeks to ensure that specific problems of the fishing industry are taken into account more effectively than was previously possible.

[64] Review of the CFP, House of Lords Select Committee on the European Communities, HL(1992–93)9, 11. See also the European Parliament Resolution of 15 May 1992 (OJ 1992 C150/317) on the CFP and the adjustments to be made, para 2.

[65] Establishing a Community system for fisheries and aquaculture (OJ 1992 L389/1).

[66] Relating to the objectives and detailed rules for restructuring the Community fisheries sector over the period 1 Jan 1994 to 31 Dec 1996 with a view to achieving a lasting balance between the resources and their exploitation (OJ 1994 L10/20).

[67] cf, regarding the account taken of special regional needs in the allocation of fishing quotas, Case C–4/96 *Northern Ireland Fish Producers' Organization Ltd and Northern Ireland Fishermen's Federation v Dept of Agriculture for Northern Ireland* [1998] ECR I–681.

[68] Resolution of 15 May 1992 (OJ 1992 C150/317) on the CFP and the adjustments to be made, para 28. See also Resolution of 28 Oct 1992 (OJ 1992 C305/56) on the MGPs 1993–96, para 3.

[69] Opinion of 27 May 1992 (OJ 1992 C223/30) on the 1991 report on the CFP, para 2.6.3.

[70] Laying down the criteria and arrangements regarding Community structural assistance in the fisheries and aquaculture sector and the processing and marketing of its products (OJ 1993 L346/1).

[71] The European Parliament had called for the establishment of a European Guidance and Guarantee Fund for Fisheries in its Resolution of 17 Nov 1983 (OJ 1983 C342/88) on ways of increasing the effectiveness of the Community's structural funds, especially that of the EAGGF, Guidance Section, para 22. In 1989, ch 47 of the Budget (OJ 1989 L26/3) had been entitled 'European Fisheries Guidance Fund'.

Objectives of assistance

The Commission favoured the creation of Objective 6 of the Structural Funds,[72] which would have covered structural measures in the fishing industry.[73] However, the Member States apparently proved unenthusiastic about creating a new Objective for this sector, and the idea was dropped by the Commission. Instead, the Commission took note[74] of the conclusion of the Edinburgh European Council that 'appropriate attention should be given to the needs of areas dependent on fishing within the relevant Objectives'.[75] Hence, Objective 5a was redefined to refer to fishing, with a view to integration of fisheries policy and 'the Union's cohesion effort'.[76] Thus, according to Article 1.5 of Regulation 2081/93,[77] 'in the framework of the review of the common fisheries policy, measures for the adjustment of fisheries structures come under Objective 5a.'

In accordance with the redefinition of this Objective, the Financial Instrument for Fisheries Guidance is to: contribute to achieving a sustainable balance between fishery resources and their management; strengthen the competitiveness of structures and the development of economically viable businesses in the fisheries sector; and improve market supply and the value added to fishery and aquaculture products.[78]

This redefinition has been criticized for its failure to ensure that sufficient account is taken of cohesion requirements. For example, the Economic and Social Committee considers that the Objective should have been redefined more broadly, to include social measures for the workforce.[79] The European Parliament favours more radical reform. According to the Parliament, assistance should be designed to guarantee the preservation of economic activities in coastal areas and to promote the appropriate exploitation of their resources.[80]

The Instrument should now, it is proposed, be limited to providing assistance in pursuit of Objective 1 or 2.[81]

[72] According to the European Parliament, it should have been Objective 5c. See the Resolution of 10 Dec 1991 (OJ 1992 C13/37) on the CFP and the adjustments to be made, para 16.

[73] Community finances between now and 1997, COM(92)2001, 25.

[74] Community Structural Fund operations 1994–99, COM(93)67, 11.

[75] Conclusions of the Presidency (Bull EC 12–1992, I.55).

[76] Community Structural Fund operations 1994–99, COM(93)67, 11.

[77] Amending Reg 2052/88 on the tasks of the Structural Funds and their effectiveness and on the co-ordination of their activities between themselves and with the operations of the EIB and the other existing financial instruments (OJ 1993 L193/5).

[78] ibid, Art 1(2).

[79] Opinion of 26 May 1993 (OJ 1993 C201/52) on the amendment of the Structural Fund regulations, para 2.5.6.2. See, earlier, the Opinion of 26 Sept 1991 (OJ 1991 C339/75) on the communication on the CFP, para 2.3.1.1; and the Opinion of 27 May 1992 (OJ 1992 C223/30) on the 1991 report on the CFP, para 3.4.1.

[80] Resolution of 6 Nov 1997 (OJ 1997 C358/43) on the CFP after 2002.

[81] Proposal of 19 Mar 1998 (OJ 1998 C176/1) for a regulation laying down provisions on the Structural Funds, Art 2(2).

Eligibility for assistance

Eligibility for assistance depends not only on the requirements of Objective 5a, particularly the requirements of the common fisheries policy and multi-annual guidance programmes.[82] Most regions suffering from a decline in fishing and fish-processing activities are also likely to be covered by Objective 1, 2, or 5b. Restructuring problems in this sector are, therefore, taken into account in the overall assessment of the infrastructure, training, and job-creation needs in these regions. Such regions which were not already covered by these Objectives have been brought within their scope.[83] Their selection is based on 'simple socio-economic parameters such as the relative and absolute number of jobs in the fisheries sector and the contribution to the local economy'.[84] The question of whether they are included under Objective 2 or 5b depends essentially on whether industrial and urban development or rural development is required.[85]

The Instrument should now, it is proposed, be limited to providing assistance in regions covered by Objective 1 or 2.[86]

Allocation of assistance

Indicative allocations of assistance for Objective 5a (fisheries) are made to Member States.[87] For Objective 1 regions, allocations are part of the general assistance arrangements under this Objective. Elsewhere allocations are based on the relative importance of the fishing industry in the Member State concerned in comparison with all the regions outside Objective 1 and the exact structural situation of the sector in each Member State.[88]

Scope of assistance

Assistance may be granted for the implementation of measures directly contributing towards ensuring compliance with the requirements of the common fisheries policy. In particular, assistance may be granted to: redeployment operations; temporary joint enterprises; joint ventures; and adjustment of capacities.[89] Assistance may also be granted for: restructuring and renewal of

[82] Art 4(3) of Reg 3699/93 (OJ 1993 L346/1). [83] Sects 2.4.2 and 2.4.3 above.

[84] Community Structural Fund operations 1994–99, COM(93)67, 12. [85] ibid.

[86] Proposal of 19 Mar 1998 (OJ 1998 C176/1) for a regulation laying down provisions on the Structural Funds, Art 2(2).

[87] Dec 94/447 (OJ 1994 L183/50) establishing the indicative allocation by Member State of the commitment appropriations from the Structural Funds for Objective 5a (fisheries structures) 1994–99.

[88] Structural Funds, adaptation of fisheries structures (Objective 5a): allocation of financial resources between Member States, COM(94)421, 2.

[89] Reg 2080/93 (OJ 1993 L193/1) laying down provisions for implementing Reg 2081/93 as regards the FIFG, Art 2(1). It was proposed that only the scrapping of vessels should be eligible for assistance to permanent withdrawal from fishing activities. See the Explanatory memorandum to the Proposal of 8 Oct 1993 for a regulation laying down detailed rules for implementing Reg 2080/93, COM(93)481, 5. However, this limitation was only partly acceptable to the Council. See Reg 3699/93 (OJ 1993 L346/1), Art 8(2).

the fishing fleet; modernization of the fishing fleet;[90] improvement of the conditions under which fishery and agricultural products are processed and marketed;[91] development of aquaculture and structural works in coastal waters; exploratory fishing; facilities at fishing ports; the search for new markets; and 'specific measures'.[92]

It seems that the specific measures may include assistance to short-term operations of collective interest undertaken by 'members of the trade',[93] and assistance for the temporary cessation of activities.[94] However, the latter kind of assistance may be granted only where the temporary cessation entails a loss of income and is caused by unforeseen and non-repetitive events, particularly those resulting from biological phenomena.

At the same time, 'socio-economic' assistance may be granted. In particular, such assistance may be granted to: early retirement schemes for fishermen; individual compensatory payments to fishermen whose vessels are permanently withdrawn from fishing or transferred to a third country; and establishment of bad-weather unemployment funds and mechanisms for the financial compensation of fishermen, when the market value of products landed fluctuates sharply.[95]

It is now proposed that the Instrument may assist: achieving a sustainable balance between fishery resources and their exploitation; strengthening the competitiveness of structures and developing economically viable enterprises in this sector; improving market supply and the value added to fishery and aquaculture products; and revitalizing regions dependent on fishing.[96]

Forms of assistance

Assistance is to be provided within the framework of Community programmes.[97] The latter are to be drawn up in accordance with the objectives of the common fisheries policy and provisions of multiannual guidance programmes.[98] Assistance may take the form of the part-financing of operational

[90] It was proposed that assistance for the building of fishing vessels should only be provided in particular circumstances and where it was compatible with MGP objectives. See the explanatory memorandum to the proposal of 8 Oct 1993 for a regulation laying down detailed rules for implementing Reg 2080/93, COM(93)481, 5. The legislation is less restrictive. See Reg 3699/93 (OJ 1993 L346/1), Art 10.

[91] See also Reg 2636/95 (OJ 1995 L271/8) laying down conditions for the grant of specific recognition and financial aid to producers' organizations in the fisheries sector in order to improve the quality of their products.

[92] Art 3(1) of Reg 2080/93 (OJ 1993 L193/1). See also the Proposal of 4 Sept 1998 for a decision on a specific measure to encourage diversification out of certain fishing activities and amending Dec 97/292, COM(1998)515.

[93] Art 13 of Reg 3699/93 (OJ 1993 L346/1).

[94] ibid, Art 14.

[95] ibid, Art 14a, as introduced by Reg 2719/95 (OJ 1995 L283/3) amending Reg 3699/93. See also Crisis in the Community's fishing industry, COM(94)335, 22–23.

[96] Art 1(2) of the Proposal of 19 Mar 1998 (OJ 1998 C176/44) on structural measures in the fisheries sector.

[97] Art 4(2) of Reg 3699/93 (OJ 1993 L346/1).

[98] ibid, Art 4(3). See, currently, the MGPs for 1997–2001 (OJ 1998 L39/1).

programmes; part-financing of national aid schemes; provision of global grants; part-financing of projects; or support for technical assistance.[99] In addition, specific operations may be adopted in favour of small-scale fisheries and small-scale coastal fishing.[100] Finally, socio-economic studies may be financed.[101]

5.3 ECSC ASSISTANCE

Article 2 of the ECSC Treaty seeks the rational distribution of coal and steel production at the highest possible level of productivity, while the continuity of employment is safeguarded and care is taken not to provoke fundamental and persistent disturbances in the economies of Member States. Thus, according to Article 3(g) of the Treaty, the orderly expansion and modernization of production and the improvement of quality are to be encouraged. At the same time, according to Article 3(e) of the Treaty, improved working conditions and an improved standard of living for workers are to be promoted.[102] For these purposes, Article 5 provides for financial resources to be placed at the disposal of coal and steel undertakings[103] to encourage investment and to bear part of the cost of 'readaptation'.

5.3.1 Establishment of the common market

ECSC assistance was seen as having an important role to play in facilitating rapid adaptation of undertakings to the establishment of the common market for coal and steel.[104] More particularly, the Convention on the Transitional Provisions was concluded with the ECSC Treaty. It provided that the Community might provide Luxembourg with assistance to deal with any repercussions for its steel industry of the special arrangements made for the Belgian coal industry.[105]

[99] OJ 1993 L346/1, Art 3(2).

[100] Art B2–910 of the 1998 Budget (OJ 1998 L44/3). See eg Call for proposals concerning pilot projects to assist small-scale coastal fishing (OJ 1997 C216/30); and Call for proposals for pilot projects to assist women family members in small-scale coastal fishing communities (OJ 1997 C216/31).

[101] In accordance with Art 4(1) of Reg 3760/92 (OJ 1992 L389/1), CFP measures are to be drawn up in the light of the available biological, socio-economic, and technical analyses. See eg 1997 Call for proposals for socio-economic study projects in the context of the CFP (OJ 1997 C232/21).

[102] Art 46(6) ECSC provides for the Commission to obtain information to assess possibilities for such improvements.

[103] 'Undertakings' are defined in Art 80 ECSC, and 'coal' and 'steel' are defined in Annex I (Art 81 ECSC).

[104] Principles of High Authority action for the financing of investments (JOCECA 1954 457), para 1.

[105] Art 31 of the Convention.

Objectives of assistance

Assistance was originally intended to correct 'anomalies' in the operation of the common market[106] or to take account of 'market realities'.[107]

Scope of assistance

Article 23(1) of the Convention on the Transitional Provisions recognized that, in consequence of the establishment of the common market for coal and steel, some undertakings or parts of undertakings might be compelled to discontinue or alter their activities during the transitional period for its establishment. If so, the Community was to assist in ensuring that workers did not have to bear the brunt of the readaptation, and in affording them productive employment. Accordingly, the Community was to provide assistance for the conversion of undertakings and for the creation of new and economically sound activities capable of reabsorbing redundant workers into productive employment.[108] Moreover, the Community was to finance: tideover allowances; allowances to temporarily laid-off workers; resettlement allowances; and training.[109] Finally, assistance could be granted to undertakings which had to close as a result of the establishment of the common market. The closure had to be directly and solely due to the fact that the common market was confined to the coal and steel sectors and was leading to a relative increase in the production of other ECSC undertakings. The assistance was to be limited to the amount required to enable the assisted undertakings to meet their immediate liabilities.[110]

Article 56(1) of the ECSC Treaty itself recognized that establishment of the common market might also be accompanied by the introduction of new technical processes or equipment. As a result, there might be an exceptionally large reduction in labour requirements in the coal and steel industries, and it might be particularly difficult in certain regions to re-employ redundant workers. Accordingly, Article 56(1)(b) provided for assistance known as 'conversion loans'. Such assistance was to be granted for the creation of new and economically sound activities capable of reabsorbing redundant workers into productive employment. At the same time, under Article 46(4), the Community might participate in studies and research concerning the possibilities for re-employing, in existing industries or through the creation of new activities, workers made redundant by market developments or technical changes.

[106] R Quadri, R Monaco, and A Trabucchi, *Trattato istitutivo della Comunità europea del carbone e dell'acciaio* (Giuffré, Milan, 1970) ii. 692.

[107] Joined Cases 17 & 20/61 *Klöckner-Werke AG and Hoesch AG v ECSC High Authority* [1962] ECR 325, 340; and Case 19/61 *Mannesmann AG v ECSC High Authority* [1962] ECR 357, 370–371.

[108] Art 23(3) of the Convention.

[109] ibid, Art 23(4).

[110] ibid, Art 23(5).

Moreover, Article 56(1)(c) provided for assistance known as 'readaptation aid'. Such assistance was to be granted towards: the payment of tideover allowances to workers; the payment of resettlement allowances to workers; and the financing of vocational retraining for workers having to change employment.

Forms of assistance

Assistance might take the form of grants, loans, or guarantees on the loans.

5.3.2 Development of the Common Market

The development of the common market for coal and steel and the associated development of policies for these industries made new demands on ECSC assistance. In the early years emphasis was placed on increasing output of both coal and steel through concentrating production at efficient works and closing down non-viable mines and steelworks. However, it became clear in the era of cheap oil in the 1960s that the Community's coal industry needed to be trimmed back drastically. The same fate soon befell the steel industry, as it entered a phase of serious world overproduction.[111]

Objectives of assistance

Article 54 of the ECSC Treaty envisaged assistance compatible with the general objectives referred to in Article 46. Article 46(3) required the Commission periodically to lay down general objectives for modernization, long-term planning of manufacture, and expansion of productive capacity in the coal and steel industries.

However, the original version of the Treaty appeared inadequate for pursuit of such objectives. In particular, Article 56(1) did not address the need for the coal and steel industries to adjust to fundamental changes in marketing conditions other than those directly connected with establishment of the common market,[112] such as expansion of the oil and gas market and increased imports of coal from third countries.[113] To address this need, in 1960 paragraph 2 was added to Article 56.[114] Its addition was based on Article 95(3), which authorized Treaty amendments on grounds of 'fundamental economic or technical changes directly affecting the common market'.

Article 56(2) recognized that fundamental changes,[115] not directly connected with the establishment of the common market, in market conditions

[111] H Clout, *Regional Variations in the European Community* (Cambridge University Press, 1986) 38. Cf Report on the application of Dec 3632/93, COM(98)288, 16.

[112] *Procedure for Amendment Pursuant to Art 95(3) and (4) ECSC* [1959] ECR 259, 271.

[113] ibid, 263–264.

[114] Amendment of Art 56 ECSC (JO 1960 781).

[115] ie structural rather than conjunctural changes. See Quadri, Monaco, and Trabucchi, n 106 above, ii. 734.

for the coal or the steel industry might compel some undertakings permanently to discontinue, curtail, or change their activities. It provided for assistance to promote the rationalization of the market necessitated by such changes.[116]

Eligibility for assistance

Basically, only coal and steel undertakings and workers in these industries were eligible for ECSC assistance. However, under Article 54(2) of the ECSC Treaty the Commission might, with the unanimous consent of the Council, also provide assistance to other industries, where the coal and steel industries would benefit indirectly.[117]

At the same time, assistance might, in practice, be limited to regions particularly affected by the restructuring of ECSC industries because of the loss of jobs and their dependence on such industries in employment terms. The more particular condition might apply that earlier assistance had not yet allowed a number of new jobs to be created which was equivalent to the number of ECSC jobs lost during the restructuring process.[118] Assistance might only be granted outside such regions, if jobs were created for former ECSC workers.[119]

Allocation of assistance

Assistance might be allocated according to priorities laid down in Commission guidelines.[120] In practice, however, the allocation might be controversial. For example, the lack of geographical balance in the distribution of assistance under Article 56(2) of the ECSC Treaty was criticized.[121] In fact, the location of the assisted action might be of less importance to the Commission[122] than its contribution to improved competitiveness.[123]

Scope of assistance

Some assistance might concern the development of the coal and steel industries. Thus under Article 54(1) of the ECSC Treaty the Commission might

[116] *Procedure for Amendment Pursuant to Art 95(3) and (4) ECSC* [1960] ECR 39, 51.

[117] cf under Art 95 ECSC, Dec 1006/92 (OJ 1992 L106/8) on the extension of readaptation aid to workers retired on bridging pensions who freed jobs not covered by the ECSC Treaty and were replaced by workers hitherto employed by the same undertaking in sectors of activity not covered by the Treaty.

[118] Point 8.1 of the Guidelines for conversion loans (JO 1990 C188/9).

[119] ibid, point 8.3.

[120] Investments which would be given priority were originally indicated in Guidance for the presentation of loan applications under Art 54(2) ECSC (JO 1961 715). See, more particularly, Granting of industrial loans at reduced interest rates under Art 54 ECSC for safety and hygiene purposes and particularly for the prevention of nuisances (OJ 1974 C146/1).

[121] COA annual report concerning the ECSC for 1993 (OJ 1994 C346/1), para 2.27.

[122] Quadri, Monaco, and Trabucchi, n 106 above, ii. 724.

[123] cf Invitation to submit project proposals for the ECSC technical coal-research programme in the fields of mining engineering and coal utilization (OJ 1996 C165/30 and OJ 1998 C218/21).

assist investments by coal[124] or steel undertakings.[125] Under Article 54(2) the Commission might go further. It might, with the unanimous consent of the Council, assist the financing of works and installations which contributed, directly or indirectly, to increasing production, reducing the production costs, or facilitating the marketing of ECSC products. Hence, 'consumption of Community coal' loans,[126] 'consumption of Community steel' loans,[127] which might benefit major infrastructure projects,[128] and 'raw materials' loans might be granted.[129] Assistance might also be granted under Article 53b, which envisaged making financial arrangements necessary for performance of ECSC tasks.[130]

However, in so far as there were development possibilities in the coal and steel industries, it came to be felt that the necessary investments could often be more appropriately supported by loans from the European Investment Bank.[131]

More particularly, Article 55(2)(b) and (c) provided that assistance might be granted to technical and economic research. Such assistance had to relate to the production and increased use of coal and steel and to occupational safety in the coal and steel industries. More detailed arrangements for such assistance were first set out in a communication on requests and the grant of financial assistance for technical and economic research (coal, iron, and steel).[132] Separate guidelines for coal[133] and steel[134] were later adopted.

[124] Industrial loans carrying interest rebates available to the coal industry from the Commission pursuant to Art 54(1) ECSC (OJ 1988 C131/2).

[125] Industrial loans at reduced rates granted by the Commission to the iron and steel industry under Art 54(1) ECSC (OJ 1980 C99/2; see, earlier, JO 1970 C73/20).

[126] Industrial loans at reduced rates of interest available under Art 54(2) ECSC for investments aimed at promoting the consumption of Community coal (OJ 1982 C343/2). Cf, under Art 235 EEC, the proposal of 31 Dec 1976 (OJ 1977 C22/4) for a regulation on Community financial measures to promote the use of coal for electricity generation.

[127] Loans which might be granted pursuant to Art 54(2) ECSC for investment aimed at promoting the consumption of Community steel (OJ 1987 C291/3; see, earlier, OJ 1985 C121/3). Their effectiveness has never been evaluated by the Commission. See COA annual report concerning the ECSC (1996) (OJ 1997 C380/1), para 2.13.

[128] cf, more generally, the proposal of 23 Dec 1986 (OJ 1987 C80/7) for a decision on financing major infrastructure projects, which was based on Art 235 EEC.

[129] Future of the ECSC Treaty borrowing/lending activity, COM(93)512. Loans are now only to be granted for large infrastructure projects of particular Union interest. See Adjustment of borrowing and lending policy with a view to the expiry of the ECSC Treaty (23 July 2002) (OJ 1994 C175/5).

[130] See eg Dec 22/54 (JOCECA 1954 286) establishing a financial mechanism to allow for the equal distribution of scrap imported from third countries.

[131] Future of the ECSC Treaty borrowing/lending activity, COM(93)512.

[132] JO 1963 1433. See, now, Communication concerning application for and the grant of financial aids for technical research pursuant to the provisions of Art 55 ECSC (OJ 1997 C213/5).

[133] Medium-term guidelines for technical coal research 1994–99 (OJ 1994 C67/7); and Invitation to submit project proposals for the ECSC technical coal research programme in the fields of mining engineering and coal utilization (OJ 1997 C227/13).

[134] Medium-term guidelines for the ECSC programmes of technical steel research and of steel pilot/demonstration projects (1991–95) (OJ 1990 C252/3). See, for 1996–2002: OJ 1995 C294/4; OJ 1996 C373/6; and OJ 1998 C326/2.

Moreover, finance might be provided for programmes involving transfers of coal or steel technology, including technological know-how in fields such as repairing mining damage or civil engineering.[135] Finance might also be provided for programmes for participation in the capital of enterprises, particularly small and medium-sized enterprises, which introduced new technology or innovative features.[136]

Other assistance might support the restructuring of coal and steel undertakings. Thus assistance under Article 56(2)(a)[137] might be used to co-finance productive investments which helped to create new and economically sound activities or to transform enterprises which could be expected to generate additional employment.[138]

Moreover, assistance under Article 53a[139] might be used to facilitate the restructuring of the coal and steel industries[140] or the implementation of closure programmes in the steel industry.[141]

At the same time, infrastructure investment might be assisted. Such assistance might concern the redevelopment of land becoming derelict because of the closure of ECSC plants. The assistance might also concern the installation of large work sites, including communications routes, where these contributed to the creation of new activities likely to provide productive jobs.[142]

Finally, housing assistance might be provided under Article 54(2).[143] Such assistance was designed to facilitate the restructuring of coal and steel industries. It was also designed to prevent the deterioration of industrial areas dominated by the coal and steel industries and affected by the withdrawal or

[135] Guidelines and operational rules for the granting of conversion loans under Art 56 ECSC (OJ 1990 C188/9), point 7.2(c).

[136] ibid, point 7.2(d).

[137] Reconversion loans granted at reduced interest rates, under Art 56 ECSC, for investments which created alternative employment opportunities in areas affected by a decline in the activities of the coal or steel industries (OJ 1977 C178/2 and OJ 1983 C191/3). In principle, such loans are no longer to be granted. Instead, EIB loans are envisaged. See Adjustment of borrowing and lending policy with a view to the expiry of the ECSC Treaty (23 July 2002) (OJ 1994 C175/5).

[138] Guidelines and operational rules for the granting of conversion loans under Art 56 ECSC (OJ 1990 C188/9).

[139] It provides for the Commission to authorize financial arrangements common to several undertakings necessary for performance of Art 3 ECSC tasks.

[140] Future of the ECSC Treaty borrowing/lending activity, COM(93)512, 8.

[141] Intermediate report on the restructuring of the steel industry, COM(94)125, 5. See eg Dec 94/6 (OJ 1994 L6/30) authorizing common financial arrangements in respect of individual programmes involving the closure of production capacity in the Community steel industry for heavy sections, hot-rolled wide coils and strip, and reversing-mill plate.

[142] Guidelines and operational rules for the granting of conversion loans under Art 56 ECSC (OJ 1990 C188/9), point 7.2(b). See, earlier, point II.C(ii) of Reconversion loans granted at reduced interest rates, under Art 56 ECSC, for investments which created alternative employment opportunities in areas affected by a decline in the activities of the coal and steel industries (OJ 1977 C178/2).

[143] It seems that such assistance could also be granted under Art 54(1) ECSC. See Quadri, Monaco, and Trabucchi, n 106 above, ii. 711.

contraction of these industries.[144] While such assistance might originally have been seen as increasing production through preserving and increasing manpower,[145] it came increasingly to be seen simply as alleviating the social costs of restructuring.[146]

Other assistance was intended from the start to provide social protection for workers affected by restructuring and to promote the reintegration of these workers into productive life by facilitating their access to new employment.[147]

In particular, Article 56(2)(b) provided for the grant of the same kind of assistance as Article 56(1)(c),[148] except that a new category of assistance was added. The new category concerned the payment of allowances to undertakings to enable them to continue paying workers who had to be temporarily laid off as a result of their change of activity. The extension of these arrangements to other industries with similar restructuring problems was advocated.[149]

Increasingly, the emphasis of such assistance was on using 'social back-up measures'[150] to gain acceptance of steel industry restructuring by those involved and to secure withdrawals from the labour force.[151] Indeed, it was envisaged that continued availability of such assistance should be conditional on presentation of 'a credible capacity reduction programme'.[152]

However, it came to be felt that such assistance could be more appropriately provided by the European Social Fund.[153]

[144] Guidelines for implementing the twelfth ECSC low-cost housing programme over the period 1993–97 (OJ 1994 C19/14). See, earlier, Loans at reduced interest rates which might be granted by the Commission under Art 54 ECSC (OJ 1979 C299/2).

[145] AG Roemer in Joined Cases 41 & 50/59 *Hamborner Bergbau AG and Friedrich Thyssen Bergbau AG v ECSC High Authority* [1960] ECR 493, 530.

[146] Resolution of the ECSC Consultative Committee of 4 Oct 1988 (OJ 1988 C277/7) on the implementation of an 11th ECSC housing programme. See also Future of the ECSC Treaty borrowing/lending activity, COM(93)512, 11.

[147] Procedures concerning the social measures in connection with the restructuring of the coal industry (1994–97) (OJ 1994 C108/3). See also Report on ECSC assistance to readaptation (1990), SEC(91)2394. Cf, regarding assistance for maintenance of employment during a 'crisis', Art 58(2) ECSC.

[148] sect 5.3.1 above.

[149] ECSC Consultative Committee, Memorandum on social aspects connected with the expiry of the ECSC Treaty in 2002 (OJ 1996 C334/3), Part IV.

[150] Steel policy, COM(87)388.

[151] COA annual report concerning the ECSC for 1994 (OJ 1995 C329/1), para 3.45.

[152] Intermediate report on the restructuring of the steel industry, COM(94)124, 7.

[153] Vocational training assistance under Art 56(1)(c), third indent and (2)(b), fourth indent and employment assistance under the first indent of Art 56(1)(c) and (2)(b) are to be suspended and, it is envisaged, will be replaced by ESF assistance (Suspension of funding for certain ECSC social assistance (OJ 1994 C178/21), para II).

Forms of assistance

Assistance might take the form of grants and loans, including global loans to small and medium-sized enterprises[154] and housing loans. Interest rebates[155] and guarantees on the loans[156] might also be provided.

In practice, a distinction was made between 'traditional aid' and 'supplementary aid'.[157] The former kind of assistance was granted according to bilateral agreements with each Member State and covered assistance for early retirement, employment, internal transfer, external transfer, and training. The latter kind of assistance also concerned early retirement, redeployment, and unemployment benefits (including benefits for short-time workers and work sharers). However, it was designed to 'enable a more significant part of the costs of restructuring' in the coal[158] and steel industries[159] to be covered. Contributions were made from the General Budget of the European Communities[160] until 1984.[161] Commission proposals of 1983,[162] 1987,[163] and 1988[164] for further contributions were not successful, though in 1988 an interim programme of accompanying social measures was adopted. The programme provided assistance to facilitate early retirement of younger workers in the coal and steel industries.[165]

[154] The EIB, the other financial instruments and strengthening economic and social cohesion, COM(88)244, 2.

[155] Point 13 of the Guidelines and operational rules for the granting of conversion loans under Art 56 ECSC (OJ 1990 C188/9).

[156] Art 54 ECSC.

[157] Report on ECSC readaptation aid for workers 1993, COM(94)247, 3.

[158] Procedures concerning the social measures in connection with the restructuring of the coal industry (1994–97) (OJ 1994 C180/3); Social measures in connection with the restructuring of the coal industry (1998–99/2000) (OJ 1997 C198/6); and Criteria for the grant of readaptation aid under Art 56 ECSC available under the Rechar programme (OJ 1990 C185/18).

[159] Implementation of the social measures for the restructuring of the steel industry (1993–95) (OJ 1993 C146/5), para 2.

[160] See eg Art 650 'Contribution to the ECSC for social measures in connection with the restructuring of the steel industry (Art 56(2)(b) ECSC)' in the Budget for 1982 (OJ 1982 L31/3).

[161] Dec 84/384 (OJ 1984 L208/55) concerning a contribution to the ECSC from the General Budget.

[162] Proposal of 18 Apr 1983 (OJ 1983 C119/7) for a decision relating to a contribution to the ECSC from the General Budget.

[163] Proposal of 18 Sept 1987 (OJ 1987 C272/3) for a decision concerning a contribution to the ECSC from the General Budget to finance measures connected with the restructuring of the steel industry.

[164] Proposal of 16 June 1988 (OJ 1988 C194/29) for a decision on a contribution from the General Budget to the ECSC to finance social measures connected with the restructuring of the steel industry.

[165] *Twenty-First EC General Report* (EC Commission, Brussels, 1988) 181–182.

5.3.3 Cohesion

While the importance of securing capacity reductions in the coal and steel industries is increasingly stressed,[166] the Commission considers that ECSC assistance should be employed so as more effectively to contribute to cohesion. Accordingly, the Commission has introduced a programme of information-gathering in relation to such assistance and its possible use, especially in regions which have not previously been granted adequate assistance. The Commission has also sought: the delegation of greater responsibility to regional authorities to co-ordinate the implementation of the assistance; a greater geographical concentration of assistance, in order to give priority to regions covered by the European Regional Development Fund; the concentration of assistance in line with the priorities for the Structural Funds; and the provision of supplementary assistance in exceptional social and economic conditions.[167]

In practice, procedures for the co-ordination of ECSC conversion loans with Structural Fund programmes[168] have been adopted. They state that when the Commission carries out its periodic revision of regions eligible for ECSC assistance,[169] it must do so in conjunction with the revision of the regions eligible for Structural Fund assistance and be consistent therewith.[170]

More radical action is favoured by the European Parliament. The Parliament has underlined the necessity for improved co-ordination between ECSC assistance and the Structural Funds. Such co-ordination should be directed towards the integration of the former within the operations of the latter, upon expiry of the ECSC Treaty.[171] According to the Parliament, unreserved use should be made of all possible measures under the ECSC and EC Treaties, so that the impact of restructuring on the regions is cushioned.[172]

5.4 TRANS-EUROPEAN NETWORKS

In the transport sector Community assistance was originally seen as addressing problems associated with the development of the common market. Such assistance now has the function of promoting trans-European networks.

[166] See eg Forward programme for steel for the first half of 1994 and for 1994 as a whole (OJ 1994 C10/2).

[167] *European Report* 1746 (14 Mar 1992).

[168] OJ 1992 C59/4.

[169] Point 8.3 of the Guidelines for conversion loans (JO 1990 C188/9).

[170] Para 3.3 of the Procedures for the co-ordination of ECSC conversion loans with Structural Fund programmes (OJ 1992 C59/4).

[171] Resolution of 22 Feb 1992 (OJ 1992 L127/23) on the COA report on the ECSC accounts for 1990 and on the COA report on the management of the accounts and the financial management of the ECSC, para 7.

[172] Resolution of 29 Oct 1992 (OJ 1992 C305/145) on the situation in the European steel industry, para 6.

5.4.1 Development of the Common Market

Early arrangements for consultation regarding transport infrastructure of Community interest were said to have proved inadequate to the needs of developing the common market[173] and were revised by Decision 78/174.[174] Article 1(2) of the Decision provided that a transport infrastructure project was of Community interest where it: was a major project designed to create new transport links, remove a bottleneck, or appreciably increase the capacity of transport links and concerned cross-frontier routes; had a significant effect on traffic between Member States or with third countries; affected a Community policy, particularly regional policy; or made use of new transport technologies relevant to long-distance interurban transport.

A Commission proposal of July 1976 for a regulation providing for Community assistance to such projects[175] was not accepted by the Council. However, from 1982 the Council annually adopted regulations, to make use of amounts entered in the General Budget for supporting projects of this kind. These regulations were originally based simply on 'the EEC Treaty'[176] and subsequently on Article 75 of this Treaty, concerning transport policy.[177] Loans might also be provided by the European Investment Bank. In addition, by 1988 around 45 per cent of assistance from the European Regional Development Fund had been spent on transport infrastructure.[178]

Such practice was regarded by the European Parliament as unsatisfactory, because assistance was granted without regard to Community priorities.[179] Indeed, it was doubted whether the assistance had any real influence on transport planning by Member States. According to the Court of Auditors, in the absence of a multiannual Community plan, Member States were unable to develop their own transport infrastructure plans—which were of a long or

[173] *Development of the Common Transport Policy*, Bull EC, Supp 8/71, 5.

[174] Instituting a consultation procedure and setting up a committee in the field of transport infrastructure (OJ 1978 L54/16). See, regarding the work of the committee, the Triannual report (1984–87), COM(88)289.

[175] Proposal of 5 July 1976 (OJ 1976 C207/9) for a regulation on support for projects of Community interest in transport infrastructure. See also Art 373 of the Budget for 1977 (OJ 1977 L79/3).

[176] Reg 3600/82 (OJ 1982 L376/10) on the granting of limited support in the field of transport infrastructure. See also Art 781 of the Budget for 1982 (OJ 1982 L31/3). See, later, Reg 3620/84 (OJ 1984 L333/58) on a specific measure in the field of transport infrastructure (see eg Dec 85/66 (OJ 1985 L30/19) granting financial support to implement the modernization of the Mulhouse-Nord railway junction project).

[177] Reg 4059/86 (OJ 1986 L378/24) on the granting of financial support to transport infrastructure projects (1985); Reg 4070/87 (OJ 1987 L380/33) (1986 and 1987); and Reg 4048/88 (OJ 1988 L356/5) (1988 and 1989).

[178] EEC regional development policy, House of Lords Select Committee on the European Communities, HL(1991–92)20, 15.

[179] Report of the Committee on Transport and Tourism on the development of the common transport policy in the run-up to the completion of the internal market, EP Doc A–0306/90, 8.

medium-term character—with a knowledge of the particular projects that would attract Community assistance. At the planning stage they did not even know the overall amount of assistance likely to be received in the years of implementation. In most cases, therefore, Member States proposed for assistance projects which they had already decided to undertake on the basis of national criteria. The grant of Community assistance might have been welcome to a Member State, but it was not a determining factor in the decision to go ahead with a project.[180] The Committee on Transport and Tourism of the European Parliament considered that such problems should be tackled through the creation of a transport infrastructure fund.[181]

5.4.2 Cohesion

Regulation 3359/90,[182] adopted under Article 75 of the EEC Treaty, established a triennial plan for an action programme in the field of transport infrastructure with a view to the completion of an integrated transport market in 1992. The plan was to promote the harmonious development of transport infrastructure in the Community.[183] Assistance for transport infrastructure projects was envisaged from appropriations designated for the purpose in the General Budget, the Structural Funds, the European Investment Bank, and other financial instruments.[184] In particular, projects might be assisted where they contributed to the integration of areas which were either landlocked or situated on the periphery of the Community.[185]

The Commission maintained that integration of the peripheral regions into the Community's transport network should be a priority for assistance. Accordingly, criteria for the grant of assistance should include the degree to which the isolation of such regions might be reduced. The criteria should also include the coherence of the project with other Community actions in the field of transport or with other Community policies.[186]

In practice, however, the possibility may not be excluded that regional disparities were increased by the assistance granted, in that the main interregional links were strengthened and peripheral regions marginalized.[187] Certainly, the triennial plan emphasized establishment of a European high-speed rail network and promotion of combined transport. The plan thus gave

[180] COA annual report for 1988 (OJ 1989 C312/1), para 10.

[181] Report of the Committee on Transport and Tourism on transport and regional development, EP Doc A3–255/92, 11–13.

[182] OJ 1990 L326/1.

[183] ibid, 5th recital in the preamble.

[184] ibid, Art 2.

[185] ibid, Art 1. See, later, Art 2 of Reg 1738/93 (OJ 1993 L161/4) for an action programme in the field of transport infrastructure with a view to the completion of an integrated transport market in 1992.

[186] Community action programme, COM(90)585, 16.

[187] Report of the Committee on Transport and Tourism on transport and regional development, EP Doc A3–255/92, 12–13.

the impression that assistance was designed basically to meet the operational needs of trans-European transport systems rather than to promote regional development. Hence, the European Parliament criticized the lack of attention to connecting lines and extensions necessary to provide services to the peripheral and inaccessible regions of the Community.[188]

Essentially the same issues now arise in connection with assistance to trans-European networks. However, the introduction of specific provisions in the Treaty for the grant of such assistance means that these provisions must now be used to enact measures providing for its grant.[189]

Objectives of assistance

Article 154(1) of the EC Treaty now requires that to achieve cohesion 'and to enable citizens of the Union, economic operators and regional and local communities to derive full benefit from the setting up of an area without internal frontiers, the Union shall contribute to the establishment and development of trans-European networks in the areas of transport, telecommunications and energy infrastructures.' More particularly, Article 154(2) of the Treaty requires that, within the framework of a system of open and competitive markets, assistance shall aim at promoting the interconnection and interoperability of national networks as well as access to such networks. It shall take particular account of the need to link island, landlocked, and peripheral regions with the central regions of the Union.

As regards transport networks, the objective is to integrate land, sea, and air transport infrastructure throughout the Union.[190] According to the Commission, this objective does not simply entail the equalization of endowments. Geographically remote and sparsely populated regions are likely to need greater provision in terms of road or rail track-length per head of population than other regions.[191]

As regards telecommunications networks, the objectives are: the interconnection of networks in the sphere of telecommunications infrastructure, the establishment and development of interoperable services and applications, and improvement of access to them. Transition to an information society, increased competitiveness, cohesion, and job creation are to be facilitated thereby.[192]

[188] Resolution of 13 Dec 1990 (OJ 1991 C19/267) on the Commission proposal for a Council decision concerning the establishment of a network of high speed trains.

[189] Case C–22/96 *European Parliament v EU Council: telematic networks* [28 May 1998].

[190] Art 2(1) of Reg 1692/96 (OJ 1996 L228/1) on Community guidelines for the development of the trans-European transport network.

[191] Fifth periodic report on the situation and socio-economic development of the regions of the Community, COM(94)322, 67. See also Trans-European transport network: report on progress and implementation of the 14 Essen Projects 1998, COM(1998)345.

[192] Art 2 of Dec 97/1336 (OJ 1997 L183/12) on a series of guidelines for trans-European telecommunications networks. See also Rolling call for proposals for support and co-ordination actions in the field of trans-European telecommunications networks (OJ 1998 C79/14).

As regards energy networks, the objective is to help to reduce energy supply costs. To this end, the interconnection, interoperability, and development of such networks are envisaged.[193] A higher rate of economic growth, more employment, and enhanced competitiveness of the European economy are to be sought thereby.[194]

Eligibility for assistance

According to Regulation 2236/95,[195] projects are eligible for assistance if they are covered by guidelines[196] adopted by the Council and Parliament under Article 155(1) of the Treaty. Account is to be taken of the contribution of the project to the smooth running of the internal market and to cohesion. Particular account is to be taken of: the contribution to the connection of island, landlocked, and peripheral regions to the central regions of the Union; the importance to development of trade at European level; the contribution to increasing the competitiveness of the European economy; compliance with environmental considerations; and consistency with Union regional planning.

Allocation of assistance

The European Parliament proposed that priority in the allocation of assistance should be given to regions eligible under the Structural Funds. However, this proposal did not win the approval of the Council. The latter felt that the proposal disregarded 'the balance apparent in Article 154(1) of the Treaty, which [referred] to a multiplicity of objectives'.[197] As a result, priority in the allocation of assistance depends on the contribution to: the establishment of trans-European networks; harmonization of technical standards; interconnection and interoperability of national networks; integration of the various networks; and the reliability and safety of networks.[198]

Scope of assistance

The Union may not only assist trans-European transport networks. It may also assist telecommunications networks and energy networks.

[193] Dec 1254/96 (OJ 1996 L161/147) laying down a series of guidelines on trans-European energy networks, Art 3.

[194] See also Dec 96/391 (OJ 1996 L161/154) laying down a series of measures aimed at creating a more favourable context for the development of TENs in the energy sector, Art 3.

[195] Laying down general rules for the granting of Community financial assistance in the field of TENs (OJ 1995 L228/1), Art 2(1).

[196] Dec 1254/96 (OJ 1996 L161/147); Dec 1692/96 (OJ 1996 L228/1); and Dec 1336/97 (OJ 1997 L183/12).

[197] Common Position 3/95 (OJ 1995 C130/1).

[198] Art 6(1) of Reg 2236/95 (OJ 1995 L228/1).

Forms of assistance

Assistance may, according to Article 155 of the Treaty, take the form of project financing. It may also take the form of: assistance to studies related to projects; interest subsidies; contributions to fees for loan guarantees; direct grants to investments; or any combination of these forms.[199] In addition, the Commission has proposed that feasibility studies and innovative measures should be assisted[200] and that risk capital should be provided.[201]

Closer co-ordination of such assistance with operations of the European Regional Development Fund is sought. In particular, since both this Fund and assistance to trans-European networks seek to improve the accessibility of disadvantaged regions, clearer organizational links between the two are demanded.[202] The Commission response has been to draft guidelines and to investigate the possibility of establishing a central data bank on assisted projects.[203]

However, co-ordination may be more than a matter of organizational links. It may require a broader view of transport policy, including recognition of the desirability of assistance to the maintenance of loss-making routes. For example, the Committee on Regional Policy and Regional Planning of the European Parliament favours 'a system of specific subsidies for transport costs linked to the additional costs imposed on Irish traders [in trade with the rest of the Union] by distance and the sea-crossing'.[204] The Court of Auditors favours similar assistance for the outermost regions.[205]

More fundamental issues are raised by the literature. According to the literature, modern transport and communications technology means that geographically peripheral regions need not necessarily be economically peripheral. Peripheral regions are those lacking in mutual interactions between natural and built-up environments and social and economic actors within the region. In such a region economic actors belong to networks which

[199] Art 6(1) of Reg 2236/95 (OJ 1995 L228/1) Art 4(1).

[200] Art 4(1) of the proposal of 9 Oct 1996 (OJ 1996 C343/4) for a regulation concerning the granting of financial assistance for actions to promote combined goods transport. See, earlier, Dec 93/45 (OJ 1993 L16/55) concerning the granting of financial support for pilot schemes to promote combined transport.

[201] Art 4 of the Proposal of 19 Mar 1998 (OJ 1998 C175/7) for a regulation amending Reg 2236/95.

[202] COA annual report for 1988 (OJ 1989 C312/1), para 10.7. See, more particularly, regarding inadequate co-ordination of transport assistance and ERDF assistance, COA special report 1/93 (OJ 1993 C69/1) on the financing of transport infrastructure, paras 5.3–12.

[203] Commission Reply by Mr Matutes to WQ E–1217/93 (OJ 1994 C240/4) by Leen van der Waal.

[204] Report on the Community's regional development activities in Ireland, EP Doc A3–0275/90, 18.

[205] COA special report 5/97 (OJ 1997 C159/1) on management of the Community cereals trade involving export refunds, special import arrangements, and regional aid schemes.

have few contact points within the region.[206] Creation of networks favouring the integration of such regions into the Union economy may depend on more than simply physical transport infrastructure. It may also depend on the relationship between assistance for trans-European networks and more general cohesion efforts.

5.5 EURATOM LOANS AND GUARANTEES

Under the Euratom Treaty the development of nuclear energy may be assisted.[207]

5.5.1 Objectives of Assistance

The objectives of Euratom assistance include promoting research, facilitating investment, and ensuring the establishment of the basic installations necessary for the development of nuclear energy.[208]

5.5.2 Allocation of Assistance

The bulk of Euratom assistance is allocated to nuclear power stations and industrial installations involved in the fuel cycle within Member States.[209] Only the criteria for allocation of assistance to research expressly refer to the contribution to the strengthening of cohesion. Even in the case of such assistance, its consistency with the pursuit of scientific and technical quality is required.[210]

According to the European Parliament, however, nuclear-energy policy should be treated as an essential element of cohesion. The Parliament has demanded that, to this end, the allocation of Euratom assistance for construction of nuclear plants should have regard to regional development considerations.[211] In practice, despite parliamentary demands, such assistance

[206] F Snickars, 'Structural Change in Peripheral and Rural Areas—An Introduction' in U Wiberg and F Snickars (eds), *Structural Change in Peripheral and Rural Areas* (Swedish Council for Building Research, Stockholm, 1987) 7–14, 7.

[207] The proposal for the Euratom Treaty was apparently seen by Germany as an attempt by France to gain subsidies for the development of its nuclear industry. See S Weber and H Wiesmith, 'Issue Linkage in the European Community' (1991) 29 JCMS 255–267, 256.

[208] Art 2 Euratom; and Dec 77/270 (OJ 1977 L88/9) empowering the Commission to issue Euratom loans for the purpose of contributing to the financing of nuclear power stations, as amended by Dec 94/179 (OJ 1994 L84/41).

[209] Commission Reply by Mr de Silguy to WQ E–2878/94 (OJ 1995 C103/47) by Undine-Uta Block von Blottnitz.

[210] Annex II to Dec 94/268 (OJ 1994 L115/31) concerning a framework programme of Community activities in the field of research and training for Euratom (1994–98).

[211] Resolution of 27 June 1966 (JO 1966 2427) on regional policy in the EEC.

apparently remains primarily concerned with reduction of Union dependence on imported energy.[212] Consequently, its allocation may be ill adapted to the promotion of cohesion.

5.5.3 Scope of Assistance

Assistance may be provided for research,[213] training, and investment,[214] particularly in the case of joint undertakings.[215]

5.5.4 Forms of Assistance

Assistance may take the form of loans[216] and loan guarantees.[217] There is also a Framework Programme of Community activities in the field of research and training for Euratom.[218] It provides assistance to research and technological development, demonstration projects, dissemination and optimization of results, and training in the fields of nuclear-fission safety and controlled thermonuclear fusion.[219] It is implemented by two specific programmes. One concerns the Joint Research Centre.[220] The other concerns research and training in the field of nuclear-fission safety.[221]

5.6 MEASURES ACCOMPANYING REFORM OF THE COMMON AGRICULTURAL POLICY

Measures accompanying reform of the common agricultural policy are financed by the Guarantee Section of the European Agricultural Guidance and Guarantee Fund.[222] This financing is designed to make available

[212] M Quévit, J Houard, S Bodson, and A Dangoisse, *Impact régional 1992: Les Régions de tradition industrielle* (De Boeck, Brussels, 1991) 351.

[213] Arts 6(a) and 7 Euratom.

[214] Art 172(4) Euratom.

[215] Art 47(a) Euratom.

[216] Annex II to Part B of the Budget for 1998 (OJ 1998 L44/3).

[217] See eg Art B0–201 (ibid). See, generally, Guarantees covered by the General Budget, COM(97)464.

[218] Dec 94/268 (OJ 1994 L115/31). See, now, the proposal of 30 Apr 1997 (OJ 1997 C173/30) for a decision concerning the Framework Programme for Euratom for research and training activities; and the proposal of 10 June 1998 (OJ 1998 C236/10) for a decision adopting a specific programme (Euratom) for research and training on 'Preserving the ecosystem' (1998–2002).

[219] Art 1(2) of Dec 94/268 (OJ 1994 L115/31).

[220] Dec 94/919 (OJ 1994 L361/132) adopting a specific RTD programme, including demonstration, to be implemented by the JRC for Euratom (1995–98). See now the proposal of 10 June 1998 (OJ 1998 C236/20) for a decision adopting a specific programme for research and training to be implemented by the JRC by means of direct actions for Euratom (1998–2002).

[221] Dec 94/920 (OJ 1994 L361/143) adopting a specific RTD programme of research and training in the field of nuclear fission safety (reactor safety, waste management, and radiation protection) (1994–98).

[222] Art 2(2) of Reg 2085/93 (OJ 1993 L193/44) amending Reg 4256/88 laying down provisions for implementing Reg 2052/88 as regards the EAGGF, Guidance Section.

resources additional to those of the Structural Funds for agricultural restructuring.[223]

This Section is now, it is proposed, to contribute more generally to achievement of Objective 2.[224] It will finance measures which used to be financed pursuant to Objective 5a or 5b,[225] including assistance to less favoured agricultural areas.[226]

5.6.1 Environmentally Friendly Farming

Regulation 2078/92[227] provides for assistance to agricultural production methods compatible with the protection of the environment and the maintenance of the countryside. The objective is not only to encourage farmers to serve society as a whole by protecting the environment,[228] but also to help to adapt agriculture to market requirements by encouraging less intensive production methods.[229]

The assistance envisaged is to relate to: the use of farming practices which reduce the polluting effects of agriculture; environmentally favourable extensification of crop farming and sheep and cattle farming; ways of using agricultural land which are compatible with protection and improvement of the environment; the upkeep of abandoned farmland and woodlands, where this is necessary for environmental reasons or because of natural hazards and fire risks, thereby averting the dangers associated with depopulation of agricultural areas; long-term set-aside of agricultural land for reasons connected with the environment;[230] land management for public access and leisure activities; and education and training for farmers in types of farming compatible with the requirements of environmental protection and upkeep of the countryside.[231]

By promoting sustainable use of rural resources, the provision of such assistance may be said to contribute to cohesion. However, in practice, the bulk of the assistance tends to go to regions outside Objective 1.[232] More fundamentally, there are objections that its provision is marginalized in the common agricultural policy and is not integrated with other measures, such as

[223] See eg the 12th recital in the preamble to Reg 2079/92 (OJ 1992 L215/91) instituting a Community assistance scheme for early retirement from farming.

[224] Proposal of 19 Mar 1998 (OJ 1998 C176/1) for a regulation laying down provisions on the Structural Funds, Art 2(3).

[225] *Agenda 2000*, Bull EC, Supp 5/97, 33.

[226] ibid, 32.

[227] On agricultural production methods compatible with the requirements of the protection of the environment and the maintenance of the countryside (OJ 1992 L215/85).

[228] ibid, 8th recital in the preamble.

[229] ibid, 9th recital.

[230] Environmental set-aside and afforestation are counted as meeting part of the set-aside obligation under Regulation 1765/92 (OJ 1992 L181/12) establishing a support system for producers of certain arable crops. See Reg 1460/95 (OJ 1995 L144/1) amending Reg 1765/92.

[231] OJ 1992 L181/12, Art 2.

[232] Report on the application of Reg 2078/92, COM(97)620.

set-aside measures.[233] In accordance with such measures, the withdrawal of land from food production is encouraged by assistance from the Guarantee Section.[234]

If integration between such measures and assistance under Regulation 2078/92[235] is to be achieved, set-aside objectives must be widened to incorporate environmental objectives. Thus specific environmental management criteria, which farmers must fulfil to receive assistance, should be attached to all land set aside. Moreover, any alternative use of such land must be subject to strict environmental criteria. In practice, however, biofuel production, which may involve continued intensive agricultural production and environmental damage, may be encouraged by set-aside measures.[236] In defence of such practice, the Commission maintains that 'it is unwise to complicate a set-aside which is designed for supply control with unrelated secondary functions.'[237]

The impression is that environmental policy is enlisted almost exclusively to give cultural and ideological substance to limiting food production. Thus there is no incentive to produce higher quality products, particularly those which are more healthy. Equally, there is no incentive to produce the typical local products which are in many ways a mainstay of agritourism. Hence, it is said, Union practice fails to grasp the full potential of environmental policy for supporting the production of high-quality foodstuffs and agritourism and, by implication, the development of the most disadvantaged regions.[238]

The underlying problem is that the interests at stake cannot satisfactorily be contained within ideas of environmentally friendly farming practices. According to the Worldwide Fund for Nature, real integration of environmental protection and agricultural production will only result from an agricultural policy that encourages a move towards more sustainable farm practices. Such practices need to be based on the natural characteristics of the region, with a regionally flexible approach to the grant of assistance being adopted.[239]

5.6.2 Early Retirement

Assistance for early retirement is provided for under Regulation 2079/92.[240] The assistance is to be granted within the framework of multiannual pro-

[233] Implementation of the reform of the CAP, House of Lords Select Committee on the European Communities, HL(1992–93)28, 8.

[234] See eg Art B1–106 of the Budget for 1998 (OJ 1998 L44/3).

[235] OJ 1992 L215/85.

[236] Implementation of the reform of the CAP, n 233 above, 66–67.

[237] Commission Reply by Mr Steichen to WQ 3143/92 (OJ 1993 C145/21) by Mr Peter Crampton.

[238] ESC Opinion of 27 Nov 1991 (OJ 1992 C40/56) on the development and future of the CAP, para 5.4.

[239] Implementation of the reform of the CAP, n 233 above, 66–67.

[240] Instituting a Community assistance scheme for early retirement from farming (OJ 1992 L215/91).

grammes drawn up at national or regional level.[241] No reference is made to cohesion in the legislation. Rather, the emphasis is on improving the viability of agricultural holdings.[242]

5.6.3 Afforestation

Afforestation is considered important not only from the point of view of soil use and the environment. It is also considered important as a contribution to reducing the shortage of forestry products in the Union and as an accompaniment to control of food production.[243]

According to Article 2 of Regulation 2080/92,[244] assistance may be provided to investments: for afforestation; for the improvement of woodlands by the provision of shelterbelts, firebreaks, waterpoints, and forest roads; and for the improvement of cork oak stands. Assistance may also be granted to cover maintenance costs for the first five years and an annual premium per hectare paid to cover losses of income resulting from the afforestation of agricultural land.[245] No reference to cohesion is made in the legislation.

5.6.4 'Transitional Aids'

'Transitional aids' were introduced by Regulation 768/89,[246] because Member States were introducing their own schemes.[247] The former were designed to assist family agricultural holdings to adjust to reforms in the common agricultural policy. Such assistance could be granted where overall family income was below a threshold to be fixed by the Member States. The threshold might be no higher than 70 per cent of the national gross domestic product or 90 per cent of the regional gross domestic product per member of the working population.[248] The assistance was originally provided from a special chapter in the General Budget,[249] but it became the responsibility of the Guarantee Section in the 1993 Budget.[250]

241 ibid, Art 4(1).

242 ibid, 6th and 7th recitals in the preamble and Art 1(2).

243 5th recital in the preamble to Reg 2080/92 (OJ 1992 L215/96) instituting a Community assistance scheme for forestry products in agriculture. Other assistance to forestry has been financed from the General Budget. See eg Reg 3528/86 (OJ 1986 L326/2) on the protection of the Community's forests against atmospheric pollution; and Reg 3529/86 (OJ 1986 L326/5) on protection of the Community's forests against fire. See, now, Art B2–515 of the Budget for 1998 (OJ 1998 L44/3).

244 OJ 1992 L215/96.

245 ibid, Art 6. See also Report on the application of Reg 2080/92, COM(97)630.

246 Establishing a system of transitional aids to agricultural income (OJ 1989 L84/8).

247 Explanatory memorandum to proposals for regulations establishing a Community system of aids to agricultural income; a framework system for national aids to agricultural income; and a Community scheme to encourage the cessation of farming, COM(87)166, 2.

248 Art 4(1) of Reg 768/89 (OJ 1989 L84/8).

249 Item 3901 in the Budget for 1989 (OJ 1989 L26/3).

250 OJ 1993 L31/3, Art B1–410.

In some regions assistance under the above measures is considered indispensable to avoid depopulation of the countryside and to preserve the natural environment.[251] However, it has been questioned whether the resources allocated are adequate for these purposes.[252] In particular, according to the European Parliament, the reduction in other payments from the Guarantee Section, associated with reform of the common agricultural policy,[253] is being implemented without adequate compensation in terms of cohesion.[254]

5.6.5 Fisheries

It is proposed that the Guarantee Section will contribute to assisting measures for the restructuring of the fishing fleets outside regions covered by Objective 1. It is also proposed that it will assist all structural measures in this sector outside regions covered by Objective 1 or 2.[255]

5.7 'OTHER BUDGETARY RESOURCES'

Use of 'other budgetary resources' has been advocated in the case of various industries, such as shipbuilding. Their use has been particularly prominent in relation to development of, or conversion from, textiles, energy, and armaments production.

5.7.1 Proposed Instruments for Shipbuilding

Various kinds of assistance have been proposed for the shipbuilding sector. In particular, provision of assistance for the restructuring of shipbuilding and the development of alternative industries in the regions concerned by such restructuring was proposed by the Commission in 1979.[256] Introduction of a scheme to assist the scrapping and building of ships was also proposed in the

[251] cf Perspectives for the CAP, COM(85)333, vi; and the Twenty-first financial report on the EAGGF, Guarantee Section, SEC(92)1865, 8.

[252] The ESC has called for the establishment of a specific DG with overall responsibility for all rural areas. See the Own-Initiative Opinion of 28 Apr 1993 (CES(93)476) on extra-urban and/or rural areas, para 4.2.

[253] cf Joined Cases C–36 & 37/97 *Hilmar Kellinhausen and Amt für Land- und Wasserwirtschaft Kiel* [22 Oct 1998].

[254] Resolution of 22 Nov 1991 (OJ 1991 C326/262) on the Community's regional development activities to assist Greece, recital G in the preamble. See also the ESC Opinion of 24 Apr 1991 on the annual report on the implementation of the reform of the Structural Funds, CES(91)576, 17.

[255] Proposal of 19 Mar 1998 (OJ 1998 C176/44) for a regulation on structural measures in the fisheries sector, Art 3.

[256] Proposal of 11 Jan 1979 (COM(78)769) for a decision on Community assistance for restructuring or conversion investments in the shipbuilding industry. See also Item 3750 of the Budget for 1980 (OJ 1980 L242/3).

same year.[257] According to the proposed scheme, the building of new ships would be assisted by the Community,[258] provided that the owner scrapped twice the tonnage represented by the new ships. However, the proposals were not accepted by the Council.

Provision of assistance for research and development in the shipbuilding sector has also been advocated by the Commission,[259] with the support of the Economic and Social Committee[260] and the European Parliament.[261] However, no specific provision for such assistance in this sector has been made in Council legislation.[262]

Increasingly, the concern of the Commission has been not so much with development of the industry as that reduction of shipbuilding capacity should not be impeded by fear of consequential social problems.[263] Thus in 1987 the Commission proposed the grant of assistance to workers in the shipbuilding industry who were made redundant or threatened with redundancy.[264] Assistance going beyond that available from the European Social Fund and the European Regional Development Fund was envisaged. The former Fund concentrated on job creation for young people under 25 and vocational training for workers over 25 affected by restructuring.[265] Operations of the latter Fund were, in turn, limited to certain regions. The proposed new assistance would have covered: measures to encourage absorption into economic life and socio-occupational integration; measures to promote geographical mobility; and measures to ease the transition to permanent retirement from working life. However, the Council failed to adopt the proposal. This failure

257 *Shipbuilding: State of the Industry and Crisis Measures*, Bull EC, Supp 7/79.

258 In its Resolution of 13 June 1974 (OJ 1974 C76/41) on the proposal for a directive on aid to the shipbuilding industry and on the memorandum on procedures for action in the shipbuilding industry, para 2, the European Parliament had maintained that, if necessary, the Commission should help to provide credit for shipbuilding investments generally.

259 Proposals on the shipbuilding industry, COM(73)1788, 5. Such assistance was considered to be necessitated, *inter alia*, by the deficiencies of small and medium-scale shipyards. See the *Third Report on Competition Policy* (EC Commission, Brussels, 1974) 83. See, later, Policy guidelines for restructuring the shipbuilding industry, COM(83)65, 12.

260 Opinion of 28 Mar 1974 (OJ 1974 C97/40) on the proposals on the shipbuilding industry, para III.

261 Resolution of 12 Dec 1986 (OJ 1987 C7/325) on the proposal for a sixth directive on aid to shipbuilding, para 14(v).

262 Though various Community R & D programmes may be available to assist shipbuilders. See Shipbuilding: industrial, social, and regional aspects, COM(87)275, 18.

263 See eg State of the shipbuilding industry in the Community (situation as at 1 Jan 1982), COM(82)564, 21.

264 Proposal of 31 July 1987 (OJ 1987 C291/11) for a regulation instituting a specific Community programme of accompanying social measures to assist workers in the shipbuilding industry who were made redundant or threatened with redundancy; and the amended proposal of 12 Sept 1988 (OJ 1988 C249/5). See also Shipbuilding—industrial, social, and regional aspects, COM(87)275. See, regarding assistance for retraining, the proposed amendment of the European Parliament to the proposal for a directive on aid to shipbuilding (OJ 1990 C324/343).

265 Reg 2950/83 (OJ 1983 L289/1) on the implementation of Dec 83/516 on the tasks of the ESF.

is said to have exacerbated the social problems associated with the reduction of shipbuilding capacity.[266]

5.7.2 Textiles

The textiles industry is regarded as excessively fragmented and is said to be in urgent need of restructuring.[267] Such restructuring is needed above all in less developed regions and will have a serious impact on employment.[268] More particularly, the abolition of national quotas on imports from third states, associated with completion of the internal market,[269] may be a heavy blow for some regions. These are regions where a labour-intensive textiles industry has not been modernized to the same extent as elsewhere. Consequently, Union assistance is considered necessary for modernization of this sector, vocational training, and redeployment of workers.[270]

Assistance to synthetic fibres was provided for in Regulation 2914/79.[271] Such assistance could be granted to investments to help create new jobs intended primarily for workers made redundant by the reduction of production capacity or by the total or partial closure of undertakings in this sector. Assistance could also be provided for conversion by undertakings in this sector to activities other than the production of synthetic fibres for textile purposes. At the same time, assistance could be provided for restructuring which would lead to a significant reduction in the production capacity of the recipients.[272] However, only EUA 14 million were made available under the Regulation. Moreover, decisions to grant such assistance had to be taken by the end of 1979, and the intensity of the assistance was low. It was limited to 5.7 per cent of a qualifying investment or to 9.5 per cent where the investment was undertaken in a 'least favoured region' or a region particularly affected by restructuring operations.[273]

Moreover, research and development assistance for the footwear industry[274] was introduced by Decision 75/266[275] and Decision 77/188.[276] Such

[266] ESC Opinion of 19 Sept 1990 (OJ 1990 C332/131) on the proposal for a directive on aid to shipbuilding, para 1.3.

[267] Report on a Community initiative for regions heavily dependent on the textiles and clothing sector (Retex), EP Doc A3–0110/92.

[268] Report of the Committee on Economic and Monetary Affairs and Industrial Policy on restructuring the textile and clothing industry in the Community, EP Doc A3–0257/91, 8–9.

[269] See eg A Evans, *The Integration of the European Community and Third States in Europe: A Legal Analysis* (Clarendon Press, Oxford, 1996), 63–64.

[270] European Parliament Resolution of 22 Oct 1991 (OJ 1991 C305/19) on restructuring the textile and clothing industry in the Community, paras 30–38.

[271] On Community assistance for industrial restructuring and conversion operations in the man-made fibres sector (OJ 1979 L326/36).

[272] ibid, Art 1.

[273] ibid, Art 2(2).

[274] See eg Item 3.7.2.1 of the Budget for 1980 (OJ 1980 L242/3).

[275] Establishing a programme of technological research in the textile sector (OJ 1975 L111/34).

[276] Adopting a technological research programme for the footwear industry (OJ 1977 L61/29).

assistance was extended to textiles more generally by Decision 81/1014.[277] However, a more 'horizontal' approach to research and development assistance came to be preferred. Accordingly, in 1983 the Commission proposed adoption of a programme relating to the application of new technologies, which was to apply to textiles as a first experiment.[278] Since this proposal was not accepted by the Council, research and development assistance to this sector was left to depend on the Brite programme.[279]

5.7.3 Portuguese Textiles

A specific programme for the modernization of the Portuguese textile and clothing industry has been established by Regulation 825/95,[280] according to the last paragraph of Article 159 of the EC Treaty. This paragraph provides for the grant of assistance outside the operations of the Structural Funds.[281] The programme is seen as promoting cohesion[282] and as assisting this industry to face increased competition resulting from World Trade Organization agreements.[283] However, paragraph 1 of the Annex to the Regulation stipulates that there should be no overall increase in Portuguese production capacity in this industry. This stipulation is controversial, particularly from the perspective of cohesion. According to the Committee of the Regions, it should be reviewed, given that this industry 'has been identified as a strategic element in the Portuguese economy'.[284]

[277] Adopting a second research and development programme in the field of textiles and clothing (indirect action 1981–83) (OJ 1981 L367/29).

[278] Proposal of 24 June 1983 (OJ 1983 C230/6) for a decision adopting a multiannual R & D programme in the field of the application of new technologies.

[279] Dec 85/196 (OJ 1985 L83/8) concerning a multiannual R & D programme in the fields of basic technological research and the application of new technologies (1985–88). It was followed by Dec 91/506 (OJ 1991 L269/30) adopting a specific programme of RTD in the field of industrial and materials technologies (1990–94).

[280] On the grant of financial assistance to Portugal for a specific programme for the modernization of the Portuguese textile and clothing industry (OJ 1995 L86/10). See also Art B5–420 of the Budget for 1996 (OJ 1996 L22/3). Item B5–3201 of the Budget for 1991 (OJ 1991 L30/3) had envisaged assistance for restructuring the textile and clothing industry in Greece, Portugal, Spain, and the former GDR.

[281] It was originally proposed as a Community initiative. See Notice laying down guidelines for the initiative concerning the modernization of the Portuguese textile and clothing industry (OJ 1994 C180/15). However, the European Parliament opposed financing of the programme under the Structural Funds, because Community initiatives should not be used in favour of one sector in one Member State. See the Resolution of 3 May 1994 (OJ 1994 C205/121) on this notice, paras 6–12.

[282] 1st recital in the preamble to Reg 825/95 (OJ 1995 L86/10).

[283] ibid, 2nd recital.

[284] Opinion of 17 May 1994 (OJ 1994 C217/14) on the Community initiative on the modernization of the textile and clothing industry of Portugal.

5.7.4 Energy

Various kinds of assistance to non-nuclear energy have been granted,[285] a programme for research and development having been introduced in 1975.[286] More particularly, assistance has been granted for: technological development relating to hydrocarbons;[287] development of new techniques in the fields of prospecting, use, storage, and transportation of hydrocarbons;[288] exploitation of alternative energy sources;[289] demonstration projects relating to the exploitation of alternative energy sources, energy saving, and the substitution of hydrocarbons; and industrial pilot projects and demonstration projects relating to the liquefaction and gasification of solid fuels,[290] energy saving,[291] and reduction of emissions.[292] Assistance is also granted to regional energy-planning studies, priority being given to studies relating to frontier regions, outlying regions, and industrial and agricultural regions in economic difficulties.[293]

[285] cf the Council Resolution of 13 Feb 1975 (OJ 1975 C153/6) concerning measures to be implemented to achieve the Community energy policy objectives adopted by the Council on 17 Dec 1974, para 1.B; Reg 625/83 (OJ 1983 L73/8) establishing specific measures of Community interest relating to energy strategy, and Art 707 of the Budget for 1984 (OJ 1984 L12/3); and Reg 2744/80 (OJ 1980 L284/4) establishing supplementary measures in favour of the UK, as amended by Reg 624/83 (OJ 1983 L73/6), and Art 580 of the Budget for 1980 (OJ 1980 L242/3).

[286] Dec 75/510 (OJ 1975 L231/1) establishing an energy R & D programme.

[287] Reg 3639/85 (OJ 1985 L350/25) on a programme of support for technological development in the hydrocarbons sector; and Item 7000 in the Budget for 1986 (OJ 1986 L358/3).

[288] Reg 3056/73 (OJ 1973 L312/1) on the support of Community projects in the hydrocarbon sector; and Art 393 of the Budget for 1974 (OJ 1974 L115/1). See also the proposal of 29 Nov 1974 (OJ 1975 C18/3) to assist undertakings engaged in prospecting for oil.

[289] Reg 1302/78 (OJ 1978 L158/3) on the granting of financial support for projects to exploit alternative energy sources; and Item 3.2.4.1 of the Budget for 1980 (OJ 1980 L242/3). Implementing arrangements in the solar energy sector were introduced by Reg 727/79 (OJ 1979 L93/3) on the implementation in the solar energy sector of Reg 1302/78. See, now, Dec 98/352 (OJ 1998 L159/33) concerning a multiannual programme for the promotion of renewable energy sources in the Community; and Item B4–1030 of the Budget for 1998 (OJ 1998 L44/3). It 'complements' the Framework Programme for R & D (para 15 of the preamble to Dec 98/352).

[290] Reg 3640/85 (OJ 1985 L350/29) on the promotion, by financial support, of demonstration projects relating to the exploitation of alternative energy sources, to energy saving and to substitution of hydrocarbons, and of industrial pilot projects and demonstration projects relating to the liquefaction and gasification of solid fuels; and Item 7030 of the Budget for 1985 (OJ 1985 L358/3).

[291] Dec 91/565 (OJ 1991 L307/34) concerning the promotion of energy efficiency in the Community (Save programme); and Item B4–1031 of the Budget for 1992 (OJ 1992 L26/3). See, now, Dec 96/737 (OJ 1996 L335/50) concerning a multiannual programme for the promotion of energy efficiency in the Community—Save II. See also Progress report on Save II, COM(1998)458.

[292] Reg 2008/90 (OJ 1990 L185/1) concerning the promotion of energy technology in Europe (Thermie programme); and Item B4–1000 of the Budget for 1991 (OJ 1991 L30/3). See also the Communication on the provision of financial support to projects for the promotion of energy technology—Thermie programme (OJ 1992 C179/14).

[293] Regional and urban planning: Commission invitation to submit proposals (OJ 1991 C12/12; OJ 1994 C163/29).

As a rule, such assistance takes little specific account of cohesion.[294] Therefore, according to the European Parliament, existing arrangements must be reformed, so that the assistance may encourage development of the energy industry in line with the requirements of cohesion and environmental protection.[295]

5.7.5 Armaments

Various regions may face major structural problems both because of arms industry conversion to civil production and because of cuts in military installations.[296] Accordingly, in Article B2–610 of the General Budget for 1991[297] ECU 40 million were committed for the Perifra programme. The Community territory as a whole was eligible for assistance, but preference was given to regions covered by Objective 1, 2, or 5b. However, the limited sums available[298] meant that assisted actions were of small scale and generally of a demonstration nature.

Perifra was replaced by the Konver programme,[299] for which ECU 130 million, including ECU 85 million from the European Regional Development Fund, were allocated.[300] Assistance could be provided for training, innovation, and 'environmental rehabilitation'. However, arrangements for the grant of such assistance remained problematic. For example, many of the regions affected by cuts in military expenditure, including a large part of Aquitaine and Provence–Alpes–Côte d'Azur in France, were not eligible for assistance. The programme has now become a Community initiative.[301]

5.8 CONCLUSION

In practice, Member States and their representatives in the Council seem more willing to approve measures to reduce the costs of implementing agreed sectoral policies than they are to design such measures according to cohesion

[294] Increased attention to cohesion issues is envisaged in the Proposal of 15 Apr 1994 (OJ 1994 C158/6) for a regulation concerning a Community programme providing financial support for the promotion of European energy technology 1995–8 (Thermie-II); and Item B4–1000 of the Budget for 1998 (OJ 1998 L44/3).

[295] Resolution of 12 Mar 1992 (OJ 1992 C94/279) on a common energy policy, para 11.

[296] Resolution of the European Parliament of 22 Nov 1991 (OJ 1991 C326/267) on the Perifra programme.

[297] OJ 1991 L30/3.

[298] Though some increase in expenditure was envisaged for 1992 and 1993. See the Budget for 1992 (OJ 1992 L26/3), Art B2–61.

[299] It was launched at the request of the European Parliament on 'an *ad hoc* basis' (Bull EC 4–1993, 1.2.100).

[300] Budget for 1993 (OJ 1993 L31/3), Items B2–142 (ERDF) and B2–143 (ESF).

[301] See sect 2.4.6 above.

requirements. As a result, the operation of sectoral instruments may be ill adapted to pursuit of such requirements.

For example, the allocation of assistance to transport may have tended to increase rather than decrease the relative isolation of peripheral regions. In other sectors, such as coal and steel, Union assistance may be used to encourage conversion away from declining sectors or to reduce the social costs of adjustment. The very focus of such assistance on particular industries may mean that it is also ill adapted to the promotion of cohesion.[302]

[302] ESC Opinion of 29 Apr 1981 (OJ 1981 C185/20) on the revision of the ERDF Regulation, para 4.

6

Horizontal Instruments

6.1 INTRODUCTION

'Horizontal' instruments provide assistance which is not limited to particular regions or sectors.[1] Some such assistance was envisaged in the EEC Treaty as a necessary accompaniment to establishment of the common market. Other such assistance originated with the emergence of policies associated with development of the common market.

6.2 LOANS AND GUARANTEES FROM THE EUROPEAN INVESTMENT BANK

The European Investment Bank (EIB) is independent in the management of its financial affairs, though it is intended to contribute to attainment of Union objectives.[2] It may thus be described as an 'instrument' of the Union.[3] It is now, according to Commission proposals, to 'co-operate in attaining the Objectives' of the Structural Funds.[4]

6.2.1 Establishment of the Common Market

The Spaak Report[5] envisaged the creation of an investment fund for financing 'global aids' to Member States to support conversion efforts and the creation of new activities. During negotiation of the EEC Treaty, however, the preference emerged for a financial institution with the characteristics of a bank,[6] which was created as the European Investment Bank.

[1] cf the distinction in DJ Neven and J Vickers, 'Public Policy towards Industrial Restructuring: Some Issues Raised by the Internal Market Programme' in K Cool, DJ Neven, and I Walter (eds), *European Industrial Restructuring in the 1990s* (Macmillan, London, 1992) 162–198, 174 between sectoral assistance and 'functional' assistance. The latter is defined as assistance which affects the use of inputs, such as energy and investment, or outputs, such as exports, pollution, and R & D.

[2] Case 85/86 *EC Commission v Board of Governors of the EIB* [1988] ECR 1281, 1320.

[3] AG Roemer in Joined Cases 27 & 39/59 *Alberto Campolongo v ECSC High Authority* [1960] ECR 391, 418.

[4] Art 2(6) of the Proposal of 19 Mar 1998 (OJ 1998 C176/1) for a regulation laying down provisions on the Structural Funds.

[5] Comité Intergouvernemental Crée par la Conference de Messine, *Rapport des Chefs de Délégation aux Ministres des Affaires Etrangères* (Secretariat of the Committee, Brussels, 1956).

[6] R Quadri, R Monaco, and A Trabucchi, *Trattato istitutivo della Comunità economica europea: Commentario* (Giuffré, Milan, 1965) ii. 992.

Objectives of assistance

According to Article 3(j) of the EEC Treaty, the Bank was intended to facilitate the economic expansion of the Community by opening up fresh resources. This provision implied that the Bank should contribute to achievement of Article 2 objectives.[7] This implication was confirmed by Article 130. This provision required the Bank to contribute to the balanced and steady establishment of the common market.

Accordingly, its Statute provided that the Bank was to 'promote the attainment of the common market'.[8] Further details were provided in the General Directives for the Credit Policy of the Bank.[9] According to these Directives, the Bank was to participate in financing projects aimed at the modernization or conversion of enterprises or the creation of new activities furthering the progressive establishment of the common market. It was to do so as soon as the repercussions of this market on given enterprises could be seen with sufficient accuracy.[10]

In practice, assistance to the less developed regions was expected to be the 'principal task' of the Bank.[11] This expectation reflected recognition that 'mechanical integration' of the Member States could harm such regions.[12] The inference drawn was that assistance from the Bank was necessary to counter the tendency of the common market to increase the differences between developed and less developed regions.[13]

Allocation of assistance

Originally assistance was allocated to infrastructure projects[14] and large industrial projects. However, in 1968 global loans, passed on through sub-loans to small and medium-sized enterprises, were introduced.[15] The bulk of the assistance went to the poorer regions, especially in Italy.[16] For example, loans were made for irrigation and other rural projects in the Mezzogiorno, and numerous transport and industrial rehabilitation schemes benefited. These loans apparently had only a marginal impact on employment in such regions.[17]

[7] A-G Mancini in Case 85/86 *EC Commission v Board of Governors of the EIB* [1988] ECR 1281, 1305. See, regarding Art 2 EEC, sect 2.2 above.

[8] Art 20(1)(b) of the Statute of the EIB.

[9] EIB, Luxembourg, 1981, 32–33.

[10] ibid, sect II.

[11] *Second EEC General Report* (EEC Commission, Brussels, 1959), 54.

[12] Quadri, Monaco, and Trabucchi, n 5 above, ii. 962.

[13] ibid, ii. 1008.

[14] H Clout, *Regional Variations in the European Community* (Cambridge University Press, 1986) 39.

[15] *Annual Report of the EIB 1968* (EIB, Luxembourg, 1969) 79–80.

[16] Between 1958 and 1973 46% of total EIB lending related to projects in Italy.

[17] DA Pinder, 'Small Firms, Regional Development and the European Investment Bank' (1986) 24 JCMS 171–186.

Scope of assistance

Much assistance from the Bank concerned projects to develop less developed regions.[18] The regions had to be less developed by Community rather than national standards.[19] During negotiation of the Treaty Germany had favoured an express statement that the assistance should be designed to adjust the economic level of the less developed regions to that of other regions.[20] However, no such statement was included in the Treaty.

The Bank also assisted projects concerned with the modernization[21] or conversion of undertakings or the development of fresh activities called for by the progressive establishment of the common market. Such projects had to be of such a size or nature[22] that they could not be entirely financed by the various means available in the individual Member States.[23] The expression 'progressive' was seen as implying that assistance from the Bank should be limited to the transitional period for establishment of the common market.[24] However, it was recognized that operations could not be confined to problems shown to be caused by the establishment of the common market.[25]

Finally, the Bank assisted projects of common interest to several Member States. These projects also had to be of such a size or nature that they could not be entirely financed by the various means available in the individual Member States.[26] Such projects included, in particular, those which would contribute to the integration of the economies of the Member States.[27] The German Government inferred that 'supraregional' projects could be assisted.[28]

Forms of assistance

The Bank granted assistance in the form of loans and guarantees.[29]

[18] Art 130(a) EEC. [19] Quadri, Monaco, and Trabucchi, n 5 above, ii. 1009.

[20] S Neri and H Sperl, *Traité instituant la Communauté économique européenne* (Court of Justice of the European Communities, Luxembourg, 1960), 326.

[21] Germany had argued that modernization should not be covered, because it was a normal and permanent task of undertakings (ibid, 327).

[22] ie they must not be purely local or particular (Quadri, Monaco, and Trabucchi, n 5 above, ii. 1009).

[23] Art 130(b) EEC. France had proposed a stipulation in the Treaty that the projects must be viable (Neri and Sperl, n 20 above, 326). This stipulation was included, instead, in para 3 of the General Directives of the Bank (n 9 above, 3–4).

[24] Neri and Sperl, n 20 above, 327. [25] ibid. [26] Art 130(c) EEC.

[27] *Second EEC General Report*, n 11 above, 54.

[28] Neri and Sperl, n 20 above, 325.

[29] Art 20(2) of its Statute prohibits the Bank, in principle, from participating in risk capital.

6.2.2 Development of the Common Market

The New Community Instrument (NCI)[30] was established by Decision 78/870.[31] It assisted investment projects to strengthen the link between the European Investment Bank and the implementation of policies demanded by the development of the common market.[32] Its administration and the selection of projects to be assisted were responsibilities of the Bank, though the Commission was responsible for determining the eligibility of projects.[33]

Objectives of assistance

Projects assisted by the Instrument were to contribute to greater convergence and integration of the economic policies of the Member States. More particularly, the projects were to help attain Community objectives for energy, industry, and infrastructure. Account was to be taken, *inter alia*, of the regional impact of the projects and the need to combat unemployment.[34]

Allocation of assistance

The allocation of assistance from the Instrument was to take account of three priorities.[35] The first priority concerned investment projects, mainly those of small and medium-sized enterprises, in industry and directly allied services. These were to promote, in particular, the dissemination of innovative ideas and new technology, and job creation. The second priority concerned projects for the rational use of energy, replacement of oil by other sources of energy, and infrastructure projects facilitating such replacement. The third priority concerned infrastructure projects associated with the development of productive activities. These had to contribute to regional development or to be of Community interest, as in the case of telecommunications, including information technology, and transport, including the transmission of energy.

[30] C André, 'Le Nouvel instrument communautaire d'emprunts et de prêts (N.I.C.)' (1980) RMC 66–71; and L Battistotti, 'I Finanziamenti concessi della banca europea per gli invetimenti ed il nuovo strumento communitario' (1985) *Cronache Economiche* 63–68.

[31] Empowering the Commission to contract loans for the purpose of promoting investment within the Community (OJ 1978 L298/9); and Dec 83/200 (OJ 1983 L112/26) empowering the Commission to contract loans under the NCI for the purpose of promoting investment within the Community.

[32] Recession and UK entry implied the need for increased attention to declining industries. See Clout, n 14 above, 39.

[33] Art 5 of Dec 78/870 (OJ 1978 L298/9).

[34] ibid, Art 1. However, where government policies aimed to bring down inflation through control of public borrowing, the NCI facility merely added to public spending and might, therefore, not be available in practice. See the ESC Opinion of 28 Oct 1981 (OJ 1981 C343/53) on the new regional policy guidelines and priorities, para II.5.2.

[35] Art 3 of Dec 84/383 (OJ 1984 L208/53) implementing Dec 83/200.

Scope of assistance

Assistance from the Instrument was provided for investment projects of small and medium-sized enterprises, especially innovatory projects. Infrastructure and energy projects were also assisted.[36] Such assistance was to be directed, in particular, to the application of new technologies and innovation and to improving the rational use of energy. At the same time, account was to be taken of the need to reduce regional disparities.[37]

Forms of assistance

Loans were provided by the New Community Instrument. Guarantees on the loans might be financed from the General Budget.[38]

6.2.3 Cohesion

Article 130 of the EEC Treaty has now been replaced by Article 267 of the EC Treaty. The new provision contains the same wording as its predecessor. It thus maintains the original tasks of the European Investment Bank. However, a final paragraph is added. According to this paragraph, in carrying out its tasks, the Bank is to facilitate the financing of investment programmes in conjunction with assistance from the Structural Funds and other financial instruments. Moreover, according to the Protocol on Economic and Social Cohesion, the Bank should continue to devote the majority of its resources to the promotion of cohesion.[39] Article 267 of the Treaty and the Protocol are said to have established the Bank as a 'real regional development bank'.[40]

Accordingly, the preamble to Regulation 2081/93[41] envisages that the Bank 'will continue to devote the majority of its resources to promoting cohesion and in particular to developing further loans in the Member States which benefit from the cohesion financial instrument and in the Community's Objective 1 regions'.[42] However, it may be problematic to ensure that the

[36] Art 3 of Dec 87/182 (OJ 1987 L71/34) empowering the Commission to borrow under the NCI for the purpose of promoting investment within the Community.

[37] ibid, 8th recital in the preamble. See, regarding assistance to rural regions through the NCI, the explanatory memorandum to the amended proposal for a decision empowering the Commission to borrow under the NCI for the purpose of promoting investment within the Community, COM(89)440, 4–5.

[38] See eg Art B0–202 of the Budget for 1998 (OJ 1998 L44/3). See, generally, Guarantees covered by the General Budget, COM(97)464.

[39] Para 13 of the Protocol.

[40] C Mestre and Y Petit, 'La Cohesion économique et sociale après le Traité sur l'union européenne' (1995) RTDE 207–243, 231.

[41] Amending Reg 2052/88 on the tasks of the Structural Funds and their effectiveness and on the co-ordination of their activities between themselves and with the operations of the EIB and the other existing financial instruments (OJ 1993 L193/5).

[42] ibid, 19th recital in the preamble. See also the declaration of the European Council meeting in Dec 1992, regarding the importance of the EIB to cohesion (Bull EC 12–1992, I.55). See, regarding the cohesion financial instrument, sect 6.5 below.

Bank makes the envisaged contribution to cohesion, because it is subject to no democratic control.[43]

European Investment Fund

In response to a declaration of the European Council meeting in December 1992 on promoting economic recovery in Europe,[44] the Board of Governors of the Bank has established a European Investment Fund.[45] This Fund is to contribute to the strengthening of the internal market, the promotion of economic recovery in Europe, and the furthering of cohesion.[46]

The Fund provides loans for large infrastructural projects, particularly those related to trans-European networks in the areas of transport, telecommunications, and energy. It also provides loans for the development of small and medium-sized enterprises,[47] particularly in Union-assisted regions.[48] In addition, the Fund may provide guarantees for loans in whatever form is permitted by the rules of law applicable. In practice, such guarantees are provided in respect of investments by small and medium-sized enterprises which result in significant environmental benefits.[49] Finally, the Fund may acquire, hold, and manage equity participations in any enterprise.[50]

Temporary Lending Facility

The Board of Governors of the Bank has established a Temporary Lending Facility.[51] This Facility provides loans designed to accelerate the financing of infrastructure projects, notably those connected with trans-European networks. Small and medium-sized enterprises which obtain such loans receive interest subsidies from the Union Budget.[52]

[43] cf the European Parliament Resolution on giving discharge to the Commission in respect of the implementation of the Budget for 1994 (OJ 1996 L148/44), para 53. See, regarding the EIF, the COA annual report 1997 (OJ 1998 C349/1), para 7.14–15.

[44] Bull EC 12–1992, I.30.

[45] Act amending the Protocol on the Statute of the EIB empowering the Board of Governors to establish an EIF (OJ 1994 L173/14).

[46] 5th recital in the preamble to Dir 94/7 (OJ 1994 L89/17) adapting Dir 89/647 (OJ 1989 L386/14) on a solvency ratio for credit institutions as regards the technical definition of 'multilateral development banks'; and Dec 94/375 (OJ 1994 L173/12) on Community membership of the EIF.

[47] Art 2 of the Statute of the Fund (OJ 1994 L173/1).

[48] European Investment Fund, COM(93)3, 2.

[49] Co-ordination of activities to assist SMEs and the craft sector 1997, COM(97)610.

[50] Art 3(1) of the Statute, n 47 above. The European Parliament considers that the COA should have full audit access to the operations of this Fund, so that it can report to the Budget authority on matters relating to the Budget. See the Resolution on giving discharge to the Commission in respect of the implementation of the General Budget for 1994 (OJ 1996 L148/44), para 53. According to Art 248(3) EC, the COA is only to have 'access to information necessary for the audit of Community expenditure and revenue managed by the Bank'.

[51] *EIB Annual Report 1993* (EIB, Luxembourg, 1994) 12–13. See also Notice of implementation of the ETF start-up facility and the SME guarantee facility under the growth and employment initiative (OJ 1998 C302/8).

[52] Dec 94/217 (OJ 1994 L107/57) on the provision of Community interest subsidies on loans

Special Action Programme

The Board of Governors of the Bank has established a Special Action Programme.[53] According to this Programme, the Bank will extend its assistance in the areas of education, health, urban environment, and environmental protection. It will also step up its interventions in relation to large infrastructure projects and small and medium-sized enterprises.

However, the contribution of the work of the Bank to cohesion is disputed.[54] Its security and credit-worthiness requirements are no less than for loans from the national banking systems. Moreover, loans are subject to other conditions, such as very high minimum qualifying conditions, which make them still less attractive to small and medium-sized enterprises. At the same time, its interest rates must respect market conditions,[55] and any interest subsidies from the Member State concerned must comply with Article 87 of the Treaty,[56] concerning state aid. In addition, its lending is related to specific projects. Hence, its time-perspective will necessarily be shorter than that adopted by the Commission in the multiannual programming used for the Structural Funds. For these reasons, comprehensive integration between the work of the Funds and that of the Bank[57] is difficult to achieve.[58]

6.3 FRAMEWORK PROGRAMMES FOR RESEARCH AND TECHNOLOGICAL DEVELOPMENT

Given the tendency of the market to underprovide in the field of research and development, policy implementation in this field may be found to demand the grant of assistance. In particular, such assistance may be seen as remedying

for SMEs extended by the EIB under its temporary lending facility; and Art B5–322 of the Budget for 1996 (OJ 1996 L22/3). See also the Fourth report on the SME facility, COM(97)645.

[53] Board of Governors: Endorsement of the Bank's Amsterdam special action programme (OJ 1998 C10/10).

[54] cf, regarding the limited utilization of EIB loans within the framework of IMPs, Annual report on the implementation of the IMPs—1991–92, COM(93)485, 8. Cf also, regarding the limitations of EIB loans in the coal and steel sectors, Future of the ECSC Treaty borrowing/lending activity, COM(93)512, 6, 8, and 11.

[55] According to Art 19(1) of the Statute of the EIB, interest rates on EIB loans and commissions on guarantees shall be adjusted to capital market conditions and enable the Bank to meet its obligations, cover its expenses, and build up a reserve fund.

[56] ibid, Art 19(2).

[57] cf the formal requirement of Art 21(1) (ibid) that applications for assistance from the EIB should be forwarded to the Commission for its opinion.

[58] ESC Opinion of 25 May 1992 (OJ 1992 C106/20) on the annual report on the implementation of the reform of the Structural Funds, para 2.6.3. See also the Opinion of 23 Feb 1994 (OJ 1994 C133/1) on the role of the EIB in regional development, para 3.2. See, most recently, the COA annual report 1997 (OJ 1998 C349/1), para 3.2.1 (Commission reply).

market imperfections,[59] associated with 'free riders' and inadequate information.[60] Indeed, it is argued that there exists an optimum level of competition. Beyond this level competition has an adverse impact on innovation because of the difficulty of allocating gains and the greater risks existing in highly competitive markets. The optimum market-structure from the standpoint of innovation ought, rather, to promote strategic rivalry between firms.[61]

6.3.1 Development of the Common Market

The research and development policy of the Community[62] had its origins in concerns for particular sectors,[63] such as nuclear energy, data processing,[64] aerospace,[65] agriculture,[66] and ceramics.[67] Various instruments, such as the Esprit programme for research and development in information technologies[68] and the Joint European Torus for nuclear research,[69] were employed in implementation of this policy.[70]

[59] cf the authorization of French and German aid for technological development by SMEs in the *Fourth Report on Competition Policy* (EC Commission, Brussels, 1976) 99–100. Cf also the block exemptions in Reg 2349/84 (OJ 1984 L219/15) on the application of Art 85(3) EC to certain categories of patent-licensing agreements; Reg 418/85 (OJ 1985 L53/5) on the application of Art 85(3) EC to categories of R & D agreements; and Reg 556/89 (OJ 1989 L61/1) on the application of Art 85(3) EC to certain categories of know-how licensing agreements. Co-operation agreements between undertakings leading to innovation are also favoured. See eg Dec 90/46 (OJ 1990 L32/19) relating to a proceeding under Art 85 EC (IV/32.006—Alcatel Espace/ANT Nachrichtentechnik).

[60] K Bhaskar, *The Effect of Different State Aid Measures on Intra-Community Competition* (EC Commission, Brussels, 1990) 103.

[61] M Emerson, M Aujean, M Catinat, P Goybet, and A Jacquemin, *The Economics of 1992* (Oxford University Press, 1988) 162.

[62] See, generally, J Elizade, 'Legal Aspects of Community Policy on Research and Technological Development (RTD)' (1992) 29 CMLRev 309–346.

[63] See eg the Memorandum on industrial policy in the EEC, COM(70)100.

[64] Council Resolution of 15 July 1974 (OJ 1974 C86/1) on a Community policy on data processing, para 3. See also the Proposals of 22 Sept 1975 (OJ 1976 C14/5) for a development project for a common language for real-time programming; projects in data-processing concerning software portability; studies in support of the use of data-processing; and projects for applications and studies in the field of data-processing.

[65] Action programme for the European aeronautical sector, COM(75)475.

[66] Reg 1728/74 (OJ 1974 L182/1) on the co-ordination of agricultural research (Art 314 of the Budget for 1975 (OJ 1975 L54/1)); and Dec 83/641 (OJ 1983 L358/36) adopting joint research programmes and programmes for co-ordinating agricultural research (Art 384 of the Budget for 1984 (OJ 1984 L12/5)).

[67] Proposal of 5 June 1979 (OJ 1979 C155/4) for a decision on the adoption of a programme of technological research in the field of clay minerals and technical ceramics.

[68] Dec 84/130 (OJ 1984 L67/54) concerning a European programme for R & D in information technologies. Cf, earlier, Dec 82/878 (OJ 1982 L369/37) on a preparatory phase for a Community R & D programme in the field of information technologies.

[69] Dec 78/471 (OJ 1978 L151/10) on the establishment of the JET Joint Undertaking.

[70] Eureka (see Eureka and the European technology community, COM(86)664) was not integrated into Community programmes. See CA Colliard, 'Eureka ou une co-opération technologique européenne' (1988) RTDE 5–22. Indeed, the Commission apparently used Eureka to fund collaborative R & D which was not clearly precompetitive and could not be conducted

The first Framework Programme for assistance to research and development was adopted in 1983,[71] and the second in 1987.[72] The second Programme was intended, along with other financial instruments, to contribute to strengthening scientific and technological infrastructures and potential throughout the Community. Assisted activities concerned: quality of life; development of an information and communications society; modernization of industrial sectors; exploitation and optimum use of biological resources; energy; science and technology for development; exploitation of the seabed and use of marine resources; and improvement of European co-operation in science and technology.[73]

More particularly, the strategic programme for innovation and technology transfer (Sprint) was established by Decision 83/624.[74] Assistance was envisaged for development of an innovation infrastructure, to enable Member States with weaker infrastructures to participate fully in transnational projects.[75]

The impact of such assistance on regional disparities might be 'only an indirect one',[76] and there was a risk that such disparities might be increased.[77] In practice, recipients tended to be located in regions which were already well developed.[78] For example, the share of Esprit assistance allocated to the less developed Member States was substantially lower than their share of Community gross domestic product and population. Even the Esprit assistance which was allocated to these Member States was 'highly concentrated' in capital cities and more developed regions.[79] A solution might be sought through orienting assistance towards the less prosperous regions,[80] though

easily under the Framework Programme because of conflicts with competition law. See J Peterson, 'Technology Policy in Europe: Explaining the Framework Programme and Eureka in Theory and Practice' (1991) 29 JCMS 269–290.

[71] Council Resolution of 25 July 1983 (OJ 1983 C208/1) on framework programmes for Community research, development, and demonstration activities and a first Framework Programme 1984–87. It was adopted under Art 235 EEC and Art 7 Euratom.

[72] Dec 87/516 (OJ 1987 L302/1) concerning the Framework Programme for Community activities in the field of RTD (1987–91). It was adopted under Art 130q EEC, but prepared under Art 235 EEC.

[73] OJ 1987 L302/1, Art 1. Further details of the activities envisaged were given in Annex II (ibid).

[74] Concerning a plan for the transnational development of the supporting infrastructure for innovation and technology transfer (1983–85) (OJ 1983 L353/15).

[75] ibid, Art 3.

[76] Common policy for science and technology: impact of Community R & D on horizontal policies, COM(81)66, 5–6.

[77] A Community strategy to develop Europe's industry, COM(81)639, 14.

[78] ESC Opinion of 29 Jan 1986 (OJ 1986 C75/12) on national regional development aid, para 4.3.

[79] COA special report 6/93 (OJ 1994 C45/1) concerning the Esprit programme, paras 2.19–2.20.

[80] Common policy for science and technology: impact of Community R & D on horizontal policies, COM(81)66, 7.

such orientation might not apparently mean that the assisted activities had to take place in such regions.[81]

6.3.2 Cohesion

An express basis for the grant of assistance to research and development was introduced by Articles 130f to 130q of the EEC Treaty, as amended by the Single European Act.[82] These provisions have now been replaced by Articles 163 to 173 of the EC Treaty.

Objectives of assistance

Article 163(1) of the EC Treaty lays down the objectives of assistance for research and development. According to this provision, they are 'strengthening the scientific and technological bases of European industry and encouraging it to become more competitive at international level,[83] while promoting all the research activities deemed necessary by virtue of other chapters of this Treaty'. To this end, Article 163(2) requires that 'the Community shall, throughout the Community encourage undertakings, including small and medium-sized undertakings, research centres and universities in their research and technological development activities of high quality.'[84]

According to Article 130f(3) of the EEC Treaty, pursuit of such objectives had to take account of 'the establishment of the internal market and the implementation of common policies, particularly as regards competition and trade'.[85] This requirement was removed by the Treaty on European Union.

Eligibility for assistance

According to Article 163(2) of the EC Treaty, undertakings, research centres, and universities are eligible for assistance.

Allocation of assistance

According to Article 163(2) of the EC Treaty, assistance is to be allocated throughout the Union to 'research and technological development activities of high quality'.

[81] COM(81)66, 3–4. The changes proposed to the Union's regional policy in 1981 (ERDF—revision of the regulation, COM(81)589) were said fully to accommodate this objective. See A Community strategy to develop Europe's industry, COM(81)639, 13.

[82] OJ 1987 L169/1.

[83] Art 157(1) EC also provides that the Union and the Member States shall foster better exploitation of the industrial potential of policies of innovation, research, and technological development.

[84] See also *Growth, Competitiveness, and Employment* (Bull EC, Supp 6/93).

[85] See, regarding the kind of reconciliation problems involved, M van Empel, 'Technology and Common Market Law' in Aspen Institute Colloquium on European Law, *Technological Development and Cooperation in Europe—Legal Aspects* (TMC Asser Institute, The Hague, 1986) 57–71. See also B Hawk, 'La Recherche et le développement en droit communautaire et en droit antitrust americain' (1987) *Revue Internationale de Droit Economique* 211–269.

In practice, assistance may seek to reconcile the promotion of the competitiveness of Community industry with the strengthening of cohesion. In particular, the Framework Programme for 1990 to 1994 was adopted by Decision 90/221.[86] It emphasized the importance of rendering Community industry more competitive. According to the Commission, assistance was to be directed towards the needs of business and boosting the competitiveness of the Community economy.[87] Thus industry-relevant, 'high-tech' research topics were to be assisted. A possible implication is that the Programme was designed primarily as a response to the needs of larger corporations and stronger Member States.[88]

At the same time, references were made to cohesion. For example, according to Annex II, Paragraph III.6 of Decision 90/221,[89] the creation of research networks was envisaged. These networks were to extend to all Community regions. Particular attention was to be paid to the needs of peripheral regions and regions that were currently lagging behind. Highly qualified scientific and technical potential was thus to be built up in these regions.[90]

Somewhat greater significance is attached to cohesion requirements in the Fourth Framework Programme,[91] which covers the period 1994 to 1998 and was adopted by Decision 94/1110.[92] The preamble to this Decision refers to the obligation to take account of cohesion requirements. It also maintains that the programme should play its part, along with other Union instruments, in contributing to the strengthening of scientific and technological capacity and potential throughout the Union.[93] Accordingly, criteria for the provision of assistance include the contribution of the research to the strengthening of cohesion and the promotion of the overall harmonious development of the Union, though there must be consistency with the pursuit of scientific and technical quality.[94] Moreover, the research priorities set for the 'first activity' by Article 164 of the Treaty[95] must take account of the interests and capacities of all Member States, including the less advanced ones.[96]

[86] Concerning the Framework Programme of Community activities in the field of RTD (1990–94) (OJ 1990 L117/28).

[87] Community's finances between now and 1997, COM(92)2001, 26. See, more particularly, The European motor vehicle industry: situation, issues at stake, and proposals for action, COM(92)166, 10.

[88] *Evaluation of the Effects of the EC Framework Programme for Research and Technological Development on Economic and Social Cohesion in the Community* (EC Commission, Brussels, 1991) 35.

[89] OJ 1990 L117/28.

[90] See also the 11th recital in the preamble (ibid).

[91] See, now, the proposal of 30 Apr 1997 (OJ 1997 C173/10) for a decision concerning the Fifth Framework Programme for RTDD activities.

[92] Concerning the Fourth Framework Programme of the EC activities in the field of RTDD (OJ 1994 L126/4).

[93] ibid, 16th recital in the preamble.

[94] ibid, Annex II.

[95] p 224 below.

[96] Annex III to Dec 94/1110 (OJ 1994 L126/4). Research activities which may also be of interest to the coal and steel industries (sect 5.3 above) will be incorporated into the relevant themes under the first activity, on condition that they comply with the eligibility criteria of the Framework Programme, in particular as regards their precompetitive and multisectoral nature.

The European Parliament has proposed that greater synergy between such assistance and the other policies designed to strengthen cohesion should be sought. To this end, the Commission should establish an internal decision-making procedure designed to achieve close co-operation between Commissioners and the services responsible. More particularly, priority should be given to actions aimed at developing the scientific potential of the less advanced Member States.[97]

However, as the Economic and Social Committee has put it,[98] there is a 'chicken and egg' situation in the less favoured regions. Since, almost by definition, there are few or no indigenous bodies in such regions which can participate in Union research and development programmes, these regions have little chance to obtain assistance. Yet, the products of some new industries, such as data processing, data transmission, and office automation, may be particularly suitable for peripheral regions, because they are relatively insensitive to transport costs.[99] Hence, it is argued that the creation of entirely new bodies in such regions should be assisted. Equally, their creation should be assisted in regions, such as the older industrial regions of the United Kingdom, where the educational and training infrastructure for new technology exists. Apart from promoting regional development, such assistance may also unlock unused technological talent and add to the total capabilities of the Union. If assistance is not so directed, recipients may tend to be in regions which are already well developed. The assistance may, therefore, be at cross-purposes with assistance provided by the European Regional Development Fund.[100]

It is questionable whether the needs of research and development and those of cohesion can be easily reconciled. Rather, there may be conflict between regional-development needs and the 'excellence' criterion for allocation of assistance.

This criterion does not necessarily discriminate against the less favoured regions. For example, the Race programme concerned research and development in relation to advanced telecommunications.[101] Over the period 1988 to 1992 fifty-three assisted projects (60 per cent of the total) 'involved organizations from the less favoured regions of the Community'.[102]

[97] Resolution of 18 Nov 1993 (OJ 1993 C329/282), amendment 123.

[98] Opinion of 28 Oct 1981 (OJ 1981 C343/53) on the new regional-policy guidelines and priorities, para II.3.3.

[99] cf the argument that Union assistance should encourage producers in peripheral regions to adopt production structures in favour of products with higher value-to-weight ratios in Fair payment for infrastructure use, COM(1998)466, 32.

[100] ESC Opinion of 29 Jan 1986 (OJ 1986 C75/12) on national regional development aid, para 43.

[101] Dec 88/28 (OJ 1988 L16/35) on a Community programme in the field of telecommunications technologies—R & D in advanced communications technologies in Europe. See, now, Dec 94/801 (1994 L334/1) adopting a specific programme for RTDD in the field of telematics applications of common interest (1994–98).

[102] Final report on phase I (1988–92) of the 10-year Race programme, COM(93)118, 18.

Indeed, according to the Commission, the criterion has played a part in promoting cohesion. It has done so because it constitutes an attainable standard of reference for such regions.[103] It stimulates them continuously to upgrade their scientific performance and to reach common technical, managerial, and cultural standards for further collaborative transnational research and development.[104]

In practice, however, application of the excellence criterion may favour regions with large firms already enjoying a relative technological advantage[105] and links with similar regions.[106] For example, the participation rate of small and medium-sized enterprises in specific programmes under the Second Framework Programme varied from 2 per cent to 18 per cent. This participation rate was much lower in relative terms than the contribution of such enterprises to gross domestic product.[107] Again, the participation rate of Objective 1 regions under the Fourth Framework Programme as a whole was 12.6 per cent.[108] Hence, it is argued that new efforts are necessary to help small and medium-sized enterprises from such regions to participate. Indeed, in certain sectors barriers to market entry, which include research and development costs, may render entry by such enterprises effectively dependent on public assistance.[109]

At the same time, in so far as research and development assistance is granted to less favoured regions, there may be detrimental effects. Scarce science and technology resources in the region concerned, particularly personnel, are committed to projects which often have little direct relevance or spin-offs to the region.[110] Indeed, since such resources are inelastic in the short and medium term, assisted projects may simply 'crowd out' unassisted ones.[111] The possibility cannot be excluded that the latter projects would,

[103] *Evaluation of the Effects of the EC Framework Programme for Research and Technological Development on Economic and Social Cohesion in the Community* (EC Commission, Brussels, 1991) 29.

[104] ibid, 45.

[105] cf, earlier, Common policy for science and technology: impact of Community R & D on horizontal policies, COM(81)66, 3.

[106] European Parliament Resolution of 15 July 1993 (OJ 1993 C255/195) on the Community response to the problem of restructuring in East Germany and the economic and social crisis, para 17.

[107] *Evaluation of the Effects of the EC Framework Programme for Research and Technological Development on Economic and Social Cohesion in the Community* (EC Commission, Brussels, 1991) 31.

[108] R & TD activities of the EU 1998, COM(1998)439, 11.

[109] *Evaluation of Economic Effects: Relevance and Impacts of EC Programmes promoting Industrial R & D with Special Emphasis on Small and Medium-Sized Enterprises* (EC Commission, Brussels, 1992) 112–113.

[110] J Howells and D Charles, 'Research and Technological Development in the "Less-Favoured" Regions of the European Community: A UK Dimension' in K Dyson (ed), *Local Authorities and New Technologies: The European Dimension* (Croom Helm, London, 1988) 24–58, 45.

[111] J Gilchrist and D Deacon, 'Curbing Subsidies' in P Montagnon (ed), *European Competition Policy* (Pinter, London, 1990) 31–51.

if implemented, be of greater benefit to regional development than the former.

Therefore, influencing the sectoral and spatial distribution of technological advantage through technology transfer[112] and promotion of 'human capital mobility'[113] may be favoured.[114] However, the need for planning and the allocation of substantial resources to technology transfer in parallel with the scientific effort is said not to be reflected in the Framework Programmes.[115]

Scope of assistance

The Union is required by Article 164 of the EC Treaty to carry out four 'activities'. First, it is to implement research, technological development, and demonstration programmes, by promoting co-operation with and between undertakings, research centres, and universities. Secondly, it is to promote co-operation in this field with third countries and international organizations. Thirdly, it is to disseminate and optimize the results of the activities. Finally, it is to stimulate the training and mobility of researchers in the Union.

This provision may be seen as confirming the importance of assistance for technology transfer, which had already been sought under the EEC Treaty. In particular, the Sprint programme[116] was revised in 1989.[117] The programme was now to be concerned with: strengthening the innovative capacity of European producers of goods and services; enhancing the effectiveness and coherence of existing instruments and policies, whether at regional, national, or Community level, in the field of innovation and technology transfer; and promoting the rapid penetration by new technologies and the dissemination of innovation throughout the economic fabric of the Community, thus strengthening cohesion in the field of innovation and technology transfer.[118] Accordingly, science parks[119] and networks[120] might be assisted.

[112] Dec 89/412 (OJ 1989 L200/23) adopting a specific programme for the dissemination and utilization of scientific and technological research results (Value) 1989–92; and Dec 92/272 (OJ 1992 L141/1) on the dissemination and exploitation of knowledge resulting from the specific RTD programmes of the Community.

[113] Cohesion and RTD policy, COM(93)203, 12.

[114] ESC Opinion of 28 Mar 1990 (OJ 1990 C124/22) on the declining industrial areas, para 2.5.

[115] *Evaluation of the Effects of the EC Framework Programme for Research and Technological Development on Economic and Social Cohesion in the Community* (EC Commission, Brussels, 1991) 30.

[116] See sect 6.3.1 above.

[117] Dec 89/286 (OJ 1989 L112/12) on the implementation at Community level of the main phase of the strategic programme for innovation and technology transfer (1989–93). See also Report on the implementation of the main phase of the Sprint programme (1989–93), SEC(92)2352.

[118] Art 2(2) of Dec 89/286 (OJ 1989 L112/12).

[119] Call for proposals to take part in the science-park consultancy scheme launched within the Sprint programme (OJ 1992 C185/18).

[120] Communication regarding calls for proposals concerning the implementation of network support measures under the Sprint programme (OJ 1992 C205/8).

More particularly, assistance was to extend to projects having a transnational character, emphasizing industrial co-operation, and involving the application of generic technologies to targeted industrial sectors in regions of lagging development or of industrial decline.[121] Higher rates of assistance might be available to such regions.[122]

Moreover, the Community action programme in education and training for technology (Comett)[123] was concerned with, *inter alia*, facilitating the balanced economic and social development of the Community[124] and promoting cohesion.[125] Hence, particular efforts were to be made in regions where co-operation between universities and industry was 'not very highly developed'.[126] Special attention in the selection of projects was to be paid to the question whether universities and industrial partners from less developed regions would be associated in the execution of the projects.[127] Support was extended to preparatory activities, particularly in the case of such regions.[128]

Such programmes may have favoured technology transfer. It is uncertain, however, whether they could compensate for the apparent failure of the Framework Programme to reconcile research and development efforts with cohesion objectives.

Forms of assistance

All Union activities in support of research and technological development are now to be set out in a multiannual Framework Programme. This Programme shall establish the scientific and technological objectives to be achieved by the activities, fix the relevant priorities, and indicate the broad lines of such activities. It shall also fix the maximum overall amount of, and the detailed rules for, Union financial participation in the Programme and the respective shares in each of the supported activities.[129]

Implementation of the Framework Programmes is to be based on specific programmes developed within each activity. A specific programme shall define the detailed rules for implementing it, fix its duration, and provide for the financial resources deemed necessary. The sum of the amounts deemed necessary shall not exceed the overall maximum amount fixed for the Framework Programme and each activity.[130]

Accordingly, the Sprint programme has been replaced by a specific programme for the dissemination and optimization of the results of activities in

[121] Para B of the Annex to Dec 89/286 (OJ 1989 L353/15).

[122] ibid, Art 6(4).

[123] Dec 89/27 (OJ 1989 L13/28) adopting the second phase of the programme on co-operation between universities and industry regarding training in the field of technology (Comett II) (1990–94). See, now, Dec 94/819 (OJ 1994 L340/8) establishing an action programme for the implementation of an EC training policy: Leonardo da Vinci.

[124] OJ 1989 L13/28, Art 3.

[125] ibid, Annex, para 1.

[126] ibid, Annex, para 2.

[127] ibid, Annex, para 2.C. (e)(iv).

[128] ibid, Annex, para 2. D. (a)(i).

[129] Art 166(1) EC.

[130] Art 166(3) EC.

the field of research and technological development, including demonstration, for 1994 to 1998.[131] This programme is seen as benefiting, in particular, small and medium-sized enterprises in the Member States and regions least involved in research and technological development. It is thus viewed as contributing to improved cohesion.[132] However, even this programme may not necessarily be adequate to compensate for the failure of the Framework Programme generally to reconcile assistance to research and development with cohesion requirements.

6.4 FINANCIAL INSTRUMENT FOR THE ENVIRONMENT

The EEC Treaty originally made no provision for environmental policy. However, the need for Community assistance to environmental protection became clear as the common market developed.

6.4.1 Development of the Common Market

Assistance for environmental protection was first envisaged in the General Budget for 1975.[133] More particularly, in 1980 assistance to develop 'clean' technologies was envisaged.[134] Moreover, in 1982 assistance for pilot projects for such technologies was envisaged.[135] The possibility was also foreseen of Community contributions to the investment needed for implementation of certain Community obligations, particularly those concerning water quality, air quality, and the management of toxic waste.[136]

Such plans led to establishment of the Ace (Action by the Community relating to the environment) programme. According to Regulation 1872/84,[137] this programme was originally to run for three years. It involved the grant of ECU 13 million to finance demonstration projects concerning habitat protection and clean technologies. Regulation 2247/87[138] extended the range of activities concerned, their geographical scope, and the resources available.[139] ECU 24 million was provided for a further four years.

[131] Dec 94/917 (OJ 1994 L361/101).

[132] ibid, 18th recital in the preamble. See eg the Call for proposals for the implementation of regional innovation and technology transfer strategies and regional technology transfer projects (OJ 1995 C240/15).

[133] OJ 1975 L54/2, Art 357, on 'environmental projects'. Assistance for studies of the environment had been envisaged in the Budget for 1974 (OJ 1974 L115/1), Art 267. See also Dec 73/126 (OJ 1973 L153/11) adopting a research programme for the EEC on the protection of the environment.

[134] Item 3.5.1.1 of the Budget for 1980 (OJ 1980 L378/3).

[135] Item 6610 of the Budget for 1982 (OJ 1982 L31/3).

[136] ibid, Item 6612.

[137] On action by the Community relating to the environment (OJ 1984 L176/1).

[138] On action by the Community relating to the environment (OJ 1987 L207/8).

[139] However, the proposal of 11 Mar 1987 (OJ 1987 C141/3) for a decision establishing a five-year Community programme of projects to demonstrate how environmental measures could help to create jobs was not accepted by the Council.

Article 1(1) of the latter Regulation stated that the Community might grant financial assistance for: demonstration projects aimed at developing new clean technologies, which caused little or no pollution and which might also be more economical in the use of natural resources; demonstration projects aimed at developing techniques for recycling and reusing waste, including waste water; demonstration projects aimed at developing techniques for locating and restoring sites contaminated by hazardous wastes or substances; demonstration projects aimed at developing techniques and methods for measuring and monitoring the quality of the natural environment; projects favouring the maintenance or re-establishment of seriously threatened biotopes which were the habitat of endangered species and were of particular importance to the Community under Directive 79/409;[140] and projects favouring the protection or re-establishment of land threatened or damaged by fire, erosion, or desertification.

6.4.2 Cohesion

Article 175(4) of the EC Treaty now provides that 'without prejudice to certain measures of a Community nature, the Member States shall finance and implement the environmental policy measures'.[141] The implication is that the Union may provide certain environmental assistance.[142]

In the case of the Cohesion Fund,[143] the implication is confirmed by Article 175(5) of the Treaty. According to this provision, 'without prejudice to the principle that the polluter should pay, if a measure . . . involves costs deemed disproportionate for the public authorities of a Member State, the Council shall, in the act adopting that measure, lay down appropriate provisions [for] financial support from the Cohesion Fund'.[144]

Moreover, Medspa was established by Regulation 563/91.[145] It provided for the grant of assistance for environmental protection in the Mediterranean, to

[140] On the conservation of wild birds (OJ 1979 L103/1).

[141] Item B4–304 of the Budget for 1998 (OJ 1998 L44/3) is entitled 'Legislation and other general action based on the fifth action programme on the environment'; Art B4–305 'Urban environment'; and Art B4–306 'Awareness and subsidies'. See also the proposal for a decision on a Community action programme promoting non-governmental organizations primarily active in the field of environmental protection (OJ 1997 C104/11). See, generally, Progress report on implementation of the Life regulation, COM(95)135, 18.

[142] Assistance to nature-protection projects was provided for in Reg 3907/91 (OJ 1991 L370/17) on action by the Community relating to nature conservation.

[143] Reg 1164/94 (OJ 1994 L130/1) establishing a Cohesion Fund. See also the Proposal of 19 Mar 1998 (OJ 1998 C159/7) for a regulation amending Reg 1164/94.

[144] Art 130r(4) EEC previously required that in the application of the 'polluter pays' principle particular account should be taken of the economic and social development of the Community as a whole.

[145] On action by the Community for the protection of the environment in the Mediterranean region (OJ 1991 L63/1).

complement the Integrated Mediterranean Programmes.[146] Similarly, Regulation 3908/91[147] established Norspa. It provided for the grant of assistance to protect the environment in the coastal areas and coastal waters of the Irish Sea, North Sea, English Channel, Baltic Sea, and North-East Atlantic Ocean.

However, the Commission considered that the Union should provide more general assistance for: preparing studies and gathering information to substantiate Commission proposals for legislation;[148] securing coherence between legislation in this and other areas; and promoting implementation of legislative rules through technical assistance, awareness campaigns, pilot projects, and demonstration projects.[149]

Regulation 1973/92[150] has gone some way towards providing for the grant of such assistance. It has established a Financial Instrument for the Environment (Life), which replaces Ace, Medspa, and Norspa. The new instrument may assist actions of Union interest which contribute significantly to the implementation of Union environmental policy and meet the conditions for implementation of the 'polluter pays' principle.[151] According to this principle, polluting may not be subsidized, though action to reduce pollution may be.[152]

Objectives of assistance

The objectives of the Financial Instrument for the Environment are: to strengthen and increase the effectiveness of administrative structures or services designed to ensure the implementation of environmental provisions; to help control and reduce the various forms of pollution; and to help protect sensitive areas and maintain biogenetic diversity.[153] As refined by Regulation 1404/96,[154] the general objective of this Instrument is to contribute to the development and, if appropriate, implementation of Union environmental policy and legislation.[155]

[146] Annex II(a) of Reg 2088/85 (OJ 1985 L197/1) concerning the IMPs, provided that in the agricultural sector such programmes might provide for operations aimed, *inter alia*, at operations to protect the environment.

[147] On Community action to protect the environment in the coastal areas and coastal waters of the Irish Sea, North Sea, English Channel, Baltic Sea, and North-East Atlantic Ocean (OJ 1991 L370/28).

[148] cf Reg 1210/90 (OJ 1990 L120/1) on the establishment of the European Environment Agency and the European Environment Information and Observation Network.

[149] Community finances between now and 1997, COM(92)2001, 29.

[150] Establishing a financial instrument for the environment (OJ 1992 L206/1).

[151] ibid, Art 2(2). See also the Communication in pursuance of Reg 1973/92 concerning priority actions to be implemented in 1993 (OJ 1992 C331/11); and Life 1998 call for proposals (OJ 1997 C282/19) and for 1999 (OJ 1998 C282/6).

[152] OECD Council Recommendation of 26 May 1972 (C(72)12) on guiding principles concerning international economic aspects of environmental policies.

[153] Art 2(1) of Reg 1973/92 (OJ 1992 L206/1).

[154] OJ 1996 L181/1.

[155] ibid, Art 1.

Eligibility for assistance

The Instrument may assist activities of Union interest which contribute significantly to the implementation of Union environmental policy and respect the 'polluter pays' principle.[156] In particular, activities eligible for assistance are: nature conservation; other activities designed to implement Union environmental legislation and policy; and monitoring and evaluation measures and dissemination of results.[157]

Allocation of assistance

Assistance provided by the Instrument is to be differentiated according to: the seriousness of the specific, notably regional, environmental problems to be tackled; the special importance attaching to the measures from a Union viewpoint; and the capacity of the Member State or of the beneficiary to contribute.[158] The need to help the less prosperous Member States to honour their environmental commitments is stressed by the European Parliament. To this end, the Parliament has called for a substantial increase in the funds earmarked for the Instrument.[159]

Scope of assistance

The Commission considers that the Instrument should assist 'translation' of concepts of environmental responsibility and sustainable development into everyday actions. Hence, such assistance should relate to: defining and promoting models of production and behaviour which are in line with the principles of sustainable development; practical demonstration of the technical viability and economic efficiency of chosen models and actions;[160] supporting specific demonstrations, pilot projects, 'horizontal information', education, and training designed to influence economic actors through practicable examples; and strengthening administrative structures.[161]

The Commission is to secure co-ordination and coherence as between such assistance and operations of the other Union funds.[162] The problems facing such co-ordination[163] were impliedly recognized by the Envireg initiative.[164] However, this initiative was too limited to overcome problems of reconciling

[156] ibid, Art 2(2). [157] ibid, Art 2. [158] ibid, Art 9.

[159] Resolution of 8 Apr 1992 (OJ 1992 C125/122) on the implementation of EC environmental legislation, paras 12–13.

[160] Presumably, such action may complement that envisaged in Dec 94/911 (OJ 1994 L361/1) adopting a specific programme of RTDD in the field of environment and climate (1994–8).

[161] Towards sustainability, COM(92)23, ii. 71.

[162] Art 6 of Reg 1973/92 (OJ 1992 L206/1). See eg ERDF: List of projects larger than ECU 50 million satisfying Community environmental legislation 1997 (OJ 1998 C322/29).

[163] J Scott, *Development Dilemmas in European Community Law* (Open University Press, Buckingham, 1995).

[164] Notice laying down guidelines for operational programmes within the framework of a Community initiative concerning the environment (OJ 1990 C115/3). See sect 2.4.6 above.

environmental assistance and Union spending generally[165] and, in any case, has been discontinued.

6.5 COHESION FUND

In accordance with the Protocol on Economic and Social Cohesion and Article 130d of the EC Treaty,[166] a Cohesion Fund has been established.[167] The Fund provides assistance to projects concerning environmental protection or trans-European networks in Member States which meet two conditions. First, they must have a per capita gross domestic product of less than 90 per cent of the Union average. Secondly, they must have a programme leading to the fulfilment of the conditions of economic convergence, as set out in Article 104 of the Treaty. In effect, the Fund is designed to assist Ireland, Portugal, Spain, and Greece in meeting the economic convergence requirements for participation in the third stage of monetary union. Participants in this stage replace their national currencies with the Euro.

However, the principle of conditional assistance[168] is embodied in the legislation establishing the Fund. According to this principle, Fund assistance may be suspended in the case of a Member State not making satisfactory progress towards fulfilment of the convergence conditions. In practice, this means that government deficits are examined by reference to targets set annually by the Council. If the deficit is 'significantly off the mark for reasons other than exceptional circumstances outside the control of the Member State', assistance will be suspended.[169]

The possibility is thus raised that assistance may be stopped at an 'inopportune moment' for the purposes of regional development.[170] In essence, therefore, the Cohesion Fund appears more an instrument of convergence than cohesion.[171] As a result, cohesion efforts which are not favoured by 'liberal market economics' may be starved of resources.[172]

[165] See eg COA annual report for 1994 (OJ 1995 C303/1), para 6.42.

[166] Now Art 161 EC.

[167] Reg 1164/94 (OJ 1994 L130/1) establishing a Cohesion Fund.

[168] ibid, Art 6. Cf Art 1 of Reg 792/93 (OJ 1993 L79/74) establishing a cohesion financial instrument, adopted under Art 235 EEC.

[169] Annual report on the Cohesion Fund 1996, COM(97)302, 8.

[170] ESC Opinion of 23 Feb 1993 (OJ 1993 C108/53) on the proposal for a regulation establishing a cohesion financial instrument and the revised draft proposal for a regulation establishing a Cohesion Fund, para 2.3.1.

[171] See also the European Parliament Resolution of 19 Apr 1996 (OJ 1996 C141/265) on the complement to the Commission's annual report on the Cohesion Fund (1994), paras 25–29.

[172] cf A Cutler, C Haslam, J Williams, and K Williams, *1992—the Struggle for Europe* (Berg, New York, 1989) 102.

6.6 PHARE

The Phare programme is primarily concerned with economic restructuring in Central and East European countries.[173] However, co-operation between border regions in these countries and border regions within the Union is also envisaged.[174] Such co-operation may receive complementary assistance from this Programme, the Structural Funds,[175] and a special heading in the General Budget.[176]

In particular, co-ordination of activities of the European Regional Development Fund, notably Interreg,[177] and Phare activities is envisaged.[178] In addition, network support is provided under the Ecos-Ouverture programme.[179]

6.7 OTHER BUDGETARY RESOURCES

Other Budgetary resources may be used to support small and medium-sized enterprises, to meet commercial policy requirements, to tackle balance-of-payments problems, to assist the outermost regions, and to assist reconstruction after natural disasters.

[173] See also the Proposal of 19 Mar 1998 (OJ 1998 C164/4) establishing an Instrument for Structural Policies for Pre-Accession.

[174] cf the Jopp Programme (OJ 1991 C46/11) for promoting the establishment of joint ventures in the countries of central and eastern Europe; Reg 1279/96 (OJ 1996 L165/1) concerning the provision of assistance to economic reform and recovery in the New Independent States and Mongolia; and Reg 1488/96 (OJ 1996 L189/1) on financial and technical measures to accompany the reform of economic and social structures in the framework of the Euro-Mediterranean partnership.

[175] 7th recital in the preamble to Reg 2082/93 (OJ 1993 L193/20) amending Reg 4253/88 laying down provisions for implementing Reg 2052/88 as regards co-ordination of the activities of the different Structural Funds between themselves and with the operations of the EIB and the other existing financial instruments.

[176] Art B7–502, 'Transfrontier co-operation in the field of structural operations', in the Budget for 1996 (OJ 1996 L22/3).

[177] Notice laying down guidelines for operational programmes in the framework of a Community initiative concerning border development, cross-border co-operation, and selected energy networks (OJ 1994 C180/60), para 19. See also Future of Community initiatives under the Structural Funds, COM(93)282, 16; and Phare Baltic Sea region cross-border co-operation programme: funding for joint projects with Interreg (OJ 1997 C336/14).

[178] Reg 1628/94 (OJ 1994 L171/14) concerning the implementation of a programme for cross-border co-operation between countries in Central and Eastern Europe and Member States in the framework of the Phare programme. See also A global approach to promote regional and social conversion and to facilitate industrial restructuring in the Central and Eastern European countries: the case of steel, COM(98)220.

[179] sect 2.4.6 above.

6.7.1 Small and Medium-Sized Enterprises

Article 157(1) of the EC Treaty provides that the Union and the Member States shall encourage an environment favourable to initiative and to the development of undertakings throughout the Union, particularly small and medium-sized enterprises.[180] This provision reflects a long-standing recognition of the desirability of assistance for such enterprises.[181]

This recognition is based on the view that financial structures are ill suited to the launching of new developments by small and medium-sized enterprises, even though such enterprises have an important role to play in the Union economy. In particular, assistance may be necessary because they are too small to benefit from the economies of scale expected to result for their larger competitors from integration.[182]

Establishment of the common market

In 1960 the European Parliament stressed that small and medium-sized enterprises should receive technical and financial assistance enabling them to carry out the necessary adaptations and conversions for increased productivity demanded by establishment of the common market.[183] However, at the time little interest was shown by the other Community institutions in the provision of Community assistance for such purposes.

Development of the common market

The Commission Memorandum on Industrial Policy in the European Community[184] in 1970 referred to the importance of small and medium-sized enterprises in the development of the common market. The Economic and Social Committee also published a *Study of the Situation of Small and Medium-Sized Enterprises in the EC*[185] in 1974. However, an action programme for such enterprises was not adopted by the Council until November 1986.[186]

On the other hand, Business and Innovation Centres (BICs) have been supported by the Commission since 1983.[187] The development of a network of

[180] Such enterprises were first defined in Dir 78/660 (OJ 1978 L222/11) on the annual accounts of certain types of companies, Arts 11 and 27; and Dir 94/8 (OJ 1994 L82/33) amending Dir 78/660 as regards the revision of amounts expressed in ECUs.

[181] cf N Moussis, 'Small and Medium Enterprises in the Internal Market' (1992) ELR 483–498.

[182] cf Public procurement: regional and social aspects, COM(89)400 and, more particularly, Promoting SME participation in public procurement in the Community, COM(90) 66.

[183] Resolution of 17 May 1960 (JO 1960 827) on conjunctural, regional, and structural aspects of Community long-term economic policy, para III.3.

[184] COM(70)100.

[185] CES(74)714.

[186] Resolution of 3 Nov 1986 (OJ 1986 C287/1) concerning the action programme for SMEs.

[187] Explanatory memorandum to the proposal for a decision concerning a Community programme to create and develop BICs and their network, COM(86)785, 3.

these bodies, the European Business and Innovation Centre Network (EBN), has also been assisted by the Commission.[188] They operate in regions assisted by the European Regional Development Fund, regions covered by Integrated Mediterranean Programmes, ECSC regions, and other regions adversely affected by major industrial decline.[189] They are designed to create innovative activities with growth potential through: detecting and selecting entrepreneurs; finding, assessing, and developing technologies; management training; rigorous business-planning; and the supply of common premises. In other words, they seek to assist regions in developing their indigenous potential.[190] They follow a Community model, but depend at local level on agreement between the public and the private sectors. They concentrate their work on new or existing firms which put forward innovative development projects which add value to the economy of the region.[191]

Such assistance fell short of what was once envisaged. In particular, the creation of a 'Regional Development Company' was proposed by the Commission in 1972[192] and recommended by the European Parliament in 1976.[193] However, the creation of such a body was not favoured by the Council.

At the same time, the performance of the Business and Innovation Centres has been criticized by the Court of Auditors. Their performance has been criticized partly because 'innovation' has been interpreted as any activity, product, or process that is new to the industrial environment of the area concerned.[194] There has also been criticism that the self-financing requirement, supposedly applicable to the Centres, has been diluted. The implied risk is that assistance to them will be perpetuated.[195]

Cohesion

Decision 89/490[196] sought to promote the development of small and medium-sized enterprises. Promotion was to take place particularly through

[188] Bull EC 11–1984, 2.1.82.

[189] Art B2–601 of the Budget for 1996 (OJ 1996 L22/3).

[190] Explanatory memorandum to the proposal for a decision concerning a Community programme to create and develop BICs and their network, COM(86)785, 1.

[191] Commission Reply by Mr Millan to WQ 1939/91 (OJ 1992 C126/16) by Mr François Musso.

[192] Proposal of 19 June 1972 (JO 1972 C94/7) for a Council resolution on instruments of Community regional policy. Cf the idea of creating a European Company for Industrial Parks in *Les Régimes d'aide régionale dans la communauté européenne: Étude comparative* (EC Commission, Luxembourg, 1979) 306. Cf also the proposal of 23 Dec 1986 (OJ 1987 C80/7) for a decision on financing major Community infrastructure projects, which envisaged Community contributions in the form of equity holdings.

[193] Resolution of 16 Dec 1976 (OJ 1977 C6/86) on the first annual report on the ERDF, para 9. See, later, the Resolution of 16 Feb 1982 (OJ 1982 C66/26) on a 'Mediterranean plan' for the benefit of Mediterranean countries belonging to the EC and the applicant countries, Portugal and Spain, para 7.

[194] Special report 5/93 (OJ 1994 C13/1) concerning BICs, para 13.

[195] ibid, para 10.

[196] On the improvement of the business environment and the promotion of the development of enterprises, and in particular SMEs, in the Community (OJ 1989 L239/33).

increasing the opportunities for such enterprises to receive assistance from the Structural Funds,[197] the Framework Programme for research and development, and other programmes.[198] Such action was to include information and assistance to small and medium-sized enterprises regarding Community policies, regulations, and activities which concerned or were likely to concern them. It was also to include encouragement of co-operation and partnership between such enterprises from different regions of the Community.[199] This action was expected to favour increased competitiveness of the European economy and employment growth.[200]

The approach to small and medium-sized enterprises is now laid down by Decision 91/319.[201] This measure is designed to revise existing arrangements so as to take account of the impact of completion of the internal market. The preamble refers to the importance of such enterprises for economic activity in general and regional development in particular.[202] Their importance is said to derive from their dynamism, productivity, adaptability, and innovation.[203]

Accordingly, a multiannual programme for assistance to such enterprises has been instituted under Decision 93/379.[204] At the same time, to facilitate co-ordination between the various measures in their favour, an integrated programme has been established.[205]

Moreover, a definition of small and medium-sized enterprises[206] has been adopted.[207] A medium-sized enterprise is defined as an enterprise which:

[197] Member States are invited to take care that both public and private financial intermediaries, specialized in financing SMEs, are in a position to call on the EIB for the granting of guarantees to SMEs (Council Resolution of 22 Nov 1993 (OJ 1993 C326/1) on strengthening the competitiveness of enterprises, in particular SMEs and craft industries, and developing employment, para 5(a)).

[198] 10th recital in the preamble to Dec 89/490 (OJ 1989 L239/33).

[199] ibid, Art 2.

[200] ibid, 8th recital in the preamble.

[201] Revising the programme on the improvement of the business environment and the promotion of the development of enterprises, in particular SMEs in the Community (OJ 1991 L175/32).

[202] See eg Assistance in the field of transnational co-operation between small enterprises and the craft sector—call for proposals (OJ 1996 C232/47). See also the Council Resolution of 22 Nov 1993 (OJ 1993 C326/1) on strengthening the competitiveness of enterprises in particular SMEs and craft enterprises and developing employment.

[203] See also Assistance for craft enterprises and small enterprises: call for proposals (OJ 1997 C117/43).

[204] Dec 93/379 (OJ 1993 L161/68) on a multiannual programme of Community measures to intensify the priority areas and to ensure the continuity and consolidation of policy for enterprise, in particular SMEs, in the Community. See, now, Dec 97/15 (OJ 1997 L6/25) on a third multiannual programme for SMEs in the EU (1997–2000).

[205] Integrated programme in favour of SMEs and the craft sector, COM(94)207.

[206] The definition of an SME used by the EIB was an independent undertaking with less than 500 employees and fixed assets (net of depreciation) of less than ECU 75 million. See P Aitken, 'SMEs, Research and Development and Technology Policies and the European Community: Issues in Implementation' in K Dyson (ed), n 110 above, 59–83, 59. Problems of inconsistency in the definitions arose in Case T–478/93 *Wafer Zoo Srl v EC Commission* [1995] ECR II–1479.

[207] Rec 96/280 (OJ 1996 L107/4) concerning the definition of SMEs.

- has no more than 250 employees;
- has an annual turnover not exceeding ECU 40 million or
- has a balance sheet total not exceeding ECU 27 million;
- is not more than 25 per cent owned by one or more companies not falling within this definition, except public investment corporations, venture-capital companies or, provided no control is exercised, [208] institutional investors.

A small enterprise is one which

- has no more than fifty employees;
- has an annual turnover not exceeding ECU 7 million or
- has a balance sheet total not exceeding ECU 5 million;
- is not more than 25 per cent owned by one or more companies not falling within this definition, except public investment corporations, venture-capital companies or, provided no control is exercised, institutional investors.[209]

Assistance to enterprises covered by this definition is expected to favour cohesion.[210] Accordingly, there is to be co-ordination between such assistance and the operations of the Structural Funds.[211] Thus in allocating assistance from the Structural Funds to part-finance national aid schemes, the Commission takes into account, *inter alia*, the priority given to small and medium-sized enterprises and the encouragement of services supplied to them, such as management advice and market surveys.[212]

Moreover, in accordance with a pilot scheme launched in 1989,[213] the Commission has provided financial assistance for the creation and development of seed-capital funds to acquire equity holdings in new or embryonic companies.[214] Repayable advances may be available from Directorate-General XXIII (Enterprise Policy), to meet part of the operating costs of a fund. A capital contribution may also be made by Directorate-General XVI (Regional Policy) to the Business and Innovation Centre established in the

[208] cf, regarding the meaning of control, Notice C42/97 (ex NN121/96) (OJ 1998 C37/8) on aid granted by the German Government to Everts Erfurt GmbH, Thuringia.

[209] Art 1 of the Annex to Rec 96/280 (OJ 1996 L107/4). According to Art 1(5), 'micro-enterprises' are those having fewer than ten employees. Craft enterprises 'continue to be defined at national level' owing to their specific characteristics (ibid, 28th recital in the preamble).

[210] 8th recital in the preamble to Dec 89/490 (OJ 1989 L239/33). Art 777 of the Budget for 1987 (OJ 1987 L86/3) had envisaged financing for analysis of problems specific to SMEs in peripheral regions and of their solutions.

[211] Art 5 of Dec 89/490 (OJ 1989 L239/33).

[212] Art 4(2) of Reg 2083/93 (OJ 1993 L193/34) amending Reg 4254/88 laying down provisions for implementing Reg 2052/88 as regards the ERDF. See, similarly, regarding the allocation of assistance under Objective 4, Art 1(2) of Reg 2084/93 (OJ 1993 L193/39) amending Reg 4255/88 laying down provisions for implementing Reg 2052/88 as regards the ESF.

[213] Pilot action to create and develop seed-capital funds (OJ 1988 C306/12).

[214] *Twenty-Fifth EC General Report* (EC Commission, Brussels, 1992) 93.

region, if the Centre is willing to invest in the fund. The funds established, sixteen of which are in assisted regions, have formed themselves into a network.[215]

Risk capital may also be available to small and medium-sized enterprises generally through Union-supported arrangements such as 'Venture consort' and 'Eurotech capital'.[216] In relation to such schemes, the importance of 'integrating the outlying regions' is recognized, but is not apparently treated as a priority.[217]

More particularly, assistance is provided for the creation of joint ventures by small and medium-sized enterprises.[218] For this purpose, risk-capital participations are provided from the General Budget and managed by the European Investment Fund.[219] For the same purpose, the General Budget finances guarantees and counter-guarantees issued by the European Investment Fund.[220] Similar assistance is available for innovation and job creation by small and medium-sized enterprises.[221]

6.7.2 Commercial Policy

Considerations of commercial policy, that is policy regarding trade with third states, may affect the grant of assistance, particularly through other Budgetary resources.

Establishment of the common market

It was recognized that establishment of the common market would affect the position of Community undertakings in their trade with third states. An example was provided by Protocol III to the Agreement on the determination of the Common Customs Tariff in respect of the products in List G in Annex I to the EEC Treaty. It recognized that fixing a zero duty for crude sulphur raised special problems for Italian industry.[222] Accordingly, Decision 66/740[223] provided for Community assistance for workers and their children

[215] *Twenty-Fifth EC General Report* (EC Commission, Brussels, 1992) 163; and Extension of the seed-capital fund pilot action in the new *Länder* in Germany (OJ 1992 C115/36).

[216] *Twenty-Sixth EC General Report* (EC Commission, Brussels, 1993) 25; and Improvement of the fiscal environment of SMEs, COM(94)206.

[217] Financial engineering, COM(86)723, 3; and ch B5–33 of the Budget for 1996 (OJ 1996 L33/2).

[218] Dec 97/761 (OJ 1997 L310/28) approving a support mechanism for the creation of transnational joint ventures by SMEs in the EU. See, more particularly, the Initiative to encourage partnership between industries and/or services in Europe, Interprise—Call for proposals (OJ 1997 C329/17; and OJ 1998 C291/5).

[219] OJ 1997 L310/28, Art 3.

[220] ibid, Art 5.

[221] Dec 98/347 (OJ 1998 L155/43) on measures of financial support for innovative and job-creating SMEs—the growth and employment initiative.

[222] JO 1960 1849, para 3.

[223] On Community aid for Italy towards the granting of assistance to sulphur-mine workers affected by dismissal and of a number of scholarships for their children (JO 1966 4168). It was adopted under Art 235 EEC.

in this sector. More generally, the European Social Fund might be seen as compensating France and Italy for the lowering of protectionist barriers resulting from establishment of the common market.[224]

Similarly, it was recognized that establishment of common organizations of agricultural markets would affect the position of Community producers in relation to traders from third states. Most recently, the establishment of a common organization of the banana market, which entailed abolition of national restrictions on imports from third states, was accompanied by introduction of assistance for Union producers.[225]

Development of the common market

In the implementation of the common commercial policy[226] required for development of the common market, the Community might conclude agreements with third states having restrictive implications for the provision of Community assistance. At the same time, in so far as trade liberalization was entailed by implementation of the policy, the Community might feel compelled to grant various kinds of assistance.

On the one hand, such agreements might be seen as entailing constraints on the grant of assistance. For example, it was recognized that assistance under Article 55(2)(c) of the ECSC Treaty for research, pilot, and demonstration projects should comply with the provisions of the 'consensus' with the United States concerning trade in steel.[227] Similarly, the Memorandum of Understanding on Oil Seeds,[228] reached with the United States within the GATT framework, necessitated changes in assistance for cereal producers.[229]

On the other hand, some agreements might be portrayed as implying the need for undertakings 'which [were] less competitive internationally to move progressively into more viable types of production or into other sectors of the economy'. Community assistance might, as in the case of textiles,[230] be seen as necessary to facilitate such adjustment.

224 J Tessier, 'Le Fonds social européen' (1960) RMC 325–337, 333.

225 Reg 404/93 (OJ 1993 L47/1) on the common organization of the market in bananas, Arts 6–14.

226 Arts 110–116 EEC.

227 OJ 1989 L368/185. Cf the Agreement with the US Government concerning the application of the GATT Agreement on Trade in Civil Aircraft to trade in large civil aircraft (OJ 1992 L301/32).

228 OJ 1993 L147/25.

229 Reg 232/94 (OJ 1994 L30/7) amending Reg 1765/92 establishing a support system for producers of certain arable crops. See, now, the Proposal of 19 Mar 1998 (OJ 1998 C170/4). Again, multiannual, regional, viticultural adjustment programmes are envisaged to secure a production level balancing the Union market 'bearing in mind our international commitments'. See Development and future of wine sector policy, COM(93)380, 4–5.

230 See, in connection with the GATT Arrangement regarding international trade in textiles, the 10th recital in the preamble to Reg 219/84 (OJ 1984 L27/22) instituting a specific Community regional development measure contributing to overcoming constraints on the development of new economic activities in certain zones adversely affected by restructuring of the textiles and clothing industry.

At the same time, the promotion of self-sufficiency within the Community might be seen as a possible justification for Community assistance. For example, as regards investment in the development of waste-paper processing, the Commission considered that major benefits would accrue to the Community from at least maintaining the percentage share of the Community's indigenous resources in the overall supplies of fibrous matter. Hence, the Commission examined the possibility of providing assistance to processors.[231]

'Strategic' assistance might also be advocated in fields of high technology. For example, the Commission proposed, in relation to microelectronics, that assistance should be provided to foster co-operation among Community producers. Such assistance should enable them to catch up and even take over the leadership again in the development of products and services which had a strategic impact on the whole of Community industry.[232]

Cohesion

Article 157(1) of the EC Treaty now provides for Union assistance to speed up the adjustment of industry to structural changes.[233] This provision may be seen as demanding assistance to protect or develop the competitive capacity of Union industry.[234] Such assistance should, it is argued, be designed to ensure that Union companies effectively and in the first place benefit from integration.[235]

Accordingly, the Prisma initiative[236] provided for the grant of assistance to industries in Objective 1 regions previously benefiting from protection under Article 134 of the Treaty.[237] Again, Perifra[238] was designed to support regions affected by the opening of Union markets to Central and East European

[231] Community action programme regarding forestry and forest-based industries, COM(83)222, 31.

[232] A Community strategy to develop Europe's industry, COM(81)639, 14.

[233] cf the ESC Opinion of 21 Dec 1993 (OJ 1994 C52/35) on the proposal for a regulation laying down detailed rules for implementing Reg 2080/93 on Community structural assistance in the fisheries and aquaculture sector and the industry processing and marketing its products, para 1.9.

[234] See eg the Report of the Committee on Regional Policy, Regional Planning, and Relations with Regional and Local Authorities on a Community initiative for regions heavily dependent on the textiles and clothing sector (Retex), EP Doc A3–110/92, 11.

[235] ibid, 17.

[236] Notice laying down guidelines for operational programmes in the framework of a Community initiative concerning the preparation of enterprises for the single market (OJ 1991 C33/9).

[237] According to this provision, in order to ensure that the execution of measures of commercial policy taken in accordance with the Treaty by a Member State was not obstructed by deflection of trade, or where differences between such measures led to economic difficulties in one or more of the Member States, the Commission could authorize Member States to take the necessary protective measures.

[238] Budget for 1991 (OJ 1991 L30/3), Item B2–610.

countries, with preference being given to regions covered by Objective 1, 2, or 5b.[239]

More particularly, adoption of the Retex initiative[240] was influenced by recognition of the problems likely to result for certain regions from liberalization of trade in textiles with Hungary, Poland, and the then Czechoslovakia. Assistance was also introduced to improve the competitiveness of Union raspberry producers in the face of imports from such countries.[241] Likewise, GATT liberalization led to adoption of a special programme to assist Portuguese textiles.[242] Extension of such liberalization to agriculture and introduction of assistance through measures accompanying reform of the common agricultural policy were also apparently linked.[243]

Commercial policy may have greater influence on the grant of such assistance than cohesion requirements. Thus where the assistance aims to promote the development of networks within the Union, it may lawfully be denied to subsidiaries tightly controlled by third-state owners.[244] However, weaker regions may be more dependent for their network participation on such subsidiaries than stronger regions.

6.7.3 Balance-of-Payment Loans

Balance-of-payment loans were introduced by Regulation 397/75,[245] and are now provided for in Regulation 1969/88.[246] They were originally designed to assist Member States in tackling balance-of-payment difficulties attributable to the increase in oil prices without disruption of the common market. However, the original arrangements were reformed by Regulation 682/81,[247]

[239] cf Dec 89/10 (OJ 1989 L7/30) on a concerted measure for the grant of a standby indemnity to fishermen from certain Member States who had to suspend their fishing activities in waters under the sovereignty or jurisdiction of Morocco.

[240] Notice laying down guidelines for operational programmes within the framework of a Community initiative for regions heavily dependent on the textiles and clothing sector (OJ 1992 C142/5).

[241] Reg 1991/92 (OJ 1992 L199/1) establishing a special scheme for raspberries intended for processing. This assistance was provided by the Guarantee Section of the EAGGF.

[242] Reg 852/95 (OJ 1995 L86/10) on the grant of financial assistance to Portugal for a specific programme for the modernization of the Portuguese textile and clothing industry. Cf, regarding the possibilities of a Union response to the difficulties implied for the Greek textiles industry by the 'new terms of international competition', Council Reply to WQ E–0067/96 (OJ 1996 C280/8) by Yannos Krandiotis.

[243] Commission Reply by Mr Fischler to WQ E–0802/96 (OJ 1996 C297/28) by Sebastiano Musumeci.

[244] T–369/94 & 85/95 *DIR International Film Srl v EC Commission* [19 Feb 1998].

[245] Concerning Community loans (OJ 1975 L46/1). Cf, earlier, Dec 71/143 (JO 1971 L73/15) setting up machinery for medium-term financial assistance.

[246] Establishing a single facility providing medium-term financial assistance for Member States' balances of payments (OJ 1988 L178/1).

[247] Adjusting the Community loan mechanism designed to support the balance of payments of Member States (OJ 1981 L73/1).

and such loans now seek more generally to assist Member States with monetary problems that may hamper investment and growth.[248]

For example, a loan to France in 1983 was to support national measures to strengthen the competitiveness of firms and to create conditions which would favour investment in the sectors subject to competition.[249] Loans to Greece have been concerned with more fundamental structural problems.[250] They have been designed to assist the strengthening and modernization of productive structures, and use of the latest loan is to have regard to the Community Support Framework[251] for Greece.[252] Guarantees on these loans are financed from the General Budget.[253]

6.7.4 Poseidom, Poseican, and Poseima Programmes

The Poseidom, Poseican, and Poseima programmes were adopted under Article 235 of the EEC Treaty. According to this provision, if Community action proved necessary to attain, in the course of the operation of the common market, one of the objectives of the Community and the Treaty had not provided the necessary powers, the Council should, acting unanimously on a proposal from the Commission and after consulting the European Parliament, take the appropriate measures.

The programmes concern, respectively, the French overseas departments,[254] the Canary Islands,[255] and Madeira and the Azores.[256] They are based on the principle that such regions form an integral part of the Union. However, the programmes also recognize features and constraints specific to the regions concerned as distinct from the Union as a whole.[257] Accordingly, assistance is granted to take account of their remoteness and insularity.[258]

[248] The EIB, the other financial instruments and strengthening economic and social cohesion, COM(88)244, 2. See, most recently, Dec 93/67 (OJ 1993 L22/121) concerning a Community loan in favour of Italy.

[249] Dec 83/298 (OJ 1983 L153/44) concerning a Community loan in favour of France.

[250] Dec 85/543 (OJ 1985 L341/17) concerning a Community loan in favour of Greece.

[251] See, regarding CSFs, sect 7.4.4 below.

[252] 8th recital in, and para 4 of, the preamble to Dec 91/136 (OJ 1991 L66/22) concerning a Community loan in favour of Greece.

[253] See eg Art B0–200 of the Budget for 1998 (OJ 1998 L44/3). See, generally, Guarantees covered by the General Budget, COM(97)464.

[254] Dec 89/487 (OJ 1989 L399/39) establishing a programme of options specific to the remote and insular nature of the French overseas departments (Poseidom).

[255] Dec 91/314 (OJ 1991 L171/5) setting up a programme of options specific to the remote and insular nature of the Canary Islands (Poseican).

[256] Dec 91/315 (OJ 1991 L171/10) setting up a programme of options specific to the remote and insular nature of Madeira and the Azores (Poseima).

[257] See eg para 1 of the Poseidom Programme (OJ 1989 L399/39).

[258] ibid, para 12.2.

6.7.5 Reconstruction after Natural Disasters

Budgetary resources may be used to assist reconstruction after natural disasters. For example, grants and interest subsidies were provided following an earthquake in Italy in 1976.[259] Again, following earthquakes in Greece in 1986, the Budget was used to fund interest rate subsidies on loans granted by the European Investment Bank in the regions stricken.[260] Similar assistance was provided following earthquakes in Italy in 1980[261] and in Greece in 1981[262] and a cyclone in Madeira in 1993.[263]

6.8 EFTA FINANCIAL MECHANISM

When the European Economic Area (EEA) Agreement[264] was concluded with EFTA States,[265] Member States demanded compensation for trade liberalization with the comparatively developed EFTA States. According to the preamble to the Agreement, the contracting parties aim to promote a harmonious development of the European Economic Area. They are convinced of the need to contribute through the application of this Agreement to the reduction of economic and social regional disparities.[266] Article 115 confirms the concern of the parties to reduce such disparities. To this end, Article 116 provides for the establishment by the EFTA States of a Financial Mechanism, details of which are set out in Protocol 38 to the Agreement.[267]

The Protocol provides for assistance in the form of grants and interest rebates.[268] Decisions regarding such assistance are subject to approval by the EFTA States and to a Commission opinion.[269]

[259] Reg 1506/76 (OJ 1976 L168/11) on the Community contribution towards repairing the infrastructural damage caused by the earthquake in May 1976 in the region of Friuli/Venezia Giulia; grants were provided for in Reg 1505/76 (OJ 1976 L168/9) on the Community contribution towards repairing the damage caused to agriculture by the earthquake in May 1976 in the region of Friuli/Venezia Giulia; and chs 58 and 59 of the Budget for 1976 (OJ 1976 L66/3).

[260] Dec 88/561 (OJ 1988 L309/32) relating to exceptional Community aid for the reconstruction of the areas stricken by earthquakes which took place in Greece in Sept 1986. See, now, ch B5–20 of the Budget for 1998 (OJ 1998 L44/3). Cf, regarding ch B4–3400 'Emergency aid to disaster victims in the Community' of the Budget for 1997 (OJ 1997 L44/3), the Commission Reply by Mr Santer to WQ E–3765/97 (OJ 1998 C223/21) by Cristiana Muscardini.

[261] Dec 81/19 (OJ 1981 L37/21) on Community aid granted by way of exception for the reconstruction of the regions affected by the Italian earthquake in Nov 1980.

[262] Dec 81/1013 (OJ 1981 L367/27) on Community aid granted by way of exception for the reconstruction of the regions affected by the Greek earthquakes in Feb and Mar 1981.

[263] Dec 95/250 (OJ 1995 L159/16) relating to exceptional Community aid for the reconstruction of the areas stricken by the cyclone that hit Madeira in Oct 1993.

[264] OJ 1994 L1/3. See, generally, A Evans, *European Community Law, including the EEA Agreement* (Kluwer, Deventer, 1994).

[265] Iceland, Liechtenstein, and Norway.

[266] 6th recital in the preamble to the EEA Agreement.

[267] Art 117 EEA.

[268] Art 1(2) of Prot 38.

[269] Report of the Committee on External Economic Relations on economic and trade relations between the EC and the EFTA countries in the EEA, EP Doc A3–306/92.

Over the period 1993 to 1997 inclusive the total amount of grants provided was to be ECU 500 million.[270] The total volume of loans to be eligible for interest rebates[271] over the same period was to be ECU 1,500 million.[272] Finance was to be provided by the EFTA States, and operations were to be administered by the European Investment Bank.[273]

Assistance is to be limited to projects in Greece, the island of Ireland, Portugal, and the regions of Spain listed in the Annex to the Agreement.[274] The shares allocated to each beneficiary region are to be determined for a five-year period in the light of the region's relative level of economic development, population size, and 'other relevant factors'.[275] Priority is to be given to projects emphasizing the environment (including urban development), transport (including transport infrastructure), or education and training. Among projects submitted by the private sector, special consideration is to be given to small and medium-sized enterprises. The maximum grant element for any project supported by the Financial Mechanism shall be fixed at a level which is not inconsistent with Union policies in this regard.[276]

6.9 CONCLUSION

The assistance provided through horizontal instruments may not necessarily be effective in securing the objectives of these instruments. For example, Life operations are said often to be incompatible with the principle, embodied in Article 174(2) of the EC Treaty, that the polluter should pay for the pollution which he causes.[277] More particularly, these instruments do little to direct assistance to less developed regions and may be ill adapted to the specific problems of such regions.

Some horizontal instruments, such as loans and guarantees from the European Investment Bank, may by their nature be ill adapted to the promotion of cohesion. More usually, the operations of horizontal instruments tend to be determined primarily by the perceived requirements of the particular policy pursued. The legal rules embodying these requirements may not neces-

[270] Art 3(1) of Prot 38.

[271] The percentage fixed for the interest rebates was reduced from 3% to 2% by Art 16 of the Protocol adjusting the EEA Agreement.

[272] Art 2(5) of Prot 38.

[273] ibid, Art 1(2). A co-operation agreement has been concluded between the EFTA States and the EIB, and the EFTA Standing Committee has established a Financial Mechanism Committee. The latter provides guidelines for the EIB and, on the basis of EIB proposals, decides on the provision of assistance in individual cases. See EFTA Standing Committee Dec 4/94 (OJ 1994 L85/79) establishing a financial mechanism committee.

[274] Art 4(1) of Prot 38.

[275] Art 8(1) of Reg 2894/94 (OJ 1994 L305/6) concerning arrangements for implementing the EEA Agreement.

[276] Art 4(2) of Prot 38.

[277] COA annual report for 1994 (OJ 1995 C303/1), para 6.34.

sarily attach the same importance to questions of profitability as does Commission practice controlling the grant of state aid under Article 87 of the Treaty.[278] Hence, Union assistance may not necessarily promote efficient use of resources. Even in so far as the assistance is capable of doing so, its effect may be to increase rather than decrease regional disparities. It may have this effect because the more developed regions may be best qualified to obtain and to use the assistance efficiently.[279] Hence, the possibility cannot be excluded that the work of horizontal instruments may sometimes be positively harmful to cohesion.

The inference may be drawn that the more assistance is provided by such instruments, the less effective assistance from the European Regional Development Fund will be. Indeed, the latter assistance may be alleged merely to offset the additional geographical distortions of competition resulting from the operations of horizontal instruments.[280] An efficient approach to promotion of cohesion would, it is said, be either to eliminate such operations, so as to reduce the overall level of assistance, or to adapt them to cohesion requirements and channel them to less developed regions.[281]

[278] A Evans, *EC Law of State Aid* (Oxford EC Law Series; Clarendon Press, Oxford, 1997).

[279] D O'Hearn, 'Global Competition, Europe and Irish Peripherality' (1993) *The Economic and Social Review* 169–197.

[280] cf, regarding disputes in the Commission as to whether assistance to car companies for training would drain Union funds away from regional and social objectives with no guarantee that competitiveness would be improved, the *Financial Times*, 29 Apr 1992.

[281] ESC Opinion of 29 Jan 1986 (OJ 1986 C75/12) on national regional development aid.

Part Three
Procedures

7

Organic Procedures

7.1 INTRODUCTION

'Organic' decision-making procedures have their origins in the practice of the Union institutions. Close contacts between Union and national officials, tending towards 'bureaucratic interpenetration',[1] may be involved. This tendency may be most developed in committee work, particularly that associated with 'partnership'. The outcomes take as their main legal forms legislation, budgetary provision, 'soft law', individual administrative decisions, contracts, and judicial decisions.

Such procedures are not insulated from those of the intergovernmental kind, which are discussed in Chapter 8. Indeed, both kinds of procedures may focus on and seek to elaborate the same legal rules. However, the differences between their respective legal contexts imply the possibility that their substantial results may diverge.

7.2 LEGISLATION

Union legislation has to be adopted, or at least authorized, by representatives of Member States in the Council of the Union. Hence, such legislation may offer a means of implementing intergovernmental bargains embodied in the Treaties or other instruments or informally reached through negotiations in the Council.

However, attitudes to the role of such legislation may vary between Member States. For example, net recipients may see Council legislation[2] as ensuring that they receive their share of resources from the Union funds, as allocated by such bargains. Net payers, for their part, may see such legislation as ensuring that the resources are genuinely devoted to promotion of cohesion or, at least, that distortion of competition is minimized.[3] Indeed, the

[1] S Cassese, 'Theoretical Sketch of the Cooperative and Multidimensional Nature of Community Bureaucracy' in J Jamar and K Wessels (eds), *Community Bureaucracy at the Crossroads* (de Tempel, Bruges, 1985) 39–46; and S Cassese, 'La Costituzione europea' (1991) *Quadri Costituzionali* 487–508.

[2] Such as Reg 1164/94 (OJ 1994 L130/1) establishing a Cohesion Fund.

[3] cf regarding the concern of net payers to secure 'value for money' from the Union funds without prejudicing their own freedom to pursue their regional policies, S George, *Politics and Policy in the European Union* (Oxford University Press, 3rd edn, 1996) 240.

latter Member States may regard the effective operation of organic Union procedures as a precondition for progress in intergovernmental bargaining. In 1982, for example, the House of Lords Select Committee warned that Member States which had little direct return from the European Regional Development Fund were becoming more determined to ensure that the Fund should not be simply a mechanism for transferring resources to the less developed Member States. Therefore, 'a genuine Community dimension to regional development had to be guaranteed' by organic Union procedures, if the net payers were to continue to support the Fund.[4] Such divergence of attitudes within the Council may reduce the matters on which the Council can agree and, hence, may limit the role played by Council legislation in regulating the operations of the Union funds.

The same divergence of attitudes may also limit the readiness of the Council to authorize the Commission to adopt implementing legislation.[5] Even where such authorization is granted, it tends to relate to 'technical' matters, such as calculation of the amount of assistance payable from the Union funds and procedures for applications for such assistance. For example, in connection with the European Social Fund, the Commission was each year to determine the amounts of assistance to be granted per person and per unit of time for each Member State.[6] Under Regulation 950/97[7] the Commission may adopt rules governing applications by Member States for reimbursement of expenditure eligible for assistance from the Guidance Section of the European Agricultural Guidance and Guarantee Fund[8] and regarding monitoring of assisted operations.[9] More generally, Regulation 2082/93[10] empowers the Commission to draw up detailed legislation on information and publicity concerning assistance from the Structural Funds and the Financial Instrument for Fisheries Guidance. The Commission has adopted Decision 94/342[11] on this

[4] Revision of the ERDF, House of Lords Select Committee on the European Communities, HL(1981–82)126, xix–xx. See, later, EEC regional development policy, House of Lords Select Committee on the European Communities, HL(1991–92)20, 37. Cf, regarding Danish attitudes, L Lyck, 'Regional Policy' in L Lyck (ed), *Denmark and EC Membership Evaluated* (Pinter, London, 1992) 158–164.

[5] R Priebe, 'Le Droit communautaire des structures agricoles' (1988) CDE 3–38, 15. See, generally, regarding such legislation, A Evans, *A Textbook on EU Law* (Hart Publishing, Oxford, 1998) sect 2.3.1.

[6] Art 2(2) of Reg 2950/83 (OJ 1983 L289/1) on the implementation of Dec 83/516 on the tasks of the ESF. See eg Dec 83/621 (OJ 1983 L350/25) on the rates of assistance from the ESF towards expenditure on recruitment and employment premiums.

[7] On improving the efficiency of agricultural structures (OJ 1997 L142/1).

[8] ibid, Art 32(3).

[9] ibid, Art 35.

[10] Amending Reg 4253/88 laying down provisions for implementing Reg 2052/88 as regards co-ordination of the activities of the different Structural Funds between themselves and with the operations of the EIB and the other existing financial instruments (OJ 1993 L193/20), Art 32(2).

[11] Concerning information and publicity measures to be carried out by the Member States concerning assistance from the Structural Funds and the FIFG. Cf Dec 96/455 (OJ 1996 L188/47) concerning information and publicity measures to be carried out by the Member States and the Commission concerning the activities of the Cohesion Fund under Reg 1164/94.

subject. In such cases concern to secure efficiency-gains may militate in favour of the grant of some legislative powers to the Commission.[12] In other cases the Council may be reluctant to grant such powers.

Such features of Council practice may lead to conflict between the Council and other Union institutions. The latter institutions may perceive legislation as having a function other than that of giving effect to intergovernmental bargains. In fact, they may perceive it as a means of establishing and developing the Union's own policies for cohesion. For example, according to the European Parliament, it is necessary to impress on Member States that operations of the Union funds are intended to reduce regional disparities and not to overcome financing difficulties in national treasuries.[13] Such conflict may add to controversy surrounding legislative activity in this area.

7.2.1 Unanimity Issues

Particular controversy may attach to the question whether the Council should be required to act unanimously or by a qualified majority.[14] For example, in the case of specific Community regional development measures, Article 13(3) of Regulation 214/79[15] provided that the Council, acting unanimously on a Commission proposal, was to adopt a special programme for each measure. The programme was to determine: the nature of the operations to which the European Regional Development Fund might contribute; the regions which the Fund might assist;[16] the national aid taken into consideration in granting Fund assistance; the contribution of the Fund; the categories of beneficiaries of Fund assistance; and the detailed rules for financing. The European Parliament objected that the requirement of Council unanimity entailed a right of veto which was contrary to the rules governing the Fund since its creation.[17] Possibly in response to such objections, Article 7(4) of Regulation 1787/84[18] subsequently provided that frameworks for Community programmes were to be established by a Council decision adopted by qualified majority.

Article 161 of the EC Treaty now provides that basic principles concerning the Structural Funds are to be established by the Council acting unanimously

[12] Priebe, n 5 above, 16. See eg Reg 2064/97 (OJ 1997 L290/1) establishing detailed arrangements for the implementation of Reg 4253/88 as regards the financial control by Member States of operations co-financed by the Structural Funds.

[13] Resolution of 15 July 1993 (OJ 1993 C255/171) on the annual report on the implementation of the reform of the Structural Funds in 1991, para 9.

[14] See, regarding such a majority, Art 205(2) EC.

[15] Amending Reg 724/75 (OJ 1979 L35/1).

[16] The Commission proposal (Art 13 of the proposal of 3 June 1977 (OJ 1977 C161/11) for a regulation amending Reg 724/75) that the eligible regions should be decided by a qualified majority vote in the Council was rejected by the latter.

[17] Resolution of 19 June 1981 (OJ 1981 C172/117) on the fifth annual report on the ERDF, para 10.

[18] On the ERDF (OJ 1984 L169/1).

with the assent of the European Parliament. However, 'implementing decisions'[19] regarding the European Regional Development Fund are to be adopted by the Council according to the 'co-decision' procedure under Article 162 of the Treaty. This procedure means that such decisions may usually be adopted by a qualified majority. Their adoption only requires unanimity in situations where the Council wishes to overrule the European Parliament or to amend a Commission proposal.[20]

7.2.2 Regulatory Failure

Whether Council unanimity or merely a qualified majority is required for legislative enactments or whether legislative powers are delegated to the Commission, the role of legislation in regulating the operations of the Union funds may be criticized as too limited. According to the European Parliament, the resulting regulatory shortcomings may lead to confusion and abuses in the grant of assistance.[21] They may also restrict the scope of internal controls and prevent applicants for assistance from bringing proceedings before the European Courts to uphold their legitimate interests.[22] Hence, the Parliament will seek to ensure that future legislation establishes rules that are as detailed as possible.[23] The Commission itself now seeks authorization to adopt detailed implementing rules for the European Regional Development Fund[24] and the European Social Fund.[25]

7.3 BUDGETARY PROVISION

The General Budget may be used simply to give effect to the financial implications of legislation. Provision may also be made in the Budget for the financing of preparatory actions[26] or pilot schemes,[27] pending adoption of

[19] See, regarding the meaning of this expression, Art 3(4) of Reg 2081/93 (OJ 1993 L193/5) amending Reg 2052/88 on the tasks of the Structural Funds and their effectiveness and on co-ordination of their activities between themselves and with the operations of the EIB and the other existing financial instruments.

[20] Art 251 EC.

[21] cf, regarding doubts whether the legislation on the Structural Funds is 'properly applied', the COA annual report 1997 (OJ 1998 C349/1), para 8.6.3.

[22] Resolution giving discharge to the Commission in respect of the General Budget for 1994 (OJ 1996 L148/44), para 44.

[23] ibid, para 48.

[24] Art 5 of the Proposal of 19 Mar 1998 (OJ 1998 C176/35) for a regulation on the ERDF.

[25] Art 8 of the Proposal of 19 Mar 1998 (OJ 1998 C176/39) for a regulation on the ESF.

[26] Case C–106/96 *UK v EC Commission: social assistance* [12 May 1998].

[27] Interinstitutional Agreement of the Commission, Parliament, and Council of 13 Oct 1998 (OJ 1998 C344/1) on legal bases and implementation of the budget, para 2(a).

the necessary legislation. More problematic is the use of the Budget as a long-term substitute for the enactment of legislation.[28]

7.3.1 Integrated Mediterranean Programmes

In the case of Integrated Mediterranean Programmes, the General Budget offered an instrument for ensuring the availability of finance to implement legislative requirements.[29] Thus legislation governing these Programmes provided for resources under Article 551 of the Budget[30] to be devoted to measures which were ineligible for assistance from the Structural Funds.[31] These resources were concentrated on: assisting measures in the Mezzogiorno for promotion of new or traditional crops and varietal improvement of agricultural products supported by research, experiments, dissemination of information and, if necessary, irrigation; special animal-husbandry operations; the establishment of new small businesses or craft units, including economic activities and training; and factoring.

7.3.2 Integrated Development Operations

A pilot project for an Integrated Development Operation was established for Naples in 1979,[32] and another was planned for Belfast.[33] The Naples operation was considered to have been successful in making it possible to detect a significant number of bottlenecks for a number of investments planned for that region. At the same time, the operation made it possible to exert some pressure on national authorities to take decisions which had been delayed.[34]

Accordingly, in the Budget for 1982, ECU 2 million were assigned under Item 5410 to 'Preparatory studies for integrated operations'. Moreover, under Item 5411 ECU 16 million were assigned to 'Community measures in the framework of integrated operations'.[35] These sums enabled the Commission to contribute to financing the preliminary studies needed to

[28] Joined Cases C–239 & 240/96R *UK v EC Commission: social assistance* [1996] ECR I–4475, I–4489–91.

[29] From 1983 the Commission had been using the General Budget to support preparatory pilot actions for IMPs (Art 550 of the Budget for 1983, OJ 1983 L19/3). See eg Dec 84/70 (OJ 1984 L44/1) instituting in the area of Ogliastra (Italy) a pilot action in preparation for the IMPs.

[30] See eg for 1986, OJ 1986 L358/3.

[31] Art 3 of Reg 2088/85 (OJ 1985 L197/1) concerning the IMPs.

[32] Commission Reply of Mr Schmidhuber to WQ 1033/87 (OJ 1988 C46/17) by Mr Francesco Compasso.

[33] *Fifth Annual Report on the ERDF* (EC Commission, Brussels, 1980) 27–28.

[34] Report of the Committee on Regional Policy and Regional Development on the fifth annual report on the ERDF, EP Doc 1–181/81, 15–16.

[35] OJ 1982 L31/1.

prepare integrated operations.[36] They also enabled the Commission to finance measures which were not eligible for assistance from the Structural Funds.

However, the perceived need for legislative intervention might affect such use of the Budget. For example, the Commission proposed to the Council in November 1981 a Regulation instituting a specific action on behalf of housing in Northern Ireland within the framework of the integrated operation for Belfast.[37] This proposal sought to make finance available for housing projects. It was a response to a Resolution of the European Parliament,[38] which stressed the worsening social and economic problems of Northern Ireland, particularly Belfast, and requested remedial measures. The Commission had hoped to use funds from Item 5411 of the Budget to finance the proposed action. However, the Council was unable to agree on the proposal. Instead, the Council adopted a new Commission proposal for a regulation introducing an exceptional Community measure to promote urban renewal in Northern Ireland (Belfast).[39]

7.3.3 International Fund for Ireland

A contribution to the International Fund for Ireland was first made from the General Budget in 1989.[40] For several years the Budget apparently continued to be used to substitute legislative action. However, in 1994 the Commission sought through the enactment of a Council regulation 'a more formal legal basis',[41] which would constitute 'a framework for continued Community support'.[42] Accordingly, Regulation 2687/94, on Community financial contributions to the International Fund for Ireland,[43] was enacted.

[36] See also the Commission Reply by Mr Varfis to WQ 1877/87 (OJ 1989 C202/2) by José Garcia Raya.

[37] Proposal of 23 Nov 1981 (OJ 1981 C346/1). See also the *Seventh Annual Report of the ERDF* (EC Commission, Brussels, 1982), 18–19.

[38] Of 19 June 1981 (OJ 1981 C172/122) on Community regional policy and Northern Ireland.

[39] Reg 1739/83 (OJ 1983 L171/1). According to Art 2 (ibid), infrastructure projects contributing to urban renewal in the Belfast area would be assisted.

[40] OJ 1989 L26/3, Art 547.

[41] Proposal of 2 Mar 1994 for a regulation on Community financial contributions to the International Fund for Ireland, COM(94)60, explanatory memorandum, 2.

[42] ibid, 15th recital in the preamble.

[43] OJ 1994 L286/5; and Art B2–604 of the 1998 Budget (OJ 1998 L44/3). Cf Item B2–1412 (ibid), Special programme for regions in both parts of Ireland; and Notice laying down procedures for an initiative in the framework of the special support programme for peace and reconciliation in Northern Ireland and the border counties of Ireland (OJ 1995 C186/3). See also Special support programme for peace and reconciliation in Northern Ireland and the border counties of Ireland (1995–99), COM(97)642.

7.3.4 BICs

The Commission submitted proposals for the creation of Business and Innovation Centres (BICs) to the Council on 23 January 1987[44] and 7 July 1988,[45] but these proposals were not adopted. Hence, Union funding of these Centres has been based on Budget headings alone.[46] The Court of Auditors considers that, if this funding is to continue, it should be placed within a more formal framework, in order to define its objectives and improve transparency.[47] The Commission view, however, is that these ends can satisfactorily be achieved through the Community Support Frameworks.[48] In other words, the Commission apparently considers that 'soft law'[49] can satisfactorily combine with Budgetary provision to substitute legislation.[50]

However, according to a Joint Declaration by the European Parliament, the Council, and the Commission,[51] the implementation of Budgetary appropriations for significant new Union action requires a 'basic regulation'.[52] This requirement is confirmed in the Financial Regulation.[53] According to the case law, the requirement applies, unless it is demonstrated that action is 'non-significant'.[54] In the absence of such a demonstration, there may be a breach of the Regulation and of Article 7(1) of the Treaty,[55] according to which Union institutions must act within the limits conferred on them by the Treaty. Whether such breaches really can be avoided through resort to soft law is uncertain.[56]

44 OJ 1987 C33/5.

45 OJ 1988 C214/65.

46 See eg Art B2–601 in the Budget for 1996 (OJ 1996 L22/3).

47 Special report 5/93 (OJ 1994 C13/1) concerning BICs, para 23.

48 ibid, para 23 (reply of the Commission).

49 CSFs may be regarded as an example of 'soft law'. See sect 7.4.4 below.

50 cf the implicit Commission view that a call for proposals may be an adequate substitute for legislation in COA special report 4/94 (OJ 1994 C383/1) on the urban environment, para 3.5 (Commission reply), regarding studies on the conservation of European cities (Item B2–6023 of the Budget for 1992, OJ 1992 L26/1).

51 On various measures to improve the budgetary procedure (OJ 1982 C194/1).

52 ibid, para IV.3(c). See, regarding the actions which may be financed without a regulation, directive, or decision, Interinstitutional Agreement of the Commission, Parliament, and Council of 13 Oct 1998 (OJ 1998 C344/1) on legal bases and implementation of the budget, para 2.

53 Art 22(1) of the Financial Regulation of 21 Dec 1977 (OJ 1977 L356/1), as amended by Reg 610/90 (OJ 1990 L70/1). See also the Report on the implementation of the interinstitutional agreement of 29 Oct 1993 on budgetary discipline and improvement of the budgetary procedure, COM(98)165, 10.

54 Case C–106/96 *UK v EC Commission: social assistance* [12 May 1998].

55 ibid.

56 eg, because of a Council failure to adopt the necessary legislation, the Commission may cancel a call for proposals. See Financial support for co-operatives, mutual societies, associations, and foundations: cancellation of the call for proposals (OJ 1997 C233/81). However, the Commission still took a 'specific decision' to finance twelve of the projects which had been submitted. See the Commission Reply by Mr Papoutsis to WQ E–3169/97 (OJ 1998 C196/2) by Raymonde Dury.

7.4 'SOFT LAW'

'Soft law'[57] may be defined as 'rules of conduct which, in principle, have no legally binding force but which nevertheless may have practical effect'.[58] A possible problem with this definition is that rules having practical effect may not always be readily distinguishable from those having binding legal force.

Indeed, such law usually 'elaborates' rules contained in Union legislation. In doing so, it may create legitimate expectations about the maintenance of established Commission practice.[59] For example, the Commission must not depart from an 'internal directive' without giving the reasons which lead it to do so. Otherwise, the principles of legitimate expectation and equality of treatment may be infringed.[60] The inference may be drawn that soft law constitutes 'rules of law which the Community judicature must enforce'.[61] However, in compliance with 'the order of preference of legal rules', soft law must be interpreted in the light of the purpose of the legislation, which it elaborates.[62]

The forms taken by soft law may be various. Its effects on the operations of the Union funds may also be various.

7.4.1 Regional Development Programmes/Plans

Regional development programmes (or plans, as they are now called) are produced by Member States. They are formally supposed merely to indicate the approaches of each Member State to its cohesion problems. However, they may affect the practice of the Union institutions and Member States regarding the operations of the Union funds. Hence, they may represent a version of soft law.

[57] See, generally, KC Wellens and GM Borchardt, 'Soft Law in European Community Law' (1989) ELR 267–321. Cf, regarding the use of such law by national administrations, G Ganz, *Quasi-Legislation* (Sweet and Maxwell, London, 1987).

[58] F Snyder, 'The Effectiveness of European Community Law: Institutions, Processes, Tools, and Techniques' (1993) 56 MLR 19–54, 32.

[59] See, regarding a form attached to a Commission decision and a Commission working document submitted to the Permanent Representatives of the Member States, Case 84/85 *UK v EC Commission: assistance for part-time employment* [1987] ECR 3765, 3796.

[60] See, regarding internal Commission rules for determining the maximum contribution available from the Guidance Section of the EAGGF under Reg 355/77 (OJ 1977 L51/1) on common measures to improve the conditions under which agricultural products were processed and marketed, which were based on the power of the Commission to organize its own departments, AG Mischo in Case 15/85 *Consorzio Cooperative d'Abruzzo v EC Commission* [1987] ECR 1005, 1015.

[61] Joined Cases T–369/94 & 85/95 *DIR International Film Srl v EC Commission* [19 Feb 1998]. This is so even when the 'rules' are drawn up by a private body and approved and applied by the Commission (ibid).

[62] ibid.

Regional development programmes

The *First Communication on Regional Policy in the Community*[63] of 1965 envisaged that Member States would prepare regional development programmes. The programmes were to be based on a detailed study of economic and demographic trends. They were to be designed to co-ordinate public and private efforts, concentrating on a few, well-chosen regions. Particular attention was to be paid to: large, predominantly agricultural, peripheral regions; certain agricultural regions affected by structural weaknesses; declining industrial regions; regions lying along the frontiers between Member States; and regions adjacent to the Soviet Zone.

Commission review of regional development programmes was envisaged in the 1969 Commission proposal on the organization of Community means of action in the field of regional policy.[64] The proposal provided, more particularly, for the Commission to direct to the Member State concerned opinions or recommendations regarding such programmes. The aim was to ensure that account was taken of: the need for better co-ordination of measures adopted by the Member States, especially in frontier regions; Community needs, where improvements were to be made to infrastructure; the implications of agricultural structural policy; the demands of industrial policy in the common market and the need to avoid uneconomic production; and vocational training and guidance needs.[65]

Legislation governing the preparation, rather than merely providing for Commission review, of such programmes was envisaged in the 1973 proposal for a regulation establishing a Regional Development Fund.[66] According to Article 6(3) of the proposal, the programmes were to indicate the objectives and the means of regional development. Furthermore, they were to indicate in sufficient detail: the evolution of the economic and social situation of the region in respect of demography, employment, regional product, sectoral structure, infrastructure, ecology, and land usage; the measures proposed in respect of infrastructure and the creation of economic activity, together with an implementation schedule; the intended financing; and the bodies responsible for these measures.

Regulation 724/75,[67] as adopted by the Council, was less elaborate. According to Article 6(1), to benefit from assistance from the European Regional Development Fund, investments had to fall within the framework of a regional development programme. Article 6(4) of the same Regulation required that the programme indicate the objectives and the means of developing the region. These requirements were taken to mean that the programme should justify the projects to be assisted, though the latter did not necessarily

[63] SEC(65)1170.

[64] Of 17 Oct 1969 (JO 1969 C152/6), Art 1.

[65] ibid, Art 5.

[66] Of 31 July 1973 (OJ 1973 C86/7).

[67] Establishing an ERDF (OJ 1975 L73/1).

have to be listed explicitly. In particular, the programme had to show the need for Fund assistance to infrastructure projects contributing to the development of the region concerned.[68] The Regional Policy Committee[69] was to study the technical methods for preparing these programmes and to draw up by the end of 1975 an outline of the information to be included in the programmes.

The outline produced by the Committee[70] was 'indicative'. It was to be 'interpreted in a flexible manner, bearing in mind the considerable differences between Member States in the nature and scale of regional problems faced, the geographical size of regional programming units, the regional policy measures in force, and regional administrative systems'. Subject to this proviso, the programmes had to contain an analysis revealing the main regional problems and their causes.[71] Moreover, details were to be given of measures envisaged for development, including state aid, and measures under other policies, including industrial, agricultural, and social policies.[72] Information was also expected about the financial means which would be allocated to programme implementation.[73]

Such programmes were regarded by the Commission as frameworks for co-ordination of the Structural Funds and of national regional policies.[74] In practice, however, Member States might receive assistance from the European Regional Development Fund, before the Commission had finished examining their programmes.[75] Besides, as the Commission complained in the *Third Annual Report on the European Regional Development Fund*,[76] the programmes 'mostly lack[ed] the detail needed to serve as a guide to the allocation of the Fund's resources or to co-ordinate them more closely with assistance from the other Community financial instruments'.[77]

On the one hand, the statistical basis of the information contained in the programmes might be inadequate. According to the Economic and Social

[68] *Regional Development Programmes of the Second Generation for the Period 1981–85* (EC Commission, Brussels, 1985) 7–8. Note also the implication in Art 6(2) and (6) of Reg 724/75 (OJ 1975 L73/1) that the programmes were to include the information indicated in the latter paragraph. See, similarly, Art 6(5) (ibid), as amended by Reg 214/79 (OJ 1979 L35/1).

[69] sect 7.7.1 below.

[70] Outline for regional development programmes (OJ 1976 C69/2).

[71] ibid, para 1.

[72] ibid, para 3.

[73] ibid, para 4.

[74] Fourth medium-term economic policy programme (OJ 1977 L101/1), para 139.

[75] Report of the Committee on Regional Policy and Regional Planning on second-generation regional development programmes for 1981–85, EP Doc A2–63/85, 13.

[76] EC Commission, Brussels, 1978.

[77] ibid 68. Further co-ordination might be advocated. According to the Committee on Regional Policy, Regional Planning, and Transport, there should be co-ordination at European level of major public and private investments in problem regions. To this end, the requirements imposed on ECSC undertakings, notably compulsory notification of major investments and publication of the Commission's opinion, might usefully be extended to all sectors of the Community's economic activity. See the Report on aspects of the Community's regional policy to be developed in the future, EP Doc 35/77, 50.

Committee, such information should, at least, be sufficient to provide internationally and inter-regionally comparable data relating to certain key development indicators. To secure this end, minimum requirements for the programmes should be made mandatory.[78] More particularly, the Committee wished to see a more precise indication in future programmes of the actual number of jobs created or maintained as a result of the previous implementation of regional policies. There was also a need, where appropriate, for statistics to be presented at a sub-regional level, so that account could be taken of variations within, as well as between, regions. Finally, it would be desirable for the programmes to include information regarding demography and migration. Such factors materially affected interpretation of unemployment statistics. They were, therefore, relevant to assessing the effectiveness of regional policy.[79]

On the other hand, the scope of the information provided in the programmes might be too limited. The programmes were said, for example, to pay insufficient attention to the effects of other national and Community policies, such as social, transport, energy, and agricultural policies, on the socio-economic situation of the weaker regions.[80] The implication was that they should indicate not only direct aid granted by Member States to the regions, but also financial transfers between the various public authorities and indirect aid entailed by other policy interventions.[81]

These were the very kind of criticisms made by the Commission in an Opinion of 1979,[82] issued under Article 155 of the EEC Treaty. In particular, the programmes might not provide the Commission with the detailed knowledge required to permit it to define with sufficient precision the regions to be assisted by the European Regional Development Fund.[83] The conclusion drawn by the Commission in this Opinion was that the programmes needed to be developed, if they were to offer a sufficiently detailed reference framework for assessing projects to receive assistance from the Fund.

To this end, the Commission issued at the same time a Recommendation, also under Article 155, to the Member States regarding future programmes.[84]

[78] Opinion of 24 Nov 1976 (OJ 1977 C56/49) on the first annual report on the ERDF 1975 and the summary analysis of annual information 1976, para 4.2.

[79] Opinion of 30 Apr 1980 (OJ 1980 C205/22) on the regional development programmes, para 4.1.

[80] According to the Committee on Regional Policy, Regional Planning, and Transport, all the 'sectoral' policies (transport, energy, social, financial, fiscal, etc) should be comprised within regional development programmes, through which a comprehensive regional policy should be implemented. See the Report on aspects of the Community's regional policy to be developed in the future, EP Doc 35/77, 49.

[81] Report of the Committee on Regional Policy and Regional Planning on second-generation regional development programmes for 1981–85, EP Doc A2–63/85, 6.

[82] Opinion 79/534 (OJ 1979 L143/7) on the regional development programmes.

[83] See eg the ESC Opinion of 29 Apr 1981 (OJ 1981 C185/20) on the revision of the ERDF Regulation, para 5.3.2.

[84] Rec 79/535 (OJ 1979 L143/9) on the regional development programmes. See, more particularly, Rec 81/879 (OJ 1981 L321/27) on transfrontier co-ordination for regional development.

Like opinions, recommendations were under Article 189(5) of the Treaty to have no binding force.[85] According to the Recommendation, the programmes should not only indicate the national measures envisaged by each Member State for regions where the European Regional Development Fund was to provide assistance. In so far as regional policy measures were applied in other regions, the programmes should also indicate the principal measures which sought an improved regional balance within the Member State as a whole.[86]

Moreover, programmes should take fuller account, in the analysis of the economic and social situation in each region, of the implications of national policies or measures for industrial restructuring, transport, energy, agriculture, fishing, the environment, physical planning, welfare, and vocational training. They should also take greater account of the most significant effects of Community policies and measures, particularly in the fields of agriculture, external trade relations, and industrial restructuring.[87]

At the same time, they should bring out more clearly, when setting infrastructure objectives, the link between infrastructure investments and the conditions affecting the development of a region. By doing so, they would make it possible for the Commission to assess better the need for such investments. More particularly, they would make it possible for the Commission to consider not only regional infrastructure proper but also national infrastructure of regional importance.[88]

Finally, they should include more detailed information about the intentions of Member States for future use of resources from the European Regional Development Fund. They should also include information concerning use of the other funds. They would thereby permit, at regional level, greater concentration of the various assistance measures adopted by the Community.[89]

Such demands, though not legally binding, may have had some impact on the drafting of the programmes. According to a Commission Opinion of 1984,[90] the second-generation programmes, those for the period 1981 to 1985, taken as a whole represented a substantial improvement on those for the preceding period. Even so, the effects of past development measures were treated only in a general manner, and the implications of Community or national policies other than those specifically for regional development were not taken sufficiently into account. Moreover, links between infrastructure investment and regional development were not shown. More particularly, the priority ratings of development measures were not indicated.

[85] Though they may have interpretative significance. See AG Warner in Case 113/75 *Giordano Frecassetti v Amministrazione delle Finanze dello Stato* [1976] ECR 983, 996–997; and Case C–322/88 *Salvatore Grimaldi v Fonds des Maladies Professionnelles* [1989] ECR I–4407, I–4421.

[86] Para 2 of Rec 79/535 (OJ 1979 L143/9).

[87] ibid, para 4.

[88] ibid, para 7.

[89] ibid, para 12.

[90] Opinion 84/389 (OJ 1984 L211/18) on the regional development programmes, sect 5.

Presumably because of these problems, a more 'legalistic' approach to programming was adopted in Regulation 1787/84.[91] According to Article 2(3) of the Regulation, the programmes were to be drawn up in accordance with the Regional Policy Committee Outline and the Commission Recommendation of 1979. They were to be indicative in character but had to specify the objectives of, and the operational means for, development of the regions concerned. Their consistency with Community programmes and objectives was to be examined by this Committee and the Commission.

Nevertheless, according to the Commission, the programmes remained deficient in their definition of 'industrial development policies and strategies or specific objectives capable of promoting job creation'.[92] The Court of Auditors criticized the programmes on the same grounds. According to the Court, such deficiencies in the programmes meant that the procedures for selecting projects to be assisted were weakened. As a result, the grant or refusal of assistance depended simply on whether the projects concerned were in line with the formal conditions specified in the legislation, or were located in sectors where assistance might disturb market operations.[93]

Plans

To tackle problems with the old regional development programmes, the legislation now lays down more detailed requirements as to the contents of the new plans. It also requires separate plans to be drawn up for Objectives 1 to 4 and 5b.

It is proposed that the plans must provide an analysis of the situation prepared by a Member State in the light of the Objectives of the Structural Funds and the priority needs for attaining these Objectives. It is also proposed that they must indicate the strategy, the planned action priorities, their specific goals, and the related indicative financial resources.[94]

According to existing legislation, plans for Objectives 1, 2, and 5b regions are to be drawn up by competent authorities designated by Member States at national, regional, or other level. The plans must be presented by the Member State itself.[95] Thus the role played by regional authorities depends on national law. It is now proposed, however, that the 'partners'[96] must at least be consulted.[97]

[91] OJ 1984 L169/1.

[92] Introduction of the CSFs was expected to reduce these problems (COA annual report for 1988 (OJ 1989 C312/1), paras 8.15–16 (Commission reply)).

[93] ibid, para 8.15–16.

[94] Art 9(1)(b) of the Proposal of 19 Mar 1998 (OJ 1998 C176/1) for a regulation laying down provisions on the Structural Funds.

[95] Art 5(1) of Regulation 2082/93 (OJ 1993 L193/20).

[96] See, regarding 'partnership', sect 7.7.7 below.

[97] Art 14(1) of the Proposal of 19 Mar 1998 (OJ 1998 C176/1) for a regulation laying down provisions on the Structural Funds.

The plans are to include: a description of the current situation; a description of an appropriate strategy to achieve the Objective concerned; an appraisal of the environmental situation of the region concerned and an evaluation of the environmental impact of the strategy and operations envisaged; and an indication of the planned use of assistance from the Structural Funds and other financial instruments.[98] The plans must also meet further, specific requirements, depending on whether they concern Objective 1, 2, or 5b regions.

'Regional development plans' concerning Objective 1 regions must, according to Regulation 2083/93,[99] include: a succinct analysis of the socio-economic situation of the region, indicating, *inter alia*, its demographic outlook; a description of the development strategy envisaged by the Member State, with an indication of the national and regional financial resources to be used; and the priorities for action of the Member State and the regional development measures for which it intends to request Union assistance, together with the estimated sums to be requested. As a rule, these plans are to be for a period of six years and may be updated annually.[100]

'Regional and social conversion plans'[101] relating to Objective 2 regions must, according to the same Regulation, contain: a description of the conversion strategy envisaged by the Member State, with an indication of the national or regional financial resources to be used; the priorities for action of the Member State and the regional conversion measures for which it intends to request Union assistance, together with the estimated sums to be requested; and information allowing an assessment to be made of the overall regional economic situation. As a rule, these plans should be for a period of three years, though they may be updated annually.[102]

'Rural development plans'[103] relating to Objective 5b regions must, according to Regulation 2081/93,[104] include an indication of the problems of agricultural structures at a relevant geographical level and any link with the consequences of reform of the common agricultural policy and the common fisheries policy.[105] As a rule, they should last six years.[106]

[98] OJ 1993 L193/5, Arts 8(4), 9(8), and 11a(5).

[99] Amending Reg 4254/88 (OJ 1993 L193/34) laying down provisions for implementing Reg 2052/88 as regards the ERDF.

[100] ibid, Art 2(2).

[101] It is proposed that they will in future be known as 'regional conversion plans'. See Art 12(2) of the Proposal of 19 Mar 1998 (OJ 1998 C176/1) for a regulation laying down provisions on the Structural Funds.

[102] OJ 1993 L193/34, Art 2(3).

[103] They replace the 'development plans for rural areas' required by Art 11(3) of Reg 2052/88 (OJ 1988 L185/9).

[104] Amending Reg 2052/88 on the tasks of the Structural Funds and their effectiveness and on co-ordination of their activities between themselves and with the operations of the EIB and the other existing financial instruments (OJ 1993 L193/5).

[105] ibid, Art 11a(5).

[106] Art 7 of Reg 2085/93 (OJ 1993 L193/44) amending Reg 4256/88 laying down provisions for implementing Reg 2052/88 as regards the EAGGF, Guidance Section.

Plans for Objectives 3 and 4 must, according to Regulation 2084/93,[107] describe: imbalances between demand and supply in employment, including female employment; the nature and characteristics of unfilled vacancies; the employment opportunities which exist on labour markets; the types of measures to be implemented and the number of persons involved; and the expected contribution of the operations concerned towards the promotion of equal opportunities for men and women in the labour market.[108]

More particularly, plans for Objective 3 must also indicate the way in which the Member State will, where appropriate, secure the participation of bodies providing services in the regions concerned in the preparation and management of the operations.[109] Plans for Objective 4 must, in turn, also indicate: imbalances between the qualifications which are offered and those which are in demand in the employment market, with particular reference to workers of either sex affected by industrial change and changes in production systems; the way in which the Member State will, within the procedures available under its institutional rules and existing practices, secure participation in the preparation of operations by the economic and social partners and vocational training bodies at the appropriate level; and the relationship between the operations and other Union policies relating to industrial change and changes in production systems, particularly the link with vocational training policy.[110]

All such plans may be simultaneously presented with applications for assistance.[111] This facility may be regarded as favouring administrative convenience. Certainly, the earlier legislation was said to have failed in its objective of securing delegation of most day-to-day management by the Commission to Member States.[112] More fundamentally, the close relationship between the 'soft law' terms of the plans and the operation of the legislative provisions governing the grant of Union assistance is highlighted.

7.4.2 Periodic Reports

Periodic reports produced by the Commission constitute a form of soft law. They enable the Commission to seize from Member States the initiative in regional planning. At the same time, perhaps, they inform the Commission of the difficulties of pursuing cohesion without effective participation by regional representatives.

[107] Amending Reg 4255/88 laying down provisions for implementing Reg 2052/88 as regards the ESF (OJ 1993 L193/39).

[108] ibid, Art 4(1).

[109] ibid, Art 4(2).

[110] ibid, Art 4(3). It is now proposed that 'development plans' will be drawn up for the new Objective 3. See Art 12(3) of the Proposal of 19 Mar 1998 (OJ 1998 C176/1) for a regulation laying down provisions on the Structural Funds.

[111] Reg 2082/93 (OJ 1993 L193/20), Art 5(2).

[112] EEC regional development policy, House of Lords Select Committee on the European Communities, HL(1991–92)20, 21.

The *Report on the Regional Problems in the Enlarged Community*[113] was a precursor of such reports. It was supposed to analyse regional disparities throughout the Community. However, definitions of socio-economic categories, dates of data collection, and the size of spatial unit by which they were ordered varied considerably. Moreover, some information was incomplete or highly dubious, and so the analysts were restricted in the number of indicators which could be used. They also had to face the fundamental problem of defining disadvantaged regions at the Community level rather than relying on the perceptions of each Member State.

The Council subsequently resolved that the Commission, working in close collaboration with the Regional Policy Committee, should prepare a periodic report on the situation and socio-economic developments in the regions of the Community.[114] On the basis of this report the Council would discuss the priorities and guidelines proposed by the Commission. Five such reports have been produced.

More formal support for this practice was introduced by Article 8 of Regulation 4254/88[115] and maintained by Regulation 2083/93.[116] According to Article 8(1) of the latter Regulation, Member States must supply the Commission with the relevant information enabling it to make an analysis of all the Union regions on the basis of statistics which are as comparable and as up to date as possible. With such information the Commission is to prepare, at three-yearly intervals, periodic reports on the social and economic situation and development of the regions of the Union.[117] The reports are to indicate the macro-economic effects of Union regional action and make it possible to assess the regional impact of other Union policies. Moreover, according to Article 8(2) of the same Regulation, they are to constitute a basis for the establishment of Commission guidelines for use of the Union funds. The implication is that the reports play an integral role in practice concerning the application of legislative provisions governing the operation of these funds.

Article 159 of the EC Treaty itself requires the Commission to submit a report to the European Parliament, the Council, the Economic and Social Committee, and the Committee of the Regions every three years on the progress made towards achieving cohesion. The report must detail the man-

[113] Bull EC, Supp 8/73.

[114] Resolution of 6 Feb 1979 (OJ 1979 C36/10) concerning the guidelines for Community regional policy, para 1.

[115] Laying down provisions for implementing Reg 2052/88 as regards the ERDF (OJ 1988 L374/15).

[116] OJ 1993 L193/34. Cf, earlier, Art 2(2) of Reg 1787/84 (OJ 1984 L169/1), which required the reports to be submitted to the Council.

[117] The Commission is also to produce annual reports on the Structural Funds under Art 16 of Reg 2081/93 (OJ 1993 L193/5) and Art 31 of Reg 2082/93 (OJ 1993 L193/20). See, currently, the Ninth annual report of the Structural Funds 1997, COM(1998)562.

ner in which the Union funds have contributed to this progress. The report may, if necessary, be accompanied by appropriate proposals. It is to include an analysis of the regions and their economic and social development.[118] The first such 'cohesion report' was published in 1996.[119]

7.4.3 Guidelines

Guidelines produced by the Union institutions have the explicit function of 'regulating' the operations of the Union funds. In particular, the Commission negotiates with Member States to secure respect for the guidelines in the Community Support Frameworks and Single Programming Documents.[120]

ERDF guidelines

Regional policy guidelines were laid down by a Council Resolution of 6 February 1979.[121] According to this Resolution, regional development programmes drawn up by Member States were the most appropriate framework for co-ordination of national and Community assistance. These guidelines, therefore, tended to treat the regional development efforts of Member States as their starting-point.

Commission guidelines have not exhibited the same tendency. According to the guidelines in the *Report on the Regional Problems in the Enlarged Community*,[122] Community regional policy was to involve not only measures of encouragement and discussion. It was also to involve co-ordination of the Structural Funds. More particularly, to be eligible for assistance from the European Regional Development Fund, the most important projects proposed by Member States were to be subject to prior approval by the Community.[123]

More detailed guidelines were set out by the Commission in *Community Regional Policy: New Guidelines*.[124] The guidelines envisaged: a comprehensive system of analysis and policy formulation; regional impact assessment; co-ordination of national regional policies; the strengthening of the role of the Regional Policy Committee; the strengthening and diversification of regional policy instruments employed by the Community; and an information campaign.

A 'sharper focus' was sought in the 1981 Commission guidelines.[125] They set out seven 'prime objectives': creation of productive jobs; improved

[118] Proposal of 19 Mar 1998 (OJ 1998 C176/1) for a regulation laying down provisions on the Structural Funds, 53rd recital in the preamble.

[119] First cohesion report, COM(96)542.

[120] New regional programmes 1997–99 under Objective 2, COM(97)524, 8. See sects 7.4.4 and 7.4.5 below, regarding CSFs and SPDs respectively.

[121] Concerning the guidelines for Community regional policy (OJ 1979 C36/10).

[122] Bull EC, Supp 8/73, 11.

[123] ibid, 13.

[124] Bull EC, Supp 2/77, 8–14.

[125] New regional policy guidelines and priorities, COM(81)152.

productivity in weaker regions; exploitation of the regions' indigenous potential; concentration of resources in the regions with especially serious structural problems and increased resources for the non-quota section of the European Regional Development Fund; closer co-ordination between operations of this Fund and operations of other Community or national financial instruments; greater consistency between regional policy and other Community policies; and tighter co-ordination between Community regional policy and national regional policy.

A formal legislative basis for the adoption of such guidelines was provided by Regulation 4254/88.[126] According to this Regulation, the guidelines were to be applied in the various stages of planning, notably in establishing the Community Support Frameworks, and in the operations of the European Regional Development Fund. They were to be forwarded to the Council and the European Parliament and be published for information in the Official Journal.[127]

However, guidelines for assistance under Objectives 1 and 2 were simply embodied in a 'note' of 15 February 1989.[128] The note set out Commission priorities: job creation; joint financing through loans and grants; development of local initiatives; diversification of economic activities, with the emphasis on new technologies; and continuation of regional development measures at Community level through the financing of studies and pilot projects, especially transfrontier projects, and the pooling of experience gained at regional level.[129]

Current legislation also provides that the Commission is to lay down regional policy guidelines. They are to be applied in the various stages of planning, notably in establishing the Community Support Frameworks and in the operations of the European Regional Development Fund.[130] They shall be forwarded to the Council and the European Parliament and be published for information in the Official Journal. Such procedural requirements reflect the idea that to be 'effective', soft law must concern matters within the competence of the Commission, be published in the Official Journal, and be clearly written and informative.[131] More fundamentally, they not only demonstrate the importance which legislation may attach to soft law. They also indicate the extent to which procedures for adoption of soft law may

[126] OJ 1988 L374/15.

[127] ibid, Art 8(2).

[128] In contrast, in accordance with Arts 7 and 8 of Reg 2053/88 (OJ 1988 L185/21) on financial assistance for Portugal for a special industrial development programme, the Commission published in the OJ general guidelines for the implementation of Pedip in 1988 and 1989 (OJ 1988 C336/4); in 1990 (OJ 1989 C322/3); in 1991 (OJ 1990 C326/5); and in 1992 (OJ 1992 C7/8).

[129] Bull EC 2–1989, 2.1.91.

[130] Art 8(2) of Reg 2083/93 (OJ 1993 L193/34).

[131] A Mattera, *Le Maré unique européen: Ses règles, son fonctionnement* (Jupiter, Paris, 2nd edn, 1990), 45. See, generally, M Melchior, 'Les Communications de la Commission' in *Mélanges en honneur de Fernand Dehousse* (Labor, Brussels, 1979) ii. 243–258.

approximate to those for adoption of implementing legislation by the Commission.[132]

In practice, however, the guidelines are rarely published.[133] Hence, they do little to add to the transparency of the relevant decision making. Equally, the procedure for their adoption does little to render the decision making more pluralist. For example, the guidelines for 1997 to 1999 were adopted without consultation of regional authorities or the social partners. Account was merely taken of the views of the Member States.[134] Even the European Parliament may complain about the adoption of 'legally binding' guidelines without securing the consent of the Parliament, as required by Article 161 of the EC Treaty.[135]

EAGGF guidelines

Guidelines have played a limited role in relation to the operations of the Guidance Section of the European Agricultural Guidance and Guarantee Fund. Their limited role is presumably a reflection of the reliance placed on formal legislation governing the work of this Fund. Even so, 'criteria' regarding projects which would be supported under Regulation 355/77[136] were published by the Commission.[137] They were said to improve transparency and to be binding on the Commission. Indeed, they were described as establishing 'quasi-norms', which were used because the Commission was not empowered to adopt implementing legislation under this Regulation.[138] However, these criteria have now been replaced by those annexed to Commission Decision 94/173,[139] which was adopted under Regulation 866/90.[140] All 'decisive' selection criteria must be included in the Annex or, possibly, published in another form.[141] By virtue of such annexation, the criteria, which 'reflect the lines of the common agricultural policy',[142] have binding force identical to that of the Decision itself.[143]

[132] A Evans, *A Textbook on EU Law* (Hart Publishing, Oxford, 1998) sect 2.3.1.

[133] eg, the Note for guidance concerning operations in the declining industrial areas (Objective 2) for the second programming period (C(96)952, 29 Apr 1996) is unpublished.

[134] Commission Reply by Mrs Wulf-Mathies to WQ E–0471/98 (OJ 1998 C323/39) by Richard Howitt.

[135] sect 7.2.1 above.

[136] On common measures to improve the conditions under which agricultural products were processed and marketed (OJ 1977 L51/1).

[137] OJ 1983 C152/2; OJ 1985 C78/7; OJ 1986 C319/2.

[138] Priebe, n 5 above, 24.

[139] On the selection criteria to be adopted for investments for improving the processing and marketing conditions for agricultural and forestry products and repealing Dec 90/342 (OJ 1994 L79/29).

[140] On improving the processing and marketing conditions for agricultural products (OJ 1990 L91/1), Art 8(3).

[141] Case T–478/93 *Wafer Zoo Srl v EC Commission* [1995] ECR II–1479, II–1496.

[142] Commission Reply by Mr Fischler to WQ E–0611/96 (OJ 1996 C297/11) by Carmen Fraga Estevez.

[143] cf Joined Cases T–551/93 & 231–234/94 *Industrias Pesqueras Campos SA, Transacciones Maritimas SA, Recursos Marinos SA, Makuspesa SA v EC Commission* [1996] ECR II–247, II–281.

ESF guidelines

Fluidity as between different legal forms for substantially the same rules is highlighted by the variety of forms which have been taken by the 'management guidelines' for the European Social Fund. The initial guidelines[144] were contained in unpublished Commission Decisions of 28 November 1973[145] and 23 July 1975.[146] The guidelines for 1977,[147] the first to be published, appeared in the Official Journal. They were subsequently published for three-year periods, with annual updating.[148] Their purpose was to ensure that the legislative provisions governing the operations of the Fund were applied in 'a homogeneous manner'. Their purpose was also to determine by areas of intervention the types of operation most compatible with the objectives and terms of the legislation governing the Fund.[149] For these purposes, they sought to promote close co-ordination between action of the Member State concerned and Community action as well as between Community operations themselves, while respecting Community policies.[150] They also sought to tackle the problem that qualifying requests for Fund assistance were always in excess of Fund resources.[151] In seeking to do so, they effectively 'amended' the Council legislation.

Article 6(1) of Dec 83/516[152] formally required such guidelines to be adopted. They were to be adopted annually for the following three years, taking into account the need to promote the harmonious development of the Community. They were to determine those operations which reflected Community priorities as defined by the Council and, in particular, the action programmes for employment and vocational training. According to Article 6(2), they were to be drawn up in close consultation with Member States. Account was to be taken of any views expressed by the European Parliament, and they were to be published in the Official Journal. Although Article 6(2) simply required such publication, in 1985 the guidelines were adopted as Commission Decision 85/261.[153]

Article 10(1) of Regulation 2052/88[154] also provided for the Commission to establish, for a period covering a number of years, 'general guidelines'. They were to set out and clarify the 'Community choices and criteria' concerning Objectives 3 and 4.[155] Accordingly, guidelines concerning intervention by the Fund in respect of action against long-term unemployment and occupational

[144] Art 3(a) of Reg 2396/71 (JO 1971 249/54) implementing the Dec of 1 Feb 1971.
[145] CFS/inf 1/74. [146] CFS/inf 1/75. [147] OJ 1977 C141/2.
[148] Guidelines for the management of the ESF during 1980–82 (OJ 1979 C159/2), para D.2(c).
[149] para I.A of the 1977 Guidelines (OJ 1977 C141/2).
[150] ibid, para I.B. [151] sect 4.3.3 above.
[152] On the tasks of the ESF (OJ 1983 L289/38).
[153] On the guidelines for the management of the ESF in 1986–88 (OJ 1985 L133/26). See, later, Dec 87/329 (OJ 1987 L167/56) on the guidelines for the management of the ESF for 1988–90.
[154] OJ 1988 L185/9.
[155] More detailed requirements were contained in Art 4 of Reg 4255/88 (OJ 1988 L374/21).

integration of young people[156] were published in 1989. They were less detailed than earlier guidelines because of the importance attached to 'partnership',[157] though they would be taken into account by the Commission when it drew up Community Support Frameworks.[158]

However, in the light of the legislative reforms of 1993, it is now considered that policy aims for the European Social Fund are sufficiently defined in the current Council legislation. In particular, the obligation to concentrate on the most important actions is considered to be adequately established by this legislation.[159] Therefore, the Commission no longer publishes guidelines for this Fund.[160] To this extent, formal legislation is seen as rendering resort to soft law unnecessary.

However, the Commission will in future, it is proposed, have to publish guidelines for each of the new Objectives in the Official Journal. They are to set out the 'Community priorities' for each Objective. They are to be taken into account by the Member States and the Commission at the various stages of the planning of assistance.[161]

7.4.4 Community Support Frameworks

A Community Support Framework[162] may be defined as the document approved by the Commission following appraisal of the development plan submitted by a Member State and containing the strategy and priorities for action, their specific objectives, and the contribution of the European Regional Development Fund and other financial resources. It shall be divided into priorities and implemented by means of one or more operational programmes.[163]

These Frameworks are a response of the Commission to requests for assistance in the plans drawn up by Member States. Union legislation does not specify the role to be played by regional representatives in establishment of these frameworks.[164] In their establishment, Commission guidelines

156 OJ 1989 C45/6. 157 sect 7.7.7 below.

158 para III.4 of the 1989 Guidelines (OJ 1989 C45/6).

159 Art 3 of Reg 2084/93 (OJ 1993 L193/39), and the last recital in the preamble.

160 Operation of the Community Structural Funds, COM(93)124, 24.

161 Art 9(4) of the Proposal of 19 Mar 1998 (OJ 1998 C176/1) for a regulation laying down provisions on the Structural Funds.

162 In the case of Objective 2 regions, Art 9(8) of Reg 2081/93 (OJ 1993 L193/5) describes them as Community conversion support frameworks.

163 Art 9(1)(c) of the Proposal of 19 Mar 1998 (OJ 1998 C176/1) for a regulation laying down provisions on the Structural Funds.

164 The original CSFs for Objective 1 regions were described as having been 'negotiated between the Member State concerned and the Commission' (see eg *CSF 1989–93 for Objective 1 Regions of Italy* (EC Commission, Brussels, 1989) 6). Those for Objective 2 regions were described as having been 'negotiated between the Member State and region concerned and the Commission' (see eg *CSF 1989–91 for Objective 2 Regions of Italy* (EC Commission, Brussels, 1990) 6).

concerning regional policy are to be applied.[165] They are to be established by Commission decisions[166] and may cover a period of three or six years.[167]

The information to be included in the Frameworks is specified by Article 8(3) of Regulation 2082/93.[168] There must be: a statement of the priorities for joint Union and national action in relation to the Objectives of the Structural Funds, together with information concerning their consistency with the economic and social policies of the Member State concerned; an outline of the assistance which is to be provided but is not decided at the same time as the Framework, including the specific objectives of operational programmes and the main types of measure involved; an indicative financing plan specifying the financial allocations envisaged for the various forms of assistance and the duration thereof, including those of the Structural Funds, the European Investment Bank, and other financial instruments, where they contribute directly to the financing plan concerned; where appropriate, information concerning the means available for any studies or technical assistance relating to the preparation, implementation, or adaptation of the measures concerned; the procedures for verifying additionality and an initial evaluation of the latter; and appropriate information concerning the transparency of the relevant financial flows, particularly those from the Member State concerned to the recipient regions. For Objectives 1, 2, and 5b the arrangements for associating the environmental authorities designated by the Member States in the implementation of the Framework must also be indicated.

Frameworks are not required for Objective 5a. However, in establishing Frameworks for Objectives 1 and 5b, the Commission considers the impact of Objective 5a actions on the development of regions covered by these two Objectives.[169]

The Frameworks are said to constitute 'programme contracts', which bind the Commission and the national authorities.[170] However, according to Article 10(2) of Regulation 2082/93,[171] the Commission decision on a Community Support Framework shall be sent as a declaration of intent to the Member State. The decision shall be published in the Official Journal. At the request of the European Parliament, the Commission shall also transmit to the Parliament the decision and the Framework approved for information. It is thus the decision rather than the Framework itself which has formal legal status.[172]

[165] Art 8(2) of Reg 2083/93 (OJ 1993 L193/34).

[166] Art 8(1) of Reg 2082/93 (OJ 1993 L193/20). [167] ibid, Art 8(2). [168] ibid.

[169] See eg Dec 92/78 (OJ 1992 L31/38) on the establishment of the CSF for Community structural assistance on the improvement of the conditions under which agricultural and forestry products are processed and marketed in Germany (with the new *Länder*).

[170] F Celimene, 'La Reforme de l'action des fonds structurels européens' (1991) AJDA 251–266, 259.

[171] OJ 1993 L193/20.

[172] Similarly, SPDs (sect 7.4.5 below) are not themselves published in the OJ. See eg Dec 98/586 (OJ 1998 L282/20) on the approval of the multiregional SPD for the conversion of the activities of defence in the areas concerned by Objective 2 in France.

At the same time, according to the Commission, the legislation provides a consistent and precise definition of the content of the Frameworks. Hence, the legislation makes it possible for the Frameworks to take account of the problems peculiar to individual regions and of possible solutions.[173] The implication is that the relationship between soft law and legislation may be so complicated that the latter may be seen as an integral element of the former.

In practice, however, while the Frameworks adopted may incorporate the outline legislative requirements, their content is left to depend largely on negotiations between the Commission and the Member States. Legislation merely authorizes and structures such negotiation. The results of the negotiation may be controversial.

Indeed, it is said that the Frameworks lack an assessment of strengths and assets on which a development strategy can rely and to which both specific and general interventions can be targeted.[174] Thus they do not generally constitute strategic documents in the strict sense.

For example, according to the European Parliament, the original Framework for Greece required amendment because of the doubtful prospects for certain important traditional sectors of Greek manufacturing industry. It also required amendment because of the need for a transformation of industry in Greece and for an emphasis on building up production capacity in the higher technology sectors.[175] Again, the Parliament criticized the generalization and dispersal of the priority regions in the Italian Frameworks for regions covered by Objectives 1 and 2. They implied an insufficient application of the integrated approach and contributed to the failure of Union assistance to concentrate sufficiently on precise regional development objectives.[176]

At the same time, the Frameworks may be criticized as facilitating centralization within Member States. For example, the introduction by the Italian Government of 'centralized guidelines for the regional proposals concerning preparation of the Frameworks' was criticized.[177] In fact, regional authorities may play only a limited role in their preparation,[178] particularly in the case of Objectives 3 and 4, where the Frameworks are usually drawn up at national level.[179]

[173] Annual report on the implementation of the reform of the Structural Funds 1989, COM(90)516, 301.

[174] RP Camagni, 'Development Scenarios and Policy Guidelines for the Lagging Regions in the 1990s' (1992) *Regional Studies* 361–374.

[175] Resolution of 22 Nov 1991 (OJ 1991 C326/262) on the Community's regional development activities to assist Greece, para 9.

[176] Resolution of 22 Nov 1991 (OJ 1991 C326/260) on the Community's regional development activities to assist the Italian regions covered by Objectives 1 and 2, para 10.

[177] ibid, para 4.

[178] C Engel and J van Ginderachter, *Le Pouvoir régional et local dans la Communauté européenne* (Pedone, Paris, 1992) 40.

[179] Report of the Committee on Regional Policy, Regional Planning, and Relations with Regional and Local Authorities on the annual report on the implementation of the reform of the Structural Funds in 1990, EP Doc A3–0152/92.

It is now proposed that they will be drawn up for Objective 1 regions by the Commission on the basis of the regional development plans and in agreement with the Member State concerned. The Commission will appraise operational programmes for consistency with the relevant Framework.[180] Continued use of such Frameworks in Objective 1 regions is considered justified because of the scale of funding involved. It is also considered justified because the frameworks offer the opportunity to implement multiregional programmes relating to a particular topic or sector, including the development of human resources.[181]

7.4.5 Single Programming Documents

Single Programming Documents must be approved by the Commission and contain the same information as Community Support Frameworks and operational programmes.[182] Under existing legislation they may replace Community Support Frameworks. Member States may submit in such documents the information required in the plans and in applications for assistance.[183] They are to be adopted by the Commission under Article 10(1) of Regulation 2082/93.[184]

Their use, instead of Community Support Frameworks, highlights the favourable attitude of the Union legislature towards linking formulation of regional policy by Member States and operations of the Union funds. Implicit in this attitude is recognition of the utility of the soft law documents as instruments by which negotiation may give detailed application to legislative rules regarding the grant of Union assistance. In practice, however, 'red tape' may lessen the attractiveness of such documents.[185] Their adoption requires just as much data and preparatory work as does separate presentation of plans and applications for assistance.[186] Hence, their negotiation may be lengthy.[187] At the same time, their preparation involves no greater guarantee of regional participation than does the preparation of Community Support Frameworks.

[180] Art 14(3) of the Proposal of 19 Mar 1998 (OJ 1998 C176/1) for a regulation laying down provisions on the Structural Funds.

[181] Explanatory memorandum to the Proposal of 19 Mar 1998 for a regulation laying down provisions on the Structural Funds, COM(98)131, 21.

[182] Art 9(1)(f) of the Proposal of 19 Mar 1998 (OJ 1998 C176/1) for a regulation laying down provisions on the Structural Funds.

[183] Art 5(2) of Reg 2082/93 (OJ 1993 L193/20).

[184] ibid.

[185] It is recognized that, in the case of Objectives 1, 3, and 4 at least, Member States may not always be able to provide the information necessary for the Commission to adopt operational programmes at the same time as it adopts the SPD. See Community Structural Funds 1994–99, COM(93)67, 18.

[186] COR Opinion of 21 Mar 1996 (OJ 1996 C182/7) on the new regional programmes under Objectives 1 and 2, para 16.

[187] See eg the Commission Reply by Mrs Wulf-Mathies to WQ E–0472/98 (OJ 1998 C310/78) by Richard Howitt.

It is now proposed that Single Programming Documents will be drawn up for the new Objectives 2 and 3.[188]

7.4.6 Commission Notices

Commission notices may, in contrast to the (bilateral) Community Support Frameworks and Single Programming Documents, unilaterally lay down conditions for the grant of Union assistance. Such notices may determine the scope of the procedure for approval of applications for various kinds of assistance, including that provided pursuant to Community initiatives, pilot and demonstration projects, and environmental measures. In doing so, they have legal consequences.[189]

Community initiatives

Community initiatives are adopted by the Commission on the basis of notices. The notices lay down guidelines for operational programmes or global grants,[190] which Member States are invited to establish with financial assistance from the Structural Funds.[191] Such notices apparently constitute 'acts' for the purposes of judicial review of their legality by the European Courts.[192]

The guidelines for Community initiatives are adopted by the Commission in accordance with the management committee procedure and after their notification for information to the European Parliament. They are published in the Official Journal.[193] It is now required that they shall describe the aims, scope, and the appropriate implementation method for each initiative.[194]

However, the proliferation of such initiatives has been criticized by Member States.[195] According to the European Council meeting in December 1992, they should mainly promote cross-border, transnational, and interregional co-operation[196] and assist the outermost regions, in accordance with the principle of subsidiarity.[197] This principle is defined in Article 5 of the EC

[188] Art 14(4) of the Proposal of 19 Mar 1998 (OJ 1998 C176/1) for a regulation laying down provisions on the Structural Funds.

[189] Joined Cases C–239 & 240/96R *UK v EC Commission: social assistance* [1996] ECR I–4475, I–4486.

[190] Art 3(2) of Reg 2083/93 (OJ 1993 L193/34).

[191] ibid, Art 6(3).

[192] Joined Cases C–239 & 240/96R *UK v EC Commission: social assistance* [1996] ECR I–4475, I–4486. See, regarding judicial review, sect 7.8 below.

[193] Art 3(2) of Reg 2083/93 (OJ 1993 L193/34).

[194] Art 20(1) of the Proposal of 19 Mar 1998 (OJ 1998 C176/1) for a regulation laying down provisions on the Structural Funds.

[195] Commission Reply by Mr Christophersen to WQ 3093/91 (OJ 1992 C168/32) by Mr Jean-Pierre Raffarin.

[196] Art 11(1) of Reg 2082/93 (OJ 1993 L193/20) provides for joint applications by two or more Member States in the case of operations of transnational interest.

[197] Conclusions of the Presidency (Bull EC 12–1992, I.56). See also Future of Community initiatives under the Structural Funds, COM(93)282, 14.

Treaty. It states: 'in areas which do not fall within its exclusive competence, the Community shall take action, in accordance with the principle of subsidiarity, only if and in so far as the objectives of the proposed action cannot be sufficiently achieved by the Member States and can therefore, by reason of the scale or effects of the proposed action, be better achieved by the Community'.

Hence, the Commission now considers that Community initiatives should be organized around a few selected priorities, so that there will be real concentration and effectiveness.[198] Apparently, then, even in the absence of legislative intervention, the Commission may regard attitudes of Member States as decisive for its use of soft law.

Pilot and demonstration projects

Calls for proposals for pilot and demonstration projects may be made by Commission notices. According to the notices, applications for assistance may be submitted by public or private bodies. Where they are submitted by the latter, they must be accompanied by proof that the local, regional, and national authorities have been consulted and have consented to the implementation of the project and, where applicable, that they will provide financial and/or practical support.[199]

Environmental measures

Legislation regarding applications for assistance from the Financial Instrument for the Environment is comparatively elaborate. According to this legislation, the Commission may ask any legal or natural person established in the Union to submit applications for assistance in respect of measures of particular interest to the Union. The Commission may do so by means of a notice published in the Official Journal.[200] Where assistance is to be granted, 'a contract or agreement governing the rights and obligations of the parties' is concluded with the person concerned.[201]

[198] From the Single Act to Maastricht and beyond: the means to match our ambitions, COM(92)2000. See also sect 2.4.6 above.

[199] See eg Call for proposals for pilot projects and demonstration projects relating to the adjustment of agricultural structures and the promotion of rural development (OJ 1994 C303/17), para 1.

[200] Art 9(2) of Reg 1404/96 (OJ 1996 L181/1) amending Reg 1973/92 establishing a financial instrument for the environment. See eg Life 1997: call for proposals (OJ 1996 C363/11). See, similarly, in the RTD field, second call for proposals for RTD actions for the specific programme for RTDD in the field of advanced communications technologies and services (1994–98) (OJ 1995 C240/7).

[201] Art 9(5) of Reg 1404/96 (OJ 1996 L181/1).

7.5 ADMINISTRATIVE DECISIONS

Legislation may confer on the Commission powers to take individual decisions on the grant of Union assistance. Article 249(4) of the EC Treaty states that decisions are binding in their entirety upon those to whom they are addressed. In principle, such decisions merely entail application of pre-existing rules. In practice, they may modify such rules or even generate new ones. Certainly, in so far as actors can induce 'general principles' from such decisions, they may 'spontaneously' modify their conduct accordingly.[202] Much may depend, however, on whether the decisions are published and in what detail they are published.

Such decisions were required in the case of: intervention programmes within a Community programme,[203] as well as decisions determining eligible regions in each Member State;[204] national programmes of Community interest;[205] integrated development programmes;[206] Integrated Mediterranean Programmes[207] and pilot actions to prepare such programmes;[208] and programmes under Regulation 355/77.[209] Alternatively, the Commission may, as under Regulation 950/97,[210] be required to take decisions approving national implementing measures.[211]

Commission decisions are also required regarding determination of regions eligible under Objectives 2[212] and 5b[213] and regarding indicative allocations of assistance by Member State.[214] It is proposed that they will be required for determination of regions covered by the new Objectives 1 and 2.[215]

[202] Melchior, n 131 above, 246.

[203] Arts 7(5), 13, and 40 of Reg 1787/84 (OJ 1984 L169/1). See eg Dec 88/48 (OJ 1988 L30/25) approving the intervention programme for Greece implementing the Valoren programme.

[204] See eg regarding Spain, Dec 91/91 (OJ 1991 L50/24) on the areas referred to in Art 3(2) of Reg 2506/88 instituting a Community programme to assist the conversion of shipbuilding areas.

[205] Arts 11(5), 13, and 40 of Reg 1787/84 (OJ 1984 L169/1). See eg Dec 89/523 (OJ 1989 L272/16) on the granting of a contribution from the ERDF for measures under a national programme of Community interest (Azores).

[206] See eg Dec 87/227 (OJ 1987 L94/27) approving an integrated approach for the area Oost-Groningen/Oost-Drenthe, Netherlands.

[207] Art 7 of Reg 2088/85 (OJ 1985 L197/1). See eg Dec 88/259 (OJ 1988 L107/41) approving an IMP for the Abruzzo region.

[208] See eg Dec 84/70 (JO 1984 L44/1) instituting in the area of Agliastra, Nuoro Province, Sardinia, a pilot action in preparation for the IMP.

[209] OJ 1977 L51/1. See eg Dec 87/384 (OJ 1987 L203/49) approving an Italian programme on the treatment and marketing of feed grains and green fodder. Cf Dec 85/597 (OJ 1985 L373/44) withholding approval from the Bavarian market structure programme for Franconian wine.

[210] On improving the efficiency of agricultural structures (OJ 1997 L142/1), Arts 29–30.

[211] See eg Dec 89/79 (OJ 1989 L30/78) on improving the efficiency of agricultural structures in Italy (Calabria).

[212] Art 9(3) of Reg 2081/93 (OJ 1993 L193/5).

[213] ibid, Art 11a(3).

[214] ibid, Art 12(4). See, now, Art 7(3) of the Proposal of 19 Mar 1998 (OJ 1998 C176/1) for a regulation laying down provisions on the Structural Funds.

[215] ibid, Arts 3 and 4.

However, the Commission may wish to avoid 'seriously burdening' the Official Journal by publishing the decisions in full.[216] The difficulties caused by the resulting lack of transparency in decision making have not passed entirely unnoticed by the Union legislature. Thus Article 10 of Regulation 4253/88[217] provided for the publication in the Official Journal of the 'declaration of intent' contained in decisions approving Community Support Frameworks.[218] The legislation now requires publication of the decisions themselves. It is also provided that, at the request of the European Parliament, the Commission must transmit to the Parliament the decision together with the relevant Framework.[219] However, other decisions concerning assistance from the Union funds may remain unpublished. Thus, for example, regional operational programmes[220] are adopted as decisions,[221] but the decisions are not published.

In the case of the Cohesion Fund, the legislation requires that the 'key details' of Commission decisions granting assistance be published in the Official Journal.[222] In the case of agricultural structure decisions, the Commission itself had decided in 1989 to amend its practice along similar lines. This category of decisions, which took effect on notification to the respective Member States, would no longer be published in full, 'except in exceptional cases'.[223]

7.6 CONTRACTS

Contracts may be seen as a suitable legal form for giving content to administrative decisions.[224] Such contracts may have as parties regions and individu-

[216] Commission submission in Joined Cases 10 & 18/60 *Società 'Eridania' Zuccherifici Nazionali v EC Commission* [1969] ECR 459, 464.

[217] Laying down provisions for implementing Reg 2052/88 as regards co-ordination of the activities of the different Structural Funds between themselves and with the operations of the other existing financial instruments (OJ 1988 L374/1).

[218] cf A-G Darmon in Case C–157/90 *Infortec Projectos & Consultadoria, Lda v EC Commission* [1992] ECR I–3525, I–3547, who apparently interpreted the requirement as applying to assistance decisions more generally.

[219] Art 10(2) of Reg 2082/93 (OJ 1993 L193/20).

[220] sect 2.4.6 above.

[221] See, regarding operational programmes under Community initiatives, the Commission Reply by Mr Millan to WQ E–1735/93 (OJ 1994 C255/9) by Alexandros Alavanos.

[222] Reg 1164/94 (OJ 1994 L130/1), Art 10(7). See eg Publication of main points of decisions to grant financial assistance under Reg 1164/94 (OJ 1996 C325/1). Cf Communication of decisions to grant Community financial support for demonstration projects forwarded under the Life instrument (OJ 1998 C68/4; and OJ 1998 C154/5).

[223] Communication of agricultural structure decisions (OJ 1989 L174/31).

[224] The European Parliament had called for the implementation of regional development programmes in the agricultural sector to be founded on a contractual relationship between the Community, the Member State and, whenever possible, the region concerned. See the Resolution of 17 Nov 1983 (OJ 1983 C342/98) on new guidelines for the Community's structural policy in the agricultural sector, para 41(c). Cf Art 3 of the proposal for a regulation instituting a specific Community programme of accompanying social measures to assist workers in the shipbuilding industry who were made redundant or threatened with redundancy, COM(87)275.

als as well as the Commission and Member States. However, their enforcement through proceedings under Article 288(1) of the EC Treaty[225] may be precluded, in so far as operations of the Union funds are characterized as 'unilateral acts falling within the province of public law'.[226] On the other hand, conditions annexed to a decision granting assistance have binding force for the purposes of other proceedings.[227]

In particular, a Community programme or national programme of Community interest had to be adopted by the Commission after consultation of the Committee for the European Regional Development Fund.[228] It then became the subject of agreement between the Commission and the Member State or Member States concerned and constituted a 'programme agreement' for the purposes of Regulation 1787/84.[229] Moreover, implementation of Integrated Mediterranean Programmes was, according to Article 9 of Regulation 2088/85,[230] to be regulated by programme contracts. These contracts were to be concluded between the parties concerned (the Commission, Member States, regional authority, or any other authority designated by the Member States) and were to set out their respective commitments. The standard contents of the contracts were specified[231] in Annex IV to the Regulation.[232]

In practice, implementation of such contracts proved more effective in some Member States than in others. For example, in 1989 the Integrated Mediterranean Programmes for France and Greece had recorded out-turn rates (that is, commitments and payments in relation to estimates) of 97 per cent and 93 per cent, respectively. In the case of the Italian programmes, the out-turn rate was just 47 per cent. According to the Commission, the greatest difficulties in Italy arose from 'demarcation disputes' between national and regional authorities and within the latter authorities.[233]

The European Parliament suggested that the Commission should transfer appropriations from regions running seriously behind schedule to those which had already completed their programmes and were able to submit further programmes.[234] The effect of such transfers, however, might well be to penalize regions suffering from the most serious administrative obstacles to development.

[225] It provides that the contractual liability of the EC shall be governed by the law applicable to the contract in question.

[226] A-G Verloren van Themaat in Case 44/81 *Germany v EC Commission: deadline for claiming payment of ESF assistance* [1982] ECR 1855, 1881.

[227] Case T–331/94 *IPK-München GmbH v EC Commission* [1997] ECR II–1665, II–1682.

[228] sect 7.7.2 below.

[229] OJ 1984 L169/1, Art 13(1).

[230] OJ 1985 L197/1.

[231] The relevant clauses may have 'mandatory status'. Cf Case C–324/96 *Odette Nikon Petridi Anonymos Kapnemporiki v Athanasia Simou* [26 Mar 1998].

[232] See eg Dec 88/62 (OJ 1988 L32/23) approving an IMP for Corsica.

[233] IMP—progress report for 1989, SEC(91)553.

[234] Resolution of 14 Feb 1992 (OJ 1992 C67/216) on the IMPs, para 5.

Apparently, the limits to the capacity of contracts to resolve such problems are recognized. Thus current legislation seeks to rely, instead, on 'declarations of intent' associated with Community Support Frameworks and Single Programming Documents. Their operational content is apparently to depend not so much on their terms as on committee work.

7.7 COMMITTEE WORK

Committees may be seen as supplementing, implementing, or modifying decision-making procedures. They may be: advisory; designed to alter relations between the Commission and Council or relations between the Commission and individual Member States; designed to assist Commission implementation efforts; or designed to increase the pluralism of Union decision making.

7.7.1 Regional Policy Committee

A Regional Policy Committee was established by Decision 75/185.[235] Each Member State and the Commission were to appoint two members to the Committee. Those appointed by the Member States were to be selected from senior officials responsible for regional policy.[236] The function of the Committee was to examine problems relating to regional development, the progress made or to be made towards solving them, and measures needed to further the achievement of the Community's regional objectives.[237] Thus, for example, the Committee was to examine the regional development programmes presented by the Member States.[238] It was also required to examine national systems of aid which were regional in purpose or in effect.[239] It was abolished in 1988.[240]

[235] Setting up a Regional Policy Committee (OJ 1975 L73/47), as amended by Dec 79/137 (OJ 1979 L35/9). The Rules of Procedure of the Committee were laid down in 1975 (OJ 1975 L320/17).

[236] Art 3 of Dec 79/137 (OJ 1979 L35/9). An official from a German *land* also participated, and there were 'silent observers' from Flanders, Northern Ireland, Scotland, Wales, and Wallonia, when regional development programmes concerning them were being discussed. See H Haenel, 'L'Europe: Une chance pour les collectivités locales' (1991) *Revue Française d'Administration Publique* 583–586, 584.

[237] Art 2(3)(e) of Dec 75/185 (OJ 1975 L73/47) envisaged that the result would be a common approach to the concept of a regional development programme.

[238] Art 6(5) of Reg 724/75 (OJ 1975 L73/1).

[239] Art 2(1) of Dec 75/185 (OJ 1975 L73/47).

[240] Art 30(2) of Reg 4253/88 (OJ 1988 L374/1).

7.7.2 Structural Funds Committees

Committees for each of the Structural Funds are well established. However, the evolving character of these committees may be controversial.

ERDF committees

A Committee for the European Regional Development Fund was originally established by Article 11 of Regulation 724/75.[241] It was composed of representatives of the Member States and chaired by the Commission. It constituted a 'management committee'.

Management committees adopt opinions on Commission decisions by a qualified majority, the votes being weighted, as in the Council, according to Article 205(2) of the EC Treaty. If such an opinion does not accord with a Commission decision, the Commission may defer application of the decision for up to two months. Within that period the Council may adopt a different decision, also by a qualified majority. Therefore, if such a committee objects to the decision concerned, the Council may effectively take back decision-making powers delegated to the Commission.[242]

The main function of the Committee for the European Regional Development Fund was to deliver opinions on Commission decisions regarding the grant of Fund assistance in individual cases.[243]

The Commission is now assisted, in connection with implementation of Objectives 1 and 2,[244] by an advisory committee. It is known as the Advisory Committee on the Development and Conversion of Regions. It is similarly composed to the original Committee. However, the Commission must merely 'take utmost account of the opinions of the Advisory Committee'.[245]

It is proposed that the Commission will in future have to inform this Committee of the manner in which it takes account of its opinions. These opinions are to be delivered on draft Commission decisions regarding Community Support Frameworks for Objective 1 and Single Programming Documents for Objective 2. In addition, they are to be delivered on the drawing-up and revision of the list of Objective 2 regions.[246]

241 OJ 1975 L73/1. A new committee was established by Art 39 of Reg 1787/84 (OJ 1984 L169/1).

242 Art 2 of Dec 87/373 (OJ 1987 L197/33) laying down the procedures for the exercise of implementing powers conferred on the Commission.

243 Art 12(3) of Reg 724/75 (OJ 1975 L73/1).

244 Art 17(1) of Reg 2081/93 (OJ 1993 L193/5). See also, regarding the organization of the Advisory Committee on Rural Development, Dec 98/235 (OJ 1998 L88/59) on the advisory committees dealing with matters covered by the CAP.

245 Art 27 of Reg 2082/93 (OJ 1993 L193/20).

246 Art 47 of the Proposal of 19 Mar 1998 (OJ 1998 C176/1) for a regulation laying down provisions on the Structural Funds.

The management committee procedure applies in relation to Objective 5b[247] and was extended by Regulation 2081/93[248] to Community initiatives.[249] The latter extension was 'deplored' by the Commission.[250] Nevertheless, the Commission does not now propose to exempt adoption of such initiatives from this procedure.[251]

EAGGF committees

A Committee on Agricultural Structures was originally established by the Decision of 4 December 1962.[252] It has become the Management Committee on Agricultural Structures and Rural Development.[253] It is composed of representatives of the Member States and chaired by the Commission. It is to be consulted on Commission decisions, which are to be adopted by the Commission and apply immediately. If the decisions are not in accordance with the Committee opinion, they are to be communicated forthwith to the Council. The Commission may defer their application for not more than one month from the date of the communication. The Council may, by a qualified majority, take a different decision during that month.[254]

It is now proposed that the Committee will deliver opinions on Commission decisions relating to the establishment of Objective 2 regions and to Single Programming Documents under Objective 2. It is also to be consulted on operations concerning agricultural structures and rural development included in draft Commission decisions regarding Community Support Frameworks for Objective 1 regions.[255]

In addition, there is to be a Management Committee on Fisheries and Aquaculture. It is to deliver opinions on Commission decisions relating to the establishment of Objective 2 regions and to Single Programming Documents under Objective 2. It is also to be consulted about operations concerning fisheries structures included in draft Commission decisions on Community

[247] Art 17(1) of Reg 2081/93 (OJ 1993 L193/5); Management Committee on Agricultural Structures and Rural Development and the Standing Management Committee on Fisheries Structures (ibid, Art 29).

[248] ibid.

[249] Art 17(1) (ibid) and Arts 3(2) and 29a of Reg 2082/93 (OJ 1993 L193/20); Management Committee for Community Initiatives (ibid). Account is also to be taken of guidelines from the European Parliament, and the Parliament is to be informed of Commission proposals.

[250] Explanatory memorandum to the re-examined proposals of 15 July 1993, COM(93)379, 1.

[251] Art 20(1) of the Proposal of 19 Mar 1998 (OJ 1998 C176/1) for a regulation laying down provisions on the Structural Funds.

[252] On the co-ordination of agricultural structural policies (JO 1962 2892). Art 11 of Reg 729/70 (JO 1970 L94/13) on the financing of the CAP established a new EAGGF committee.

[253] Art 29(1) of Reg 2082/93 (OJ 1993 L193/20).

[254] ibid. There is also a Standing Management Committee on Fisheries Structures (ibid, Art 29(2)).

[255] Art 49 of the Proposal of 19 Mar 1998 (OJ 1998 C176/1) for a regulation laying down provisions on the Structural Funds.

Support Frameworks or Single Programming Documents for Objective 1 regions.[256]

ESF committee

An Advisory Committee for the European Social Fund was provided for in Article 124 of the EEC Treaty and was established in 1960.[257] It is composed of representatives of Member States, trades unions, and employers' organizations. It delivers opinions on draft Commission decisions. The Commission is to inform the Committee of the manner in which it has taken account of these opinions.[258]

It is now proposed that the Committee will deliver opinions on draft Commission decisions relating to Single Programming Documents under Objective 3. Moreover, in the case of assistance from the European Social Fund, it will also deliver opinions on Community Support Frameworks and Single Programming Documents for Objectives 1 and 2.[259]

Similar procedures may apply to use of other financial instruments.[260] The relevant committees may be mainly intended to provide the means of establishing a link between the representatives of the Member States and the Commission. Their work may, however, be criticized on the ground that they do not aim specifically to ensure that the price of the operations financed is a fair one.[261]

7.7.3 IMP Committee

An Advisory Committee on Integrated Mediterranean Programmes, consisting of representatives of the Member States and chaired by the Commission, was established by Article 7(1) of Regulation 2088/85.[262] According to Article 7(2) of the same Regulation, the Committee was to consider draft programmes submitted by the Commission. If the Committee delivered a negative opinion on such a draft, the Commission had to amend the draft, taking into consideration the Committee's opinion, and resubmit the amended draft. Within a month of the second submission the Commission was required finally to decide on implementation of the programme.

[256] ibid, Art 50.

[257] Reg 9/60 on the ESF (JO 1960 1189), Arts 27–30.

[258] Art 28 of Reg 2082/93 (OJ 1993 L193/20).

[259] Art 48 of the Proposal of 19 Mar 1998 (OJ 1998 C176/1) for a regulation laying down provisions on the Structural Funds.

[260] See eg in the case of Thermie, Reg 2008/90 (OJ 1990 L185/1) concerning the promotion of energy technology in Europe, Art 29(1) and (2).

[261] COA special report 3/92 (OJ 1992 C245/1), para 2.8.

[262] OJ 1985 L197/1.

7.7.4 Monitoring Committees

Monitoring Committees, which were originally introduced for each Integrated Mediterranean Programme,[263] are now established for Structural Fund operations generally. Their establishment is based on agreement between the Member State concerned and the Commission within the 'partnership'[264] framework. The committees may, subject to confirmation by the Commission and Member State concerned, adjust both the procedure for granting assistance as initially approved and the financing plan envisaged.[265]

The legislation does not expressly prescribe the composition of these committees, though it is provided that the Commission and, where appropriate, the European Investment Bank, may delegate representatives.[266] The European Parliament considers that regional authorities and the economic and social partners should be represented on the committees.[267] The Parliament has also sought the right for MEPs to be members of the committee for their region,[268] but no provision has been made to this effect in the legislation. At the same time, these committees are said by the Commission[269] to obviate the need for the network of regional observers suggested by the Economic and Social Committee.[270]

In practice, the composition of these committees is left to be largely determined by each Member State. For example, the Commission has gone no further than 'successfully arguing' with the United Kingdom Government that local authorities should have the right to decide how they are to be represented on monitoring committees for Merseyside. However, the Government rejected the Commission request that the social partners be represented.[271]

The legislation governing the Cohesion Fund apparently does more to ensure decentralization. According to this legislation, where regional and local authorities are competent for the execution of a project supported by this Fund and where they are directly concerned by a project, they are to be represented on the relevant monitoring committee.[272]

[263] OJ 1985 L197/1 Art 9.

[264] See sect 7.7.7 below.

[265] Art 25(5) of Reg 2082/93 (OJ 1993 L193/20).

[266] ibid, Art 25(3).

[267] Resolution of 5 May 1994 (OJ 1994 C205/438) on the draft guidelines for operational programmes or global grants within the framework of a Community initiative on Employment and Development of Human Resources, proposed amendment 43.

[268] Resolution of 22 Jan 1993 (OJ 1993 C42/211) on Community structural policies: assessment and outlook (mid-term review), para 26(a).

[269] Commission Reply by Mr Millan to WQ 295/92 (OJ 1992 C207/46) by Mrs Raymonde Dury.

[270] Opinion of 25 Sept 1991 (OJ 1991 C339/6) on the fourth periodic report on the economic situation of the regions, para 4.16.

[271] Commission Reply by Mr Millan to WQ E–2500/94 (OJ 1995 C103/15) by Kenneth Stewart.

[272] Art F.3 of Annex II to Reg 1164/94 (OJ 1994 L130/1).

The committees are now, it is proposed, to be set up by agreement between the designated managing authority[273] and the partners. Representation of local and environmental authorities and economic and social partners will be obligatory.[274] There is to be one committee for each Community Support Framework or Single Programming Document.[275] The representatives of all the partners which contribute to the financing of the assistance shall have the right to vote, when the committee adopts its decisions. Moreover, in the case of decisions concerning human resources, the representatives of the other partners shall have the same right. Generally, however, the representatives of partners who do not contribute to the financing of the assistance serve only in an advisory capacity.[276] The rationale for this limitation to voting rights is, according to the Commission, to ensure that 'procedures are not slowed down'.[277]

In any case, these committees are concerned with monitoring the *implementation* of Union decision making,[278] and such decision making may take place without effective participation by regional institutions.[279] Hence, while the establishment of such committees implicitly recognizes the lack of pluralism of the Union decision-making system, the system is allowed to remain essentially intact.

7.7.5 Consultative Council of Regional and Local Authorities

Partly in response to calls from the European Parliament for the Commission to establish direct relations with representatives of regional and local authorities,[280] the Commission established the Consultative Council of Regional and Local Authorities.[281] It was attached to the Commission[282] and might be

[273] ie the authority authorized by the Member State to manage Union assistance. It is to be responsible for the efficiency and correctness of the overall management. See Art 33(1) of the Proposal of 19 Mar 1998 (OJ 1998 C176/1) for a regulation laying down provisions on the Structural Funds.

[274] Explanatory memorandum to the Proposal of 19 Mar 1998 for a regulation laying down provisions on the Structural Funds, COM(98)131, 22.

[275] Art 34(1) of the Proposal of 19 Mar 1998 (OJ 1998 C176/1) for a regulation laying down provisions on the Structural Funds.

[276] ibid.

[277] Explanatory memorandum to the Proposal of 19 Mar 1998 for a regulation laying down provisions on the Structural Funds, COM(98)131, 10.

[278] The emphasis of their work is to be securing 'greater cost-effectiveness' (ibid, 5 and 11). They shall satisfy themselves as to the effectiveness and quality of the implementation of assistance (Art 34(2) of the Proposal of 19 Mar 1998 (OJ 1998 C176/1) for a regulation laying down provisions on the Structural Funds).

[279] See, regarding their role in the different Member States, the Seventh annual report on the structural funds, COM(96)502, 229–234.

[280] Resolution of 13 Apr 1984 (OJ 1984 C127/240) on the role of the regions in the construction of a democratic Europe and the outcome of the Conference of the Regions, para 7.

[281] Dec 88/487 (OJ 1988 L247/23) setting up a Consultative Council of Regional and Local Authorities.

[282] ibid, Art 1.

consulted by the latter on any matter relating to regional development. In particular, it might be consulted about the formulation and implementation of Community regional policy and about the regional and local implications of other Community policies.[283] It consisted of fifty-two members holding elected office at regional or local level.[284] They were appointed by the Commission on the basis of a joint proposal from the Assembly of Regions in Europe, the International Union of Local Authorities, and the Council of European Municipalities and Regions.[285]

The Consultative Council was said to have established very good working relations with the Commission, particularly as regards regional policies. Greater participation by regional authorities in 'the building of Europe' would, according to the Commission, be problematic, because of the need to allow for the varying structures of power in the Member States, institutional organization being entirely a matter of national sovereignty.[286]

This idea approaches constitutional issues essentially by reference to the relationship between Union law and national law. This approach may seem consistent with the definition of subsidiarity in Article 5 of the EC Treaty.[287] Its consistency with the requirement in Article A of the Treaty on European Union that decisions should be 'taken as closely as possible to the citizen' is more questionable. At the same time, it allows for little recognition of the constitutional dimensions to cohesion.

Instead, it embodies the question-begging idea that Member States have transferred to the Union only the sovereignty necessary for fulfilment of Treaty obligations.[288] The particular question asked is whether cohesion is achievable so long as the position of regions in the internal organization of Member States and, hence, their participation in Union decision making, depend on national law. In any event, following the creation of the Committee of the Regions, the Consultative Council was abolished.[289]

7.7.6 Committee of the Regions

Article 7(2) of the EC Treaty provides for a Committee of the Regions to assist the Council and Commission in an advisory capacity. This Committee is established by Article 263 of the Treaty. According to the same provision, the members of the Committee may not be bound by any mandatory instructions.

[283] OJ 1988 L247/23 Art 2. [284] ibid, Art 3(1). [285] ibid, Art 3(2).

[286] Commission Reply by Mr Millan to WQ 1390/90 (OJ 1991 C164/5) by Mr Reinhold Bocklet. [287] sect 7.4.6 above.

[288] As regards the concept of sovereignty transfers, see eg Case 26/62 *NV Algemene Transport- en Expeditie Onderneming van Gend en Loos v Nederlandse Administratie der Belastingen* [1963] ECR 1, 12; and Case 6/64 *Flaminio Costa v ENEL* [1964] ECR 585, 593.

[289] Dec 94/209 (OJ 1994 L103/28) winding up the Consultative Council of Regional and Local Authorities.

Functions

According to Article 265 of the EC Treaty, the Committee shall be consulted by the Council or Commission where the Treaty so provides[290] and in all other cases in which one of these institutions considers such consultation appropriate. The Committee may also take the initiative and issue an opinion in cases in which it considers such action appropriate. Hence, this Committee is described as 'an institution through which regional and local bodies can officially be involved in drawing up and implementing Community policies'.[291] According to the Committee itself, its establishment 'enables regional and local bodies to participate, through the Committee of the Regions, in the decision-making process of the European Union'.[292] The 'inclusion' of such bodies in the legislative process is said to be entailed.[293] However, as the Treaty makes clear,[294] the function of the Committee is purely advisory.

Composition

The composition of the Committee may be problematic. In its contributions to the intergovernmental conference which produced the Treaty on European Union, the Commission favoured a stipulation that, as in the case of the Consultative Council of Regional and Local Authorities,[295] membership should be limited to those holding elective office at regional or local level.[296] The European Parliament, in turn, considers that Committee members should be 'elected representatives at immediate sub-central government level and/or that they should derive direct democratic legitimacy from a regional or local assembly'.[297]

No such stipulation is included in Article 263 of the EC Treaty. According to this provision, the members of the Committee shall be appointed by the Council, acting unanimously on proposals from the respective Member States. Hence, each Member State is free, but not obliged, to propose elected representatives as members of the Committee.[298] This arrangement is

290 Arts 149(4), 151(5), 152(4), 156, 159, 161, and 162 EC.

291 Preamble to Dec 94/209 (OJ 1994 L103/28), 3rd recital.

292 Opinion of 17 May 1994 (OJ 1994 C217/10) on the draft notice laying down guidelines for operational programmes in the framework of a Community initiative concerning urban areas, para 4 of the preamble.

293 European Parliament Resolution of 18 Nov 1993 (OJ 1993 C329/279) on the participation and representation of the regions in the process of European integration: the Committee of the Regions, recital G in the preamble.

294 Arts 7(2) and 257 EC.

295 sect 7.7.5 above.

296 Art 198a(2) of the Commission draft (Bull EC, Supp 2/91, 178).

297 Resolution of 18 Nov 1993 (OJ 1993 C329/279) on the participation and representation of the regions in the process of European integration: the Committee of the Regions, para 9. See also the Resolution of 23 Apr 1993 (OJ 1993 C150/329) on the Committee of the Regions, para 4.

298 Commission Reply by Mr Millan to WQ 1206/92 (OJ 1993 C6/10) by Mr Jaak Vandemeulebroucke.

designed to allow for the fact that 'the Member States have very different institutional structures which are exclusively within their purview'.[299] In other words, these structures are matters of national sovereignty. However, a consequence is that the 'autonomy' of members of the Committee in relation to the national authorities of their Member State may be uncertain.[300] To this extent, it may be said that the Treaty fails to guarantee effective opportunities for regional participation in Union decision making through the Committee.

More fundamentally, it may be questioned whether centralized representation through such a body can ever be an adequate mechanism for regional participation in Union decision making. In fact, the inadequacy of such representation is implicitly recognized by the Committee of the Regions itself. The Committee argues that it should be represented on various committees consulted by the Commission, to ensure that views of *individual regions* affected by Union decisions will be 'heard'.[301] This argument reflects doubt in the literature whether an established role for regional representatives at Union level can compensate for their exclusion from day-to-day management of development planning and approval of fund operations.[302]

7.7.7 'Partnership'

The concept of 'partnership' has gradually emerged as the principal basis for participation by individual regions in committee work concerning operations of the Union funds. The concept is consistent with ideas of endogenous development. According to these ideas, regional development depends on a local organizational structure, which enables firms to generate successive innovations or to handle the implementation of technology effectively.[303] Such a structure depends, in turn, on collaboration between public and private bodies at the regional level and, hence, on sufficient autonomy being enjoyed by the former bodies.[304]

[299] Commission Reply by Mr Millan to WQ 1405/92 (OJ 1993 C16/15) by Mr Sotiris Kostopoulos.

[300] See eg M Vellano, 'Coesione economica e sociale e ripartizione di competenze: Le nuove iniziative comunitarie' (1995) RDE 193–208, 195.

[301] Opinion of 17 May 1994 (OJ 1994 C217/26) on the proposal for a decision laying down a series of guidelines on trans-European energy networks, para A.5.1.

[302] J Scott, *Development Dilemmas in European Community Law* (Open University Press, Buckingham, 1995) 34.

[303] P Grindley, 'Turning Technology into Competitive Advantage' (1991) *Business Strategy Review* 35–48.

[304] ESC Opinion of 5 Apr 1979 (OJ 1980 C53/61) on the role and influence of local and regional authorities and socio-economic organizations in the field of the common regional policy; and Opinion of 29 Oct 1981 (OJ 1981 C343/53) on the new regional policy guidelines and priorities, para II.3.5. See, similarly, EEC regional development policy, House of Lords Select Committee on the European Communities, HL(1991–92)20, 38–39.

At the same time, partnership may be decisive for the articulation of cohesion requirements. If a 'genuine partnership' is established, their articulation may be adapted to the diversity of regional problems within the Union.[305]

Such thinking has, it seems, particularly influenced the European Parliament. The Parliament has long stressed the need for the involvement of representatives of local and regional authorities in the development of Union regional policy[306] and, even more controversially,[307] for transfrontier institutions to be established by Union acts.[308] For example, the Commission proposal for the creation of a Committee for Regional Policy[309] merely provided in Article 5 that the Committee might 'take evidence from interested parties from the regions'. This proposal was considered inadequate by the Parliament. The Parliament proposed an amendment to require consultation of 'the competent representatives of the region concerned' and to require the Committee to seek the opinions of regional business organizations.[310] However, this amendment was not adopted in Decision 75/185,[311] by which the Committee was established.

Moreover, the Parliament advocated participation by local authorities in frontier regions in the preparation, implementation, and control of regional development programmes under what became Regulation 724/75.[312] Their participation was only to be within the field of competence assigned to such authorities by the legislation of Member States.[313] However, no such participation was required by the legislation adopted.

Regulation 1787/84[314] also failed to provide for the regional representation sought by the Parliament.[315] It did, however, contain a number of exhortations to the Member States to promote participation of regional and local authorities in decision making regarding use of the European Regional Development Fund. With regard to regional development programmes, the regional authorities concerned were to be involved as far as possible in their

305 cf J Scott, n 302 above, 30.

306 Resolution of 27 June 1966 (JO 1966 2427) on regional policy in the EEC.

307 cf regarding the investigation of Italian–Austrian regional co-operation as 'an attack on the integrity, independence, and unity' of the Italian State contrary to Art 241 of the Italian Penal Code, WQ 0640/96 (OJ 1996 C305/13) by Astrid Lulling.

308 Interim report of the Committee on Regional Policy and Transport on regional policy as regards regions at the Community's internal frontiers, EP Doc 467/75; and the draft proposal of the European Parliament of 18 Nov 1976 (OJ 1976 C293/40) for a regulation on the creation of transfrontier regional authorities (European Joint Authorities).

309 Of 31 July 1973 (OJ 1973 C86/11).

310 Resolution of 15 Nov 1973 (OJ 1973 C108/51), para 13.

311 OJ 1975 L73/47.

312 OJ 1975 L73/1.

313 See also Resolution of 18 Nov 1976 (OJ 1976 C293/37) on the Community's regional policy as regards the regions at the Community internal frontiers, para 30.

314 OJ 1984 L169/1.

315 Report of the Committee on Regional Policy and Regional Planning on the role of the regions in the construction of a democratic Europe—outcome of the Conference of the Regions, EP Doc 1–91/84.

preparation.[316] In the case of regions situated near internal Community frontiers, the Member States were to endeavour to pursue, within the framework of their bilateral relations, transfrontier co-ordination of regional development by means and at the levels which they jointly considered appropriate. In this context they were to support co-operation between the regional and local bodies involved.[317] Moreover, national programmes of Community interest were to be drawn up by the Member State concerned 'in collaboration with the authorities or bodies concerned, within the limits laid down by the national legislation'.[318] Finally, the Community and the national and local authorities in Member States were to contribute in a closely co-ordinated manner to the implementation of integrated development operations.[319] At the same time, Article 15 of the Regulation did not require any formal participation by regional or local authorities in measures to exploit local development potential. However, the nature of those measures was seen as being such that the role of these authorities had to be 'a major one in defining and implementing them'.[320]

More generally, a Joint Statement by the Council, Commission, and Parliament was issued following the conciliation procedure[321] on the reform of the European Regional Development Fund.[322] In this Statement the three institutions recognized the importance of a more effective relationship between the Commission and the regional, or where appropriate, the local authorities. Due regard was to be had for the internal jurisdiction of the Member States and the provisions of Community law. Even so, such a relationship, it was stated, would enable the interests of the regions to be taken more fully into account, when regional development programmes and intervention programmes were produced.[323]

It is ends of this kind which are now sought through express legislative provisions on partnership.

Definition of 'partnership'

Article 4 of Regulation 2081/93[324] provides for operations of the Union funds[325] to be conducted on the basis of 'partnership'. 'Partnership' is defined in Article 4(1) of this Regulation as 'close consultations between the Commission, the Member State concerned, and the competent authorities and bodies, including within the framework of each Member State's national

316 Art 2(3)(a) of Reg 1787/84 (OJ 1984 L169/1).
317 ibid, Art 1(3).
318 ibid, Art 11(1).
319 ibid, Art 34(2)(b).
320 Statement of Commissioner Varfis to the European Parliament (EP Debs No 2–322, 107, 13 Feb 1985).
321 See, regarding the conciliation procedure, A Evans, *A Textbook on European Union Law* (Hart Publishing, Oxford, 1998) sect 3.3.1.
322 OJ 1985 C72/59.
323 ibid, para 4.
324 OJ 1993 L193/5. See, regarding the ERDF and 'regional partnership', Art 9 of Reg 2083/93 (OJ 1993 L193/34).
325 Including the drawing up of CSFs (Art 8(2), ibid).

rules and current practices, the economic and social partners, designated by the Member States at national, regional, local, or other levels, with all parties acting as partners in pursuit of a common goal'.[326] It must, according to the same provision, 'be conducted in full compliance with the respective institutional, legal and financial powers of each of the partners'. This provision thus seeks to facilitate the participation of regional institutions in Union decision making. However, it also seeks to avoid challenging rules of national law which may preclude their effective participation.

The latter feature of the legislation is tacitly recognized in the case law. Thus partnership has been judicially defined as 'a kind of dialogue . . . between the Commission and the Member State concerned'.[327] Moreover, the legal status of dialogue outcomes may be problematic. According to the Court of Justice 'negotiated acts', if not provided for in Union legislation, cannot affect the legal position of Member States under the relevant legislation.[328]

Nevertheless, within this dialogue the Commission is expected to perform its duty to 'take steps and implementing measures to ensure that Community operations are in support of the Objectives of the Structural Funds and impart an added value to national initiatives'.[329] In practice, according to the Commission, partnership needs to ensure that decisions on regional economic development are taken collectively by all those involved, notably the Commission, the Member States, and the local or regional authorities concerned. Thus the Commission seeks to ensure that partnership arrangements involve all authorities and bodies which are competent for the regions and sectors in which fund operations are to be performed.[330] Ideally, the partnership needs to incorporate other relevant economic actors, such as Chambers of Commerce, employers, and trades unions, all of whom have a valuable role to play in the success of a region's economy.[331]

The Commission, however, considers that the legislation does not fully meet these needs. According to the Commission, the Council wrongly watered down its proposals for greater involvement of the social partners.[332] In particular, the Commission criticized the Council for stipulating that their involvement must take place 'within the framework of each Member State's national rules and current practices' and 'in full compliance with the respective institutional, legal, and financial powers of each of the partners'.[333] The

[326] 'Verification' arrangements are not covered. See Case C–303/90 *France v EC Commission: code of conduct* [1991] ECR I–5315, I–5348.

[327] AG Tesauro, ibid, I–5338.

[328] ibid, I–5349.

[329] Art 4(2) of Reg 2081/93 (OJ 1993 L193/5).

[330] Community Structural Funds 1994–99, COM(93)67, 21.

[331] Address by Bruce Millan at the European League for Economic Cooperation's Conference on 'Developing Europe's Regions after 1992: New Ideas for the New Europe', Cleveland, 10 July 1992 (IP92/563).

[332] Explanatory memorandum to the re-examined proposals of 15 July 1993, COM(93)379, 2.

[333] Art 4(1) of Reg 2081/93 (OJ 1993 L193/5).

result is that the mobilization of regional authorities, social partners, and non-profit-making organizations is often inadequate and always too formal.[334]

The Commission now proposes that operations assisted by the Union funds shall be drawn up in close consultations between the Commission and the Member States, together with the local and regional authorities and other competent authorities, the economic and social partners, and the other competent bodies. Each Member State shall, within its own institutional, legal, and financial system, choose and designate the most appropriate representative partners at national, regional, or other level through as wide an association as possible. Where appropriate, the bodies active in the field of environment and in the promotion of equality between men and women are to be included.[335]

The Member State shall ensure the association of each of the partners. Such association shall cover all stages of programming at the appropriate territorial level. Partnership shall cover the preparation, financing, monitoring, and evaluation of assistance.[336] It is the responsibility of the Member States, as a trade-off for the decentralization of implementation envisaged, to guarantee the broadening of the partnership.[337]

The strengthening of partnership sought through these proposals is expected to render Union assistance more effective and, in particular, to reduce programming problems.[338] However, these proposals still envisage that partnership will respect the 'institutional, legal, and financial system' of each Member State.[339] Moreover, 'in pursuance of the principle of subsidiarity . . . the implementation of assistance shall be primarily the responsibility of the Member States at the most appropriate territorial level'.[340] In fact, Member States 'will maintain a central role and will ensure that national administrative rules are fully respected'.[341] Therefore, even if these proposals are adopted by the Council, regional participation in Union decision making may apparently remain inadequate and too formal.

More radical reforms may be sought. For example, in connection with the Cohesion Fund, the Committee of the Regions considers that 'the regional and local authorities directly concerned [should] play an important part in

[334] Community structural assistance and employment, COM(96)109, 26.

[335] Art 8(1) of the Proposal of 19 Mar 1998 (OJ 1998 C176/1) for a regulation laying down provisions on the Structural Funds.

[336] ibid, Art 8(2).

[337] Explanatory memorandum to the Proposal of 19 Mar 1998 for a regulation laying down provisions on the Structural Funds, COM(98)131, 19–20.

[338] COA annual report 1997 (OJ 1998 C349/1), para 3.16 (Commission reply).

[339] Art 8(1) of the Proposal of 19 Mar 1998 (OJ 1998 C176/1) for a regulation laying down provisions on the Structural Funds.

[340] ibid, Art 8(3).

[341] Explanatory memorandum to the Proposal of 19 Mar 1998 for a regulation laying down provisions on the Structural Funds, COM(98)131, 19.

determining the priorities established by the beneficiary Member States, not only in cases where these authorities have full power to frame or implement the projects within their region, but in all cases'.[342] Similarly, the involvement of social partners at the regional level going beyond 'statutory obligations'[343] is advocated by the European Parliament.

Even in the absence of such reforms, the Commission may still take account of participation by regional bodies in assessing applications for assistance.[344] In particular, the Commission may take account of the involvement of regional and local authorities and the social partners in the preparation of programmes and their implementation in a way appropriate to each Member State.[345] An example is provided by the Notice to the Member States laying down guidelines for the initiative concerning the modernization of the Portuguese textile and clothing industry.[346] According to this Notice, the 'regional and local authorities and the social partners must be involved in the most appropriate manner in the preparation and implementation of the operational programmes'.[347] Moreover, priority may be given to applications for assistance, made in co-operation with regional and local authorities, which include the creation and development of shared institutional or administrative structures.[348]

More generally, it is now proposed that in appraising the development plans submitted by Member States, the Commission will take account of the arrangements made to associate the partners, and of the opinions of the latter.[349] Moreover, the plans must include the results of consultation of the partners and the arrangements made and provisions envisaged to include them.[350]

The European Parliament wishes to go further.[351] In particular, the Parliament favours 'Community framework agreements' with each region.[352]

[342] Opinion of 5 Apr 1994 (OJ 1994 C217/1) on the proposal for a Regulation establishing a Cohesion Fund, para 2.5.

[343] European Parliament Resolution of 3 May 1994 (OJ 1994 C205/101) on the draft notice laying down guidelines for operational programmes or global grants in the framework of a Community initiative concerning the economic conversion of coal-mining areas (Rechar II), para 32.

[344] See eg Notice laying down guidelines for global grants or integrated operational programmes within the framework of a Community initiative concerning the restructuring of the fisheries sector (OJ 1994 C180/1), para VII.17.

[345] Notice laying down guidelines for operational programmes in the framework of a Community initiative concerning the most remote regions (OJ 1994 C180/44), para 14.

[346] OJ 1994 C180/15.

[347] ibid, para V.6.

[348] Para 11 of the Communication laying down guidelines for operational programmes in the framework of a Community Interreg initiative concerning transnational co-operation on spatial planning (OJ 1996 C200/23).

[349] Art 14(2) of the Proposal of 19 Mar 1998 (OJ 1998 C176/1) for a regulation laying down provisions on the Structural Funds.

[350] ibid, Art 15(2)(d).

[351] See the amendments proposed on 20 May 1988 (OJ 1988 C167/443).

[352] Resolution of 22 Jan 1993 (OJ 1993 C42/211) on Community structural policies: assessment and outlook ('mid-term review'), para 15.

Equally, development of the 'Recite model'[353] is favoured by the Parliament.[354] According to Recite, applications for assistance were to be made to the Commission by groups of regional authorities or by international associations representing such authorities at Union level.

The Committee of the Regions, in turn, considers that the final selection of applications for assistance should be made by the Commission and regional authorities.[355] Moreover, applications which have not been endorsed by regional partnerships should, according to the Committee, be rejected.[356] Such demands are partly met in the legislation governing the Poseidom Programme.[357] It requires a guarantee of the active involvement of local, regional, and national authorities in the implementation of this Programme.[358]

National constitutional arrangements

The partnership principle may be undermined by national constitutional arrangements,[359] which may allow the central governments of Member States to 'exercise authority' over regional authorities.[360] The result may be that regional authorities have difficulty implementing strategies inspired by the European Regional Development Fund because of lack of support from national authorities,[361] and Union law does not ensure that such support is provided. More particularly, in the case of efforts to promote transfrontier co-operation for regional development, the Commission may argue that co-operation 'is not served by a series of disjointed projects on either side of the border [and so] emphasis should continue to be given to measures which create and develop lasting frameworks for co-operative action in support of economic development'.[362] However, Union legislation does little to ensure that

[353] See sect 2.4.6 above.

[354] OJ 1993 C42/211, para 32.

[355] Opinion of 15 Mar 1994 (OJ 1994 C217/10) on the draft notice laying down guidelines for operational programmes in the framework of a Community initiative concerning urban areas, para 4.

[356] Opinion of 21 Mar 1996 (OJ 1996 C182/7) on the new regional programmes under Objectives 1 and 2, para 20.

[357] Dec 89/487 (OJ 1989 L239/23) establishing a programme of options specific to the remote and insular nature of the French overseas departments.

[358] ibid, 24th recital in the preamble.

[359] ESC Opinion of 25 Mar 1992 (CES(92)363) on the annual report on the implementation of the reform of the structural funds (1990), 3.

[360] See, regarding the 'structural lack of fit in Britain between the expression and pursuit of regional economic interests and a unitary political process tuned overwhelmingly to national politics', JJ Anderson, 'Business Associations and the Decentralization of Penury: Functional Groups and Territorial Interests' (1991) *Governance* 67–93, 89.

[361] K Dyson, 'Introduction' in K Dyson (ed), *Local Authorities and New Technologies: The European Dimension* (Croom Helm, London, 1988) 1–23. See eg European strategy for encouraging local development and employment initiatives, COM(97)273.

[362] Future of Community initiatives under the Structural Funds, COM(93)282, 14. See, earlier, People living in frontier areas, COM(85)529, 3. Cf the idea of 'regional compacts' co-ordinated at Union level in G Majone, *Market Integration and Regulation: Europe After 1992* (EUI Working Paper, SPS No 91/10; Florence, 1991).

regional authorities are allowed by national law effectively to participate in such measures. At the same time, according to the Commission, while Community initiatives[363] 'can bring the regions and their peoples closer together . . . differences in fiscal and legal systems and in social provisions will continue to influence relations between border regions'.[364] In short, there seems to be a conflict between the present administrative structure, at both national and regional levels, in some Member States and the structures required to implement Union-assisted operations, as envisaged by the Commission and supported by the Committee of the Regions.[365]

For example, the Italian Government has been criticized for laying down centralized guidelines to be followed by regional bodies in the drawing-up of regional development plans.[366] More particularly, Article 5(2) of Regulation 2088/85[367] provided for Integrated Mediterranean Programmes to be 'drawn up at the relevant geographical level by the regional authorities or other authorities designated by each Member State concerned'. According to Article 9 of the same Regulation, their implementation was to be regulated by programme contracts, which were to be concluded between the Commission, Member States, and regional or other designated authorities. In Italy the designated authority was the *regione*.[368] However, according to the *Corte Costituzionale*, the Italian Government could alter the Programmes drawn up by the *regioni.* It could do so, because only the Government had knowledge of the national economy and because the Government took much of the financial burden.[369]

Centralization might go further in the United Kingdom. For example, after West Cumbria was classified as an Objective 2 area, the United Kingdom Government refused to authorize the expenditure by the local authorities concerned which was necessary to 'draw down' the Union assistance, and declined to forward an operational programme to the Commission.[370]

On the other hand, in some Member States constitutional guarantees may have positive effects for the role of regional authorities in the operations of

[363] sect 2.4.6 above.

[364] Future of Community initiatives under the Structural Funds, COM(93)282, 14.

[365] COR Opinion of 11 June 1997 (OJ 1997 C244/19) on the Interreg IIC Community initiative and the potential role for local and regional authorities, para 3.3.4.

[366] Resolution of 22 Nov 1991 (OJ 1991 C326/260) on the Community's regional development activities to assist the Italian regions covered by Objectives 1 and 2, para 4.

[367] OJ 1985 L197/1.

[368] Decree of the President of the Council of Ministers of 1 Feb 1986 (Official Gazette of Italy (1986) No 32, 9). See, generally, G Tesauro, 'Partecipazione delle regioni alla formazione delle decisione comunitarie' in F Cuocolo (ed), *Istituzioni comunitarie e regioni* (Edizione Scientifiche Italiane, Naples, 1991) 37–51.

[369] *Regioni Emilia-Romagna e Liguria v Stato* [1987] Giurisprudenza Costituzionale 2807, 2814.

[370] EEC regional development policy, House of Lords Select Committee on the European Communities, HL(1991–92)20, 16.

the Union funds.[371] Thus partnership is said to operate particularly well in the framework of the 'regional structure' of Germany.[372]

Technical assistance

The effects of differences in national constitutional arrangements may be exaggerated by the impact of Union assistance on resource interdependencies within Member States. On the one hand, administrative burdens are implied for national officials. These burdens can render them more dependent on regional bodies, whose co-operation, information, and organizational capabilities are required to assemble acceptable development plans and Community Support Frameworks or Single Programming Documents.[373] On the other hand, resource deficiencies at the regional level, such as the lack of administrative capacity to develop projects suitable for Union assistance, may be exposed. The result may be that regional actors become even more dependent on national officials.[374] Indeed, it may be argued that the operation of the Union funds has put at the disposal of the central authorities of Member States new, and more refined, financial means to control regional institutions.[375]

Problems of resource deficiencies at regional level are recognized by the Commission and the European Parliament.[376] For example, the Commission considers that implementation of the Integrated Mediterranean Programmes would have been facilitated by the 'strengthening of public administration structures, centrally and regionally, through improved management training, technical support, and information processing'.[377]

The legislation does little to address these problems. The Commission may, according to Article 4(3) of Regulation 2081/93,[378] contribute to the preparation, implementation, and adjustment of operations of the Union funds. It

[371] JJ Hesse and LJ Sharpe, 'Local Government in International Perspective: Some Comparative Perspectives' in JJ Hesse (ed), *Local Government and Urban Affairs in International Perspective* (Nomos, Baden-Baden, 1991) 603–620, 612.

[372] European Parliament Resolution of 22 Jan 1993 (OJ 1993 C42/228) on the regional and social redevelopment plan and the CSF for the areas of Germany included in Objective 2, para 8.

[373] cf Hesse and Sharpe, n 371 above.

[374] JJ Anderson, 'Skeptical Reflections on a Europe of Regions: Britain, Germany, and the ERDF' (1990) *Journal of Public Policy* 417–445.

[375] F Papageorgiou and S Verney, 'Regional Planning and the Integrated Mediterranean Programmes in Greece' in R Leonardi (ed), *The Regions and the European Community: The Regional Response to the Single Market in the Underdeveloped Areas* (Frank Cass, London, 1993) 139–161.

[376] Resolution of 16 Dec 1993 (OJ 1994 C20/179) on the conclusions of the mission of inquiry of the Committee on Budgetary Control into the management and monitoring of the Structural Funds in Italy, para 4.

[377] Annual report on the implementation of the IMPs 1991–92, COM(93)485, 19–20. See, more recently, regarding problems in Italian use of Union assistance, the Commission Reply by Mrs Wulf-Mathies to WQ E-1074/97 (OJ 1998 C21/30) by Roberta Angelilli.

[378] OJ 1993 L193/5.

may contribute by financing preparatory studies and technical assistance locally in agreement with the Member State concerned and, where appropriate, the authorities and bodies designated by Member States. However, it is stipulated that such contributions must be made within the framework of the partnership. The implication is that the position of central institutions of Member States under national law, being a matter of national sovereignty, is not to be prejudiced by the grant of technical assistance. The more general implication of Articles 4(1) and (3) of this Regulation together is that national constitutional law may prevent unwanted interference by regional actors with the outcomes of intergovernmental bargaining in this area.

Again, provision of technical assistance for the social partners at regional level has been suggested,[379] and the Union may already provide financial support for the activities of various bodies. For example, assistance under Article B4–306 of the General Budget[380] may be provided to representative organizations operating in the environmental field.[381] It is recognized that organizations of this kind may play a fundamental role in fostering awareness of environmental problems.[382] In particular, checks on the use of Union funds may be carried out by regional authorities as the result of local public opinion being aroused by such organizations.[383] However, the Commission considers that it has no basis in the existing legislation for demanding their involvement in the partnership.[384]

7.8 JUDICIAL DECISION MAKING

The European Courts have plenary jurisdiction to hear claims that a Member State is in breach of Union law, to review the legality of Union acts or inaction, and to hear claims for compensation against the Union. The Court of Justice also has jurisdiction to deliver preliminary rulings on questions of the meaning and validity of Union law referred to it by national courts. The latter are to apply directly effective provisions of Union law. They are also to provide remedies for violations of Union law.

379 ESC Opinion of 10 July 1996 (OJ 1996 C295/47) on the sixth annual report on the Structural Funds and the new regional programmes under Objectives 1 and 2, para 4.7.

380 See, for 1998, OJ 1998 L44/3.

381 List of organizations having received Community funding for environmental purposes (OJ 1998 C85/3).

382 COA special report 3/92 (OJ 1992 C245/1) concerning the environment, para 2.15.

383 ibid, para 4.2.

384 ibid, para 3.1–5 (Commission reply). See above, p 288, regarding proposed legislative reforms.

7.8.1 *Locus Standi*

If a Member State does not fulfil its obligations under Union law rules governing the Union funds, the Commission has standing to bring proceedings before the Court of Justice under Article 226 of the EC Treaty.[385] A Member State may also challenge the grant or non-grant of Union assistance before the Court under Article 230 or 232 of the Treaty, respectively. Interim measures suspending the relevant Commission decisions may be sought under Article 242.[386]

In particular, at least in the context of operations under the European Social Fund, 'legitimate expectations' regarding the grant of assistance may arise for a Member State. The Court may enforce these expectations against the Commission.[387] Moreover, a Member State participates in the exercise of legislative and budgetary powers and contributes to the General Budget. Therefore, in proceedings before the Court it can rely on the damage which would arise from expenditure being incurred contrary to the rules governing the powers of the Union and its institutions.[388]

Such proceedings must be brought within the period of two months laid down by Articles 230 and 232. This requirement does not apply, however, where the alleged defect in the decision is so serious that, if substantiated, the decision 'would lack any legal foundation in the context of the Community'.[389] Moreover, where the decision in dispute is not published or notified, the period within which proceedings must be instituted cannot start to run until the challenger has precise knowledge of the content and grounds of the act in question.[390] In the absence of publication or notification, it is for the party which learns of a decision concerning it to request the whole text thereof within a reasonable period.[391]

A natural or legal person may also challenge before the Court of First Instance the legality of a decision addressed to him under Article 230, or of a failure to address a decision to him under Article 232. In the latter case there must have been an obligation on the relevant Union institution to act.[392]

385 See eg Case 272/83 *EC Commission v Italy: producer groups* [1985] ECR 1057; and Case 309/84 *EC Commission v Italy: abandonment of vine-growing* [1986] ECR 599. Another Member State may bring proceedings under Art 227 EC.

386 Case T–84/96R *Cipeke—Comércio e Indústria de Papel Lda v EC Commission* [1996] ECR II–1313.

387 Case 84/85 *UK v EC Commission: assistance for part-time employment* [1987] ECR 3765, 3798.

388 Case C–239 & 240/96R *UK v EC Commission: social assistance* [1996] ECR I–4475, I–4492.

389 Joined Cases 6 & 11/69 *EC Commission v France: export aid* [1969] ECR 523, 539.

390 Case T–109/94 *Windpark Groothusen GmbH & Co Betriebs KG v EC Commission* [1995] ECR II–3007, II–3017.

391 Case C–48/96P *Windpark Groothusen GmbH & Co Betriebs KG v EC Commission* [14 May 1998].

392 A-G Roemer in Joined Cases 10 & 18/68 *Società 'Eridania' Zuccherifici Nazionali v EC Commission* [1969] ECR 459, 494.

He may also challenge a decision which, although in the form of a regulation or decision addressed to another person, is of direct and individual concern to him.[393] However, a decision addressed to a Member State may leave the national authorities such a margin of discretion with regard to the manner of its implementation that he cannot be considered directly concerned.[394] Moreover, he will not be considered individually concerned, unless the decision affects him by reason of certain attributes peculiar to him or by reason of circumstances differentiating him from all other persons and distinguishing him individually just as in the case of the person addressed.[395]

Recipients of assistance

Persons whom the Commission has agreed to assist or even persons making an initial application for assistance,[396] at least where they have participated in protracted procedures for evaluation of their application,[397] may have standing to bring proceedings under Articles 230 and 232. Where the Commission refuses payment of assistance which it has previously undertaken to grant, it disputes a prior commitment or denies the existence of the commitment. Thus it adopts an act which has legal effects and may be challenged under Article 230.[398] If the action leads to a declaration that the refusal to make payment is void, the Commission will be obliged, pursuant to Article 233 of the Treaty,[399] to ensure that the payment which has been unlawfully refused is made. If the Commission fails to reply to a request for payment, the same result may be obtained by means of proceedings under Article 232.[400]

For example, a decision reducing assistance from the European Social Fund, though addressed to a Member State, is of direct and individual concern to the recipient. This is because it deprives the recipient of part of the assistance originally granted, the Member State having no discretion in

[393] 'The EC Treaty does not grant individuals the same capacity to act as national law' (AG Roemer, ibid 493).

[394] Case C–181/90 *Consorgan—Gestaõ de Empresas, Lda v EC Commission* [1992] ECR I–3557, I–3568.

[395] Case 25/62 *Plaumann & Co v EEC Commission* [1963] ECR 95, 107.

[396] Case 107/80 *Giacomo Cattaneo Adorno v EC Commission* [1981] ECR 1469; and Case T–478/93 *Wafer Zoo Srl v EC Commission* [1995] ECR II–1479.

[397] Case T–465/93 *Consorzio Gruppo di Azione Locale 'Murgia Messapica' v EC Commission* [1994] ECR II–361, II–373.

[398] cf the argument of the Commission in Case T–585/93 *Stichting Greenpeace Council (Greenpeace International) v EC Commission* [1995] ECR II–2205, II–2217–18 that the payment of assistance was not an act for the purposes of this provision. The CFI did not find it necessary to address this argument (ibid, II–2232).

[399] According to this provision the institution whose act has been declared void or whose failure to act has been declared contrary to this Treaty shall be required to take the necessary measures to comply with the judgment.

[400] Case 44/81 *Germany v EC Commission: deadline for claiming payment of ESF assistance* [1982] ECR 1855, 1874. However, the Commission may lawfully set a deadline for claims for payment of approved assistance to be made (ibid, 1877).

the matter.[401] Hence, the recipient has standing to challenge the legality of the decision under Article 230.

Competitors

A competitor of the recipient of assistance may challenge the legality of a decision to grant the assistance, where his market position has been 'significantly affected' by the assistance.[402] However, the mere fact that a decision may affect competition in the market in question cannot suffice to allow any trader in any competitive relationship whatever with the recipient to be regarded as directly and individually concerned by that decision. Only the existence of specific circumstances gives standing under Article 230.[403] Thus a competitor must be concerned in a particular manner,[404] as for example where he is in the same region as the recipient.[405] Account may be taken of whether the competitor has participated in the proceedings leading to the adoption of the contested decision.[406]

Locus standi requirements may be easier for a competitor to fulfil under Article 33 of the ECSC Treaty. According to this provision, undertakings may challenge 'decisions . . . concerning them which are individual in character'. Thus an undertaking may challenge a Commission decision which entails benefits for one or more undertakings that are in competition with it.[407]

Interest groups

The 'administration of justice' may imply that trade associations should be entitled to bring proceedings, given the 'valuable role' they may play in administrative procedures. In particular, they are in a better position than their individual members to put their sector's case to the Commission.[408] However, trade associations must have a 'personal' interest in bringing proceedings.[409] This condition is not met, unless the association is shown to have an interest which is distinct from the interests of the industrial policy of the

[401] Case T–85/94 *EC Commission v Eugénio Branco Lda* [1995] ECR II–45, II–55.

[402] cf Case 169/84 *Cie Française de l'Azote (COFAZ) SA* v *EC Commission* [1986] ECR 391, 415; and Joined Cases T–447–449/93 *Associazione Italiana Tecnico Economica del Cemento, British Cement Association, Titan Cement Company SA v EC Commission* [1995] ECR II–1971, II–1994–6 and II–2002.

[403] Joined Cases 10 & 18/68 *Società 'Eridania' Zuccherifici Nazionali v EC Commission* [1969] ECR 459, 481.

[404] AG Roemer (ibid, 491). [405] ibid, 492.

[406] Submission of the Commission (ibid, 473).

[407] Joined Cases 24 & 34/58 *Chambre Syndicale de la Sidérurgie de l'Est de la France v ECSC High Authority* [1960] ECR 281, 292; and Joined Cases 172 & 226/83 *Hoogovens Groep BV v EC Commission* [1985] ECR 2831, 2847.

[408] cf AG Slynn in Joined Cases 67, 68 & 70/85 *Kwekereij Gebroeders van der Kooy* [1988] ECR 219, 246. Cf also the view of the EFTA Court in Case E–2/94 *Scottish Salmon Growers Association Ltd v ESA* [1995] 1 CMLR 851, 862.

[409] A-G Roemer in Joined Cases 10 & 18/68 *Società 'Eridania' Zuccherifici Nazionali v EC Commission* [1969] ECR 459, 493.

Member State concerned.[410] Nor is the condition met in the case of an act that has consequences affecting the general interests of the category of persons the association represents.[411] Hence, an association may only bring an action for annulment where its members may also do so individually.[412] Such thinking may be appropriate in the case of trade associations representing the market interests of their members. If the latter interests are not affected, it may be argued that the association itself is not affected.[413]

The same thinking may be more problematic in the case of interest groups other than trade associations. An example is provided by *Stichting Greenpeace Council (Greenpeace International) v EC Commission*.[414] Here assistance from the European Regional Development Fund for the building of two power stations in the Canary Islands was challenged on environmental grounds by local residents and economic operators and by the environmental group, Greenpeace. The Court of First Instance was urged to go beyond consideration of 'purely economic interests' in determining whether the challengers had standing.[415] According to the Court, however, *locus standi* had to be limited to those whose competitive position was significantly affected by a contested decision. This limitation was necessary, in accordance with Article 230, to ensure that only those who were individually concerned by a decision had standing to challenge it.[416] Thus to have standing, it was not enough to be a resident, fisherman, farmer, or tourist in a region where the Union was to assist the construction of a power station.[417]

However, cohesion implies that the relationship between individuals is to be based on more than simply the market. The implication is that individuals should have standing to challenge decisions regarding the grant of assistance which may significantly affect their cohesion prospects. Assistance for building a power station in a coastal region may affect such prospects through, for example, damaging tourism and fishing.[418]

In essence, such damage may result from environmental degradation. Whereas the environment provides assets in the form of natural resources,

[410] Case 282/85 *Comité de Développement et de Promotion du Textile et de l'Habillement v EC Commission* [1986] ECR 2469, 2481.

[411] Joined Cases 16 & 17/62 *Confédération Nationale des Producteurs de Fruits et Legumes* v *EEC Council* [1962] ECR 471, 479–480; and Case T–117/94 *Associazione Agricoltori della Provincia di Rovigo v EC Commission* [1995] ECR II–455, II–466.

[412] Case T–585/93 *Stichting Greenpeace Council (Greenpeace International) v EC Commission* [1995] ECR II–2205, II–2230–1; and Case T–197/95 *Sveriges Betodlares Centralförening and Sven Åke Henrikson v EC Commission* [1996] ECR II–1283, II–1296–7.

[413] cf Joined Cases 67, 68 & 70/85 *Kwekereij Gebroeders van der Kooy* [1988] ECR 219, 268–269; and the EFTA Court in Case E–4/97 *Norwegian Bankers' Association v ESA* [1998] 3 CMLR 281, 290.

[414] Case T–585/93 [1995] ECR II–2205.

[415] ibid, II–2220.

[416] ibid, II–2227.

[417] ibid, II–2229.

[418] cf the argument of AG Cosmas in Case C–321/95P *Stichting Greenpeace Council (Greenpeace International) v EC Commission* [1998] 3 CMLR 1, 52–53 that standing could derive from particular damage to non-market interests suffered by certain individuals.

environmental degradation constitutes a restraint on development.[419] Thus, as the European Parliament has argued, cohesion efforts should be *founded* on the principle of environmentally sustainable development.[420] The inference may be drawn that environmental protection is such an integral element of cohesion that any Union assistance to environmentally harmful investments will damage cohesion prospects for residents.

In accordance with such thinking, it may be argued that groups representing such persons should have standing to challenge decisions regarding operations of the funds before the European Courts. However, Greenpeace was found to have no standing because the interests of its members were not individually affected. The possibility that the credibility and campaigning capacity of Greenpeace might be adversely affected by the denial of standing was apparently disregarded. Certainly, an earlier Opinion of Advocate-General Lenz arguing that an interest group might have standing, even if its members were not individually affected,[421] was disregarded.

Nor was it enough for Greenpeace to have complained to the Commission about the grant of assistance.[422] This was because the legislation governing the Structural Funds did not provide specific procedures for associating such bodies with decisions implementing the European Regional Development Fund.[423] Apparently, then, limitations to judicial intervention were thought to be justified by perceived limitations to the legislation. However, it is questionable whether the latter limitations were correctly perceived. Certainly, the importance attached by the Commission to involvement of the social partners in the 'partnership' required by the legislation suggests that a range of actors, including environmental groups, is to be associated with decisions concerning assistance from the Union funds.[424]

More fundamentally, the ruling conflicts with the view of the European Courts that questions of *locus standi* are to be resolved in the light of the Treaty system and the structure of the Union legal order.[425] The systemic or structural significance of cohesion for *locus standi* questions seems to be neglected by these Courts, when they decide such questions in cases relevant to promotion of cohesion.

[419] Industrial competitiveness and protection of the environment, SEC(92)1986, 11. Note also the link made between environmental policy and cohesion in Art 174(3) EC.

[420] Report of the Committee on Regional Policy, Regional Planning, and Relations with Regional and Local Authorities on the impact of Community regional policy on the environment, EP Doc A3–0170/92.

[421] Case 297/86 *Confederazione Italiana Dirigenti di Azienda* (*CIDA*) *v EC Council* [1988] ECR 3531, 3543.

[422] cf Case T–465/93 *Consorzio Gruppo di Azione Locale 'Murgia Messapica' v EC Commission* [1994] ECR II–361, II–373.

[423] [1995] ECR II–2205, II–2229.

[424] The Commission also declares that the greater involvement of regional institutions in the implementation of Union policies generally is desirable. See Sustainable urban development in the EU: a framework for action, COM(1998)605, 19.

[425] A-G Roemer in Case 25/62 *Plaumann & Co v EEC Commission* [1963] ECR 95, 114–115.

This neglect not only means that the range of cohesion requirements likely to be invoked and, hence, activated and developed in proceedings before the European Courts is narrowed down. The incentive is also reduced for other Union institutions, notably the Commission, to devise procedures consistent with promoting cohesion requirements and learning what the requirements mean for the operations of the Union funds. Even the apparent willingness of these Courts to consider arguments about the effectiveness of Union assistance[426] has reduced significance.

A contrast may be drawn with the case law concerning Commission control of state aid. Here ready recognition that competition is affected by the grant of state aid is reflected in the willingness of the European Courts to admit challenges to the legality of Commission decisions by competitors of aid recipients. Exposure to the possibility of such challenges has led the Commission to employ expert consultants to learn about the issues involved and to articulate its policy through published guidelines.[427] The Treaties now imply that cohesion is no less important in Union law than the common market,[428] but judicial restraint jeopardizes transformation of this implication into practice concerning the operations of the Union funds. True, the Commission may consult experts about applications for Union assistance submitted by individuals.[429] However, the opinions of experts are apparently considered to be of 'technical' rather than 'legal' significance, and so they are not used to articulate cohesion requirements.

The underlying thinking of the Courts is also illustrated by the case law concerning state aid. According to this case law, a distinction may be made between a decision declaring state aid compatible with the common market and a decision declaring it incompatible. Persons who consider themselves adversely affected by a decision of the first type are fully entitled to judicial protection, because the Treaty guarantees them protection against aid which distorts competition. It is not so with persons complaining of a decision of the second type, because the Treaty does not guarantee, but at most tolerates, state aid. In other words, the aid has its source not in the Treaty but in the will of the Member State concerned. Where the Commission considers the aid unlawful, the Member State may or may not challenge the Commission's decision. If it brings a challenge, the interests of the aid-recipients are indirectly protected by this challenge. If the Member State does not bring a

426 Joined Cases C–248 & 249/95 *SAM Schiffahrt GmbH and Heinz Stapf v Germany* [1997] ECR I–4475, I–4505.

427 A Evans, *EC Law of State Aid* (Oxford EC Law Series; Clarendon Press, Oxford, 1997), 408–427.

428 *Agenda 2000*, Bull EC, Supp 5/97, 21.

429 See eg regarding R & D assistance, the Commission Reply by Mrs Cresson to WQ E–1175/96 (OJ 1996 C345/36) by Gerhard Schmid. See, regarding pilot projects assisted by the ERDF, the Commission Reply by Mrs Wulf-Matthies to WQ E–1565/96 (OJ 1996 C345/84) by José Pomés Ruiz.

challenge, either because it considers the decision well founded or because its policy has changed, no one can remedy its lack of will.[430]

Such thinking concentrates on the right to free competition. It does not allow for recognition of the possibility that a right to aid, or at least to assistance from the Union,[431] may derive from the establishment of cohesion as a Union objective. Rather, in the absence of an express basis in Union legislation,[432] the Courts seem reluctant to conceptualize individual rights other than by reference to the competition sought through the common market.[433] Hence, unless market interests are at stake,[434] rights may only arise for individuals from their embodiment in legislation approved by representatives of Member States in the Council. This narrow definition of individual rights apparently may preclude the Courts from recognizing the standing of representatives of cohesion interests.

The approach of the Courts may appear to be a reasonable reflection of Commission concern that there should not be a proliferation of judicial challenges to its decision making.[435] The approach appears more problematic, if regard is had to the 'constitutionalization' of cohesion[436] and to the 'establishment' of Union Citizenship by Article 17 of the EC Treaty.[437] The apparent implication is that Union Citizens should be recognized as having rights to cohesion.[438] The further implication is that these rights should be judicially enforceable[439] and fully taken into account in the operations of Union funds.

As long as these implications remain neglected, the Courts may avoid the need to address the fundamental question of whether the constitutionalization of cohesion means that sovereignty has been transferred beyond the requirements of the common market.[440] At the same time, the function of Treaty provisions governing cohesion as instruments giving effect to the outcomes of intergovernmental bargaining may be unimpaired.

[430] AG Mancini Case 282/85 *Comité de Développement et de Promotion du Textile et de l'Habillement (DEFI) v EC Commission* [1986] ECR 2469, 2474.

[431] Case T–465/93 *Consorzio Gruppo di Azione Locale 'Murgia Messapica' v EC Commission* [1994] ECR II–361, II–373.

[432] cf Case C–321/95P *Stichting Greenpeace Council (Greenpeace International) v EC Commission* [1998] 3 CMLR 1, 38, 69.

[433] cf A Evans, 'Union Citizenship and the Constitutionalization of Equality in European Union Law' in M La Torre, *European Citizenship: An Institutional Challenge* (Kluwer, Deventer, 1997).

[434] cf AG Lenz in Case C–309/89 *Cordoniu SA v EU Council* [1994] ECR I–1853, I–1868, regarding the criterion of 'economic repercussions'.

[435] Case C–312/90 *Spain v EC Commission: Cenemesa* [1992] ECR I–4117, I–4122.

[436] sect 1.7 above.

[437] cf Case T–330/94 *Syndical des Producteurs de Viande Bovine de la Coordination Rurale v EC Commission* [1996] ECR II–1579, II–1589, where the ECJ rejected a claim under Art 288(2) EC based on harm suffered by the applicant 'like any citizen of a member country'.

[438] cf, regarding a right to development as a fundamental right, Scott, n 302 above, 71.

[439] cf, regarding Union Citizenship and equality before the law, AG Lenz in Case C–91/92 *Paola Faccini Dori v Recreb Srl* [1994] ECR I–3325, I–3340.

[440] cf the Commission approach to the question in sects 7.7.5–7 above.

Regional authorities

The Court of Justice has not ruled out the possibility that a decision addressed to a Member State may leave the latter with so little discretion, that it may be of direct concern to regional authorities affected by it.[441] However, a wide circle of persons in the region, including employers, customers, suppliers, and businessmen, may also be affected. Hence, the decision may not easily be regarded as of individual concern to a regional authority.[442]

It has also been argued that a regional authority would have standing to challenge a measure affecting its own prerogatives.[443] However, the Court of Justice apparently recognizes no link between such prerogatives and cohesion requirements. Certainly, the Court infers from cohesion requirements no need to discourage centralization within Member States. For example, according to the Court, 'the Member State is the sole interlocutor of the [European Social] Fund'[444] or at least has a 'central role' in the operations of this Fund.[445] Therefore, while regional authorities may have a vital role to play in the articulation of cohesion requirements, the Court is uncertain about securing such a role for them in judicial proceedings.

A person who lacks standing under Article 230 or 232 may still claim compensation for unlawful action or inaction under Article 288(2) of the Treaty.[446] Strictly speaking, no claim for payment of Union assistance may be brought.[447] Indeed, the Commission once maintained that claims for compensation under Article 288(2) had to be distinguished from 'actions for the provision of benefits' and that the latter were not admissible under this provision.[448] However, the Court of Justice accepts that compensation may be claimed for damage resulting from non-payment of Union assistance.[449] For such compensation to be awarded, there need only be illegality, damage, and a causal link between the two.[450]

441 cf, regarding Commission authorization of state aid, Case 222/83 *Municipality of Differdange v EC Commission* [1984] ECR 2889.

442 AG Lenz (ibid, 2905).

443 Vellano, n 300 above, 194.

444 Case C–291/89 *Interhotel v EC Commission* [1991] ECR I–2257, I–2280. Cf, earlier, Case 310/81 *Ente Italiano di Servizio Sociale v EC Commission* [1984] ECR 1341, 1353. Such case law reflected Commission practice. See eg Communication concerning the procedures laid down by the Member States for the submission of applications for assistance from the ESF and their transmission (OJ 1982 C6/4).

445 Case C–304/89 *Establicementos Isodoro M Oliveira SA v EC Commission* [1991] ECR I–2283, I–2313.

446 Case T–185/94 *Geotronics SA v EC Commission* [1995] ECR II–2795, II–2809. Conversely, the annulment of a measure does not necessarily mean that compensation is payable. See Case T–478/93 *Wafer Zoo Srl v EC Commission* [1995] ECR II–1479, II–1500.

447 Case 44/81 *Germany v EC Commission: deadline for claiming payment of ESF assistance* [1982] ECR 1855, 1874–5.

448 Joined Cases 261 & 262/78 *Interquell Starke GmbH & Co KG and Diamalt AG v EC Council and EC Commission* [1979] ECR 3045, 3050.

449 ibid, 3062.

450 Case C–200/89 *Funoc v EC Commission* [1990] ECR I–3669, I–3695.

Even so, the utility of such proceedings for representatives of cohesion may be limited. The concern of such representatives may be more with the content of decisions regarding the grant of Union assistance than with compensation for the effects of such decisions. However, proceedings for compensation constitute an abuse of procedure, if their real purpose is to secure the withdrawal of a decision which has become definitive.[451]

Opportunities to *intervene* in proceedings before the European Courts may be more generally available to consumer groups,[452] trades unions,[453] regional authorities,[454] and presumably environmental groups. However, an intervener must accept the case as he finds it at the time of his intervention.[455] Hence, he may be precluded from raising arguments of specific relevance to his interests.

7.8.2 Substantive Illegality

According to Article 230, Commission decisions may be annulled on three substantive grounds. First, they may be annulled on grounds of lack of competence. For example, Commission departments are only competent to exercise delegated powers, in the name of the Commission, and, subject to its control, to take clearly defined measures of management or administration. If they adopt a decision concerning the grant of assistance which goes beyond such limits, the decision may be annulled for lack of competence.[456]

Secondly, Commission decisions may be annulled for infringement of the Treaty or of any rule of law relating to its application. For example, they may be annulled for breach of the principles of legitimate expectations and legal certainty.[457] The rationale is that foreseeability as to the payment of assistance is necessary to enable the recipients to commit themselves to expenditure free of the risk of ultimately having themselves to bear the burden of it.[458] Consistent with this rationale, the principles may be more demanding when expenditure has been incurred than when only an application for assistance

[451] Case T–514/93 *Cobrecaf SA v EC Commission* [1995] ECR II–621, II–641.

[452] Joined Cases 41, 43–48, 50, 111, 113 & 114/73 *Société Anonyme Générale Sucrerie v EC Commission* [1973] ECR 1465.

[453] Case 22/74 *Union Syndicale v EC Council* [1975] ECR 401, 410.

[454] Case T–194/95Intv I *Area Cova SA* [1996] ECR II–591.

[455] Art 93(4) of the Rules of Procedure of the ECJ (OJ 1991 L176/7).

[456] Case T–450/93 *Lisrestal—Organizacaõ Gestaõ de Restaurantes Colectivos Lda v EC Commission* [1994] ECR II–1177, II–1191–2. See also Case T–218/95 *Azienda Agricola 'Le Canne' Srl v EC Commission* [1997] ECR II–2055.

[457] Case 15/85 *Consorzio Cooperative d'Abruzzo v EC Commission* [1987] ECR 1005, 1037; and Case T–478/93 *Wafer Zoo Srl v EC Commission* [1995] ECR II–1479.

[458] A-G Darmon in Case C–157/90 *Infortec Projectos & Consultadoria, Lda v EC Commission* [1992] ECR I–3525, I–3354 and in Case C–291/89 *Interhotel v EC Commission* [1991] ECR I–2257, I–2267.

has been made.[459] By the same token, acquired rights, which must usually be respected by the Commission, do not arise from unapproved expenditure or expenditure above the amount approved.[460]

However, in the case of withdrawal of unlawfully granted assistance, there may be conflict between the requirements of the principle of legality and the requirements of the principle of legal certainty.[461] In particular, the former principle may have priority over the latter, where the equality principle would otherwise be violated.[462] In other words, there may be conflict between the 'public interest in legality and the sound management of public funds' and 'the private interest' of the recipient of assistance.[463]

At the same time, decisions must also comply with the principle of equality of treatment.[464] Thus distinctions in the grant of assistance must be based on 'objective' criteria.[465]

However, judicial review must be circumspect where the Commission is judging economic circumstances of fact which involve elements of economic and structural policy;[466] where the Commission is assessing 'complex facts and accounts';[467] or where several Union objectives are relevant and the Commission must make the necessary reconciliation as best it can between the interests entrusted to it. In such circumstances, 'considerable, although not unlimited, discretion' is available to the Commission.[468]

For example, the Commission enjoys such discretion in assessing the existence of conditions justifying the grant of assistance and the 'overriding requirements of the proper administration of Community finances'.[469] It also enjoys such discretion in determining whether expenditure has been properly

[459] Case 44/81 *Germany v EC Commission: deadline for claiming payment of ESF assistance* [1982] ECR 1855, 1877.

[460] A-G Darmon in Case C–304/89 *Establicementos Isodoro M Oliveira SA v EC Commission* [1991] ECR I–2283, I–2298.

[461] A-G Mischo in Case 15/85 *Consorzio Cooperative d'Abruzzo v EC Commission* [1987] ECR 1005, 1025.

[462] Joined Cases T–551/93 & 231–234/94 *Industrias Pesqueras Campos SA, Transacciones Maritimas SA, Recursos Marinos SA, Makuspesa SA v EC Commission* [1996] ECR II–247, II–278.

[463] Submission of the Commission in Case C–200/89 *Funoc v EC Commission* [1990] ECR I–3669, I–3679.

[464] A-G Capotorti in Case 107/80 *Giacomo Cattaneo Adorno v EC Commission* [1981] ECR 1469, 1497–1498, where a breach of Reg 355/77 (OJ 1977 L51/1) was also involved. See also Case T–85/94 *EC Commission v Eugénio Branco Lda* [1995] ECR II–45.

[465] Case 8/57 *Groupement des Hauts Fourneaux et Aciéries Belges v ECSC High Authority* [1957–58] ECR 245, 257

[466] Joined Cases 10 & 18/68 *Società 'Eridania' Zuccherifici Nazionali v EC Commission* [1969] ECR 459, 502.

[467] Case T–142/97 *Eugénio Branco Lda v EC Commission* [15 Sept 1998].

[468] A-G Lagrange in Case 13/57 *Wirtschaftsvereinigung Eisen- und Stahlindustrie Carl Bönnhoff, Gußstahlwerk Witten, Ruhrstahl, and Eisenwerk Annahütte Alfred Zeller v ECSC High Authority* [1957–8] ECR 265, 301.

[469] A-G Da Cruz Vilaça in Case 84/85 *UK v EC Commission: assistance for part-time employment* [1987] ECR 3765, 3781.

incurred by the recipient.[470] Hence, the Court of First Instance cannot undertake a detailed re-examination of an application for assistance during proceedings before it.[471] Even less is it the function of the Court to undertake investigations into the use of assistance of the kind performed by the Court of Auditors.[472]

Nevertheless, a Commission assessment may be overturned where there is found to have been an *erreur manifeste d'appréciation* (clear error of assessment). For example, where it is clear from the description of a project proposed in an application for assistance that the project fits in with the policies adopted to meet Union priorities laid down by the Council, the Commission may commit such an error in refusing assistance.[473]

Finally, a Commission decision may be annulled for a misuse of power.[474] A decision may be annulled on this ground where it appears, on the basis of objective, relevant, and consistent factors, to have been taken with the purpose of achieving ends other than those stated.[475] It may also be annulled on the same ground where it represents a departure, without reasons being given, from 'rules of conduct' regarding the grant of assistance, by which the Commission considers itself to be bound.[476]

7.8.3 Procedural Illegality

The European Courts may, according to Article 230, annul Commission decisions on grounds of procedural illegality, that is, infringement of an essential procedural requirement. Such an infringement may take the form of a failure by the Commission to consult an advisory committee[477] or a management committee,[478] to grant a fair hearing, or to give adequate reasons for its decisions.

470 ECR 3765, 3781, 3797.

471 Case T–109/94 *Windpark Groothusen GmbH & Co Betriebs KG v EC Commission* [1995] ECR II–3007, II–3026; and Case T–465/93 *Consorzio Gruppo di Azione Locale 'Murgia Messapica' v EC Commission* [1994] ECR II–361, II–379.

472 Joined Cases T–551/93 & 231–234/94 *Industrias Pesqueras Campos SA, Transacciones Maritimas SA, Recursos Marinos SA, Makuspesa SA v EC Commission* [1996] ECR II–247, II–307. See, regarding such investigations, A Evans, *A Textbook on EU Law* (Hart Publishing, Oxford, 1998) sect 6.3.1.

473 Case C–213/87 *Gemeente Amsterdam and Stichting Vrouwenvakschool voor Informatica Amsterdam (VIA) v EC Commission* [1990] ECR I–221.

474 Case T–109/94 *Windpark Groothusen GmbH & Co Betriebs KG v EC Commission* [1995] ECR II–3007, II–3026.

475 A-G Mischo in Case 15/85 *Consorzio Cooperative d'Abruzzo v EC Commission* [1987] ECR 1005, 1024–1025.

476 ibid 1016.

477 A-G Da Cruz Vilaça in Case 84/85 *UK v EC Commission: assistance for part-time employment* [1987] ECR 3765, 3788–3789.

478 A-G Mischo in Case 15/85 *Consorzio Cooperative d'Abruzzo v EC Commission* [1987] ECR 1005, 1019.

Fair hearing

Any person who may be adversely affected by a decision should be placed in a position in which he may effectively make known his views on the evidence against him which the Commission has taken as the basis for the decision at issue.[479] For example, 'the Member State is the sole interlocutor of the [European Social] Fund'. Hence, the opportunity for it to comment before a definitive decision to reduce assistance is adopted constitutes an essential procedural requirement the disregard of which renders a decision void.[480]

A private recipient of assistance must also be placed, practical problems notwithstanding,[481] in a position in which he can effectively make known his views on the evidence against him relied on to justify a decision reducing his assistance.[482] In so far as the recipient has not been afforded the opportunity to comment on the evidence, the Commission may not use the evidence in a decision. However, for such an infringement of the right to a fair hearing to result in annulment of the decision concerned, it must be established that, had it not been for that infringement, the decision might have been different.[483]

In the case of applicants for assistance, where hundreds of applications must be evaluated and the selection procedure is conducted on the basis of the documentation submitted by the applicants, the denial of a hearing may be considered reasonable.[484] The underlying idea is that a right to a hearing only arises for an individual, where the Commission contemplates the imposition of a penalty or the adoption of a measure likely to have an adverse effect on his legal position.[485] The Commission also considers that notice to those who have an interest contrary to the grant of assistance is not required.[486]

Reasons

Article 253 of the Treaty requires that regulations, directives, and decisions 'state the reasons on which they are based'. The European Courts are entitled to review, even of their own motion, the statement of reasons for Commission

[479] Case T–450/93 *Lisrestal—Organização Gestão de Restaurantes Colectivos Lda v EC Commission* [1994] ECR II–1177, II–1194.

[480] Case C–291/89 *Interhotel v EC Commission* [1991] ECR I–2257, I–2280; see also Case 310/81 *Ente Italiano di Servizio Sociale v EC Commission* [1984] ECR 1341, 1353. Cf Case C–304/89 *Establicementos Isodoro M Oliveira SA v EC Commission* [1991] ECR I–2283, I–2313.

[481] Case C–32/95P *EC Commission v Lisrestal—Organização Gestão de Restaurantes Colectivos Lda* [1996] ECR I–5373, I–5399.

[482] Case T–109/94 *Windpark Groothusen GmbH & Co Betriebs KG v EC Commission* [1995] ECR II–3007, II–3024.

[483] Case C–142/87 *Belgium v EC Commission: Tubemeuse* [1990] ECR I–959, I–1016. This case was invoked by the Commission in Case T–109/94 *Windpark Groothusen GmbH & Co Betriebs KG v EC Commission* [1995] ECR II–3007, II–3023.

[484] ibid, II–3023.

[485] Case C–48/96P *Windpark Groothusen GmbH & Co Betriebs KG v EC Commission* [14 May 1998].

[486] Joined Cases 10 & 18/68 *Società 'Eridania' Zuccherifici Nazionali v EC Commission* [1969] ECR 459, 476.

decisions challenged before them.[487] The statement must be appropriate to the decision at issue and must not be contradictory.[488] It must disclose in a clear[489] and unequivocal fashion the reasoning of the Commission in such a way as to enable the persons concerned to ascertain the reasons for the decision and to enable the European Courts to carry out their review.[490] Moreover, sufficient detail must be given to alert the Member States and the individuals concerned to the elements of the Commission's reasoning.[491]

The duty of confidentiality imposed on the Commission by Article 287 of the Treaty may offer no defence to a failure to meet these requirements. According to this provision, the Commission must not 'disclose information of the kind covered by the obligation of professional secrecy, in particular, information about undertakings, their business relations or their cost components'. However, this provision cannot be interpreted so broadly that the duty to give reasons is 'deprived of its essential content'. In particular, recipients of assistance, their competitors, and others may not be denied the information needed to ascertain whether a decision is well founded and whether they have an interest in starting legal proceedings.[492] In any case, some relevant facts may manifestly be of a non-confidential nature. At the same time, the entry into force of a decision is not dependent on its publication in the Official Journal pursuant to Article 254 of the Treaty. Hence, information which is confidential can be omitted from the published text.[493]

On the other hand, the question of whether the statement meets the requirements of Article 253 must be assessed with regard not only to its wording. Regard must also be had to the nature of the decision,[494] to its context, and to all the rules governing the matter in question.[495] If, for example, the reduction of assistance has been proposed by the national authorities, which

[487] Case C–304/89 *Establicementos Isodoro M Oliveira SA v EC Commission* [1991] ECR I–2283, I–2312.

[488] A-G Mischo in Case 15/85 *Consorzio Cooperative d'Abruzzo v EC Commission* [1987] ECR 1005, 1023.

[489] Case T–85/94 *EC Commission v Eugénio Branco Lda* [1995] ECR II–45, II–57. See also Case C–181/90 *Consorgan—Gestaõ de Empresas, Lda v EC Commission* [1992] ECR I–3557, I–3569; and Case T–450/93 *Lisrestal—Organizacaõ Gestaõ de Restaurantes Colectivos Lda v EC Commission* [1994] ECR II–1177, II–1197.

[490] A-G Darmon in Case C–157/90 *Infortec Projectos & Consultadoria, Lda v EC Commission* [1992] ECR I–3525, I–3541.

[491] A-G Mischo in Case 15/85 *Consorzio Cooperative d'Abruzzo v EC Commission* [1987] ECR 1005, 1023.

[492] A-G Roemer in Joined Cases 10 & 18/68 *Società 'Eridania' Zuccherifici Nazionali v EC Commission* [1969] ECR 459, 488.

[493] cf Joined Cases 296 & 318/82 *Netherlands and Leeuwarder Papierwarenfabriek BV v EC Commission* [1985] ECR 809, 826. This judgment was invoked by the applicant in Case T–109/94 *Windpark Groothusen GmbH & Co Betriebs KG v EC Commission* [1995] ECR II–3007, II–3020.

[494] Case 181/90 *Consorgan—Gestaõ de Empresas, Lda v EC Commission* [1992] ECR I–3557, I–3569.

[495] Case C–213/87 *Gemeente Amsterdam and Stichting Vrouwenvakschool voor Informatica Amsterdam (VIA) v EC Commission* [1990] ECR I–221, I–222.

have given an explanation to the recipient, it may be sufficient for the Commission to refer with sufficient clarity to the national measure containing that explanation.[496] Again, reasoning requirements may be less demanding in the case of an unsuccessful applicant for assistance, who has incurred no expenditure on the project for which assistance is sought.[497] An applicant for assistance is only entitled to an objective examination of the application in the course of the selection procedure. Special features of the procedure, such as publication of the criteria for eligibility and the participation of committees in the selection of projects, may mean that there is no need for an individual, detailed statement of reasons.[498]

At the same time, the reasoning need not go beyond what is necessary, regard being had to the requirements and constraints inherent in the functioning of the Union institutions.[499] In the determination of what is necessary, account may be taken of whether the person concerned is able to defend sufficiently his point of view before the European Courts. Account may also be taken of whether the ability of these courts to review the lawfulness of the decision has been diminished or impaired.[500] For example, where the addressee of a decision has taken part in the preparation of the decision, a limited statement of reasons may be found to satisfy Article 253. The statement need contain only the indispensable elements which permit the addressee to determine whether the decision is vitiated by a defect.[501]

More particularly, a summarized statement of the reasons for rejecting an application for assistance may be regarded as 'an inevitable consequence of the computerized handling of several thousands of applications for assistance on which the Commission is required to give a decision rapidly'. In such a situation a more detailed statement of reasons in support of each decision would be likely to jeopardize the rational and efficient allocation of the Union assistance.[502]

Such case law may be consistent with the Commission argument that a distinction should be made between the performance of its public service duties (*Leistungsverwaltung*) and the exercise of its prerogatives as a public authority (*Eingriffverwaltung*). According to the Commission, its duty to give

[496] Case T–85/94 *EC Commission v Eugénio Branco Lda* [1995] ECR II–45, II–58.

[497] A-G Darmon in Case C–157/90 *Infortec Projectos & Consultadoria, Lda v EC Commission* [1992] ECR I–3525, I–3541–3542.

[498] Case C–48/96P *Windpark Groothusen GmbH & Co Betriebs KG v EC Commission* [14 May 1998].

[499] A-G Darmon in Case 157/90 *Infortec Projectos & Consultadoria, Lda v EC Commission* [1992] ECR I–3525, I–3541.

[500] A-G Capotorti in Case 107/80 *Giacomo Cattaneo Adorno v EC Commission* [1981] ECR 1469, 1496.

[501] A-G Darmon in Case C–157/90 *Infortec Projectos & Consultadoria, Lda v EC Commission* [1992] ECR I–3525, I–3542.

[502] Case C–213/87 *Gemeente Amsterdam and Stichting Vrouwenvakschool voor Informatica Amsterdam (VIA) v EC Commission* [1990] ECR I–221, I–222.

reasons should be less demanding in relation to the former than in relation to the latter. This is because only the latter limits the rights of those subject to its administration. The assumption of the Commission is that there is no right to Union assistance, and the inference drawn by the Commission is that its refusal causes no damage to applicants.[503]

Thinking of this kind may be reflected in the literature. According to the literature, where action is to benefit individuals in the framework of a largely discretionary policy, judicial control has less of a role than where the action takes place through coercive measures.[504] The underlying idea is that such control is concerned with protecting market interests. The literature thus highlights the difficulty for the market-based thinking which informs the case law to recognize the legal implications of adoption of cohesion as a Union objective.

7.8.4 Court of First Instance

Decision 93/350[505] confers jurisdiction on the Court of First Instance in relation to proceedings brought by private persons under Articles 230 and 232. The aim, particularly in respect of actions requiring close examination of complex facts, is to improve the judicial protection of individual rights. The aim is also to maintain the quality and effectiveness of judicial review in the Union legal order. The latter aim is to be achieved through enabling the Court of Justice to concentrate on its fundamental task of ensuring uniform interpretation of Union law.[506] Hence, the Court of Justice retains jurisdiction in relation to actions brought by Member States and Union institutions and in relation to references for preliminary rulings. There is also a right of appeal for individuals from the Court of First Instance to the Court of Justice on points of law.[507] Generally, the position of such persons is said to have been improved,[508] and it is anticipated that a more critical appraisal of Commission practice may be stimulated.[509]

However, at least in relation to operations of the Union funds, the primary weakness of judicial control lies in a definition of standing which takes no account of cohesion. This weakness is not affected by the work of the Court of First Instance.

[503] cf Case T–109/94 *Windpark Groothusen GmbH & Co Betriebs KG v EC Commission* [1995] ECR II–3007, II–3024.

[504] Priebe, n 5 above, 5.

[505] Amending Dec 88/59 establishing a CFI (OJ 1993 L144/21).

[506] ibid, 8th recital in the preamble.

[507] Art 49 of the Statute of the ECJ.

[508] cf H-J Priess, 'Recovery of Illegal State Aid: An Overview of Recent Developments in the Case Law' (1996) 33 CMLRev 69–91, 86.

[509] cf L Hancher, T Ottervanger, and PJ Slot, *EC State Aids* (Chancery Law Publishing, London, 1993) 15; and FY Jenny, 'Competition and State Aid Policy in the European Community' (1994) 18 *Fordham Int. Law J.* 525–554.

7.8.5 National Courts

National legislation and administrative practice must allow individuals to obtain Union assistance without particular difficulties. Thus the relevant procedures must not be different from those for obtaining national aid[510] and must respect general principles of Union law.[511] National courts may have a role in securing such respect, particularly in connection with interpretation of Union law, the validity of Union decisions, and enforcement.

Interpretation of Union law

Under Article 234(1)(a) of the Treaty, national courts may request preliminary rulings on the interpretation of Union law from the Court of Justice. Such rulings may have importance for the interpretation by Member States of Union law governing the funds. For example, the Court stresses the need for the common agricultural policy to be managed in conditions of equality between traders in the Member States. The inference drawn by the Court is that the national authorities of a Member State should not, by the expedient of a wide interpretation of a Union law provision regarding assistance from the European Agricultural Guidance and Guarantee Fund, favour traders in that Member State to the detriment of those in Member States applying a stricter interpretation.[512] With the help of preliminary rulings national courts may prevent such divergent interpretations.

Validity of Union decisions

Individuals may take proceedings before national courts against national measures implementing a Commission decision. Such courts may refer questions of the validity of the decision being implemented to the Court of Justice under Article 234(1)(b) of the Treaty. There is no requirement in this provision that the decision be of direct and individual concern to the litigant.[513] In considering the validity of the decision, the Court of Justice may apparently have regard to cohesion requirements in the Treaty.[514] A ruling that the decision is invalid means that it cannot provide a defence to the challenge to national implementing action.

However, this procedure only operates where there is a basis in directly effective Union law or in national law for challenging the national action. It seems unlikely that provisions such as Article 158 of the Treaty or many

[510] Priebe, n 5 above, 30.

[511] Joined Cases 201 & 202/85 *Marthe Klensch v Secrétaire d'État à l'Agriculture et à la Viticulture* [1986] ECR 3477, 3507.

[512] Case 11/76 *Netherlands v EC Commission: EAGGF* [1979] ECR 245, 279.

[513] Case T–271/94 *Eugénio Branco Lda v EC Commission* [1996] ECR II–749.

[514] cf, regarding Arts 39 and 40(3) EC and the general principles of proportionality and non-discrimination, Case C–27/97 *Woodspring* v *Nilsea* [1997] ECR I–1847.

provisions of the current legislation governing the Union funds have the characteristics of directly effective provisions.[515] Consequently, the challenge may have to be based on national law.[516] In essence, then, the procedure may merely allow for national law consistent with cohesion requirements to be protected from being undermined by Commission decisions. Thus activation and development of such requirements are left to depend on national law. Therefore, where a narrow definition of individual rights underlies lack of standing in plenary proceedings before the European Courts, this procedure may be unable to compensate for the consequences of lack of standing in such proceedings.

Enforcement

Directly effective provisions of the Treaties and Union legislation are to be applied by national courts, where national authorities grant or deny assistance from the Union funds contrary to such provisions.[517] For example, in *Banfi*[518] the Court of Justice ruled that legal persons could not be denied assistance under Directive 72/159[519] solely because they had assumed a specific legal form. Again, *Omada*[520] concerned cotton-producer groups recognized under Article 2 of Regulation 389/82.[521] The Court ruled that Article 5 of the Regulation obliged Member States to grant such groups assistance for investments included in national programmes to promote cotton production and marketing, which had been approved by the Commission. In both cases national denial of assistance was found to be contrary not only to the relevant Community legislation but also to the prohibition of discrimination in Article 40(2) of the EEC Treaty. Hence, the national courts concerned had to overrule the denial of assistance by their national authorities.

However, Treaty provisions governing cohesion and many of the legislative provisions governing the Union funds may lack the precision necessary for them to be directly effective.[522] As a result, the role of national courts in securing the realization of cohesion requirements may be limited.

True, damages may be awarded by a national court where a Member State, in deciding on the grant of assistance partly financed by the Union funds, has

[515] Evans n 5 above, sect 7.1.

[516] According to A-G Cosmas in Case C–321/95P *Stichting Greenpeace Council* (*Greenpeace International*) *v EC Commission* [1998] 3 CMLR 1, 38, issues of Union financing cannot *per se* be raised before national courts. According to the ECJ itself, rights recognized by Union law may only be indirectly affected by such financing (ibid, 69).

[517] D Comijs, 'Individual Legal Protection under the Structural Funds' (1995) *Maastricht Journal* 187–195.

[518] Case 312/85 *SpA Villa Banfi v Regione Toscana* [1986] ECR 4039, 4055. See, now, Case C–164/96 *Regione Piemonte v Saiagricola SpA* [1997] ECR I–6129.

[519] On the modernization of farms (JO 1972 L96/1).

[520] Case 8/87 *Omada Paragogon Vamvakiou Andrianou-Gizinou & Co v Greece* [1988] ECR 1001, 1014.

[521] On producer groups and associations thereof in the cotton sector (OJ 1982 L51/1).

[522] A-G Warner in Case 152/79 *Kevin Lee v Minister for Agriculture* [1980] ECR 1495, 1514.

violated a Union law provision intended to confer rights on individuals.[523] Thus the grant or denial of assistance contrary to such a provision may be challenged before a national court. However, there is nothing to suggest that the law governing the Union funds is interpreted as being intended to confer rights on individuals other than recipients of assistance and their competitors. Consequently, no provision on which to base the challenge may be available to representatives of cohesion interests.

7.9 CONCLUSION

While all organic Union decision making takes place within the framework of the Treaties, these Treaties embody several 'sub-frameworks' for such decision making. Formally, the sub-frameworks may represent legislative (or 'soft legislative'), budgetary, administrative, or judicial perceptions of Treaty requirements.

Operation of one sub-framework rather than another in any given instance may be assumed to be decisive for the effects of the resulting decisions. For example, according to this assumption, soft law may be seen simply as implementing Council legislation. Again, individual administrative decisions may be seen simply as entailing application of the rules embodied in such legislation. Thus the Commission may distinguish between 'the legislative process and . . . actual execution',[524] while an Advocate-General may distinguish between 'substantive rules of policy and administrative rules.'[525]

In reality, the relationship between the different legal forms is more complicated. It may, in fact, be of a horizontal rather than vertical kind, with cohesion requirements established pursuant to adoption of one legal form articulating the requirements established pursuant to adoption of another such form.[526] An example is provided by the Communication laying down guidelines for operational programmes or global grants within the framework of the Community initiative on Employment and the Development of Human Resources.[527] According to paragraph 8 of the Communication, all eligible measures which may be financed under this initiative are listed in the Communication. In other words, they are listed in soft law. However, when

[523] cf Case C–66/95 *R v Secretary of State for Social Security, ex p Eunice Sutten* [1997] ECR I–2163, I–2191.

[524] Explanatory memorandum to the Proposals of 15 Oct 1979 for regulations instituting specific Community regional development projects under Art 13 of the ERDF Regulation, COM(79)540, 12.

[525] A-G Verloren van Themaat in Case 44/81 *Germany v EC Commission: deadline for claiming payment of ESF assistance* [1982] ECR 1855, 1885.

[526] cf regarding the 'recursive interaction' of Commission practice and decision making by the European Courts, F Snyder, 'Soft Law and Institutional Practice in the European Community' in S Martin (ed), *The Construction of Europe* (Kluwer, Deventer, 1994) 197–225.

[527] OJ 1996 C200/13.

preparing their proposals for operational programmes or for global grants, which are to be adopted by individual administrative decisions, Member States are invited to select, in co-operation with the Commission, a more limited list of measures on which to concentrate financial assistance. Thus successive opportunities for negotiation and renegotiation may be entailed by organic Union decision making.

However, the various sub-frameworks are such that the negotiation and renegotiation may be essentially limited to interests expressed by the Commission and national governments. Thus the resulting law may reflect relations in which regional actors have little opportunity to contribute to the articulation of cohesion requirements.[528] Even the European Parliament may object that its decision-making role in this field is more limited than in other fields.[529]

It is recognized that this situation is unsatisfactory and that Commission efforts alone may be unable to maximize the potential of the Union funds for strengthening cohesion. In particular, there is felt to be a risk that the Union will fail to secure the full benefits of the funds. It may fail to do so because of lack of care, lack of available resources to provide proper project monitoring, or the absence of a satisfactory administrative process for evaluating results.[530] The implication is that development of pluralistic, decentralized control of the operations of the funds may be necessary. However, the organic decision-making procedures of the Union are not favourable to such control.

The problems may be highlighted, if reference is made to public-choice theory. According to such theory, 'a systematic introduction of all affected interest groups and sectors into the decision-making process may improve the outcome of the political process'.[531] The practical implications of such theory may be reflected in demands made by the European Parliament. For example, according to the Parliament, the very nature of regional development is such as to render it dependent on participation in decision making by the public through their elected representatives at all levels.[532]

[528] cf European Parliament Resolution of 5 Sept 1996 (OJ 1996 C277/29) on the sixth annual report on the Structural Funds in 1994, para 9. See, more particularly, the Resolution of 5 Sept 1996 (OJ 1996 C277/40) on development problems and structural measures under Objectives 1, 2, and 5b in Spain (1994–99), para 10.

[529] cf the Code of conduct on the implementation of structural policies by the Commission (OJ 1993 C255/19), which was designed to improve arrangements for consultation of the Parliament.

[530] COA special report 3/92 (OJ 1992 C245/1) concerning the environment, para 1.21.

[531] M Teutemann, *Completion of the Internal Market: An Application of Public Choice Theory* (Economic Papers No 83; EC Commission, Brussels, 1990), 37.

[532] European Parliament Resolution of 12 Oct 1977 (OJ 1977 C266/35) on the guidelines for Community regional policy, para 10.

8

Intergovernmental Procedures

8.1 INTRODUCTION

The role of intergovernmental procedures in Union decision making reflects the original constitution of the European Communities[1] and the European Union[2] by the Member States. The natural implication of their constitution is that there were opportunities for intergovernmental bargaining (that is, bargaining between Member States, or 'intergovernmental exchange'[3]) during the drafting of the Treaties.

Further opportunities for such bargaining may derive from the express terms of the constituent Treaties.[4] These opportunities may arise in the context of the 'broadening' of integration. For example, Accession Acts[5] and agreements with third states (that is, non-member states) which involve matters left at least partly within the competence of the Member States[6] must be unanimously accepted by the latter. Similar opportunities may arise in the context of the 'deepening' of integration. For example, changes in the legal framework which are perceived as going beyond incremental implementation of the constituent Treaties and as demanding their amendment must be similarly accepted.[7] Whether the broadening or deepening of integration is involved, these unanimity requirements entail opportunities for recasting previous bargains through intergovernmental procedures.

The outcomes of such procedures may take the form of Treaty amendments, as in the case of the Single European Act[8] and the Treaty on European Union, Accession Acts, or protocols or declarations thereto. They may also take the form of resolutions of the representatives of the governments of the Member States. They may even take the form of unpublished undertakings, the existence of which can only be inferred from the context in which more formal acts are adopted.

[1] Art 1 EEC.

[2] Art 1 TEU.

[3] S Levine and PE White, 'Exchange as a Conceptual Framework for the Study of Interorganizational Relationships' (1961) 16 *Administrative Science Quarterly* 583–601.

[4] In particular, the EC Treaty and the TEU.

[5] Art 49 TEU.

[6] See eg Art 300(5) and (6) EC.

[7] Art 48 TEU.

[8] OJ 1987 L169/1.

8.2 EMU RESOLUTIONS

The deepening of integration envisaged in early plans for economic and monetary union apparently rendered the need to add to the existing two Structural Funds a pressing matter.[9] Thus in March 1971 a Resolution of the Council of Ministers and representatives of the governments of Member States on monetary union recognized that regional policy was a matter of Community interest.[10] More particularly, in a Resolution of March 1972,[11] also on monetary union, it was envisaged that the European Agricultural Guidance and Guarantee Fund could be used from 1972 for regional development actions. Moreover, it was envisaged that a Regional Development Fund should be created or 'some other system of Community resources' should be established for regional development purposes.

The Paris Summit Conference of October 1972[12] confirmed that a Regional Development Fund was 'needed to correct the structural and regional imbalance which might affect the realization of economic and monetary union'. Accordingly, the Member States not only assigned the Commission the task of drawing up a report analysing regional problems in the Community and of submitting appropriate proposals for dealing with such problems. They also committed themselves to co-ordinating their national regional policies and asked the Community institutions to create a Regional Development Fund, to be operational by 31 December 1973.

The underlying concern was expressed in the *Report on the Regional Problems in the Enlarged Community*. According to this Report, no Member State could be expected to support the disciplines of monetary union without Community solidarity involving the effective use of such a fund. Equally, Member States had to be prepared to accept the disciplines of monetary union as a condition for assistance from the fund.[13]

The Commission responded with proposals[14] for a Regional Development Fund,[15] a list of regions to be eligible for assistance from the Fund,[16] a

[9] See, generally, regarding EMU and the ERDF, E Faure and G Gelée, 'L'Union économique et monétaire et les déséquilibres régionaux' (1979) RMC 481–489; and T Buck, 'Regional Policy and European Integration' (1975) 16 JCMS 368–378.

[10] Resolution of 22 Mar 1971 (JO 1971 C28/1) on the achievement of EMU within the Community in stages, sect 1.

[11] Resolution of 21 Mar 1972 (JO 1972 C38/3) on the application of the resolution of 22 Mar 1971, sect 2.

[12] Bull EC 10–1972, 18–19.

[13] Bull EC, Supp 8/73, 8.

[14] See, generally, J van Gundesachter, 'La Politique régionale de la Communauté, justifications, modalités, et propositions' (1973) RMC 468–486.

[15] Proposal of 31 July 1973 (OJ 1973 C86/7) for a regulation establishing a Regional Development Fund.

[16] Proposal for a regulation on the list of regions and areas referred to in the Regulation establishing an ERDF, COM(73)1751.

Regional Policy Committee,[17] and a Financial Regulation.[18] The Commission maintained in the explanatory memorandum to its proposal for the Fund[19] that Community assistance was intended 'to implement regional development policies faster than Member States could alone, taking account of the discipline which economic and monetary union [would] impose on the use of their own resources'.

The undertaking to establish the Fund was reiterated at the December 1973 Summit,[20] and the December 1974 Summit decided, at Irish and Italian insistence,[21] that it should be established from 1 January 1975.[22] The European Regional Development Fund was finally established by Regulation 724/75 of 18 March 1975,[23] the preamble referring to the Summit Conference of October 1972.[24] Thus a major step in the development of the Structural Funds originated in the demands of 'loser' Member States. They demanded compensation for problems which they might face in the deepening of integration sought through economic and monetary union.

However, the Fund might not have been ideally adapted to this purpose. Thus subsequent monetary union proposals, of 1978,[25] had to be supplemented by a preamble approving 'concurrent studies' of action that might be needed to strengthen the economies of the less prosperous Member States.[26] The European Council meeting of 5 December 1978 duly agreed on measures to strengthen the economies of less prosperous Member States participating in the monetary union.[27] Accordingly, a 'facility' was established by Regulation 1736/79.[28] The facility took the form of Community interest subsidies on European Investment Bank loans in such Member States.[29]

[17] Draft decision of 31 July 1973 (OJ 1973 L86/11) on the creation of a Committee for Regional Policy.

[18] Proposal of 31 July 1973 (OJ 1973 C86/12) for a Financial Regulation concerning special provisions to be applied to the ERDF.

[19] COM(73)1170.

[20] para 7(iii) of the Communiqué (Bull EC 12–1973, 10).

[21] Ireland and Italy had threatened to boycott the Summit unless agreement was reached on the ERDF. See S George, *Politics and Policy in the European Union* (Oxford University Press, 3rd edn, 1996) 234.

[22] para 22 of the Communiqué (Bull EC 12–1974, 10).

[23] Establishing an ERDF (OJ 1975 L73/1). See, generally, P Romus, 'La Création du Fonds européen de développement régional: Début de la politique régionale européenne' (1975) RMC 149–157.

[24] 6th recital in the preamble to Reg 724/75 (OJ 1975 L73/1).

[25] Bull EC 4–1978, 1.2.2; and Bull EC 6–1978, 1.5.2.

[26] para 2 of the Conclusions of the Presidency (ibid). See also S Weber and H Wiesmeth, 'Issue Linkage in the European Community' (1991) 29 JCMS 255–267.

[27] Bull EC 12–1978, 1.1.11, para B. 3.

[28] On interest subsidies for certain loans granted under the EMS (OJ 1979 L200/1).

[29] ibid, Art 1.

8.3 SINGLE EUROPEAN ACT

Completion of the internal market, as sought by the Single European Act of 1987,[30] was seen as requiring 'accompanying' action to strengthen cohesion. In effect, liberalization efforts, particularly provision for greater use of majority voting in the Council on matters related to completion of the single market,[31] increased the demands for interventionist action by the Community.

8.3.1 Increased Finance

The sums made available for intervention by the Structural Funds had increased considerably from those originally provided. Nevertheless, they still constituted a small proportion of comparable national expenditure. More particularly, the sums had not been increased proportionately to the problems created by the accession of Portugal and Spain. Their accession meant that the number of people living in regions with a per capita gross domestic product amounting to less than 75 per cent of the Community average was doubled. Yet, European Regional Development Fund resources had increased in real terms by a mere 34 per cent. The spending of the European Social Fund had kept up more closely with increased demands. However, a large part of the increase in its spending in 1987 was apparently due to a change in accounting practices.[32]

The need further to increase the resources of the Structural Funds was recognized in a Declaration annexed to the Single European Act.[33] According to this declaration, the resources available to the Funds, having regard to the Integrated Mediterranean Programmes, would be significantly increased in real terms within the limits of financing possibilities. At its February 1988 meeting the European Council duly agreed that the resources of the Funds should be doubled by 1993. More particularly, the resources devoted to promoting the development and structural adjustment of the less developed regions should be doubled by 1992.[34] Effectively, however, this agreement seems to have been as much a belated response to the consequences of enlargement as a recognition of the effects which efforts to complete the internal market might have in such regions.

In any case, the mere transfer of resources might not constitute an adequate response to cohesion problems. Such transfers might improve the national budgetary situation. However, they would not necessarily assist disadvan-

30 OJ 1987 L169/1.

31 P Bianchi, 'La Réorientation des politiques structurelles dans la CEE' (1991) RMC 599–603, 600.

32 P Lowe, 'The Reform of the Community's Structural Funds' (1988) 25 CMLRev 503–521.

33 On Art 130d EEC.

34 Bull EC 2–1988, 1.1.1.

taged regions in making the best use of their resources, a requirement which was considered necessary for effective promotion of cohesion.[35]

8.3.2 Treaty Amendments

Articles 130a to 130e of the EEC Treaty were introduced by the Single European Act.[36] They provided a new legal framework for co-ordination of the Structural Funds and other financial instruments in support of cohesion, and created for the European Regional Development Fund a specific legal basis in the Treaty.

The Commission had proposed that the new provisions should refer to improvement of living conditions and conditions of work and employment of the peoples of the Member States. However, Italy and the 'cohesion states'[37] preferred the emphasis to be on regional development. As a result, the provisions actually introduced, though they might be said to have recognized the interest of all regions in completion of the internal market,[38] concentrated on reduction of regional disparities.[39]

Apparently, the thinking of these Member States was that exposure of their less developed regions to increased competition would be associated with completion of the internal market. Such exposure would present their national economies with problems not faced by other Member States. At the same time, an 'economic downturn' in these regions would entail national budgetary losses not faced by other Member States. Hence, they demanded Community resources to equalize (to some degree, at least) their financial capacity to pursue interventionist policies in these regions.

In other words, the Union funds were 'to assist the [Member States] to reach their objectives during the process of integration'.[40] In particular, it was said that the 'mismatch between the severity of a country's regional problems and its ability to fund it suggest[ed] a distinctive role' for these funds.[41] However, the EEC Treaty amendments did not guarantee that financial transfers between Member States through the Union funds would really be used in such a way as to reduce disparities between regions.[42]

[35] cf AJ Marques Mendes, 'Economic Cohesion in Europe: The Impact of the Delors Plan' (1990) 29 JCMS 17–36.

[36] OJ 1987 L169/1.

[37] ie Greece, Ireland, Portugal, and Spain.

[38] B Hessel and K Mortelmans, 'Decentralized Government and Community Law: Conflicting Institutional Developments' (1993) 30 CMLRev 905–937, 921.

[39] JA Valle Galvez, 'La cohesion economica y social como objetivo de la Union europea: Analisis e perspectivas' (1994) *Revista de Instituciones Europeas* 341–378, 346.

[40] T Georgakopoulos and T Hitiris, 'The Community Budget and 1992' in D Gowland and S James (eds), *Economic Policy after 1992* (Dartmouth, Aldershot, 1991) 126–146, 127.

[41] HW Armstrong and J Taylor, *Regional Economics and Policy* (Harvester Wheatsheaf, 2nd edn, London, 1993), 286.

[42] A Cutler, C Haslam, J Williams, and K Williams, *1992—the Struggle for Europe* (Berg, New York, 1989) 79.

8.4 TREATY ON EUROPEAN UNION

Negotiation of the Treaty on European Union gave fresh impetus to discussion of the role of the Union funds. The convergence criteria for adoption of a single currency[43] were expected to restrict the redistributive and the stabilizing roles traditionally played by national budgets through the manipulation of domestic fiscal and monetary policies. At the same time, regional disparities were an obstacle to sustained growth in the Union as a whole. They also made it more difficult for the Union to strengthen its role on the world stage and to co-ordinate Member States' economic policies. In these circumstances, a greater role was demanded of the Union funds, especially by the less developed Member States.[44] The Treaty went some way towards securing such a role for these funds.

8.4.1 Provisions of the Treaty on European Union

According to the preamble to the Treaty on European Union,[45] the Member States are determined to promote economic and social progress for their peoples. They will do so within the context of the accomplishment of the internal market and of reinforced cohesion and environmental protection. They are also determined to implement policies ensuring that advances in economic integration are accompanied by parallel progress in other fields. Hence, Article 1 of the Treaty provides that the task of the Union 'shall be to organize, in a manner demonstrating consistency and solidarity, relations between the Member States and between their peoples'.[46] Moreover, the objectives of the Union, as outlined in Article 2, include promoting economic and social progress which is balanced and sustainable. Such progress is to be promoted through, in particular, the creation of an area without internal frontiers, the strengthening of cohesion, and the establishment of economic and monetary union, ultimately including a single currency.

8.4.2 EC Treaty Amendments

Article 8 of the Treaty on European Union introduced various amendments to the EC Treaty. Article 2 of the latter Treaty now provides that the European Community shall have as its task, by establishing a common market and an economic and monetary union and by implementing the common

[43] Art 109j(1) EC and the Protocol on the convergence criteria.
[44] ESC Opinion of 30 Apr 1992 (OJ 1992 C169/34) on the Commission document 'From the Single Act to Maastricht and beyond—the means to match our ambitions', para 1.2.1.
[45] 7th recital in the preamble to the TEU.
[46] See also Community structural policies: assessment and outlook, COM(92)84.

policies or activities referred to in Articles 3 and 4, to promote throughout the Community a harmonious, balanced, and sustainable development of economic activities; a high level of employment and social protection; equality between men and women; sustainable and non-inflationary growth; a high degree of competitiveness and convergence of economic performance; a high level of protection and improvement of the quality of the environment; the raising of the standard of living and quality of life; economic and social cohesion; and solidarity among Member States. Hence, Article 3(k) includes among the activities of the Community the strengthening of cohesion. The latest proposals of the Commission are said to be inspired by the principles stressed in these provisions.[47]

8.4.3 Protocol on Economic and Social Cohesion

A Protocol on Economic and Social Cohesion, annexed to the EC Treaty, envisages greater flexibility in the operation of the Structural Funds than was previously available. According to this Protocol, the Member States declare their intention of allowing a greater margin of flexibility in allocating assistance from the Structural Funds to specific needs not covered by existing legislation on these Funds.[48] Moreover, they declare their willingness to modulate the levels of Union participation in programmes and projects of the Structural Funds. They will do so, with a view to avoiding excessive increases in budgetary expenditure in the less prosperous Member States.[49]

At the same time, Member States agree that the Cohesion Fund[50] will provide assistance to projects in the fields of environment and trans-European networks in Member States meeting two conditions. First, their per capita gross national product must be less than 90 per cent of the Union average. Secondly, they must have a programme leading to the fulfilment of the convergence criteria.[51]

According to this Protocol and Article 161 of the EC Treaty, the Cohesion Fund has been established.[52] By agreeing to the creation of this Fund, the Member States sought to achieve two ends. First, they sought to meet the demands for compensation for accepting the deepening of integration

[47] Explanatory memorandum to the Proposal of 19 Mar 1998 for a regulation laying down provisions on the Structural Funds, COM(98)131, 13.

[48] para 16 of the Protocol.

[49] ibid, para 17. Note also the declaration of the European Council of Dec 1992 (Bull EC 12–1992, I.53–5). This declaration and the TEU were taken into account in the 1993 reforms, though the reforms were based on Art 130d EEC. In particular, Art 1(d) of Reg 4254/88 (OJ 1988 L374/15) laying down provisions for implementing Reg 2052/88 as regards the ERDF was amended by Reg 2083/93 (OJ 1993 L193/34), to extend the tasks of the ERDF to cover operations related to education and health in Objective 1 regions.

[50] sect 6.5 above.

[51] para 15 of the Protocol.

[52] Reg 1164/94 (OJ 1994 L130/1) establishing a Cohesion Fund.

associated with monetary union which were made by the 'cohesion states'.[53] Secondly, they sought to avoid prejudicing the evolution of the Structural Funds.[54]

8.4.4 Declaration on the Outermost Regions

A Declaration on the Outermost Regions of the Union was adopted with the Treaty on European Union. In this Declaration the Member States acknowledge that the French overseas departments, the Azores and Madeira, and the Canary Islands suffer from major structural backwardness.[55] This problem is compounded by several phenomena (remoteness, island status, small size, difficult topography and climate, and economic dependence on a few products). The permanence and combination of these phenomena severely constrain the economic and social development of these regions.[56] To overcome these constraints, specific assistance should be provided. Such assistance should recognize the 'regional reality' and seek to enable the outermost regions to achieve the average economic and social level of the Union.[57]

Legislation governing the operations of the Union funds may reflect such thinking. For example, provision has been made for the outermost regions to enjoy '*ad hoc* derogations' from the restrictions which otherwise apply to Union assistance to improve the processing and marketing of agricultural and forestry products.[58]

8.5 ACCESSION ACTS

The deepening of integration and its broadening, as entailed by Accession Acts, may have mutually reinforcing effects on the evolution of the Union funds. This possibility is suggested by the apparent impact of arrangements agreed in accession negotiations.

[53] Spain argued that moves towards EMU and political union should be accompanied by creation of an 'inter-statal compensation fund'. See the *Financial Times*, 12 Mar 1991.

[54] Y Doutriaux, *Le Traité sur l'Union européenne* (Armand Colin, Paris, 1992) 152.

[55] See also the Declaration on island regions, adopted with the Amsterdam Treaty (OJ 1997 C340/1).

[56] See also Reg 2019/93 (OJ 1993 L184/1) introducing specific measures for the smaller Aegean islands, concerning certain agricultural products; and the 1995 Report on progress in implementation of the specific measures for the smaller Aegean islands, COM(98)292.

[57] The Poseidom, Poseican, and Poseima programmes had already been adopted for these regions. See sect 6.7.4 above.

[58] Dir 94/73 (OJ 1994 L79/29) on the selection criteria to be adopted for investments for improving the processing and marketing conditions for agricultural and forestry products and repealing Dec 90/342, Art 1(2).

8.5.1 First Accession Act

In accession negotiations the United Kingdom demanded financial transfers from the Community to compensate it for the costs of implementing the common agricultural policy.[59] Such compensation was demanded, because the allocation of these costs between Member States was dependent on the degree of national self-sufficiency in key, regulated products rather than on relative national wealth.[60] Italy also demanded transfers, because this policy was felt to be less favourable to its farmers than to northern European farmers.[61] The magnitude of these compensation demands may have rendered 'side-payments' alone inadequate and required policy reformulation,[62] or 'forced spillover'. Such spillover occurs, when 'the prospect of a breakthrough in one arena create[s] intense pressure for innovation in others'.[63] Establishment of the European Regional Development Fund may have been designed partly to meet this requirement. However, its establishment may have been rendered feasible only by the concern of stronger Member States to secure participation by weaker Member States in economic and monetary union.[64]

Other demands may have been met by less radical reforms. In particular, a Declaration on hill farming in the United Kingdom was attached to the Accession Act.[65] The Declaration recognized that the special conditions in certain regions of the enlarged Community might require action to resolve the problems raised by these conditions. In particular, action might be required to maintain reasonable incomes for farmers in such regions. The result was the enactment of Directive 75/268.[66] This measure provided for the grant of assistance from the Guidance Section of the European Agricultural Guidance and Guarantee Fund to hill farmers and farmers in less favoured areas.[67]

[59] G McCrone, *Regional Policy in Britain* (Allen & Unwin, London, 1969) 248.

[60] J-V Schrader, 'EC Agricultural and Regional Policy: Consistent Interventions or Cumulative Inconsistencies' (1989) *Inter-Economics* 167–173, 170.

[61] C André, J-F Drevet, and E Landaburu, 'Regional Consequences of the Internal Market' (1989) *Contemporary European Affairs* 205–214; and P Cheshire, R Camagni, J-P de Gaudemaar, and JR Cuadrado Roura, '1957 to 1992: Moving toward a Europe of Regions and Regional Policy' in L Rodwin and H Sazanami (eds), *Industrial Change and Regional Economic Transformation: The Experience of Western Europe* (Harper Collins Academic, London, 1991) 268–300, 279.

[62] cf H Wallace, 'The Best is the Enemy of the "Could": Bargaining in the European Community' in S Tarditi, KJ Thompson, P Pierani, and L Croci-Angelini (eds), *Agricultural Trade Liberalization and the European Community* (Clarendon Press, Oxford, 1989) 193–206.

[63] G Marks, 'Structural Policy in the European Community' in AM Sbragia (ed), *Europolitics: Institutions and Policymaking in the 'New' European Community* (Brookings Institution, Washington, 1992) 191–224.

[64] George, n 21 above, 233.

[65] JO 1972 L73/14.

[66] On mountain and hill farming and farming in less favoured areas (OJ 1975 L128/1).

[67] It was preceded by a Council Resolution of 15 May 1973 (OJ 1973 C33/1) on farming in certain less favoured areas.

8.5.2 Second Accession Act

Community enlargement might require not only new bargains to accommodate the demands of acceding states. It might also require revision of previous bargains between existing Member States to take account of the consequences of enlargement for the latter. The need to take account of such consequences was recognized before Greek accession. In particular, it was recognized that the less developed regions of existing Member States might find it difficult to cope with new competitors.[68] The conclusion drawn was that increased resources should be allocated to the European Regional Development Fund.[69] They should be used, in particular, to tackle any new problems that might arise as a result of enlargement.[70]

However, quota shares in the Fund were merely modified to take account of Greek accession by Regulation 3325/80.[71] The modifications followed the Declaration of the EEC on the European Regional Development Fund attached to the Accession Act.[72] At the same time, a specific Community regional development measure was established by Regulation 2615/80.[73] This measure assisted certain French and Italian regions likely to be adversely affected as a result of Greek accession.[74]

8.5.3 Third Accession Act

The third enlargement of the Community was expected to expose weaker regions of the existing Community to increased competition. It was also expected substantially to increase the magnitude of the Community's regional problems, since many regions of Spain and Portugal would qualify, according to existing criteria, as having such problems.[75] The implication was that the European Regional Development Fund would have to be strengthened accordingly.

[68] *Fourth Annual Report on the ERDF* (EC Commission, Brussels, 1979) 56.

[69] ESC Opinion of 21 Nov 1981 (OJ 1981 C346/9) on the ERDF fourth annual report, para 9.

[70] The ESC subsequently observed that the demands of the acceding countries for ERDF assistance and budgetary constraints would mean that less ambitious regional plans might have to be accepted in the existing Member States. Acknowledgement might also be necessary by those Member States whose scale of regional problems was less serious and enduring that strict priorities for Fund assistance would have to be adopted. See the Opinion of 30 Apr 1980 (OJ 1980 C205/22) on the regional development programmes, para 5.7.

[71] Amending Reg 724/79 (OJ 1980 L349/10).

[72] OJ 1979 L291/190.

[73] Instituting a specific Community regional development measure contributing to the development of certain French and Italian regions in the context of Community enlargement (OJ 1980 L271/1).

[74] ibid, 9th and 10th recitals in the preamble.

[75] *Second Periodic Report on the Social and Economic Situation of the Regions of the Community* (EC Commission, Brussels, 1984) 151.

ERDF allocations

The preamble to Regulation 2615/80[76] recognized that the southern regions of the Community could be affected by enlargement. These regions were particularly likely to be affected because of increased competition in markets for certain agricultural products and because of problems involved in adapting their economic fabric.[77] The interests of the Community required that the enlargement process should take place harmoniously. Therefore, it was necessary, even before the accessions of Portugal and Spain became effective, to undertake vigorous structural measures to enable the Mezzogiorno and the three French regions adjacent to Spain to adapt to enlargement.[78] Similarly, Regulation 215/84[79] sought to assist certain Greek regions likely to be adversely affected by enlargement. However, these measures did not affect the overall amount of resources available to the European Regional Development Fund.

At the same time, the new Member States attached importance to the Structural Funds, primarily the European Regional Development Fund. Pre-accession assistance had been allocated to Portugal under Regulation 3323/80[80] and Regulation 3598/84,[81] and the Commission noted the need for extra assistance to follow Portuguese accession.[82] However, in a Declaration annexed to the Accession Act[83] the Community merely undertook to amend Regulation 1787/84[84] before accession. It would merely amend this Regulation, in order to fix the upper and lower limits of the Fund allocations for the two new Member States. This commitment was fulfilled through Regulation 3641/85,[85] which fixed the limits for Portugal and Spain and correspondingly reduced the limits for the other Member States. In addition, Portugal could benefit until the end of 1990 from rates of assistance (up to 70 per cent)[86] above those normally permitted by Regulation 1787/84.[87] However, the overall resources available to the Fund for 1986 were insufficient either to maintain level funding for the existing Member States or to secure for Portugal and Spain the amounts proposed by the Commission.[88]

76 OJ 1980 L271/1.

77 ibid, 10th recital in the preamble.

78 ibid, 12th recital.

79 Instituting a specific Community measure contributing to the development of certain regions of Greece in the context of Community enlargement (OJ 1984 L27/5).

80 On the conclusion of the agreement in the form of an exchange of letters with Portugal concerning the implementation of pre-accession aid for Portugal (OJ 1980 L349/1).

81 On the conclusion of the agreement in the form of an exchange of letters with Portugal concerning the implementation of pre-accession aid for Portugal (OJ 1984 L333/7).

82 *Problems of Enlargement: Taking Stock and Proposals*, Bull EC, Supp 8/82, 10.

83 Declaration by the EEC on the participation of Spain and Portugal in the benefits derived from the resources of the ERDF (OJ 1985 L302/1).

84 On the ERDF (OJ 1984 L169/1).

85 Amending Reg 1787/84 (OJ 1985 L350/40).

86 ibid, Art 3.

87 OJ 1984 L169/1.

88 *Nineteenth EC General Report* (EC Commission, Brussels, 1986) 188.

It was recognized that the problems posed were too fundamental to be tackled merely through such reallocations of sums already agreed.[89] Thus in response to the call of the June 1983 European Council meeting,[90] the Commission had already produced a report with proposals for strengthening the effectiveness of the Structural Funds.[91] The proposals sought, in particular: increased discretion for the Commission in the management of these Funds; greater concentration of resources on the most serious problems; and the financing of programmes rather than projects. Limited reforms along these lines were introduced by Regulation 1787/84.[92]

Integrated Mediterranean Programmes

Before Portuguese and Spanish accession, the European Parliament had called on the Commission to draw up proposals for the creation of a Development Fund for the Mediterranean regions of the Community and the applicant countries.[93] In response, the Commission proposed the introduction of Integrated Mediterranean Programmes.[94] At the European Council meeting of December 1984 the Greek Government stated that it did not agree with enlargement of the Community unless 'a satisfactory position' was taken on the Commission proposal.[95] Agreement on the main terms of the proposal was reached by the European Council in March 1985.[96] A revised Commission proposal,[97] in which the amount of resources initially envisaged was considerably lowered,[98] was finally adopted by the Council as Regulation 2088/85.[99]

This Regulation established Integrated Mediterranean Programmes for a seven-year period. Their purpose was to facilitate the adjustment of the regions concerned to the new conditions created by the enlargement of the Community.[100] They had originally been conceived by the Community

[89] Note also the Joint Declaration concerning the economic and social development of the autonomous regions of the Azores and Madeira (OJ 1985 L302/23), which was annexed to the Portuguese and Spanish Accession Act. This declaration eventually led to Dec 91/315 (OJ 1991 L171/10) setting up a programme of options specific to the remote and insular nature of Madeira and the Azores (Poseima).

[90] Bull EC 6–1983, 1.5.5.

[91] Ways of increasing the effectiveness of the Community's structural funds, COM(83)501.

[92] OJ 1984 L169/1.

[93] Resolution of 16 Feb 1982 (OJ 1982 C66/26) on a 'Mediterranean plan' for the benefit of Mediterranean countries belonging to the EC and the applicant countries Portugal and Spain on the basis of a regulation, para 4.

[94] Proposal of 3 Nov 1983 for a regulation instituting IMPs, COM(83)541.

[95] Bull EC 12–1984, 1.2.16.

[96] Bull EC 3–1985, 1.2.8. Agreement in principle had been reached at the Mar 1984 Summit (Bull EC 3–1984, 1.1.1).

[97] Proposal of 6 May 1985 for a regulation instituting IMPs, COM(85)180.

[98] See the figures in the explanatory memorandum to the proposal of 3 Nov 1983 for a regulation instituting IMPs, COM(83)541.

[99] Concerning the IMPs (OJ 1985 L197/1).

[100] Art 11 (ibid) provided that increases in real terms accruing to the Structural Funds during the period concerned should help to finance the IMPs, but without adversely affecting transfers from the Funds to other less prosperous and priority regions.

institutions as a large-scale plan for the structural development of the Mediterranean regions. However, intergovernmental negotiations meant that they became a compensation instrument for the Member States likely to be most directly affected by the enlargement.[101]

Sectoral instruments

The adoption of an agricultural development programme for Portugal was required by Article 263(d) of the Accession Act and Protocol 24 thereto,[102] on agricultural structures in Portugal.[103] Regulation 3828/85[104] duly established a specific programme for the development of Portuguese agriculture (PEDAP), and, more particularly, a specific common measure was adopted for the improvement of vineyards in Portugal.[105]

At the same time, enlargement implied the need for reform of the fisheries structural policy, so that it would be primarily concerned with the balanced exploitation of internal resources in Community waters.[106] More particularly, the large and efficient sardine-canning industries now to be included within the Community threatened the continued economic viability of many sardine-canning plants in the existing Member States. To help such plants meet this threat, the Council adopted Regulation 3722/85.[107] This Regulation established an assistance programme for research, development, conversion, and closure in this sector.

Regulation 2053/88[108] went beyond agriculture and fishing. It established a special programme for industrial development in Portugal (PEDIP). This was a five-year programme involving the use of extra Community resources for basic and further vocational training facilities for careers in industry, productivity drives, the financing of productive investment, and development of 'industrial infrastructure'.[109]

[101] H Bourgeau, 'Programmes Mediterréens Integrés: Un defi pour la Communauté' (1983) RMC 451–456; and J Blasco Jauregui, 'Los Programas Mediterraneos Integrados: Una respuesta a la Europa del Sud' (1985) *Rivista de Instituciones Europeas* 109–136.

[102] OJ 1985 L302/23.

[103] See also the Declaration by the EEC on the adaptation and modernization of the Portuguese economy, adopted with the Accession Act (ibid).

[104] On a specific programme for the development of Portuguese agriculture (OJ 1985 L372/5).

[105] Reg 2239/86 (OJ 1986 L196/1) on a specific common measure to improve vine-growing structures in Portugal. It was argued in Case 253/86 *Sociedade Agro-Pecuaria Vicente Nobre, Lda v EC Council* [1988] ECR 2725, 2742 that this measure was less favourable than a more general Community scheme, established by Reg 777/85 (OJ 1985 L88/8) on the granting for the 1985/6–1989/90 wine years of permanent abandonment premiums in respect of certain areas under vines.

[106] 8th recital in the preamble to Reg 4028/86 (OJ 1986 L376/7) on Community measures to improve and adapt structures in the fisheries and aquaculture sector.

[107] On a system of structural aid for the conversion of sardine-canning factories (OJ 1985 L361/36).

[108] On financial assistance for Portugal for a special industrial development programme (OJ 1988 L185/21).

[109] See, regarding the implementation of this Programme, COA annual report for 1988 (OJ 1989 C312/1), ch 7; Pedip progress report, COM(90)205; and Pedip final report, COM(93)711.

8.5.4 Fourth Accession Act

During negotiations for the fourth enlargement[110] Spain, in particular, sought to tie enlargement questions to implementation of financial arrangements for the Cohesion Fund.[111] At the same time, Finland and Sweden demanded modification of Union legislation governing the Structural Funds.

In response to the demands of these two applicant states, the Commission proposed that Lapland (Finland), with a per capita gross domestic product figure of 94 per cent of the Union average, and Norrbotten (Sweden) with a figure of 80 per cent, should be classified as Objective 1 regions.[112] This proposal, however, was challenged by the Greek Presidency, which favoured a 'transitional' and '*ad hoc* effort' to be made 'in a limited number of areas'.[113] As a result, the Council of Foreign Affairs Ministers agreed that there should be a new Objective 6,[114] for Nordic regions with a population density no greater than eight persons per square kilometre.[115] This Objective was provided for in Protocol 6 to the Accession Act.[116]

In the context of the same negotiations it was also accepted[117] that latitude in Finland and Sweden would be considered as an equivalent criterion to altitude for the purposes of Directive 75/268.[118] A Declaration to this effect was duly attached by the Union to the Accession Act,[119] and the Directive was amended by Part V.C of Annex I to the Act.[120]

8.6 EUROPE AGREEMENTS

Negotiation of agreements with third states to which Member States themselves as well as one of the Communities are parties[121] entails opportunities for intergovernmental bargaining. As in the case of Accession Acts, such bargaining may lead simply to side-payments, though the results may at least potentially be more profound.

[110] cf, regarding the EFTA Financial Mechanism, sect 6.8 above.

[111] *Financial Times*, 20 May 1992.

[112] *European Report* 1905 (27 Nov 1993).

[113] *European Report* 1918 (19 Jan 1994). There were also objections from France and Spain. See *European Report* 1923 (5 Feb 1994).

[114] *European Report* 1928 (23 Feb 1993).

[115] In the Highlands and Islands the figure is nine (Fifth periodic report on the situation and socio-economic development of the regions of the Community, COM(94)322, Table A27). However, this area is now covered by Objective 1.

[116] cf the treatment of Burgenland, in Austria, as an Objective 1 region in Annex XVII to the Accession Act, as amended by Dec 95/1 (OJ 1995 L1/1) adjusting the instruments concerning the accession of new Member States to the EU.

[117] *European Report* 1905 (27 Nov 1993).

[118] OJ 1975 L128/1.

[119] Declaration 37 on mountain areas and less favoured areas.

[120] As amended by Dec 95/1 (OJ 1995 L1/1).

[121] These so-called 'joint agreements' cover some matters within the competence of the Union and some matters within the competence of Member States.

Certainly, the trade liberalization sought by the Europe Agreements with Central and East European countries was considered likely to entail increased competition for Union industry, particularly the agricultural and textiles sectors. These sectors were important for the economies of the weaker regions within the Union.[122] There were also fears of investment diversion from such regions to Central and Eastern Europe.[123] Consequently, to secure their approval of the Europe Agreements, various forms of compensation were introduced for the Member States whose regions were considered likely to suffer such adverse effects from the liberalization envisaged in these Agreements.

For example, one of the factors which led the Commission to propose a large increase in the sums available to the Structural Funds for the period up to 1997 was the likely impact on the Union, especially its weaker regions, of this liberalization.[124] More particularly, on 30 September 1991, within the framework of negotiations for the Europe Agreements, consensus was reached regarding liberalization of trade in textiles. At the same time the Commission undertook to adopt measures to improve and modernize the textile industry within the Union and to promote its competitiveness, especially in the regions most affected by such liberalization.[125] On 23 October 1991 the Commission produced the draft of its Retex programme.[126]

8.7 CONCLUSION

The outcomes of intergovernmental procedures may reflect the search for reciprocity between Member States rather than being consistent with cohesion requirements. For example, cohesion implies that in the context of accession negotiations, full account should be taken of the increased diversity of regional problems in the Union likely to result from enlargement. However, the general tendency has been limitation of such negotiations to issues perceived to have a sufficiently specific connection with enlargement. The preference in such negotiations, as in negotiations for the Europe Agreements,

[122] See, regarding the desirability of granting Union assistance to the adjustment of the 'lagging regions' generally to competition from Central and Eastern Europe, National Economic Research Associates, *Trade and Foreign Investment in the Community's Regions: The Impact of Economic Reform in Central and Eastern Europe* (Regional Development Studies No 7; EC Commission, Brussels, 1993).

[123] R Hall and D van der Wee, 'Community Regional Policies for the 1990s' (1992) *Regional Studies* 399–404.

[124] Commission Reply by Mr Millan to WQ 24/92 (OJ 1992 C285/7) by Mr Gary Titley.

[125] *European Report* 1708 (2 Oct 1991).

[126] Notice laying down guidelines for operational programmes within the framework of a Community initiative for regions heavily dependent on the textiles and clothing sector (OJ 1992 C142/5). See sect 2.4.6 above.

has been for 'side-payments' and containment of the disruption of existing Union policy.

Negotiations related to arrangements for economic and monetary union and completion of the internal market may have provided opportunities for adoption of more fundamental reforms. These reforms may have gone some way towards accommodating demands which accession negotiations failed to meet. Indeed, the Single European Act[127] and the Treaty on European Union may be said to have transformed the Union funds into instruments of cohesion.[128] However, the very considerations which made such accommodations possible—the balance of benefits and losses perceived to be entailed for Member States—may mean that such reforms are also inadequate for cohesion purposes. In fact, the net results of the overall bargains struck may be to leave regional disparities unaffected or even to exacerbate them.[129]

True, the effective requirements of a bargain may not depend solely on the terms of the legal act in which it is expressed. These terms may leave considerable scope for 'creative' interpretation by the Union institutions. While the issues may be essentially the same for these institutions as for the Member States, the decision making of these institutions does not take place within the same legal framework as that for intergovernmental bargaining.[130] However, the framework for organic decision making may be little better adapted to effective pursuit of cohesion than the framework for intergovernmental bargaining. In fact, the former may do little to counter effective control of the operations of the Union funds by Member States.

[127] OJ 1987 L169/1.

[128] C Mestre and Y Petit, 'La Cohesion économique et sociale après le Traité sur l'Union européenne' (1995) RTDE 207–243.

[129] Note, eg, regarding the possible adverse consequences for Objective 1 regions excluded from the scope of the Cohesion Fund, the COR Opinion of 5 Apr 1994 (OJ 1994 C217/1) on the proposal for a regulation establishing a Cohesion Fund, para 1.5.

[130] Note, eg, the problems in implementing the bargain regarding assistance to Portuguese textiles, which was negotiated in the Council in Dec 1993 in return for Portuguese acceptance of the GATT Uruguay Round (*European Report* 1921 (29 Jan 1994)). See sect 5.7.3 above.

9

Conclusions

Union decision making is ill adapted to the articulation of cohesion requirements in Articles 158 and 159 of the EC Treaty. In other words, it is ill adapted to determining what the reduction of regional disparities demands of the Union funds, and thus to giving real meaning to these provisions. Hence, regulation of the operations of these funds may be left to depend partly on the outcomes of intergovernmental bargaining, particularly outcomes concerned with reciprocity between Member States. It may also be left to depend partly on the needs of the common market, particularly needs expressed by competition policy.[1]

In such bargaining, the operations of the Union funds are seen as means of equalizing the financial capacity of Member States to intervene in their national economies. Such equalization is sought through the transfer of resources from the stronger to the weaker Member States.[2] In practice, the consequence is that Union assistance concentrates on infrastructure and training measures,[3] because such measures tend to be favoured by transferee Member States as being in the national economic interest. In other words, assistance is generally granted according to 'essentially Member State-initiated priorities'.[4]

At the same time, concentration on infrastructure and training measures may be broadly consistent with competition-policy requirements.[5] This is because assistance to measures of this kind may be treated as less likely to distort competition than other kinds of assistance.[6] Such concentration may thus meet the demands of net transferors that the distorting effects of fund

[1] cf Communication on the links between regional and competition policy—reinforcing concentration and mutual consistency (OJ 1998 C90/3). More particularly, the grant of Union assistance to a regional aid scheme may be withheld, pending Commission authorization of the scheme under Art 87 EC. See eg Art 7 of Dec 98/586 (OJ 1998 L282/20) on the approval of the multiregional SPD for the conversion of the activities of defence in the areas concerned by Objective 2 in France.

[2] RR Barnett and V Borooah, 'The Additionality (or Otherwise) of the European Community Structural Funds' in S Hardy, M Hart, L Albrechts, and A Katos (eds), *An Enlarged Europe* (Jessica Kingsley, London, 1995) 180–191, 189.

[3] Around 30% of the resources of the Structural Funds go to infrastructure and around 30% to training. See First cohesion report, COM(96)542, 9.

[4] Future of Community initiatives under the Structural Funds, COM(93)282, 4.

[5] A Cutler, C Haslam, J Williams, and K Williams, *1992—the Struggle for Europe* (Berg, New York, 1989) 80–82.

[6] cf Annual report of the Cohesion Fund 1997, COM(1998)543, 17. See, generally, A Evans, *EC Law of State Aid* (Clarendon Press, Oxford, 1997).

operations[7] should be limited without their own freedom to intervene being substantially affected by legislation governing these operations.[8] At this point intergovernmentalism and the needs of the common market may be reconciled. In other words, intergovernmental equality and liberal equality may be reconciled. However, the reconciliation is achieved at the expense of regional participation in Union decision making and, consequently, at the expense of the regional equality required by Article 158 of the Treaty.

Regional authorities and other actors at the regional level are denied guaranteed opportunities[9] to contribute to the articulation of cohesion requirements through participation in such decision making.[10] This denial may mean that threats to the implementation of intergovernmental bargains or to the competition sought through the common market are avoided. On the other hand, it may also explain why the operations of the Union funds 'resonate with the overarching ideology, preferred policy instruments, and institutional interests of the main actors' in the Union.[11]

In these circumstances, the concentration of Union assistance on infrastructure and training goes largely unchallenged by reference to cohesion requirements. However, such assistance does not necessarily facilitate the development of weaker regions. For example, improvements in infrastructure, particularly transport infrastructure, may render the markets of these regions more open to producers from outside and may do little to assist regional producers. Again, training may lead those acquiring new skills to migrate to more developed regions where these skills are in demand.[12] As a result, such assistance may tend to reduce disparities between Member States rather than between regions.[13]

At the same time, lack of articulation of cohesion requirements means that operations of the Union funds may depend on the requirements of various,

[7] cf, regarding concern to ensure that assistance does not lead to 'delocalization' problems, the Explanatory memorandum to the Proposal of 19 Mar 1998 for a regulation laying down provisions on the Structural Funds, COM(98)131, 26.

[8] Such demands may explain why arrangements for Commission control of fund operations have been most developed in the case of IMPs and the Cohesion Fund, where there has been only a limited number of beneficiary Member States.

[9] See, regarding the role of regional authorities in the different Member States, the Seventh annual report on the Structural Funds, COM(96)502, 229–234.

[10] cf the view that intergovernmental decision making has a negative impact on organic decision making, in that the bargains struck between Member States limit the room for manœuvre of the Union institutions, in S Padgett, 'The Single European Market: The Politics of Realisation' (1992) 30 JCMS 53–75, 54.

[11] JJ Anderson, 'Structural Funds and the Social Dimension of EU Policy: Springboard or Stumbling Block?' in S Leibfried and P Pierson (eds), *European Social Policy* (Brookings Institution, Washington, 1995) 150.

[12] cf regarding 'liberal market tutelage', A Cutler, C Haslam, J Williams, and K Williams, n 5 above, 80–82.

[13] First cohesion report, COM(96)542, 5–6. See, more particularly, regarding the limited impact of Union assistance to the Mezzogiorno, COA special report 15/98 (OJ 1998 C347/1) on the assessment of Structural Fund intervention for the 1989–93 and 1994–99 periods, para 7.2.

more articulated, Union policies. In other words, cohesion requirements risk 'dilution'.[14] This risk does not derive from the role of policy as something extraneous from the law. Rather, it illustrates the integral role which policy plays in the operation of the law, through demanding selectivity in the activation and development of the various requirements embodied in legal provisions.

Such selectivity may be heavily influenced by the role of various interest groups in Union decision making. For example, sectoral interests, such as agricultural interests,[15] may be effectively represented in the procedures leading to the adoption of decisions concerning the Union funds. Indeed, the deficient rationality of Union decision making may guarantee the success of such interests.[16] Thus they may even play a central role in drawing up guidelines applied by the Commission in the allocation of assistance.[17] The representation of regional interests may be more limited.[18] In these circumstances, the operations of the funds may tend merely to give effect to 'fair return' bargains[19] between Member States in sectoral contexts.

More particularly, in so far as sectoral interests are well entrenched in stronger regions, the result may be that more Union assistance is directed to such regions than is consistent with promotion of cohesion.[20] In other cases, in so far as sectoral policy entails denial of assistance, there may also be harmful effects for cohesion. Such effects may arise, because assistance which may enable weaker regions to exploit unrealized comparative advantages may be denied. Thus it has been argued that in 'crisis' sectors, regions with growth potential may be penalized by the denial of Union assistance.[21] For example, according to the European Parliament[22] and the Committee of the

[14] cf A Liberatore, 'The Integration of Sustainable Development Objectives into EU Policy-Making' in S Baker, M Kousis, R Richardson, and S Young, *The Politics of Sustainable Development* (Routledge, London, 1997) 107–126, 119.

[15] The 'political decision-making mechanisms at Community level have particularly favoured the promotion of the specific group interests of agriculture' (E Guth, 'European Agricultural Policy: Is There No Alternative?' (1985) *Intereconomics* 3–9, 9).

[16] cf J Habermas, *Legitimation Crisis* (Polity Press, Cambridge, 1988) 60.

[17] Joined Cases T–369/94 & 85/95 *DIR International Film Srl v EC Commission* [19 Feb 1998].

[18] An analogy may be drawn with the problems of taking specific account of consumer interests in the application of competition policy. See A Evans, 'Article 85(3) Exemption: "Allowing Consumers a Fair Share of the Resulting Benefit" ' in M Goyens (ed), *European Competition Policy and the Consumer Interest* (Bruylant, Brussels, 1985) 99–120. Cf, regarding 'latent interests' generally, M Teutemann, *Completion of the Internal Market: An Application of Public Choice Theory* (Economic Papers No 83; EC Commission, Brussels, 1990) 8.

[19] cf, regarding the practical problems involved in calculating 'fair returns', the Commission Reply by Mr Liikanen to WQ E–3815/97 (OJ 1998 C174/135) by Caroline Jackson.

[20] DJ Neven and J Vickers, 'Public Policy towards Industrial Restructuring: Some Issues Raised by the Internal Market Programme' in K Cool, DJ Neven, and I Walter (eds), *European Industrial Restructuring in the 1990s* (Macmillan, London, 1992) 162–198, 175.

[21] *The Regional Impact of Community Policies* (Regional Policy and Transport Series No 17; European Parliament, Luxembourg, 1991) 15 and 83.

[22] Resolution of 3 May 1994 (OJ 1994 C205/121) on the guidelines for the modernization of the textile and clothing industry in Portugal, para 14.

Regions,[23] the denial of assistance leading to increases in Portuguese textile-production capacity is harmful to regional development in Portugal. Similarly, criticism may be made of the lack of regional differentiation in application of the common agricultural policy to products in surplus.[24]

Again, horizontal policies may mean that assistance supporting achievement of various objectives, such as promotion of small and medium-sized enterprises and of research and development, is granted. However, limited account may be taken of cohesion requirements. In practice, such assistance tends to assist stronger regions, particularly those with an established research and development capacity or dynamic small and medium-sized enterprises. As a result, pursuit of such policies may also have harmful effects for cohesion.

The operations of the European Regional Development Fund itself may be indirectly affected by pursuit of various policies. In practice, this Fund may be viewed as a way of compensating those Member States which benefit little from other Union 'expenditure policies', such as the common agricultural policy. More generally, it may be viewed as a means of securing the consent of weaker Member States to further market integration. Less importance is attached to ensuring that the operations of this Fund effectively promote cohesion. Thus even the contribution of this Fund to the promotion of regional equality may be impaired.[25]

Therefore, the pursuit of various sectoral and horizontal policies may have the effect of reinforcing the tendency of Union assistance to reduce disparities between Member States rather than between regions. Indeed, in some cases the latter disparities are increasing.[26] The Committee of the Regions infers the need for increased participation by regional authorities in the pursuit of 'European structural policy'.[27]

The need for 'democratization' of intergovernmental bargaining is apparently implied. The Treaties may provide a basis for such reform. In particular, regard may be had to the concept of subsidiarity in Article 1 of the Treaty on European Union. According to this provision, decisions should be 'taken as closely as possible to the citizen'. Regard may also be had to the constitutional implications of the 'establishment' of Union Citizenship by Article 17 of the EC Treaty. These provisions raise questions about whether it is consistent with Union Law for the constitutional procedures mentioned in Article

[23] Opinion of 17 May 1994 (OJ 1994 C217/14) on the Community initiative on the modernization of the textile and clothing industry of Portugal.

[24] ESC Opinion of 30 Apr 1992 (OJ 1992 C169/41) on the Commission proposals on the prices for agricultural products and on related measures (1992/93), para 1.8.

[25] HW Armstrong and J Taylor, *Regional Economics and Policy* (Harvester Wheatsheaf, 2nd edn, London, 1993) 296.

[26] First cohesion report, COM(96)542, 5–6.

[27] Opinion of 19 Nov 1997 (OJ 1998 C64/5) on the views of the regions and local authorities in arrangements for European structural policy after 1999, para 1.3.6.

48 of the Treaty on European Union to be regarded as permitting national ratification of Treaty amendments agreed between Member States solely on the basis of consent from central institutions of the Member States.[28] If Article 48 were interpreted as demanding more pluralism in intergovernmental decision making, such decision making might entail increased articulation of cohesion requirements. At least, the articulation might go beyond the minimum considered necessary by national governments to secure a 'fair return' for their participation in market integration.

At the same time, reform of organic Union decision making may enable the Union funds more effectively to reduce disparities between regions.[29] For example, if the legislation governing partnership were appropriately amended, regional representatives might be able to ensure that Union assistance more closely addressed the problems of their regions.[30] Evolution in the case law may also have a role to play. In particular, recognition by the European Courts of rights for actors other than Member States and Union institutions to invoke cohesion requirements in plenary proceedings concerning the operations of the Union funds may be critical. Recognition of such rights would enable supposed beneficiaries of cohesion to participate in the articulation of its requirements through judicial proceedings.

In other words, effective pursuit of the regional equality sought through cohesion and promotion of institutional equality—that is, equal opportunities as between regions and other actors and as between regions themselves to participate in Union decision making—may be interdependent processes. Reforms which go beyond the changes to 'economic law' envisaged in the latest Commission proposals[31] and more fully recognize this interdependence of economic law and institutional law may not simply be a constitutional imperative.[32] If cohesion is to be strengthened, such reforms may also be an inherent necessity.

Obstacles to such reforms may derive from structural features of the Union legal system, which cannot be fully appreciated solely by reference to provisions governing cohesion. According to this structure, the Union is a creation of Member States,[33] and its evolution depends on progressive transfers of

[28] Art 48 TEU provides that Treaty amendments must be 'ratified by all the Member States in accordance with their respective constitutional requirements'. Cf the Belgian statement on the signing of treaties by Belgium as a Member State of the EU (OJ 1998 C351/1).

[29] See, regarding the need to broaden participation at regional and local level and to involve the social partners, First cohesion report, COM(96)542, 11.

[30] cf ibid 114. However, problems of 'departmental specialization' within the Commission (sect 1.7.3 above) may remain, where assistance is granted outside the framework programme.

[31] Proposal of 19 Mar 1998 (OJ 1998 C176/1) for a regulation laying down provisions on the Structural Funds.

[32] cf the view that 'state aid control in the EU is of constitutional nature, both with respect to substance and procedure' (C-D Ehlermann, 'State Aid Control in the European Union: Success or Failure?' (1994–95) 18 *Fordham International Law Journal* 1212–1229, 1214).

[33] Art A TEU and Art 1 EC.

sovereignty by Member States.[34] The transfers necessary for establishment of the common market may be deemed to have taken place.[35] Unless Treaty provisions concerning cohesion are interpreted as meaning that sovereignty transfers necessary for effective pursuit of cohesion have also taken place, national law may remain free to limit regional participation in the partnership sought by Union legislation.

At the same time, the European Courts infer from the structure of the Union legal system that individual rights are essentially market-based in character. Whether or not their case law reflects reluctance to confront the sovereignty implications of cohesion, the result is to limit opportunities for representatives of cohesion interests to take proceedings before these Courts. In other words, the 'constitutionalization' of cohesion may be contradicted, and reforms of the above kind may be precluded.

Failure to secure such reforms may mean that 'transaction cost' problems, implicit in the increased diversity of regional problems likely to be associated with future enlargements of the Union, may be exaggerated. According to Coase, a firm will tend to expand until the costs of organizing an extra transaction within the firm become equal to the costs of carrying out the same transaction by means of an exchange on the open market.[36] Dynamic analysis would take account of the capacity of the firm internally to reorganize and thereby to reduce the relative costs of expansion. If an analogy between the expansion of a firm and the enlargement of the Union is justified, it seems that Union practice will need to be adapted to cope with future enlargements. The importance of such adaptation may be greater for the Union than for the firm, given that Union enlargement, at least in relation to Central and East European countries, may have the characteristics of a political imperative.

The Commission acknowledges that the accession of such countries will make the Union much more heterogeneous[37] and that the nature of the likely impact on existing 'cohesion countries' is uncertain.[38] Some impact seems inevitable, given that the need is inferred for greater concentration of Union assistance and strict application of the criteria for determining eligibility.[39] The Commission further acknowledges that better targeting and a broader

[34] Opinion 1/91 *Draft Agreement between the Community and the EFTA Countries relating to the Creation of the EEA* [1991] ECR I–6079, I–6103.

[35] Case 26/62 *NV Algemene Transport- en Expeditie Onderneming van Gend en Loos v Nederlandse Administratie der Belastingen* [1963] ECR 1, 12; and Case 6/64 *Flaminio Costa v ENEL* [1964] ECR 585, 593.

[36] RH Coase, 'The Nature of the Firm' (1937) 4 *Economica* 386–405.

[37] cf the Proposal of 18 Mar 1998 for a regulation on Community support for pre-accession measures for agriculture and rural development in the applicant countries of Central and Eastern Europe in the pre-accession period, COM(98)153; and the Proposal of 18 Mar 1998 for a regulation on co-ordinating aid to the applicant countries in the framework of the pre-accession strategy, COM(98)150.

[38] *Agenda 2000*, Bull EC, Supp 5/97, 108.

[39] ibid, 112. See also Agenda 2000: the legislative proposals: overall view, COM(98)182, 4.

range of policies will be needed and that more local (or regional or national) participation in Union decision making may be appropriate.[40] Nevertheless, the Commission still thinks essentially of transfers from western countries[41] and of preventing 'discrepancies' between national and Union instruments.[42] According to such thinking, the reduction of regional disparities is assumed to be a likely consequence of reducing the 'overall gap' between Central and East European countries and the Union average.[43] The record of the Union funds suggests that this assumption is questionable.

More fundamentally, the assumption may be questioned that 'absorption' of new Member States and maintaining the 'momentum of European integration' are liable to conflict.[44] At least as regards regional disparities, the problems of absorption and of maintaining the momentum of integration are essentially the same. They revolve around the need more effectively to pursue cohesion.[45] In so far as this need is recognized in both the broadening and deepening of integration, the two processes may reinforce each other.

40 *Agenda 2000*, Bull EC, Supp 5/97, 109. 41 ibid, 108. 42 ibid, 110.
43 ibid, 111.
44 According to the European Council meeting of June 1993, 'the Union's capacity to absorb new members, while maintaining the momentum of European integration, is . . . an important consideration in the general interest of both the Union and the candidate countries' (Bull EC 6–1993, I.13).
45 This need is recognized in the preamble to the Proposal of 19 Mar 1998 (OJ 1998 C176/1) for a regulation laying down provisions on the Structural Funds. However, its achievement is seen as basically dependent on the closer monitoring and evaluation of fund operations by Member States.

Bibliography

ADDISON, JT, and SIEBERT, WS, 'The Social Charter of the European Community: Evolution and Controversies' (1991) *Industrial and Labour Relations Review* 597–623.

AITKEN, P, 'SMEs, Research and Development and Technology Policies, and the European Community: Issues in Implementation' in K Dyson (ed), *Local Authorities and New Technologies: The European Dimension* (Croom Helm, London, 1988) 59–83.

ALBRECHTS, L, MOULAERT, F, ROBERTS, P, and SWYNGEDOUW, E (eds), *Regional Policy at the Crossroads* (Jessica Kingsley, London, 1989).

ALDSKOGIUS, G, 'Regionalpolitikens utmaningar' (1991) *Nordrevy* (No 4) 7–11.

ALLEN, K, 'Requirements for an Effective Regional Policy' in L Albrechts, F Moulaert, P Roberts, and E Swyngedouw (eds), *Regional Policy at the Crossroads* (Kingsley, London, 1989) 107–124.

—— 'International Forces and Regional Policy' in *Internationalisering och regional utveckling* (NordRefo 1990: 2) 37–46.

ANDERSON, JJ, 'Skeptical Reflections on a Europe of Regions: Britain, Germany, and the ERDF' (1990) *Journal of Public Policy* 417–445.

—— 'Business Associations and the Decentralization of Penury: Functional Groups and Territorial Interests' (1991) *Governance* 67–93.

—— 'Structural Funds and the Social Dimension of EU Policy: Springboard or Stumbling Block?' in S Leibfried and P Pierson (eds), *European Social Policy* (Brookings Institution, Washington, 1995) 123–158.

ANDRÉ, C, 'Le Nouvel Instrument communautaire d'emprunts et de prêts (N.I.C.)' (1980) *Revue du Marché Commun* 66–71.

——, DREVET, J-F, and LANDABURU, E, 'Regional Consequences of the Internal Market' (1989) *Contemporary European Affairs* 205–214.

ARMSTRONG, HW, 'The Role and Evolution of European Community Regional Policy' in B Jones and M Keating (eds), *The European Union and the Regions* (Clarendon Press, Oxford, 1995) 23–53.

——, and TAYLOR, J, *Regional Economics and Policy* (Harvester Wheatsheaf, 2nd edn, London, 1993).

BACHTLER, J, 'Policy Agenda for the Decade' in S Hardy, M Hart, L Albrechts, and A Katos, *An Enlarged Europe* (Jessica Kingsley, London, 1995) 313–324.

——, and CLEMENT, K, *Regional Peripherality in the Single European Market, with Particular Reference to Ireland and Scotland* (European Policies Research Centre, Research Paper No 10; Glasgow, 1990).

BALASSA, B, *European Economic Integration* (North-Holland, Amsterdam, 1975).

BARNETT, RR, and BOROOAH, V, 'The Additionality (or Otherwise) of the European Community Structural Funds' in S Hardy, M Hart, L Albrechts, and A Katos (eds), *An Enlarged Europe* (Jessica Kingsley, London, 1995) 180–191.

BATTEN, D, *Infrastructure as a Network System: Mera Revisited* (CERUM Working Paper 1989: 2; University of Umeå).

Battistotti, L, 'I finanziamenti concessi della banca europea per gli invetimenti ed il nuovo strumento communitario' (1985) *Cronache Economiche* 63–68.

Begg, I, 'European Integration and Regional Policy' (1989) *Oxford Review of Economic Policy* 90–104.

—— 'The Regional Dimension of the "1992" Proposals' (1989) *Regional Studies* 368–376.

——, and Maye, D, *A New Strategy for Economic and Social Cohesion after 1992* (EC Commission, Luxembourg, 1992).

Bernardini, G, 'Les Operations integrées de développement communautaire' (1982) *Revue du Marché Commun* 265–271.

Bhaskar, K, *The Effect of Different State Aid Measures on Intra-Community Competition* (EC Commission, Brussels, 1990).

Biancarelli, J, 'La Communauté européenne et les collectivités locales: Une double dialectique complexe' (1991) *Revue Française d'Administration Publique* 515–527.

Bianchi, P, 'La Réorientation des politiques structurelles dans la CEE' (1991) *Revue du Marché Commun* 599–603.

Bliss, C, 'Adjustment, Compensation, and Factor Mobility in Integrated Markets' in C Bliss and J Brage de Macedo (eds), *Unity with Diversity in the European Economy: The Community's Southern Frontier* (Cambridge University Press, 1990) 18–52.

Blumann, C, 'Regime des aides d'état: Jurisprudence recente de la cour de justice (1989–92)' (1992) *Revue du Marché Commun et de l'Union Européenne* 721–739.

Bourgeau, H, 'Programmes Mediterréens Integrés: Un defi pour la Communauté' (1983) *Revue du Marché Commun* 451–456.

Buck, T, 'Regional Policy and European Integration' (1975) 16 *Journal of Common Market Studies* 368–378.

Bureau, D, and Champsaur, P, 'Fiscal Federalism and European Economic Unification' (1992) 82 *American Economic Review* 88–108.

Camagni, RP (ed), *Innovation Networks: Spatial Perspectives* (Belhaven Press, London, 1991).

—— 'Development Scenarios and Policy Guidelines for the Lagging Regions in the 1990s' (1992) *Regional Studies* 361–374.

—— and Cappellin, R, 'Policies for Full Employment and More Efficient Utilization of Resources and New Trends in European Regional Development' (1981) *Lo Spettatore Internazionale* 99–135.

Carcelen Conesa, JM, 'Hacia una politica regional comun en el marco de la CEE' (1983) *Revista de Instituciones Europeas* 475–491.

Cardieux, J-L, 'Restructuration industrielle et politique communautaire vis-à-vis des aides nationales' in J Dutheil de la Rochère and J Vandamme (eds), *Interventions Publiques et Droit Communautaire* (Pedone, Paris, 1988) 77–88.

Carney, J, Hudson, R, and Lewis, J (eds), *Regions in Crisis: New Perspectives in European Regional Theory* (Croom Helm, London, 1980).

Cassese, S, 'Theoretical Sketch of the Cooperative and Multidimensional Nature of Community Bureaucracy' in J Jamar and W Wessels (eds), *Community Bureaucracy at the Crossroads* (de Tempel, Bruges, 1985) 39–46.

—— 'La Costituzione europea' (1991) *Quadri Costituzionali* 487–508.

CAVES, R, 'Industrial Policy and Trade Policy: The Connections' in H Kierzkowski (ed), *Protection and Competition in International Trade* (Blackwell, Oxford, 1987) 68–85.

CELIMENE, F, 'La Reforme de l'action des fonds structurels européens' (1991) *Actualité Juridique Droit Administratif* 251–266.

CHESHIRE, P, CAMAGNI, R, DE GAUDEMAAR, J-P, and CUADRADO ROURA, JR, '1957 to 1992: Moving toward a Europe of Regions and Regional Policy' in L Rodwin and H Sazanami (eds), *Industrial Change and Regional Economic Transformation: The Experience of Western Europe* (Harper Collins Academic, London, 1991) 268–300.

CHRISTENSEN, PR, 'Firms in Network: Concepts, Spatial Impacts, and Policy Implications' in *Networks and Regional Development* (NordRefo 1990: 1) 11–58.

CLARK, C, WILSON, F, and BRADLEY, J, 'Industrial Location and Economic Potential in Western Europe' (1969) *Regional Studies* 197–212.

CLOUT, H, *A Rural Policy for the EEC?* (Methuen, London, 1984).

—— *Regional Variations in the European Community* (Cambridge University Press, 1986).

COASE, RH, 'The Nature of the Firm' (1937) 4 *Economica* 386–405.

COLLIARD, CA, 'Eureka ou une co-opération technologique européenne' (1988) *Revue Trimestrielle de Droit Européen* 5–22.

COLLINS, D, *The Operation of the European Social Fund* (Croom Helm, London, 1983).

COMFORT, AM, 'Alternatives to Infrastructure? Possible Ways Forward for the ERDF: A View from Luxembourg' (1988) *Regional Studies* 542–551.

COMIJS, D, 'Individual Legal Protection under the Structural Funds' (1995) *Maastricht Journal* 187–195.

COOMBES, D, and REES, N, 'Regional and Social Policy' in L Hurwitz and C Lequesne (eds), *The State of the European Community* (Lynne Rienner, Boulder, Colo., 1991) 207–228.

CUDDY, M, 'Community Policy and the Periphery' (1984) 32 *Administration* 147–162.

CURRAL, J, 'Le Fonds européen de développement regional des origines jusqu'à l'acte unique européen' (1988) *Revue Trimestrielle de Droit Européen* 39–102.

CURZON PRICE, V, *1992: Europe's Last Chance? From Common Market to Single Market* (Institute of Economic Affairs, London, 1988).

CUTLER, A, HASLAM, C, WILLIAMS, J, and WILLIAMS, K, *1992—the Struggle for Europe* (Berg, New York, 1989).

DAM, KW, 'The Economics and the Law of Price Discrimination: Herein of Three Regulatory Schemes' (1963) *University of Chicago Law Review* 1–62.

DEHOUSSE, R, 'Completing the Internal Market: Institutional Constraints and Challenges' in R Bieber, R Dehousse, J Pinder, and JHH Weiler, *1992: One European Market* (Nomos, Baden-Baden, 1988) 311–336.

VAN DEPOELE, L, 'Het Europees Fonds voor Regionale Ontwikkeling' (1975) *Sociaal Economische Wetgeving* 387–394.

DOUTRIAUX, Y, *Le Traité sur l'Union européenne* (Armand Colin, Paris, 1992).

DUNFORD, M, and BENKO, G, 'Neo-Fordism or Post-Fordism? Some Conclusions' in G Benko and M Dunford (eds), *Industrial Change and Regional Development* (Belhaven Press, London, 1991) 286–305.

DYSON, K, 'Introduction' in K Dyson (ed), *Local Authorities and New Technologies: The European Dimension* (Croom Helm, London, 1988) 1–23.

EHLERMANN, C-D, 'State Aid Control in the European Union: Success or Failure?' (1994–95) 18 *Fordham International Law Journal* 1212–1229.

ELIZADE, J, 'La Reforma del FEDER: Principios de una autentica politica regional comunitaria' (1985) *Revista de Instituciones Europeas* 93–107.

—— 'Legal Aspects of Community Policy on Research and Technological Development (RTD)' (1992) 29 *Common Market Law Review* 309–346.

EMERSON, M, AUJEAN, M, CATINAT, M, GOYBET, P, and JACQUEMIN, A, *The Economics of 1992* (Oxford University Press, 1988).

VAN EMPEL, M, 'Technology and Common Market Law' in Aspen Institute Colloquium on European Law, *Technological Development and Cooperation in Europe—Legal Aspects* (TMC Asser Institute, The Hague, 1986) 57–71.

ENGEL, C, and VAN GINDERACHTER, J, *Le Pouvoir régional et local dans la Communauté européenne* (Pedone, Paris, 1992).

ESER, TW, 'Die Kontrolle regionaler Beihilfen im Rahmen der Wettbewerbspolitik der Europäischen Gemeinschaften' (1989) *Raumforchung und Raumordnung* 202–216.

EVANS, A, 'Article 85(3) Exemption: "Allowing Consumers a Fair Share of the Resulting Benefit" ' in M Goyens (ed), *European Competition Policy and the Consumer Interest* (Bruylant, Brussels, 1985) 99–120.

—— *European Community Law, including the EEA Agreement* (Kluwer, Deventer, 1994).

—— *The Law of EU Regional Policy* (Kluwer, Deventer, 1995).

—— *EC Law of State Aid* (Oxford EC Law Series; Clarendon Press, Oxford, 1997).

—— 'Union Citizenship and the Constitutionalization of Equality in European Union Law' in M La Torre, *European Citizenship: An Institutional Challenge* (Kluwer, Deventer, 1997).

—— *A Textbook on European Union Law* (Hart Publishing, Oxford, 1998).

EVERLING, U, 'Reflections on the Structure of the European Union' (1992) 29 *Common Market Law Review* 1053–1077.

FAURE, E, and GELÉE, G, 'L'Union économique et monétaire et les déséquilibres régionaux' (1979) *Revue du Marché Commun* 481–489.

FOLEY, A, and GRIFFITH, B, 'Indigenous Manufacturing Enterprises in a Peripheral Economy and the Single Market: The Case of the Republic of Ireland' (1992) *Regional Studies* 375–386.

FRAZER, T, 'The New Structural Funds, State Aids, and Interventions on the Single Market' (1995) *European Law Review* 3–19.

GADBIN, D, 'Le Droit communautaire des structures agricoles: Organisation ou dilution?' (1991) *Revue du Marché Commun* 218–230.

GALLIZIOLI, G, *I Fondi strutturali delle Comunita europee* (CEDAM, Padova, 1992).

GANZ, G, *Quasi-Legislation* (Sweet and Maxwell, London, 1987).

GEORGE, S, *Politics and Policy in the European Union* (Oxford University Press, 3rd edn, Oxford, 1996).

GERBER, D, 'The Transformation of European Competition Law' (1994) 35 *Harvard International Law Journal* 97–147.

GIERSCH, H, 'Economic Union between Nations and the Location of Industries' (1949–50) 16 *Review of Economic Studies* 87–97.

GILCHRIST, J, and DEACON, D, 'Curbing Subsidies' in P Montagnon (ed), *European Competition Policy* (Pinter, London, 1990) 31–51.

Godin, P, 'Environment and the CAP' (1987) 219 *Green Europe*.

Grieco, JM, *Cooperation among Nations* (Cornell University Press, Ithaca, NY, 1990).

Grindley, P, 'Turning Technology into Competitive Advantage' (1991) *Business Strategy Review* 35–48.

Gruber, A, 'Le Fonds social européen à la veille d'un bilan' (1982) *Revue Trimestrielle du Droit Européen* 251–287.

van Gundesachter, J, 'La Politique régionale de la Communauté, justifications, modalités, et propositions' (1973) *Revue du Marché Commun* 468–486.

Guth, E, 'European Agricultural Policy: Is There Really No Alternative?' (1985) *Intereconomics* 3–9.

Haas, EB, *The Uniting of Europe* (Stanford University Press, Stanford, Calif., 1958).

Habermas, J, *Communication and the Evolution of Society* (Heinemann, London, 1979).

—— *Legitimation Crisis* (Polity Press, Cambridge, 1988).

Haenel, H, 'L'Europe: Une chance pour les collectivités locales' (1991) *Revue Française d'Administration Publique* 583–586.

Hall, R, and van der Wee, D, 'Community Regional Policies for the 1990s' (1992) *Regional Studies* 399–404.

Hancher, L, Ottervanger, T, and Slot, PJ, *EC State Aids* (Chancery Law Publishing, London, 1993).

Harrop, J, *The Political Economy of Integration in the European Community* (Edward Elgar, 2nd edn, Aldershot, 1992).

Hatt, P, 'Thirty Years of ESF Assistance' *Social Europe* 2:91, 78–91.

Hawk, B, 'La Recherche et le développement en droit communautaire et en droit antitrust américain' (1987) *Revue Internationale de Droit Economique* 211–269.

Heine, J, 'Les Mesures prises dans le secteur agricole pour l'intégration de la RDA dans la Communauté' (1991) *Revue du Marché Commun* 199–217.

Hesse, JJ, and Sharpe, LJ, 'Local Government in International Perspective: Some Comparative Perspectives' in JJ Hesse (ed), *Local Government and Urban Affairs in International Perspective* (Nomos, Baden-Baden, 1991) 603–620.

Hessel, B, and Mortelmans, K, 'Decentralized Government and Community Law: Conflicting Institutional Developments' (1993) 30 *Common Market Law Review* 905–937.

Howell, T, *The Microelectronics Race: The Impact of Government Policy on International Competition* (Westview Press, Boulder, Colo., 1988).

Howells, J, and Charles, D, 'Research and Technological Development in the "Less-Favoured" Regions of the European Community: A UK Dimension' in K Dyson (ed), *Local Authorities and New Technologies: The European Dimension* (Croom Helm, London, 1988) 24–58.

Jauregui, JB, 'Los Programas Mediterraneos Integrados: Una respuesta a la Europa del Sud' (1985) *Rivista de Instituciones Europeas* 109–136.

Jenny, FY, 'Competition and State Aid Policy in the European Community' (1994) *Fordham International Law Journal* 525–554.

Jordan, J, 'The Compatibility of Regional Aid Systems with the Common Market' (1976) *European Law Review* 236–242.

Jovanovic, MN, *International Economic Integration* (Routledge, London, 1992).

KARSTEN, D, 'Regional Policy' in CC Schweitzer and D Karsten (eds), *The Federal Republic of Germany and EC Membership Evaluated* (Pinter, London, 1990) 94–101.

KEATING, M, in B Jones and M Keating (eds), *The European Union and the Regions* (Clarendon Press, Oxford, 1995) 1–22.

KEOHANE, RO, and NYE, JS, *Power and Interdependence: World Politics in Transition* (Little, Brown, & Co, 2nd edn, Boston, 1988).

KRUGMAN, P, 'Introduction: New Thinking about Trade Policy' in P Krugman (ed), *Strategic Trade Policy and the New International Economics* (MIT Press, Cambridge, Mass., 1986).

KUKLINSKI, A, *Efficiency versus Equality: Old Dilemmas and New Approaches in Regional Policy* (European Policies Research Centre, Research Paper No 8; Glasgow, 1990).

LANGHAMMER, RJ, *EC Integration Widening Towards Eastern Europe* (Kiel Working Paper No 524; Kiel, 1992).

LATOUCHE, D, 'State Building and Foreign Policy at the Subnational Level' in I Duchacek and G Stevenson (eds), *Perforated Sovereignties and International Relations* (Greenwood Press, New York, 1988) 29–42.

LEBORGNE, D, and LIPIETZ, A, 'How to Avoid a Two-Tier Europe' (1990) *Labour and Society* 177–199.

LEIBFRIED, S, 'Towards a European Welfare State' (Centre for Social Policy Research 2/91; Bremen University).

LETTERON, R, 'Les Aides des collectivités territoriales aux services publics' (1993) *Actualité Juridique de Droit Administratif* 437–443.

LEVINE, S, and WHITE, PE, 'Exchange as a Conceptual Framework for the Study of Interorganizational Relationships' (1961) 16 *Administrative Science Quarterly* 583–601.

LIBERATORE, A, 'The Integration of Sustainable Development Objectives into EU Policy-Making' in S Baker, M Kousis, R Richardson, and S Young, *The Politics of Sustainable Development* (Routledge, London, 1997) 107–126.

LOWE, P, 'The Reform of the Community's Structural Funds' (1988) 25 *Common Market Law Review* 503–521.

LUNDBERG, L, 'Economic Integration, Inter- and Intra-Industry Trade: The Case of Sweden and the EC' (1992) *Scandinavian Journal of Economics* 393–408.

LYCK, L, 'Regional Policy' in L Lyck (ed), *Denmark and EC Membership Evaluated* (Pinter, London, 1992) 158–164.

MACALEAVEY, P, 'The Politics of European Regional Development Policy: The EC Commission's Rechar Initiative and the Concept of Additionality' (1993) *Regional Politics and Policy* 88–107.

MACCORMICK, N, and WEINBERGER, O, *An Institutional Theory of Law* (Reidel, Dordrecht, 1986).

MCCRONE, G, *Regional Policy in Britain* (Allen & Unwin, London, 1969).

MCINERNEY, J, 'Agricultural Policy at the Crossroads' (1986) *Countryside Planning Yearbook* 44–75.

MACMILLEN, MJ, and CHARD, JS, 'European Social Fund Aid to Textile Workers: The Early Experience' (1978) *European Economic Review* 269–290.

MAILLET, P, and DORMARD, S, 'Social Europe and Economic Cohesion' in A Pijpers (ed), *The European Community at the Crossroads* (Nijhoff, Dordrecht, 1992) 71–90.

Majone, G, *Market Integration and Regulation: Europe After 1992* (EUI Working Paper, SPS No 91/10; Florence, 1991).

Marks, G, 'Structural Policy in the European Community' in AM Sbragia (ed), *Europolitics: Institutions and Policymaking in the 'New' European Community* (Brookings Institution, Washington, 1992) 191–224.

Marques Mendes, AJ, 'Economic Cohesion in Europe: The Impact of the Delors Plan' (1990) 29 *Journal of Common Market Studies* 17–36.

Marsh, J, 'Agriculture and Structural Policy' in K Burger, M Groot, J Post, and V Zacchariasse (eds), *Agricultural Economics and Policy: International Challenges for the Nineties* (Elsevier, Amsterdam, 1991) 95–118.

Massart-Pierard, F, 'La Dialectique européanisation–régionalisation' in *L'Europe et ses régions* (Faculté de Droit de Liège, The Hague, 1975) 289–310.

Massey, D, 'In What Sense a Regional Problem?' (1979) *Regional Studies* 233–243.

Mathijsen, PSRF, 'The Role of Regional Policy in the European Economic Integration Process' in S Bates, W Finnie, JA Usher, and H Wildberg (eds), *In Memoriam JDB Mitchell* (Sweet and Maxwell, London, 1983), 171–183.

Mattera, A, *Le Marché unique européen: Ses règles, son fonctionnement* (Jupiter, 2nd edn, Paris, 1990).

Mégret, J, Louis, JV, Vignes, D, Waelbroeck, M, Dewost, JL, Brueckner, P, and Sacchettini, A, *Le Droit de la Communauté économique européenne* (University of Brussels, 1973).

Melchior, M, 'Les Communications de la Commission' in *Mélanges en honneur de Fernand Dehousse* (Labor, Brussels, 1979).

Mestre, C, and Petit, Y, 'La Cohesion économique et social après le Traité sur l'Union européenne' (1995) *Revue Trimestrielle de Droit Européen* 207–243.

Molle, W, *Regional Disparity and Economic Development in the European Community* (Saxon House, Farnborough, 1980).

—— and Cappellin, R (eds), *Regional Impact of Community Policies in Europe* (Avebury, Aldershot, 1988).

Moussis, N, 'Small and Medium Enterprises in the Internal Market' (1992) *European Law Review* 483–498.

Myrdal, G, *Economic Theory and Under-Developed Regions* (Duckworth, London, 1957).

Neri, S, and Sperl, H, *Traité instituant la Communauté économique européenne* (Court of Justice of the European Communities, Luxembourg, 1960).

Neunreither, K, 'Subsidiarity as a Guiding Principle for European Community Activities' (1993) *Government and Opposition* 206–220.

Neven, DJ, and Vickers, J, 'Public Policy towards Industrial Restructuring: Some Issues Raised by the Internal Market Programme' in K Cool, DJ Neven, and I Walter (eds), *European Industrial Restructuring in the 1990s* (Macmillan, London, 1992) 162–198.

O'Hearn, D, 'Global Competition, Europe, and Irish Peripherality' (1993) *The Economic and Social Review* 169–197.

Padgett, S, 'The Single European Market: The Politics of Realisation' (1992) 30 *Journal of Common Market Studies* 53–75.

Palard, J, 'Structural and Regional Planning Confronted with Decentralization and European Integration' (1993) *Regional Politics and Policy* 192–210.

PAPAGEORGIOU, F, and VERNEY, S, 'Regional Planning and the Integrated Mediterranean Programmes in Greece' in R Leonardi (ed), *The Regions and the European Community: The Regional Response to the Single Market in the Underdeveloped Areas* (Frank Cass, London, 1993) 139–161.

PARUCCINI, M, *Decision Support Systems for Environmental Management* (EC Commission, Brussels, 1992).

PATRICE, H, *Study on the Regional Impact of the Common Agricultural Policy* (Regional Policy Series No 21; EC Commission, Luxembourg, 1981).

PESCHEL, K, *Regional Development in a Changing Europe* (CERUM Working Paper 1990: 15, Umeå).

—— 'Spatial Effects of the Completion of the European Single Market' (1990) *Built Environment Quarterly* 11–29.

—— 'European Integration and Regional Development in Northern Europe' (1992) *Regional Studies* 387–397.

PETERSON, J, 'Technology Policy in Europe: Explaining the Framework Programme and Eureka in Theory and Practice' (1991) 29 *Journal of Common Market Studies* 269–290.

PFALLER, A, 'The Issue' in A Pfaller, I Gough, and G Therborn (eds), *Can the Welfare State Compete?* (Macmillan, London, 1991) 1–14.

PHILIPS, L, *The Economics of Price Discrimination* (Cambridge University Press, 1983).

PINDER, DA, 'Small Firms, Regional Development, and the European Investment Bank' (1986) 24 *Journal of Common Market Studies* 171–186.

POURRE, C, 'Le Cumul des aides' (1993) *Actualité Juridique de Droit Administratif* 444–450.

PRIEBE, R, 'Le Droit communautaire des structures agricoles' (1988) *Cahiers de Droit Européen* 3–38.

QUADRI, R, MONACO, R, and TRABUCCHI, A (eds), *Trattato istitutivo della Comunità economica europea: commentario* (Giuffré, Milan, 1965).

—— *Trattato istitutivo della Comunità europea del carbone e dell'acciaio: Commentario* (Giuffré, Milan, 1970).

QUÉVIT, M, *Impact régional 1992: Les Régions de tradition industrielle* (De Boeck, Brussels, 1991).

—— 'The Regional Impact of the Internal Market: A Comparative Analysis of Traditional Industrial Regions and Lagging Regions' (1992) *Regional Studies* 349–360.

ROMUS, P, 'La Création du Fonds européen de développement régional: Début de la politique régionale européenne' (1975) *Revue du Marché Commun* 149–157.

—— *L'Europe et les régions* (Nathan, Paris, 1979).

ROSENAU, JN, 'Patterned Chaos in Global Life: Structure and Process in the Two Worlds of World Politics' (1988) *International Political Science Review* 327–364.

ROSENBLATT, J, MAYER, T, BARTHOLDY, K, DEMEKAS, D, GUPTA, S, and LIPSCHITZ, L, *The Common Agricultural Policy of the European Community: Principles and Consequences* (International Monetary Fund, Washington, D.C., 1988).

DE RUYT, J, *L'Acte unique européen* (University of Brussels, 1987).

SAPIR, A, *Regional Integration in Europe* (EC Commission Economic Papers No 94; Brussels, 1992).

SBRAGIA, AM (ed), *Europolitics: Institutions and Policymaking in the 'New' European Community* (Brookings Institution, Washington, 1992).
SCHAUER, F, 'Formalism' (1988) 97 *Yale Law Journal* 509–548.
SCHRADER, J-V, 'EC Agricultural and Regional Policy: Consistent Interventions or Cumulative Inconsistencies?' (1989) *Intereconomics* 167–173.
SCOTT, A, 'Subsidiarity: A Europe of the Regions v. the British Constitution' (1994) *Journal of Common Market Studies* 47–68.
SCOTT, J, *Development Dilemmas in European Community Law* (Open University Press, Buckingham, 1995).
—— *EC Environmental Law* (Longman, London, 1998).
—— and MANSELL, W, 'European Regional Development Policy: Confusing Quantity with Quality?' (1993) *European Law Review* 87–108.
SMIT, H, and HERZOG, P, *The Law of the European Economic Community: A Commentary on the EEC Treaty* (Matthew Bender, New York, 1990).
SMITH, H, *The Power Game* (Ballantine, New York, 1993).
SNICKARS, F, 'Structural Change in Peripheral and Rural Areas—An Introduction' in U Wiberg and F Snickars (eds), *Structural Change in Peripheral and Rural Areas* (Swedish Council for Building Research, Stockholm, 1987) 7–14.
SNYDER, F, 'Ideologies of Competition in European Community Law' (1989) 52 *Modern Law Review* 149–178.
—— 'The Effectiveness of European Community Law: Institutions, Processes, Tools and Techniques' (1993) 56 *Modern Law Review* 19–54.
—— 'Soft Law and Institutional Practice in the European Community' in S Martin (ed), *The Construction of Europe* (Kluwer, Deventer, 1994) 197–225.
SPRONK, J (ed), *Multiple Criteria Decision Methods and Applications* (Springer, Berlin, 1985).
STEINLE, W, 'Labour Markets and Social Policies' in W Molle and R Cappellin (eds), *Regional Impact of Community Policies in Europe* (Avebury, Aldershot, 1988) 111–126.
STREECK, W, and SCHMITTER, PC, 'From National Corporatism to Transnational Pluralism: Organized Interests in the Single European Market' (1991) *Politics and Society* 133–164.
TESAURO, G, 'Partecipazione delle regioni alla formazione delle decisione comunitarie' in F Cuocolo (ed), *Istituzioni comunitarie e regioni* (Edizione Scientifiche Italiane, Naples, 1990) 37–51.
TESSIER, J, 'Le Fonds social européen' (1960) *Revue du Marché Commun* 325–337.
TEUBNER, G, 'Autopoiesis in Law and Society: A Rejoinder to Blankenburg' (1984) 18 *Law and Society Review* 291–301.
TEUTEMANN, M, *Completion of the Internal Market: An Application of Public Choice Theory* (Economic Papers No 83; EC Commission, Brussels, 1990).
TICHY, G, 'Theoretical and Empirical Considerations on the Dimension of an Optimum Integration Area in Europe' (1992) *Aussenwirtschaft* 107–137.
TINBERGEN, J, *International Economic Integration* (Elsevier, Amsterdam, 1954; 2nd edn, 1965).
TSOUKALIS, L, *The New European Economy: The Politics and Economics of Integration* (Oxford University Press, Oxford, 1991).
VALLE GALVEZ, JA, *La Articulación jurídica de la política regional comunitaria: El caso de los Programas Integrados Mediterráneos* (University of Granada, 1990).

VALLE GALVEZ, JA, 'La cohesion economica y social como objetivo de la Union europea: Analisis e perspectivas' (1994) *Revista de Instituciones Europeas* 341–378.

VANHOVE, N, and KLAASSEN, LH, *Regional Policy: A European Approach* (Saxon House, London, 1980).

VELLANO, M, 'Coesione economica e sociale e ripartizione di competenze: Le nuove iniziative comunitarie' (1995) *Rivista di Diritto Europeo* 193–208.

VERBRUGGEN, H, 'Subsidies as an Instrument for Environmental Policy' in R Gerritse (ed), *Producer Subsidies* (Pinter, London, 1990) 122–133.

WADLEY, D, *Restructuring the Regions* (OECD, Paris, 1986).

WÄLDCHEN, P, 'Industrial Change, New Technologies, and EC Regional Policy' in K Dyson (ed), *Local Authorities and New Technologies: The European Dimension* (Croom Helm, London, 1988) 49–58.

WALLACE, H, 'The Best is the Enemy of the "Could": Bargaining in the European Community' in S Tarditi, KJ Thomson, P Pierani, and E Croci-Angelini (eds), *Agricultural Trade Liberalization and the European Community* (Clarendon Press, Oxford, 1989) 193–206.

WEBER, S, and WIESMITH, H, 'Issue Linkage in the European Community' (1991) 29 *Journal of Common Market Studies* 255–267.

WEILER, JHH, 'The Transformation of Europe' (1991) 100 *Yale Law Journal* 2403–2483.

WELLENS, KC, and BORCHARDT, GM, 'Soft Law in European Community Law' (1989) *European Law Review* 267–321.

WHITING, A, *The Economics of Industrial Subsidies* (HMSO, London, 1976).

WILKE, H, and WALLACE, H, *Subsidiarity: Approaches to Power-Sharing in the European Community* (Royal Institute of International Affairs Discussion Paper No 27; London, 1990).

WINTER, JA, 'The ERDF and the Principle of Originality' in *In Orde, Liber Amicorum Pieter Verloren van Themaat* (Kluwer, Deventer, 1982) 365–380.

WISHLADE, FG, 'Competition Policy, Cohesion, and the Coordination of Regional Aids in the European Community' (1993) *European Competition Law Review* 143–150.

—— 'Competition Policy or Cohesion Policy by the Back Door: The Commission Guidelines on National Regional Aid' (1998) *European Competition Law Review* 343–357.

DE WITTE, B, 'The Reform of the European Regional Development Fund' (1986) 23 *Common Market Law Review* 419–440.

Index